Living *with* Purpose

GROWING EACH DAY IN YOUR
RELATIONSHIP WITH GOD

DAWN J. BARRIE

Ark House Press
arkhousepress.com

© 2023 Dawn J. Barrie

All rights reserved. Apart from any fair dealing for the purpose of study, research, criticism, or review, as permitted under the Copyright Act, no part may be reproduced by any process without written permission.

Scripture quotations marked (NIV) are taken from the Holy Bible, New International Version®, NIV®. Copyright © 1973, 1978, 1984, 2011 by Biblica, Inc.™ Used by permission of Zondervan. All rights reserved worldwide. www.zondervan.comThe "NIV" and "New International Version" are trademarks registered in the United States Patent and Trademark Office by Biblica, Inc.™

Cataloguing in Publication Data:
Title: Living With Purpose
ISBN: 978-0-6457514-3-7 (pbk)
Subjects: REL012020 [RELIGION / Christian Living / Devotional]; REL012120 [RELIGION / Christian Living / Spiritual Growth]; REL012040 [RELIGION / Christian Living / Inspirational].
Other Authors/Contributors: Barrie, Dawn J.

Design by initiateagency.com

With gratitude in my heart, I dedicate this book firstly to my late husband of fifty-three years, who taught me a great love and appreciation for worship through gospel music. He always encouraged me to pursue my goals, and it was through his encouragement, I started writing many years ago.

I would also like to acknowledge the dedication of my father and mother, who taught me, through their example, so much about praying and reading my Bible every day, even when I didn't understand what I was reading. Without the commitment of these three dear loved ones to my life, this book may never have been written. Thank you to each one for the inspiration you contributed to my life.

ACKNOWLEDGEMENTS

I would like to thank my family members for their support, encouragement and assistance on this journey, especially my sister-in-law Wendy for the mammoth task of helping me edit this work.

INTRODUCTION

Over many years, I have sent words of devotion and encouragement to my family and friends, to connect on a spiritual level. At the beginning of 2020, my son-in-law suggested I compile my words and write them into a book.

I decided it would be nice to write a series of devotions as a legacy to my family, but as I continued writing I found that within a space of time I had accumulated over three hundred devotions from having journaled and written for over thirty years. The amazing thing was that once I made the decision to do so, it often seemed that God was putting the words together for me, as sometimes I would discover a Scripture passage, an event, or even words spoken by someone that all seemed to connect to bring a devotion together.

The culmination of my thoughts and words come from my own spiritual growth throughout life as my Lord led me through many different fields of personal development, leadership and public relations both within the church family and the corporate world. These experiences have led me to become a writer and speaker, as well as a carer and encourager of others.

It is with compassion to see people find trust and faith to better live each day, that I have come to the point of sharing my work with each of you. I pray that you will be uplifted and inspired to choose to follow Christ more closely, to love Him more dearly and share His love with your family and friends.

May I encourage you to not only read the daily verse and devotion, but to read the chapter of Scripture that surrounds the verse. Through experience I can tell you that when you read these words now and in the years that follow, God will speak to you more deeply each time you read them. I personally have read the same devotional book for over fifty years and have found that each time God brings out new truth from the scripture passage to help me live closer to Him.

*"For everything that was written in the past was written to teach us,
so that through the endurance taught in the Scriptures
and the encouragement they provide we might have hope."*
Romans 15:4.

I bless you in the name of Jesus, to find His path for your life in these words.

*"I will make every effort to see that after my departure
you will always be able to remember these things."*
2 Peter 1:15.

*The man without a purpose is
like a ship without a rudder –
A waif, a nothing, a no man.
Have a purpose in life, and, having it,
throw such strength of mind
and muscle into your work as God has given you.*
Thomas Carlyle (1795-1881)

*"You will seek me and find me when you seek me
with all your heart."* Jeremiah 29:13

DAY 1
MAKING A FRESH START

Eph. 4:22-24, *"Put off your old self, which is being corrupted by its deceitful desires; to be made new in the attitude of your minds; and to put on the new self, created to be like God in true righteousness and holiness."*

Romans 13:14, *"Clothe yourselves with the Lord Jesus Christ, and so not think about how to gratify the desires of the sinful nature."* NIV

We all need a fresh start, and what better time than today. It does not matter how far we have fallen, we can make a new start, or however far we have ascended, we can always discover new heights in our walk with Jesus. We need to allow ourselves throughout the days ahead to become students of the living Lord and be taught by Him.

Whoever we may be, without Jesus as our Saviour, it will be impossible for us to rid our minds of corruption and deceitful desires. When presented with a new suite of clothes, the beggar will only take a moment to remove the old clothes and renew his appearance with the new. We need to decide today to change our bad habits, unsavoury thoughts and unkind speech by asking the Lord Jesus to renew our thinking.

We can always make a new start.

To live this way, we must continually seek the help of the Holy Spirit, who came to live within each of us at the moment we received Christ as Saviour. We must believe that God's Spirit lives in us, because of the assurance of Eph. 3:16-17 *"He may strengthen you with power through his Spirit in your inner being, so that Christ may dwell in your hearts through faith."*

To make our fresh start, we need to bring every thought to Christ. In other words, every time we are insincere in speech, have trouble forgiving, have impurity of speech, have wrong dealings in business or work, or fail to love, we need to ask Christ to change our thinking and renew the attitude of our mind. Take up the challenge to put on Christ, so that we do not grieve Him by our inconsistencies.

Prayer: *Father God, in the name of Jesus, please help me to change my attitude of mind so that my feelings and actions will reveal the graciousness of Christ to those around me. Amen*

DAY 2
EVERY DAY IS NEW

Lamentation 3:22-23, *"Because of the Lord's great love we are not consumed, for his compassions never fail. They are new every morning; great is your faithfulness." NIV*

Are you a person who has lost their home to a bushfire, flood or cyclone? Maybe you have lost your family in an accident or through terrible circumstances like war, or you have struggled with a very sick child or loved one over many years. For most of us, we can never understand the feelings that batter our emotions, often affecting our health in such circumstances.

God is always faithful and will fill you with hope every day.

This is probably how God's prophet, Jeremiah felt as he trudged through his ruined Jerusalem after the invasion by the Babylonians. He laments what was and what might have been, much like you may be feeling at this very moment. Wisely, even though he is filled with sorrow each day, he remains fixed on his sovereign God, who is more powerful than the Babylonian army.

As he focuses on the nature of the Lord, he realizes afresh that God is full of mercy and compassion, and knows, he will not be consumed for that very reason. He knows and understands that even though things could not get any worse, God's faithfulness is new every morning and there is always hope where God is.

Regardless of your circumstances, remember that your hope must be in God, not your circumstances and that your God is faithful every morning to fill you with the hope and the spiritual strength you will need for that day. The Lord told Paul, *"My grace is sufficient for you, for my power is made perfect in weakness"* (2 Cor. 12:9). We must believe in hope, even when we face destruction, for as we call on the name of Jesus, we will learn that restoration and redemption will follow destruction.

How can you help and support someone who is going through challenging times?

Prayer: *Thank you, Lord that your love and mercy is new every morning. Help me when I am without hope to come to You, for You alone are faithful. Amen*

DAY 3
USING TIME WISELY

Ephesians 5:15-16, *"Be very careful, then, how you live - not as unwise but as wise, making the most of every opportunity, because the days are evil."* NIV

When you are born, God has already put in place a plan for your life that will give you a fully developed life. But let us always remember that God has given us a free will to choose His way or our own.

None of us know how long our time on earth will last, so the discipline and lessons of life for some are crowded into a brief amount of time. But for most, each of us is intended to touch all the experiences of life, with an appointed time for us to be born and die, weep and laugh, gain and lose, to have peace or experience trials (Ecclesiastes 3.) We must be careful not to force the pace of life but wait and trust the Lord, knowing all will work out for our good and to His glory in due time. *"My times are in your hands"* (Psalm 31:15).

> God has given us a free will to choose His way or our own.

The seasons of life succeed one another very quickly, and as our life on this earth draws to a close, we look back over our lives, and it seems that each experience was but for a moment, then it vanished, never to return. We must make the most of every opportunity, being alert to the demands of every hour, for we know not when our hour will come when we will take our last breath. God opens and shuts all the doors in our lives. The same God gives us wisdom, grace, power, encouragement and everything we need to live and enjoy this earthly life.

The story is told of the sculptor who made the statue of David. When asked how he knew what to do, he replied that he knew David was there, but he just had to find him inside the rock. God's design for each of us has always been there. Let us not idly waste the time we have, for the Lord wants us to take advantage of every opportunity He gives us. We will experience true fulfilment and the greatest blessings when we use our time wisely to serve others.

"Therefore, as we have opportunity, let us do good to all people, especially to those who belong to the family of believers" (Gal.6:10).

Prayer: *Lord, keep me from wasting the precious time You have given me. Let me look for opportunities every day to bring glory to Your name. Amen*

DAY 4
RUN YOUR RACE WITH GLADNESS

Hebrews 12:1, *"Let us throw off everything that hinders and the sin that so easily entangles. And let us run with perseverance the race marked out for us."* NIV

In life, some emotions hinder and distract us from living our Christian life with joy and gladness. One of the worst is despair, for it drags us down from being useful. This was the very problem God had with the Israelites when they started murmuring and very quickly became discontented, blossoming into rebellion and ruin. It is very easy to fall into the habit of doubting God. The instant we start to wonder if God really loves us and if our hopes are in vain, we very quickly become of little use to anyone else.

As we comfort others, we will unknowingly comfort ourselves.

Let us be careful and refuse to doubt that our God, who loves without conditions, will never leave us or forsake us. Hebrews 13:5 *"Never will I leave you; never will I forsake you."*

On the other hand, when we look in the book of Nehemiah, where Ezra began to read the Sacred Book, the people understood the Divine Word and profited from it. Nehemiah 8: 3,6. *"All the people were attentive to the book of the law . . . then they bowed low and worshiped the Lord."* They worshiped because they rejoiced and were glad.

When we are overcome with despair and doubt, let us dwell on the words of scripture, until they become part of our thoughts and lives. Find a verse like Nehemiah 8:10, *"The joy of the Lord is your strength."* Every time you begin to feel down, say these verses to yourself and dwell on them; this will cultivate the spirit of gladness within your soul. The enemy does not like it when we overcome in the name of our Lord.

Sadness and despair discolour our lives and produce mental paralysis within. A sure way to shun sadness is to be helpful, because as we comfort others, we will unknowingly comfort ourselves. Let us rejoice and be glad, so that others will be glad also.

Prayer: *Thank you, God that we can fellowship with You at any time. May Your gifts fill our hearts and lives with joy and gladness. Amen.*

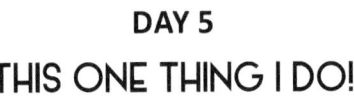

DAY 5
THIS ONE THING I DO!

Psalm 86:11, *"Teach me your way, Lord, . . . give me an undivided heart, that I may fear your name."* NIV.

I am sure we have all had disturbed sleep when we lie there wondering if we have locked the front door or some other trivial matter, and until we get up and check we are restless and unable to fall asleep. So it is, when we have a divided heart. Some of us suffer from anxiety, preventing us from taking a strong and straight course in life. Some would like to be pleasant and helpful but find themselves constantly being disagreeable, distant and awkward. Even Paul, talked of his better self who longed to do the will of God, but so often became subject to passion and selfishness.

In contrast, when Jesus came to earth to live among us and be human in every way, His heart was set on doing the will of His Father, teaching us about the love of God, before going to the cross and dying for our salvation. From the time He came as a babe, He was never 'divided' on His commitment to His Father.

> **With a divided heart, we lack the strength of the Holy Spirit and become unstable.**

When we have a divided heart, we lack the strength of the Holy Spirit in our lives, and we become unstable. If we are going to make any mark on the lives of the people we mix with, we must be united in ourselves and in God. We need to totally concentrate on Jesus and His way of life and consecrate ourselves to Him, allowing Him to teach us His ways. Only as we distance ourselves from this world and allow Christ complete control of our life will we be able to say with Paul, *"This one thing I do."* In Matthew 6:21, Jesus told us to keep our eyes on Him that our whole body would be filled with His light.

If you and I are to learn the ways of our Lord, we must make it our business to study His Word, asking for understanding and wisdom to hear just what the Spirit wants to teach us.

Prayer: *Heavenly Father, give me a faithful heart that is devoted to You and to the service of those around me, to bring Your light into their lives. Amen.*

DAY 6
LIFE IN THE SHADOW OF THE CROSS

2 Corinthians 5:21, *"For our sake He made Christ to be sin Who knew no sin, so that in and through Him we might become (viewed examples of) the righteousness of God – what we ought to be, approved and acceptable and in right relationship with Him, by His goodness"* (AMP).

Philip Yancey tells of Joanna Flanders-Thomas in Cape-Town. *"She started visiting prisoners daily, bringing them a simple gospel message of forgiveness and reconciliation. She earned their trust, got them to talk about their abusive childhoods and showed them a better way of resolving conflicts. In one year, the logged acts of violence against inmates and guards, went from 279 to 2."*

We must live knowing the gospel can transform us.

The apostle Paul and Joanna lived in the shadow of the cross. What does this mean to us? To live in the shadow of the cross means that, we live with the appreciation of the power of the gospel to transform our life to be a new creation in Christ. Christ gave Paul and Joanna the ministry of reconciliation, always being aware of their own salvation and bringing new hope to others.

As children of a Holy God, we live with the assurance of the completeness of knowing we have eternal life through the cross. Many people follow Jesus, attend church, and live good lives hoping to go to heaven. Nothing we can do, be it living a good life, or anything else, could convince God that we are worthy of heaven; nothing except the transformation of our life as we live in the shadow of the cross will get us there. Verse 17, *"Therefore, if anyone is in Christ, he is a new creation."*

Like Paul and Joanna, we must live with the constant knowledge that the blood Jesus shed saves us, together with the compulsion to share the message of the gospel with others. We must never lose sight of what the cross of Calvary cost Jesus for us. Are you living in the shadow of the cross, allowing Jesus to transform you through the work of the Holy Spirit, as you share the gospel with those you love and care about?

Prayer: *Loving Father, thank you that Jesus accomplished life for us when He died on the cross. Please help me to daily stay on track and not fall back to the old things in my life. Amen*

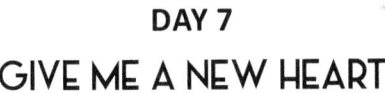

DAY 7
GIVE ME A NEW HEART

Ezekiel 36:26, *"I will give you a new heart and put a new spirit in you; I will remove from you your heart of stone and give you a heart of flesh"* NIV.

We all stand in awe of what medical doctors can do today. In 2018, some friends were overcome when they learned that their new-born baby had a badly deformed heart. Thankfully, the surgeons were hopeful that they could help. Through a lot of prayer and waiting on God, their son today lives a normal life, and his heart pumps not only with blood but he is a joy to everyone who knows him. How precious to know that God keeps our physical heart beating to give us physical life and energy, but what about our spiritual heart?

Every one of us needs a new heart that flows with the Spirit of God. As humans, we naturally have hearts that are self-seeking and self-centred. We are born with sinful hearts. *"Surely I was sinful at birth, sinful from the time my mother conceived me"* (Psalm 51:5).

> *Our sinful hearts are naturally self-seeking and self-centred.*

God promised the Israelites a new heart, one filled with His Spirit, and that He would cleanse them from all impurities (v.29). Like so many today, they had lost hope. In a spiritual sense, we are like someone with a diseased physical heart whose only hope is to trust in today's physicians. God has promised us a fresh start through Jesus Christ, the only one who can renew our lives spiritually.

His promise to us was fulfilled when He died and rose again. By trusting Him alone, He will change our self-centeredness to be Christ centred, filling us with His Holy Spirit to make our heart and life beat with the spiritual lifeblood of God.

You no longer have to struggle with guilt and shame but simply come to the Saviour, who can forgive and fill you with a heart for God.

Prayer: *Father, thank you for hope of new life in Christ. Help me to trust You each day so that Your Spirit can lead me into a new way of living for You. Amen.*

DAY 8
GETTING OUR PRIORITIES RIGHT

Proverbs 14:12, *"There is a way that seems right to a man, but in the end, it leads to death"* NIV.

Man has always been in pursuit of happiness and money. The world view is, that if we are rich, we will be happy. To be wealthy is a blessing from God. God can use it to help others, and many billionaires today give generously to charities, but money will never bring us happiness. Jesus warned us in Mark 8:36, *"What good is it for a man to gain the whole world, yet forfeit his soul".*

Money will never bring happiness.

In Matthew 19, Jesus gives counsel to the 'Rich Young Ruler' who saw his need to follow Jesus but was unwilling to sell all that he had to give to the poor, and then with nothing left except his life, to come and follow Jesus. Like good works, money will never buy us happiness. Happiness will only come when we are willing to hand everything that we have and are, over to Jesus and let Him lead our lives.

When young, we pursue our chosen career in life, we marry, have children and enjoy God's work and creation. God gives all this for our life and enjoyment here on earth, but we need to allow God to use them for His glory. Throughout life, I had many different fields of work experience, and God led me into positions in church life where He used the skills He had given me. Now that time has passed, I can see how God has always provided for my needs and taught me many skills. *"And my God shall supply all your needs"* (Phil.4:19).

Jesus told his disciples that He is Life (John 14:6). When we come to Jesus, confess that we are a sinner and ask His forgiveness, He gives us eternal life and assures us that He will supply all our needs according to His riches in glory.

True happiness and life come in building our relationship with Him, and then all of life's priorities fall into place. If you have never asked Jesus to be your Saviour, then seek Him today and know the happiness and peace He gives.

Prayer: *Lord, help me to always understand that You can supply all I need. Help me to know Your peace and happiness in my life as I serve You. Amen.*

DAY 9
DOES GOD CARE

Psalm 28:7, *"The Lord is my strength and my shield; my heart trusts in him, and I am helped"* NIV.

Throughout life, you can question whether the God you trust really cares about you especially if things you have given your life to begin to fall apart. Things like your profession, marriage, the collapse of a business, or your health. So many happenings in our lives can cause our hearts and mind to question.

When only 28 years of age with two small children, I had no other option but to just trust God and move forward. At the time, we owned a bread run (fresh bread to the door daily). Due to injury, my husband could not work, and having no money to pay someone; I had five days to learn what 500 randomly placed homes across three suburbs received and where they hid their money for safety. Thankfully, my parents came and helped by looking after our children.

Our God is always faithful and caring.

I left home at 10 pm each night to arrive home the next day at about 11 am. When I felt scared in the small hours of the morning with darkness and no one around, I just had to keep telling myself, 'Jesus is with you.'

By the time three weeks passed I was exhausted, but I knew the power and presence of my God in a new way. I knew it was God who prompted my mind to remember what each home received and where their money was, because under the circumstances, it was impossible to remember without His help.

Does He care? Yes, He does! As humans, we so often forget about just how faithful and caring God is. I, for one, often had to be reminded throughout life, but I can testify to the wonderful care our Heavenly Father has for those who love Him. Hold on to Jesus and you too will testify, *"My heart will leap for joy and I will give thanks to him in song."* There is no other way.

Prayer: *Loving Heavenly Father, thank You that even when we forget, You never do, and are always caring and faithful to us. Amen.*

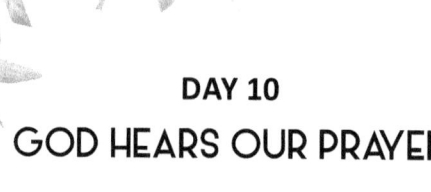

DAY 10

GOD HEARS OUR PRAYER

Psalm 18:6, *"In my distress I called to the Lord; . . . for help. From His temple He heard my voice; my cry came before Him, into His ears."* NIV

Have you ever wondered if God actually hears your prayers? John, in his vision of heaven sees, *"Another angel, . . . came and stood at the altar. He was given much incense to offer, with the prayers of all the saints."* (Rev.8:3) This gives us confidence that God does indeed hear our whispered prayer.

God does indeed hear our whispered prayer.

As a small child, whilst my parents were fishing, I would lie on the grass on the river bank and listen to the breeze blowing through the needle-like leaves of the she oaks growing there. It was a whispering sound that today reminds me that my God loves to hear even the whisper of my voice as I speak to Him.

When we are distressed and in tears, we need only whisper, and God hears and understands. Over and over in Psalms, we read of requests to God. In Psalm 4:1, *"Hear my prayer,"* then in Chapter 5:3, *"O Lord, you hear my voice."* Then we read in our verse that God heard David's voice. These verses are truly a comfort and should compel us to persist in prayer, because our whisper is precious to God.

David knew God as his rock and his deliverer (v.1), someone he could lean on and depend on. Like David, we need to recognise the greatness of our God and come to Him with our requests, knowing that He indeed hears and answers our prayers. Whisper your prayer to God today.

Prayer: *Lord, lift me up and let me stand in your presence, and through faith, lead me to a deeper relationship with You. Amen*

DAY 11
THIRSTY FOR GOD

Psalm 63:1, *"I thirst for you, my whole being longs for you, in a dry and parched land where there is no water."* NIV

Like many others, I genuinely love the Psalms, especially to use some as a prayer because many embrace everything that we can experience in life. When writing this Psalm, David was distressed and running for his life in the desert.

David thirsted after God, even though he fought on the side of God. Unlike David, we often thirst for different things like friends, recognition, a new house, or education. Deep within each of us, we thirst to love and be loved, but we seek other things to satisfy, when this deep thirst can only be filled by God. We must first get all the delights of this world in the proper perspective, for only then *"will I be fully satisfied"* (verse 5). David didn't long for food for his physical body, but to be fully satisfied with the love of God, which is better than anything life can give.

God alone can bring joy and peace to our hearts.

To desire God as David did is to know Him. Remember when Jesus asked the Samaritan woman for water, He broke every law regarding Jews and Samaritans. Yet, to Jesus, this was not as important as the desire to offer the woman the living water that comes from knowing Him. Today this invitation is just the same. Can you, honestly say with David that your whole being longs for God?

God is our God, but we must seek to know Him by speaking to Him and seeking Him in the Bible. Our God is better than anything this life can give us, for He alone can bring joy and peace to our hearts. If anyone thirsts, let them ask for "living water" from the Holy Spirit within. *"For everyone who asks receives"* (Matt.7:8).

Take pleasure today by spending time in the presence of your Saviour and Lord.

Prayer: *Lord, help us open our lives to You so our longings may be satisfied with the love and peace You give. Hear our prayer, dear Lord and save us. Amen*

DAY 12

BREAK FREE

Matthew 4:18 – 20, *"Jesus saw two brothers . . . casting a net into the lake, for they were fishermen. "Come, follow me," Jesus said, "and I will make you fishers of men . . . At once, they left their nets and followed Him."*

Simon (Peter) and Andrew immediately obeyed. Jesus adapted Himself to the understanding of their humanity. If Jesus had stood there and told Peter that within four years, he would see over 3,000 souls accept Him as Saviour (Acts 2: 41), Peter would probably have thought, *'who is this guy,'* and in turning to continue his work, would have missed the most incredible opportunity he could ever have had.

We look for any excuse not to do what God wants us to do.

Jesus still calls us to follow Him, but we have to be willing to take Him at His word, which means we may have to put our own ambitions and desires aside to allow God to use the gifts He has given us for His glory. Many of us are lethargic when an opportunity comes to us, and like Moses, we look for any excuse not to do what God wants us to do. We say, "Why me? Everyone else is doing their own thing." Decide now, that when your opportunity comes you won't find an excuse and won't lack the discipline to do what you must do, or you will miss out on what God has in store for you.

God gives you opportunity to do what nobody else will do, and sometimes you have to learn by doing little things before you are the strong and courageous person God wants you to be. Peter had to learn from Jesus for three years before he became the leader God intended. You must understand and believe, as Jesus said in Matt.19: 26, *"with God all things are possible."*

If we are willing with God's help to step out and walk with the Lord, God will reap a mighty harvest for His kingdom. Be like Peter and Andrew, commit today and go after God with all your heart, mind, soul and strength, and have a life full of purpose, joy and eternal life. Stop waiting to first 'become', know God can use you if you trust and walk with Him.

Prayer: *Dear Lord, I give my life in obedience to You and want to serve and love You so that others will be drawn to Your love and Salvation. Amen*

DAY 13
FOOLISH EXCUSES

Luke 14:17-18, *"Come, for everything is now ready, but they all alike began to make excuses"* NIV.

We might ask, *"Who would be so foolish as to find an excuse not to attend the banquet of the King of Kings?"* Jesus knows us so well. He knows that the temptations of life often lie in our property, activities or our home and family. Whilst there is nothing wrong with any of these, let's never forget that we are only on earth for a short time, and in the end, all these things will have no value at all.

Our relationship with our Lord often takes second place as we place all our time and effort into what we own. *"Set your minds on things above, not on earthly things"* (Col.3:2). So often, our profession or our social pleasures very easily and quickly consume us, allowing them to keep us from meeting with our fellow Christians in worship. Or is it your family that keeps you from a deeper spiritual life with God?

We continue to make foolish excuses.

Jesus has nothing against these things, for He honoured a wedding feast with His first miracle, but He knows that when our hearts desire something, it is easy for us to choose our desire by justifying whatever it may be to ourselves. We need to ask ourselves and decide before our Lord if our excuses are affecting our relationship with Him and keeping us from connecting with those who need salvation.

Everything that a celebration stands for your God wants to give to you. Our Lord's banquet is spread with abundant consuming love. There will be happy conversation, the sparkle of laughter, and enjoyment of the interchange of friendship and fellowship. How foolish when we allow the Evil One to entice us into forfeiting our place at God's table. The amazing thing is, we can enjoy all this and more every day in our relationship with Jesus, yet we continue to make foolish excuses. Let us respond to the love Jesus offers us daily as we meet with Him, lest He refuses us at the last.

Prayer: *Dear Lord, keep me from the cares of this life so that I don't allow them to keep me from my eternal relationship with You. Amen*

DAY 14
DON'T LOOK BACK

Psalm 46:1, *"God is our refuge and strength, an ever-present help in trouble"* NIV.

Even though we are not immune to trouble and struggles in life, we wonder, why God doesn't come to our aid sooner when we pray earnestly to Him. It is not His way because often He must adjust us to our trouble before He can lead us through it.

> **Often, He must adjust us to the trouble we face before He can lead us through it.**

As you come through a problem, you must look constructively at where you are spiritually, emotionally, and physically. Paul's quest was to have a holy character, and in Philippians 3:13-14, he gives instruction to the Christians, *"But one thing I do: Forgetting what is behind and straining toward what is ahead, I press on toward the goal to win the prize for which God has called me heavenward in Christ Jesus".* Sometimes our failure can even lead to success, though very often, our troubles can be the result of our own mistakes and choices. At all times, we must come to God who is our refuge and strength because He alone is our help. We cannot change anything in the past, not even what happened 1 hour ago, but we can look with courage and expectation to the future, which is still before us.

Look forward even when the sky is dark, and never doubt that God has a silver lining there for you. His hand is on the helm of the boat of your life, and He will guide you through the waves. There have been times in life when I felt I was drowning, especially when our business failed, and we feared for our future. As we called the Real Estate agent, fearing we may have to sell our home, I felt utterly without hope. When she came, instead of having to sell, she offered me a position that turned into 12 years of successful sales.

Paul focused on Jesus, looking forward as he pressed on through enormous difficulties toward his goal. God never forgets us, and we are never alone. God's grace is always sufficient. Yes, God's grace is always sufficient.

> *Oh, Saviour, let me hear Your voice. You give me the courage to fight on. You've promised that You'll never leave me. Thank You that I am not alone.*
>
> *Unknown*

DAY 15
TRULY BEING RICH

Luke 12:15, *"He said to them, "Watch out! Be on your guard against all kinds of greed; life does not consist of an abundance of possessions."* NIV

For most people life is about getting more possessions, but Christ warns us that life doesn't consist in what we possess but in who we are, in goodness and qualities of life. In God's eyes how much are you worth? As we age, we think about leaving a reasonable sum of money to our family, and we hear people talk about how much a person has left. Is it not better to leave the value of love, humility, generosity, and Godly characteristics of your own life on which your family can model their lives?

The rich young man in the bible story made some foolish mistakes. He thought of his wealth as though it was his, not that he had gained it wrongfully, but he forgot that it was God who gave the ability to do well. Let us be mindful of God's provision to us, both in our ability and the gifts He gives us. We must beware not to be prone to accept the praise for our ability but to give God the glory.

Wealth will never satisfy the hunger of our soul.

The young ruler excluded God from the profit and stored it away for his future. Whilst there is nothing wrong with an investment, we must never forget that our good fortune is due to God's goodness. He calls us to give Him a portion of our supply for the work of His people, whether to feed others or to help missionaries change lives. Today, people give large sums to charity, and although this is good and honouring, we need to always maintain the right attitude toward giving which makes all the difference in God's eyes. *"Each of you should give what you have decided in your heart to give, not reluctantly or under compulsion, for God loves a cheerful giver"* (2 Cor. 9:7).

The worst mistake he made was he thought his wealth would satisfy the hunger of his soul. How easily we make this mistake, and our lives are troubled daily. Christ is the only one who can satisfy our need within, and we will overflow with love, tenderness, and human sympathy, enjoying the true blessing of our Lord, as we draw on the power of the Holy Spirit.

Prayer: *Help us, Lord, to set our eyes on eternal life, not the things of this world, for when our hearts are right with You we have happiness. Amen*

DAY 16
THE LAW OF SELF

Ecclesiastes 2:10-11, *"I denied myself nothing my eyes desired... Yet when I surveyed all that my hands had done and what I had toiled to achieve, everything was meaningless, a chasing after the wind; nothing was gained under the sun."* NIV

Today the trendy trinity is me, myself, and I. We are all aware of the law of gravity, but too many are totally unaware of the down-pull of self on their spirit. With modern technology, one's phone has become the modern billboard for personal, hour-by-hour activities, spending hours connecting with friends to see who they're with, what they're doing, or what they have had to eat. It has become increasingly easy to give into the flesh and self-life.

> We have become fascinated with pleasure, and personal fulfilment.

By focusing on self, we have become fascinated with pleasure, and personal fulfilment. We seek things like yoga and exercise to relieve our stress but fail to come to God who alone can calm our fears and anxieties. The Bible tells us that *"physical exercise is of some value, but godliness has value in all things"* (1 Tim. 4: 8). The things of this earth will never bring the happiness we desire.

We need to overcome the law of self in our lives by looking to the Spirit of life as recorded by Paul in Romans 8:2, *"Through Christ Jesus the law of the Spirit who gives life has set you free from the law of sin and death."* Many of us have always been fascinated by the ability of an enormous plane to lift off from the earth and fly. Science tells us that the combination of lift (upward force), and thrust (forward push) get a plane into the air to fly by continually pushing and pulling the surrounding air. It is constantly working to maintain the ability to stay in the air, and we know the tragedy when those combined forces cease.

When you become aware of the lack of Christ's Spirit in your life, turn back, and by confession, again become conscious of God's Spirit within your soul. To enjoy life in the Spirit, you must take time to be holy, meditating, praying and especially reading God's Word. Only as you maintain your spiritual life will you have the power to overcome the spirit of self.

Prayer: *Help me, dear Lord, to find my life as I spend time with You each day. Thank You that You are always leading me onward in my upward climb to overcome self and be filled with the Spirit of Jesus. Amen.*

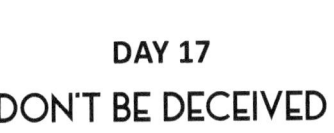

DAY 17
DON'T BE DECEIVED

John 8:44, *"The devil is a liar and the father of lies."* NIV

Back in 1935, the cane toad was brought from Hawaii to Australia with the belief that it would kill the cane beetle that destroyed the sugar cane crops in Queensland. However, they did not consider the damage it would cause to the natural wildlife of our beautiful country. Long before the beginning of the 21st century, they had wreaked havoc on Australia's delicate ecosystems and biodiversity. Our country was deceived by what appeared to be a benefit at the time.

In the story of Adam and Eve in Genesis 3: 1-7, we see how Satan used the serpent to deceive them into disobeying God. Was Eve deceived by the serpent's words, or was it something else?

> Satan still uses his God-created ability to deceive us.

God created Satan, and in Ezekiel 28: 16 we read, *"You sinned, so I drove you in disgrace from the mount of God."* Satan used the same temptation that had him thrown out of heaven to tempt Eve by telling her if she ate the fruit of the forbidden tree, that she would be like God.

Satan still uses his God-created ability to deceive us, just as he did to try to tempt Jesus in the desert by telling him lies. Just as he fell from God's grace, he tries to pull us down by placing attractive ideas into our minds and telling us that just one dose of drugs won't hurt us; that one act of adultery doesn't matter; that one lie to get a better position is okay; or that a little cruelty to our family is alright. In 2 Cor.11:14, Paul warns the church, *"Satan, himself masquerades as an angel of light."* In what way is Satan deceiving you, and what are you doing about it? Read Proverbs 4: 20-26, and act on these words of wisdom.

When Jesus is our Saviour, we can come to Him knowing that even though we have sinned, He is always willing to forgive us and to give us the strength to overcome the things of this life that Satan uses to cause us to fall from grace. Come back to Jesus today and ask for His help.

Prayer: *Dear Lord, help me to be honest with myself and with You, to look to You for forgiveness and consider what You say in your Word. Thank You that when I trust, You will give me the strength to triumph over evil. Amen*

DAY 18
FAITH WITH PATIENCE

Rev. 3:10, *"Since you have kept my command to endure patiently, I will also keep you from the hour of trial."* NIV

God has promised that if we endure with patience, He will keep us, but patience is more than endurance. Consider Paul when he was on his way to Rome to stand trial before Caeser. Whilst on the ship, they ran into a torrential storm and became shipwrecked. I am sure that as the boat got into more difficulty, Paul was beginning to feel he couldn't stand anymore, even though God had revealed to him that if he could just be faithful and wait all would be well. Regardless of what the sailors said or how he was treated, he hung his very existence on his hope in God. *"Do not be afraid, Paul. You must stand trial before Caesar; and God has graciously given you the lives of all who sail with you."* (Acts 27:24)

Faith with patience calls for total confidence that God will never fail.

Even during our storms in life, we must have patient faith until God intervenes. Faith with patience calls for total confidence that God will never fail us. *"Never will I leave you; never will I forsake you."* (Hebrews 13:5). Even when we cannot see any way forward and we don't understand what God is doing, we must continue to trust and worship Him as Sovereign. There is peace in knowing God is in control.

We will have shipwrecks in our lives, especially when we fail to trust that God cannot be anything but faithful to His promises. Even when the winds of life are against you and the 'ship' of your life does run aground, don't walk away just because it's too hard. God is still with you; know His presence and that He will bring you through.

Is your life in Christ strong enough to face anything without faltering as you wait on Him? Can you say, as Paul did, that Jesus is indeed the Lord of your life? When we can view our life with patient endurance that God will never fail us, our life will become a glorious opportunity for seeing marvellous things happening all the time.

Prayer: *Please help me to trust You more each day so when the storms of life batter me, I will be able to stand and endure with patience until you, Lord, bring new life to me. Amen*

DAY 19
TELL THEM THE STORIES OF JESUS

Deuteronomy 4:9-10, *"Do not forget the things your eyes have seen or let them fade from your heart as long as you live. Teach them to your children and to their children after them... so that they may learn to revere me as long as they live."* NIV

Through Moses, God commanded the Israelites to be sure to tell their children that the Lord had led them all the way. When I was about eight years old and attending a country primary school, the minister from the nearest town would come each week to give Religious Instruction. Over many weeks, he acted out and told the complete journey of the Children of Israel from Egypt to the Promised Land. That has remained in my memory, and still today, is one of my favourite stories from the Bible.

As parents or grandparents, it is essential for us to tell our children the events that created our lives so they can tell their children. In the latter part of life, it is of value to look back and see how God has guided you. So many events shape our lives, like when you accepted Christ as Saviour, and other spiritual signposts along the road of life. Throughout life, we struggle with problems and celebrate good times, but all the way, God's love and grace sustain us.

> **Look back to see how God has guided you.**

A child's ability to remember is pretty impressive, and the stories we tell our children when they're young will remain with them the rest of their life. The most important story we can pass on to them is the life of Jesus, teaching and telling them how He was born and died to save them from sin so they could have a home in heaven. One of the memories children will always cherish is the Bible stories and prayer times they had with their parents before bed.

Sometimes we may think it is a little above their understanding, but our Heavenly Father will enable them to understand at their level and remember as they grow. Proverbs 22:6 says, *"Train up a child in the way he should go, and when he is old, he will not depart from it."* Keep reading to them from God's Word, the most important training we can give them.

Prayer: *What can I give back to you Lord, for all Your benefits to me? I will praise and bless all your children that they may know You as Lord of their lives. Amen*

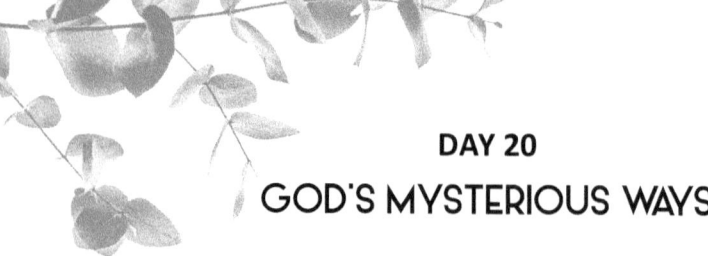

DAY 20
GOD'S MYSTERIOUS WAYS

Acts 16:26,28, *"Suddenly there was a violent earth quake ......the prison doors flew open and everybody's chains came loose. Paul shouted, "Don't harm yourself! We are all here!"* NIV

When I read this amazing story of how the Philippian jailer and his family accepted Jesus as their Saviour (Read Acts 16: 22-34), I praise God for the way He works in people's lives. The uncharacteristic actions of the prisoners, moved the jailer in such a way that he wanted to know about the God Paul and Silas worshiped.

We must always be prepared to speak on behalf of our Saviour.

When I was only 30, my dear mother had terminal cancer, and it was my privilege to nurse her in our home for the last six months of her life. A relative of my husband, a cancer research specialist, came to our home and offered his care and services to her, explaining in detail what he could do for her with treatments that were available at the time. She looked into his face and gently refused any treatment, saying, *"Thank you, but I know I am saved and am going to heaven."* He continued to care for her, despite her refusal, and just a few weeks after her passing, he and his wife were both diagnosed with cancer.

With the best the medical world could offer them their lives began to slip away. The words my mother spoke to him played in his mind and God used them to bring Salvation to both him and his wife before they passed away.

As God's children, we must always be prepared to speak on behalf of our Saviour because we never know how God, in His wisdom, can bring Salvation to the needy. 1 Peter 3:15. *"But in your hearts revere Christ as Lord. Always be prepared to give an answer to everyone who asks you to give the reason for the hope that you have. But do this with gentleness and respect."*

Prayer: *Thank You Jesus, for calling me to speak for You. Please always give me Your gentle words that will bring salvation to someone. Amen*

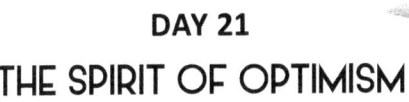

DAY 21
THE SPIRIT OF OPTIMISM

Psalm 37:3-4, *"Trust in the Lord... and feed on His faithfulness. Delight yourself also in the Lord, and He shall give you the desires of your heart"* NKJV.

It is as though these verses are saying to you and me, *"Don't worry, for you cannot remove the evil from this world by worry or anger. It is not worth losing your peace of mind, so be quiet in your heart, and look up to God in prayer, so that He can deliver you."*

> *It's all the things you suppose that make you miserable.*

The story is told of a very poor woman who, in her employment earned only a pittance to feed her family, yet she always displayed a joyful spirit. One day, a gloomy friend said to her, *"It's okay to be cheerful now, but I should think that thoughts of your future would worry you. Suppose, for instance, that you suddenly got very sick and were unable to work, or suppose you lost your job, and you could find no other work; or suppose..."*

Turning to her gloomy friend, the poor woman told her that she never supposes, but that *"The Lord is my Shepherd, I want for nothing"* (Psalm 23:1). And then she added, *"It's all the things you suppose that make you miserable, so you had better give up supposing and worrying, and just trust in Jesus."*

We must rest and delight in the Lord, for only then can you and I keep the noise of this world from filling our minds, so that we can hear His voice in our hearts. Are you prepared to receive and act on what the writer of Hebrews 13:5-6 says, *"Be content with what you have, because God has said, "Never will I leave you; never will I forsake you." So, we can say with confidence, "The Lord is my helper; I will not be afraid. What can mere mortals do to me?"*

Start today and turn all your supposes and worries over to God, and find contentment in knowing His peace and assurance in your heart.

Prayer: *Lord, help me to turn everything over to You, to trust You, and to believe and know that You understand my every circumstance and will give me Your peace. Amen*

DAY 22
NAVIGATING LIFE

Psalm 32:8, *"I will instruct you and teach you in the way you should go: I will counsel you with my loving eye on you."* NIV

Knowing God's counsel (will) for us is something most of us struggle with in life. We all have crushing moments when we feel like we are spinning out of control and being drowned by the circumstances that make up our life. Often in these moments, we try desperately to do what we can to improve our situation, as we struggle day after day. Maybe this is your life at this present moment.

> God knows just what we are able to bear, and He loves us

Take heart! God said, *"I will instruct you... I will counsel you."* In v.5, we're told to *"confess our transgression to the Lord,"* and He will forgive our sin. Granted, we may not have committed a gross error, but the mere fact that we struggle and don't bring our problem to our Heavenly Father is a big mistake. Then in v.6, we are told to pray. Unfortunately, often, when we have a problem this is the last thing we think about.

The most powerful thing we can do, even when we are busy, is to pray. Nothing is more important. We must remember that we are speaking to the God of the universe, who knows just what we can bear, and He loves us. He is our ever-present help in all our troubles. God said keep near to Him, and He will lead us through any circumstance.

Can you hear Him saying, *'Why are you worrying my child when you can just surrender yourself and everything that concerns you to me, and I will take care of it?'* Believe God's promise and let your mind dwell on the fact that, *"He will instruct us and teach us in the way we should go."*

> Every day I need you, Lord,
> but this day especially.
> I need some strength,
> to face whatever is to be.
> And so, dear Lord, I pray –
> hold onto my trembling hand,
> and be with me today.
> Unknown

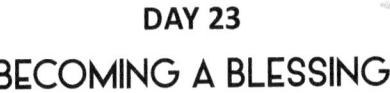

DAY 23
BECOMING A BLESSING

Jeremiah 29:11, *"For I know the plans I have for you," declares the Lord, "plans to prosper you and not to harm you, plans to give you hope and a future."* (NIV)

Ever notice how you feel alive when someone says something good about you. It is because God wants us to bless others with our words and deeds. God blesses us so we can be a blessing to others, like speaking words of encouragement or doing something to assist someone, or even cooking a meal for someone who is sick. The amazing way of God is that when we bless others, we will be blessed. God wants us to have a joyous and prosperous life, but He wants us to do it His way. Doing life God's way will bring joy and satisfaction to our own lives. When our lives are filled with the Holy Spirit and we walk each day in the Spirit, the joy of life will flow in blessing to those we come in contact with each day.

Be God's blessing to someone today.

When the Israelites were captured and went to Babylon, God sent a message to them and told them He would come to them and they would return to Jerusalem, but meantime, even though they were in exile, they were to build houses, increase in number and pray for the city where they were. He was telling them that even though their circumstances were not what they wanted, He was with them, and they could still be a blessing to those around them as they lived their lives for God.

God wants us to prosper, to be generous and a blessing to others. We don't need to be blessed with what the world calls the luxuries of life to bless others. We can bless and be generous to others in the little everyday things of life. What matters in life is your relationship with your Lord and passing on the blessing of God to others.

Through Zachariah, God told those in exile, *"I will save you, and you will be a blessing"* (Zachariah 8: 13). If you follow Jesus and live for Him, God will turn your life around to be a blessing to others. Who can you bless today?

Prayer: *Thank You Lord, for placing me just where I am, so that I can bless others for You. Please help me speak kindness and love over everyone I meet each day. Amen*

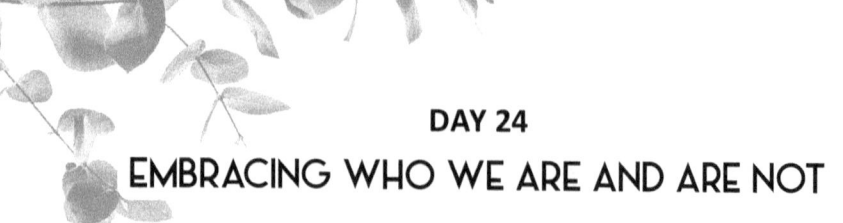

DAY 24
EMBRACING WHO WE ARE AND ARE NOT

Romans 12:3-5, *"Do not think of yourself more highly than you ought, but rather think of yourself... in accordance with the faith God has distributed to each of you. For just as each of us has one body with many members, and these members do not all have the same function, so in Christ we, though many, form one body, and each member belongs to all the others"* NIV.

We are often told who we are, but it is also important to know who we are not. Much of our weariness stems from continuously trying to be someone we are not. Nobody can be everything to everybody they know. We often feel we should help a person with their problems, so we listen, try to give advice, and often share our own experiences. The result is we end up feeling exhausted.

> We often fail to stop and take time to let the Spirit speak into our life.

We need to know what we are and are not, to be able to listen without pressure, cry with and pray for them and then if their problem is not within our ability to help them, we need, with their permission, to pass their problem onto a person who is better equipped with that area of service. We must not be afraid to step out of our comfort zone to fulfil the calling that God asks of us, but God also asks us to see ourselves with sober judgement. Sometimes it is better to focus on one-on-one conversation instead of entering into trying to help everyone.

We struggle because we want our lives to count and be helpful. More than anything, we want to be accepted and of worth to others, having a life that matters, but we often fail to stop and take time to let the Spirit speak into our life and hear Him tell us, *'You are important to me, for there is nobody else like you, made in My image, one of a kind, my original design and creation.'*

We need to know who we are not and celebrate who we are, for this is the key that will enable us to joyfully fit into our role in the body of Christ. *"Now you are the body of Christ, and each one of you is a part of it"* (1 Corinthians 12:27). Let us rejoice that together our different skills make us into the perfect instrument for God's work and glory.

Prayer: *Thanks Lord, that I am important to You and that You can use even me in the work of Your Kingdom here on earth. Help me to always listen and be prepared to obey. Amen*

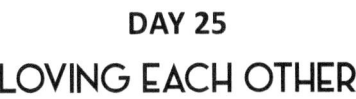

DAY 25
LOVING EACH OTHER

Leviticus 19:34, *"The foreigner residing among you must be treated as your native-born. Love them as yourself"* NIV.

In the history of our world, even as early as Moses' day, God tried to show us that every human being on earth is created in the image of God and is loved by Him. What is it that after 4,000 plus years, there is still so much hatred and discrimination between nationality and the colour of the human race? It wasn't until 1949 that the Australian Government effectively dismantled the strict immigration policies that prevented many people from other countries coming to Australia and becoming citizens.

The sad reality is that the church of Jesus Christ has been involved in discrimination as much as anyone else, to the extent that we have segregated many fellow believers from meeting together. God instructed the Israelites to welcome foreigners and live together in harmony. They were to treat foreigners kindly (v.33) and to love them as themselves. In Mark 12:31, Jesus reminds us of the commandment when He says, *"Love your neighbour as yourself."*

> Every human on earth is created in the image of God and is loved by Him.

In Nelson Mandela's Inaugural speech in 1994, he said, *"We were born to manifest the glory of our God that is within us. It is not just in some of us, it is in everyone, and as we let our light shine, we subconsciously give other people permission to do the same. As we are liberated from our own fear, our presence automatically liberates others."*

How do you react when you encounter a stranger? Our God calls us to welcome them as brothers and sisters in Christ because we are all God's children, created in the image of God. Our cultural practices though sometimes challenging must be overlooked and learnt from. Let us shine our light for Jesus so that our brothers and sisters can see our love and be liberated from fear so they can also know Jesus as their Saviour.

Prayer: *Father God, let us welcome each other with open arms, for You love and died for us, so that each of us could know You. Amen.*

DAY 26
YOUR VALUE OF JESUS

Mark 14: 6,10, *"She has done a beautiful thing to me... 10. Then, Judas Iscariot, went to the chief priests to betray Jesus to them."* NIV

When Mary came to the home of Simon the leper and poured very expensive oil over the head of Jesus, those present were indignant at the sheer waste and money spent, claiming many poor could have been fed. It certainly placed a high value on how much Jesus meant to Mary Magdalene. Perhaps her generosity was inspired because she had experienced the love of Jesus in her own life, not to mention the raising of her brother Lazarus from the dead.

> *Jesus loves you and will not turn you away.*

In contrast, Judas didn't value Jesus, immediately going to speak with the chief priests to betray Him, taking 30 pieces of silver, the price paid for a slave. A small price for the Creator of the World. Judas had listened to Jesus teach, seen Him perform miracles and yet placed no value on Him because of the greed within himself. How much do you value Jesus? With Jesus, it is all in or not at all. There is no middle road. God is looking for the heart that truly belongs to Him and trusts Him. How important is Jesus to you?

At the Passover meal, He reminded them how the Israelites were delivered from Egypt and how down through the centuries God forgave them again and again. In 1 Cor. 12:24-25, Paul reminds us of Jesus's words, *"This is my body, which is broken for you... This cup is the new covenant of my blood, do this, whenever you drink it, in remembrance of me."* We read they sang the 'Great Hallel,' a traditional hymn from Psalm 118, *"Give thanks to the Lord, for He is good; his love endures forever."* Immediately after celebrating with his disciples, He went out knowing they would forsake Him, that He would suffer ridicule and torture to then die the most humiliating and horrific death on a cross for you and me.

Eternity will not be long enough to thank Jesus, who loves you more than you can understand and will not turn you away. He died, so by trust in Him, we do not have to die; He has done it all. All you need to do is humbly give your life to Him.

Prayer: *Praise You Lord, there is no greater love. You paid the price for my sin on the cross. It is measureless and will endure forever. Amen.*

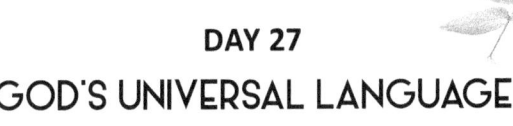

DAY 27
GOD'S UNIVERSAL LANGUAGE

Eph. 5:19,20, *"Sing and make music in your heart to the Lord, always giving thanks to God the Father for everything"* NIV.

The amount of expression and thought that goes into composing a piece of music has always fascinated me. From black dots and lines comes the language that everyone in the world can enjoy and worship God together.

I was fortunate to marry someone who was very musical. Over the 50 years of being involved with him in his musical endeavours of singing and conducting, I gained a great appreciation for those who have this gift. As my children had music lessons, at first it was a struggle but, as they learnt the notes and moved their fingers along the piano keys, the tune always rang out clear and beautiful.

Over the years, all of us have been faced with many black dots and lines in our lives, and often we cannot understand why our loving Heavenly Father has placed them there or permitted them in our life. We have to be prepared to allow God to arrange the dots and lines as He chooses, as it will only be then that the actual melody that He instilled into each of us before we were born will give the glorious harmony that He wants us to reveal to the world.

> **Allow God to arrange the dots and lines in your life as He chooses.**

Even though I can't sing in tune, God has enabled me to enjoy music and the musical ability of others while I just keep on making a joyful noise. It doesn't concern me in any way because God knows my heart, and I can sing the tune He designed for me in my spirit. Let us always give thanks for all things, the white and the black, because God has to touch all the keys to get the full capacity He has placed in us. Psalm 95: 1-2 says, *"Come, let us sing for joy to the Lord, let us shout aloud to the Rock of our salvation. Let us come before him with thanksgiving and extol (praise emphatically) him with music and song."*

Many men owe the grandeur of their lives
to their tremendous difficulties.
C. H. Spurgeon.

Spend time in prayer, giving thanks to your Heavenly Father for everything you have faced to make you who you are today.

DAY 28

SEEK GOD FIRST

Deut. 4:29, *"But if from there you seek the Lord your God, you will find him, if you seek him with all your heart and with all your soul."* NIV

Most of us would love to know Jesus more but things get in the way, and we continue our spiritual journey without any change on a daily basis. We forget that God is so loving and humble He will stoop to meet any of us in our need.

> **Focus on what matters – your relationship with God.**

A friend shared her life as a child in an atheist home, never being able to attend religious education at school. Even though she knew nothing about God or if He even existed, she felt if she prayed, He would hear her. As a child and a teenager, whenever she hurt, was scared or alone, she prayed, though still knowing nothing about God. Through marriage to a Christian, she put her trust in Jesus as her Saviour, but after their first daughter was born, and due to the pressures of life, they lost their focus on their relationship with God.

Throughout the following years, she gave birth to three more daughters. The first was severely growth-restricted being only 2kgs but survived due to miraculous intervention. During those first days, she prayed and cried, somehow knowing, that again God was there for her, resulting in both her husband and herself recommitting their lives to Jesus. They prayed together each day, which brought a remarkable change to their relationship. The birth of their third daughter at first seemed okay; however, after a few days, her baby suffered a severe stroke, resulting in cerebral palsy. Yet again, with her fourth child, God intervened by making the doctors hear her concerns that something was wrong, resulting in her life being saved at the last minute.

Could we have coped with all this? My friend learned to put her relationship with God first and leave everything else with Him. *"Be strong and courageous. Do not be afraid, . . . for the Lord your God goes with you; He will never leave you or forsake you."* (Deut. 31:6) These were the words Moses told Joshua about how to live, and they have helped countless millions. You too can find God's unconditional love and faithfulness in them as my friend has.

Prayer: *Lord, thank You for never failing us, and being there when we need Your help. You are in control of our lives. Help us to trust You in everything. Amen*

DAY 29
INVITATION TO LISTEN

Isaiah 55:2,3, *"Listen, listen to me... and you will delight in the richest of fare. Give ear and come to me; listen, that you may live."* NIV

Christ is our leader and speaks to us through Scripture and prayer. He longs for us to make Him the priority in our daily lives. We must listen intentionally by turning from the things that distract us, otherwise we will miss His voice.

There is a town called Green Bank which is known as the quietest town in America because there are no mobile phones, Wi-Fi, GPS, Bluetooth devices or microwave ovens. Can you imagine living in the 21st century without all these modcons? This town is the home of the world's largest steerable radio telescope, which needs perfect quiet to listen to the naturally occurring radio waves deep in outer space. The uninterrupted quiet enables scientists to hear the movements in the universe.

He has promised us His faithful love and forgiveness.

Like the town of Green Bank, we need to be quiet enough to hear the Creator of the universe. The Israelites were distracted from their obedience to God, so God used Isaiah to communicate His message to be quiet and listen. He told them to *"listen so that they may live."* When we listen and begin to focus on Christ more, He has promised us His faithful love and forgiveness. The amazing result will be, that loving Christ and serving others becomes a natural part of us. Psalm 4:8, *"In peace I will lie down and sleep, for you alone, Lord, make me dwell in safety."*

As Christians, it is utter foolishness to seek fulfilment outside of a close relationship with Christ because He knows just what we need and can bear and will always give us the required courage and strength. He is with us always and helps us to learn obedience, faith and hope as we follow Him, but WE MUST LISTEN.

In what way do you plan to make time to listen to Him?

Prayer: *Lord, please help me to be constantly aware of Your presence with me and to make time to be quiet and listen to You every day. Amen*

DAY 30
TAKE A CHANCE

Isaiah 30:15, *"In quietness and confidence shall be your strength."* NIV

In life, we have two paths to choose from, the path of least resistance or the path of motivation and doing. When asked to do something that we are not familiar with, most of us take the easy way out and take the path of least resistance. In doing this, we could miss the opportunity that may change our life. Joy and meaning in life come from taking responsibility. When we step up and take a chance the way to progress often opens before us.

> *Joy and meaning in life come from taking responsibility.*

Consider Moses, who, at 40 years of age murdered an Egyptian and then fled to Median, where he became a shepherd. At age 80, God asks him to lead the Israelites out of Egypt. Yes, he was old, and four times he came up with excuses as to why he should not do what God required of him, the last excuse being, *"O Lord, please send someone else to do it."* (Exodus 4:13.) We know that Moses did go and became a great man of God. Had he not taken the chance, he would never have known the power and presence of God in his life, becoming an integral part of the history of mankind.

Sound familiar? Even when we have the skills, we are still prepared to say to God, *'find someone else.'* James 4:17 says, *"So whoever knows the right thing to do and fails to do it, for him it is sin."* God wants to do amazing things in our lives but whilst we remain weak minded, we will never know the blessings God has for us. We are never too old, too young, or too inexperienced when God is with us. I know a lady who in her seventies became a youth leader, something she never expected God would require of her.

God needs people like you. Do what is wise and take the chance with God by your side. As He works through you, your walk with Him will be a relationship like no other. All you need is the Lord. You have the power of the Holy Spirit within you, so do not have any regrets. Take the chance God is giving you today. 1 Peter 3:14. *"But even if you should suffer for what is right, you are blessed. "Do not fear their threats; do not be frightened."*

Prayer: *Dear Lord, give me the courage to always be willing to take the opportunities you give me to live and work for You. Amen*

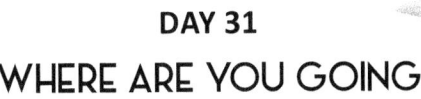

DAY 31
WHERE ARE YOU GOING

John 8:32, *"Then you will know the truth, and the truth will set you free"* NIV.

Any day, you can sit on a seat in a shopping centre and watch people pass by. As you watch, you will observe people just walking along listening to their music playing in their ears; others rushing to purchase the items on sale even though they probably don't need them; people hurrying with children; people without any time to spare, and it seems as though they are all being sucked along in what we call living in our modern world. Life as we know it for the majority, can be cold and mechanical. Are you and I allowing the majority to lead us in doing things that are against our better judgement? Are you feeling as though you are being driven by the majority?

Many of us who call ourselves Christians and believe, do not trust and live for the God we claim to believe in. We say, I pray and go to church, but God doesn't want us to have this pretend behaviour. He doesn't pretend, and He doesn't want us to pretend. Sadly, there are many false believers who think they are going to Heaven and will be disappointed. We must wise up as to how we live so that we know where we are going. *"Therefore, if anyone is in Christ, he is a new creation. The old has passed away; behold, the new has come"* (2 Corinthians 5:17).

> **We need to wise up to the way we live our lives.**

As a child of a Holy God, you must live by truth, even if it means that you are somehow persecuted. Only as you trust the Saviour and live by the truth of God, will you be the witness that the world needs. All around us, thousands are crying out because they are mistreated, abused and hurt as they are sucked along by the way of the world. As you and I stand on truth and pray, living our lives for Jesus, God's Spirit will draw men and women to Himself. We must so live our lives that we will attract others to the peace they see in us.

3 John 1:11, *"Dear friend, do not imitate what is evil but what is good."* Only then can you be sure of where you are going when you leave this life.

Prayer: *Dear Lord, help me live for You each day, that others will want to come to You and know You as Saviour. Amen*

Enter to grow in wisdom.
Depart better to serve thy country and mankind.
Charles William Eliot
(Inscription on the 1890 Gate to Harvard Yard)

"Let the wise listen and add to their learning,
and let the discerning get guidance—
The fear of the Lord is the beginning of knowledge,
but fools despise wisdom and instruction.
Proverbs 1:5,7.

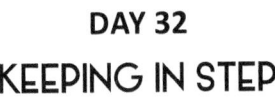

DAY 32
KEEPING IN STEP

Matthew 11:28-30, *"Come to me, all you who are weary and burdened. Take my yoke... learn of me... For my yoke is easy and my burden is light"* NIV.

If you are finding you are exhausted and drained in your Christian experience, maybe you are just practising religion rather than enjoying a relationship with Christ. When you come to the Lord and enjoy a life of being Christ conscious, He will take the load as you abide in Him. *"For my yoke is easy."*

When we yoke our life to Christ, He desires to work out the Father's will in our lives, and as His child, we know that God's will for us is perfect and brings peace. When we think only of ourselves, we will find it is the first thing that upsets our completeness in Christ. Until we come back and connect with Christ, we are outside of God's purpose for us. Amos 3:3 says, *"Do two walk together unless they have agreed to do so?"* To know completeness in Christ, there must always be cooperation between the Devine and the Human.

The most important aspect of life is to keep yourself right spiritually.

When "timber getters" of early Australia used bullocks to haul enormous logs, it was vital that the two bullocks yoked together, worked and pulled together. Training a new bullock took many hours before he could become part of the team. The yoke means hard work by ploughing the subsoil of your soul. Christ knew that He had to break the hard surface of your spirit from resistance.

Do not allow your life to be divided from Christ, who loves you so much that He died to save you. Be aware of your life being divided by the influence of friends or circumstances, of anything that will break your oneness with Jesus, to make you see yourself as separate from Him. The most crucial aspect of your life is to keep yourself right spiritually.

Is it as though Jesus is saying to you, *'Are you feeling tired and worn out spiritually? Is your life burned out trying to be religious? If this is how you feel, then you need to learn to walk in unforced rhythms of grace with Me.'* - For us all, the solution is straightforward – Jesus said, *"Come to me."*

Prayer: *Thank You, Lord Jesus for loving and dying for me. Forgive my self-conscious ways and lead me to the life you desire for me. Amen*

DAY 33
STAYING FOCUSED

2 Corinthians 4:18, *"So we fix our eyes not on what is seen, but on what is unseen. For what is seen is temporary, but what is unseen is eternal"* NIV.

As you read these words from Paul's letter to the church at Corinth, consider what is happening in your life. Are you stressed or worried about your work or family, or are you suffering pain and illness? Maybe you are experiencing depression or anxiety. In all these circumstances, we try desperately to convince ourselves that God is there and will help us, yet we don't see the answer to our prayer.

When everything around us is shaky, we must focus on God.

Like King David, we cry, *"O Lord, don't rebuke me in your anger or discipline me in your wrath. Be merciful to me, Lord, for I am faint; O Lord, heal me, for my bones are in agony* (Psalm 6;1-2). Our Heavenly Father is just like the wood craftsman when he wants strong wood to polish, he searches for a tree that has suffered. Only in the tree that has lost limbs in the storm or been damaged by an axe will he find the hardness and knots that will give beauty to his craft. We are the tree Jesus longs to heal and craft to become like Him.

In my Christian walk, it has been my experience that if I can stay focused on God and hope in the eternal home He has for me, I can find strength in my troubles. If we can stay focused, this will supersede momentary troubles (v17) and achieve eternal glory for us which, far outweighs all our problems.

When everything around us is shaky, we must turn our eyes and focus on God our loving Father, knowing that the troubles are precious and God will use them to build spiritual strength in us. For every sorrow there is compensation that will bring beauty to our lives.

Prayer: *Dear God, please help me to stay focused on You when troubles surround me. Please take my hand and lead me to the peace only You can give. Amen*

DAY 34
HIS KEEPING POWER

Deut. 32: 10-12, *"He shielded him and cared for him; he guarded him as the apple of his eye, like an eagle that stirs up its nest and hovers over its young, that spreads its wings to catch them and carries them aloft. The Lord alone led him."* NIV

We don't become God's child when we accept Jesus as our Saviour. We are already His. He made us, and Salvation brings us back to Him, *"God was reconciling the world to himself in Christ, not counting people's sins against them. We are therefore Christ's ambassadors"* (1 Cor. 5: 19-20). In Moses's song, there are three symbols of our Almighty Father's love of His own.

God said that we are the apple of his eye (v.10). Just as we instinctively raise our hand to protect our eyes, so it is with God's care for us when we are threatened. The eye is protected, from behind by a bony socket, by eyebrows and lashes which help to catch dust, by the eyelid that closes over our eye to shield it, and 'tear water' which is continually washing the eye clean. Just as our eye is completely protected, we can be sure that when God brings us into unparalleled difficulty in life, we can count on Him to protect and deliver.

When in unparalleled difficulty, count on God for deliverance.

Sometimes God has to break up the comforts we have become accustomed to and send us forward so that we may grow in Christ. Like an eagle (v11), when the young eaglets need to learn to fly, the parents break up their nest and bring them to the very edge of the cliff, thrusting them off into the air. If they falter, the parent glides gently beneath to break their fall and bear them upward to safety. We can be confident that when God pushes us forward, He puts His arms around and beneath us.

God led them. As a parent guides, teaches, and disciplines a child, so Jesus guides us through life. I encourage you to read of the countless blessings God lavishes on us and waits for us to accept. His love for us is beyond imagination with an eternal purpose. He redeemed us from sin; His grace is sufficient for our needs; we are kept by the Holy Spirit and will be presented without blemish to God. Do you have the love and protection of Almighty Father God?

Prayer: *Jesus, take my hand, I lack nothing when I am Yours. You are the Almighty loving Father and Prince of peace. You're a good, good God. Amen*

DAY 35
IT'S NOT ABOUT ME

Philippians 1:21, *"For to me, to live is Christ and to die is gain."* NIV.

In our verse today, there is only a comma standing between life and death, and that is where we all stand. If you have ever lost someone suddenly, as in a car accident, you truly understand the brevity of life. So, what is life all about?

Paul turned the pressure of life into joy. He had a very clear sense of the purpose of his life; to exalt God and bring glory to Him every day and in every way. As the beloved of Christ, we must also have the same purpose in our life. For those of this world, it may be different. For a philosopher, to live is knowledge, or for the businessman, it may be riches, but for the majority it is toil and trouble, trying to make ends meet as they struggle to provide for their families.

> *God can work through us when we don't seek recognition from others.*

Paul saw the needs of those around him and chose to make Christ his priority. He decided to share the love of Jesus with them, not allowing circumstances to overwhelm him; instead, wherever God put him, he was unfazed, even when he was in prison, because his priority in life was what was important. God was able to use him because he always gave the glory to his Heavenly Father. When we don't seek praise or recognition from others, God can work through us too.

Consciously or subconsciously, we all work with a priority to imitate someone. Paul's priority was to imitate Christ. *"And we all... are being transformed into his image"* (2 Cor.3:18, NIV). Like Paul, we must keep our perspective focused, as we endeavour to bring others to love and serve Christ as we do. External things of life will have no power over us when we can say, *"I live; yet not I, but Christ liveth in me."* Then we are triumphant over death, and like Paul... to die is gain.

Prayer: *Dear Lord, help me to always make my priority to imitate You, and to understand that life is about You and not about me. Amen.*

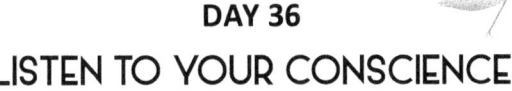

DAY 36
LISTEN TO YOUR CONSCIENCE

Romans 2:15, *"They show that the requirements of the law are written on their hearts, their consciences also bearing witness, and their thoughts sometimes accusing them, and at other times even defending them."* NIV

What is it that makes you or me who we are? When God created us, He gave us a soul, which is the centre of our personality. From it, we connect to the world through the organs of touch, sight, smell, taste and hearing. To the spiritual world, we are related as the Holy Spirit reveals and convicts our conscience through our thoughts, from which, by our choice, we can descend to the material or ascend to a relationship with our Creator God.

Our conscience shows us who we are in the light of God's truth, what a person knows about themselves, whether good or bad. This is evident when we can smile about our life, as opposed to when we are ashamed, being unable to deceive ourselves, as Paul said about himself. *"For I know that good itself does not dwell in me, that is, in my sinful nature. For I have the desire to do what is good, but I cannot carry it out."* (Romans 7:18)

> *Our conscience shows us who we are in the light of God's truth.*

Our conscience is as if it were our own judge because it is that which God speaks to, but unfortunately for some, they have not listened for so long that they are no longer hearing God's Spirit. It is God's standard, and through our conscience, we know right and wrong, good and evil.

For the Christian, it is necessary to keep on good terms with your conscience, allowing the Holy Spirit to instruct you, and by your choice and intelligence, correct your life by Christ's standard. Never say it does not matter just this once. Never let the voice of your conscience wear itself out. To do so is to tamper with the most delicate part of creation in God's universe.

Instead, *"Let us draw near to God with a sincere heart and with the full assurance that faith brings, having our hearts sprinkled to cleanse us from a guilty conscience and having our bodies washed with pure water."* (Heb. 10:22)

Prayer: *Lord, fill me to a deeper measure with Your Spirit, that my conscience may be enlightened by You, helping me to always choose right over wrong, and good over evil. Amen.*

DAY 37
GREAT FAITH

James 1:3-4, *"You know that the testing of your faith produces perseverance. Let perseverance finish its work so that you may be mature and complete, not lacking anything."* NIV

Great faith is achieved through great suffering. Jesus said to Peter just before His crucifixion, *"The cup which my Father has given me, shall I not drink it"* (John 18:11). Jesus was prepared to suffer greatly for our sin, and there is no greater faith than Jesus had that day as He bled and died for all mankind.

Through the ages, there have been prophets, apostles and great men of God, who have been able to work wondrous miracles, but could not always cope with the problems and sufferings of the life they were called to lead. The greatest of all Christian achievements is when we can suffer deeply and endure our sufferings with great faith.

Great achievement is when we endure our sufferings with great faith.

To be deprived of the everyday necessities of life, to be handicapped mentally or physically by disability, to be rejected by our family and friends, to lose everyone dear to you and to have to stand alone to meet the shocks of this life, or to bear a lifetime of extreme pain – these are the things of this life that test our faith. When you can suffer these things and say, *"I shall drink the cup my Heavenly Father has given me,"* this, my friend, is faith of the highest spiritual calling.

If we are to truly stand in our Lord's shoes and minister to others as He did, we must know something of the cost our Saviour paid for us. Only at a cost to ourselves can we do good for others, and our sufferings are the price we pay for the ability to sympathize and have genuine compassion as our Lord had for humanity. When we genuinely suffer with others, we will know the highest happiness and blessing of a life of great faith.

When you surrender your life's circumstances to Christ, they will become your Heavenly Father's tool to mould you to help others. Just trust Jesus, being careful not to reject the instrument in God's hands, lest you lose faith in God.

Prayer: *Lord, sometimes we wonder why we have troubles. Help us to hang in, trusting You, that we may receive the blessing You have for us. Amen*

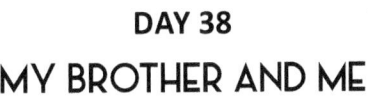

DAY 38
MY BROTHER AND ME

Genesis 4:9, *"Am I my brother's keeper?"* 1 John 2:11, *"Anyone who hates a brother or sister is in the darkness and walks around in the darkness"* NIV.

Man is made in the likeness of God, and God's nature is selfless. From the time our first parents chose to gratify their self-life, the world became what it is today because man continued to choose a lifestyle where the essence of life is the serving of self. The first children of Adam and Eve had different dispositions, hence the reason for their disagreement is somewhat veiled in mystery, except where we read in 1 John 3:12, *"Because his own actions were evil and his brothers were righteous."*

All through history, we have had sibling rivalry, jealousy, deceitfulness, and hatred, often just for the ability of a sibling's success. Sometimes it can just be a difference of personality, or a feeling of the sibling being favoured by a parent. Sad as it may seem, the troubles between siblings are often never resolved, and the family splits.

> **Man continues to choose a lifestyle where the essence of life is the serving of self.**

We are all made in the image of God, and as such, like God, we are required to be selfless, seeking to help and understand each other. Most importantly, God requires us to forgive as God in Christ has forgiven us.

Is there something that puts a barrier between you and your sibling? God tells us to look out for our brother or sister more than looking out for ourselves all the time. You are probably saying, *"but you don't know what my sibling has done."* True, but when we love God first, and open our souls to Him, He will provide us love to forgive, understand, and encourage our siblings.

The blood of Jesus cries out for those who are wronged, asking God for mercy and not judgement. Hebrews 13:1 says, *"Keep on loving one another as brothers and sisters."*

Prayer: *Dear Father, help me to consider the interests of others before myself, and help me to act generously toward them because You love them. Amen.*

DAY 39
RENEWED LOVE

Psalm 119:11, *"I have hidden your word in my heart that I might not sin against you."* NIV

We all know someone who has been passionate for Jesus, but after a time, they have stopped reading their Bible, praying, and worshiping with other believers. They have lost their first love for Jesus, or they are like the seed that was planted, and weeds choked it from becoming strong and bearing a good crop. Have you lost your first love? Do you read God's Word and pray to your Father in Heaven daily, and do you commit to meeting weekly with other believers to worship and grow?

> *God's Word will lead us to a changed heart, attitude, and conduct.*

Psalm 119: 97 tells us to *"meditate on God's Word all day long."* As we read, and meditate on God's Word, we will find the world God wants us to experience. You may say, *"I don't like reading, or I am a poor reader."* I can tell you I would have been the poorest reader there was when young, and as I read my Bible it meant nothing to me, quickly forgetting what I read until I decided to read it aloud so that it was audible. I persevered, and gradually God showed me things that made me want to read even more until I grew to love reading His Word. Today, we do not have the excuse of being a poor reader, for we all have technology which will audibly read the Bible to us. Praise God for good in technology. It is amazing what God can do for us.

Reading and studying our Bible, will permeate our lives to keep us from sin, for as we read we will become aware of our sins. Paul tells us in Romans 3:20, *"through the law (God's Word), we become conscious of sin."* When we delight in God's Word, sin becomes distasteful, and we are transformed into new life.

In the same way as food gives our body energy, so spiritual food received from the Bible empowers us to live our lives according to God's Word (v.9).

James also tells us in James 1:22. *"Do what it says."* We can only 'do' what it says, if we 'know' what it says. God's Word will lead us to a changed heart, a changed attitude, and changed conduct. Obedience to God's word is proof of the renewal of our first love.

Prayer: *Dear Lord, as I read Your Word, I pray that I will grow to love what You show me and that my life will change to bring glory to You alone. Amen*

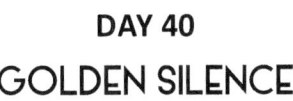

DAY 40
GOLDEN SILENCE

Rev. 4:1, *"After this I looked, and there before me was a door standing open in heaven."*

Job 4:16, *"A form stood before my eyes, and I heard a hushed voice"* NIV.

In the early 1800s, a book 'True Peace' was written expounding the message, God is deep within those who truly love Him, waiting to speak if only we would get still enough to hear His voice. From the beginning of time, there's accounts of God speaking to people, like Moses, Paul, and John on the Isle of Patmos. God has spoken to men in prison, sufferers of abuse, and people on beds of pain, each experiencing God's voice as a door opens in heaven.

Do you long for an experience of the Holy Spirit? Thinking it to be easy, I began to be still before God, only to have my thoughts interrupted by voices within and noise around me. As I tried to connect with God, I was pulled in every direction, feeling I needed to listen and answer them in my mind, voices about tomorrow, but God said, *"Be still and know that I am God."*

> The problem is we fail to get still enough to hear Him within.

When our heart is pure and obedient, putting aside everything to know God, we will enter into His Spirit. Then, somewhere deep inside we will hear the voice of the Holy Spirit impressing on our soul tenderness, comfort, and peace. But there are conditions. As we listen with ears to no other sound than God's voice, we will find within the voice of prayer and of wisdom. We will no longer need to think or pray so hard, as the still small voice of the Holy Spirit in our heart whispers God's prayer for us. As His loved children, He is always there; the problem is that we fail to get still enough in His presence to hear Him within. As He speaks, our spirit of life is then lived out in our duties and the conflicts of life.

When God is everything to us; when we live, move, and have our being in Him, it is as though we are a flower that has drunk from the fountain of life as the dew settled on it in the stillness of the night. Remember that the dew never falls on a stormy night or when the wind blows, just as God's peace never comes to the restless soul.

Prayer: *Father, let me hear Your voice within me, that I may know Your will each day. Amen*

DAY 41
A GLIMPSE INTO THE FUTURE

Revelation 7:9, *"After this I looked and there before me was a great multitude that no one could count, from every nation, tribe, people and language, standing before the throne and in front of the Lamb"* NIV.

Visualize with me the reality of this verse. My imagination cannot grasp the glory of this scene. All will be joy as the great multitude of the redeemed gathers together before the throne of God, praising and worshiping Jesus, our Saviour. What a triumphant day for every believer! Can you say, *'What a wonderful day, I'm going to be among that multitude of believers!'*

Be sure the final chapter of your life will be victory in Christ.

In Revelation 7, we're told that we will be rewarded by serving and loving Jesus. As we look around us, we see so many opportunities to serve. People are hungry and thirsty. People are hurting and homeless, and no one cares about them. It's not just the poor, for those who are physically and financially secure often carry burdens of depression, anxiety and loneliness.

God gave John the privilege of seeing the joyful culmination of man's journey here on earth. Are you numbered among this great multitude of believers, or are you carrying many burdens? Will your life be defeat or victory?

Jesus shed His blood so that when we ask Him to forgive our sins and cleanse our life, we can be sure that the final chapter of our life will be victory in Christ and not defeat. If you have never asked Jesus to cleanse you of sin, then come and ask Him right where you are. He has promised to *"wipe away every tear"* (Revelation 7:17). He will wash away your sin, and you will stand with the redeemed before the throne of Almighty God with that great multitude and sing with the angels.

> *"Holy, holy, holy is the Lord God Almighty, who was, and is, and is to come."* (Rev.4:8)

If you have never asked Jesus to forgive you and want to stand with the great multitude before the throne of Almighty God in heaven, then you can ask Jesus to be your Saviour by praying this prayer.

Prayer: *Dear Jesus, thank You for paying the price for my sin when You died on the cross. Please forgive me and fill me with Your Holy Spirit so that I might live for You from this day forward. Amen*

DAY 42
POWERFUL PRAYER

1 Corinthians 16:13, *"Be men of courage; be strong. Do everything in love."* NIV

Be careful not to pray for an easy life, instead pray for trust and faith to be a stronger Christian. Phillip Brooks said, *"Do not pray for tasks equal to your powers. Pray for powers equal to your tasks. Then doing your work shall be no miracle, but you shall be a miracle."*

As we think of some of the great men of the Bible, we can be sure they prayed for power equal to their tasks. There was Moses, who showed God's power in his life as he parted the Red Sea with a touch of his rod. Also, Elijah when he defended the worship of God over that of Baal by calling down fire from heaven. (1 Kings.18.) Not to forget the power of God that filled Joshua as he marched around Jericho to see the walls tumble.

> **Lead a self-indulgent easy life, and it will not lead to greatness in God**

If we continue to lead a self-indulgent easy life, it will not lead us to greatness in God. Yet, the power that the men of God in the Bible experienced can be ours today. We serve the same God who can give the same passion. We may not be called to do great deeds, but God will give us the power to overcome the obstacles of our life. The noble people of our present world, like Nelson Mandela or Mother Teresa, have sacrificed the easy life to help others.

Prayer and trust give the courage and strength that Paul refers to in our verse for today. Greatness in this life does not come by having the money to have whatever pleases us but by having faith and trust in reliance on God, to make our pathway in life with our own hands, through the power of the Holy Spirit within us. We have to be prepared to sometimes go without the pleasures of life to reach the mountaintop and be filled to overflowing with the love and mercy of God.

Will you reach the splendours God has for you on the mountaintop of your life?

> *'Rise up O men of God, be done with lesser things.*
> *Give heart and soul and mind and strength,*
> *To serve the King of Kings.'*
> William P. Merrill

DAY 43
VALUED FRIENDSHIP

Eccles. 4:9-10, *"Two are better than one... If one falls down, his friend can help him up."* NIV

It is sad when a person is without a close, spiritual friend. The kind of friend who, in an emergency, would ask, *"Where are you?"* and *"What do you need?"* Do you have someone you could call at 2 am, and are you someone your friends could depend on at 2 am? Having or being a friend like this is crucial in life. *"Brothers, if a man be overtaken in a fault, you which are spiritual, restore such a one in the spirit of meekness; considering yourself, lest you also be tempted"* (Gal.6:1). We must watch out for each other, always being ready to help those who have fallen. It is easier to rise above our situation when we have a friend to listen to and encourage us. This is probably why Jesus sent His disciples out in pairs, to support each other and keep each other from falling under pressure from Satan.

> **Always be ready to help those who have fallen.**

Even the person with all his wealth forfeits the joy of the satisfaction of life without companionship. It is what makes our daily lives worthwhile.

For the Christian, there is nothing quite like a friend who can give you Godly wisdom and fellowship, as you meet together. To know your friend is upholding you in prayer gives strength and courage to your soul.

Because of deep friendship, Johathan warned David of his father's plan to kill him. He grieved as Saul pursued David. The Bible tells us, (1 Samuel 20: 41), *"Then they kissed each other and wept together."* Their souls were as one.

Vital as it is to have a close spiritual friend, there is no other friendship more remarkable than our friendship with Jesus our Saviour. He lifts us when we fail, comforts us when we are distressed and guards our lives from the Tempter. *"Where two or three are gathered together in My Name, there am I in the midst of them"* (Matt.18:20). It is Jesus who makes the third person. When we are a trustworthy and loving friend to those we care for, we bring glory to our Heavenly Father.

> *I thank the Lord, for a good friend like You, always there to see me through*
> *I can't explain what You mean to me. Helpful to me, You, will always be*
> Unknown

DAY 44
THE GIFT OF UNDERSTANDING

Proverbs 4:7-8, *"Though it cost all you have, get understanding. Cherish her, and she will exalt you; embrace her, and she will honour you."* NIV

When we love someone, we want to lavish gifts on them, often going without what we may need ourselves. Jesus could have lavished anything He wished on those around Him, but He knew that more precious is understanding. He gave to them what they really needed, such as forgiveness, hope and love.

We can have good education, a good position, and everything we desire, but without understanding we won't be successful. All of life we have to deal with people, and understanding and working with them is essential to being successful. We need empathy, and a positive attitude to make others feel special. When conflict arises, it is because people lack understanding of each other. Harry Truman said, *"When we understand the other fellow's viewpoint – understanding what he is trying to do – nine times out of ten, we find that he is trying to do what is right."* When we can understand others, we can influence them and have a significant impact on their lives.

> We need empathy, and a positive attitude to make others feel special.

The Bible tells us, *"Fools find no pleasure in understanding but delight in airing their own opinions"* (Prov.18:2). Always try to see the situation from the other person's point of view. We need to seek to understand the things of God, applying His truth and wisdom in our lives so that we don't make foolish decisions or seek the things of this world. *"Lean not on your own understanding; in all your ways submit to him, and he will make your paths straight"* (Prov.3:5-6). When we understand God's truth, we will end up understanding how to have wisdom in the most challenging situations of life.

Even though we can never understand God in all His fullness... do not be discouraged in wanting to know more, for He will surely guide you through the Holy Spirit within you. By regularly reading the Bible, we will learn more about who God is and how we can better understand those around us as we influence them to learn more about Christ.

Prayer: *Please help me to have understanding each time I connect with someone, so I will see things from their point of view to guide them to Your cross. Amen*

DAY 45
THE MUSIC OF THE GOSPEL

1 Peter 3:15, *"In your heart set apart Christ as Lord. Always be prepared to give an answer . . . for the hope that you have."* NIV

> Have you heard the music of the gospel?
> Have you heard it ringing in your ear?
> It's playing sweet and low.
> It's a song I've come to know,
> It's a song I want the whole wide world to hear.
>
> Unknown

As believers in Jesus, we have each been commissioned by God to bring the gospel to the world, so that those we know and come in contact with, will not only know who Jesus is but will want to know Him personally when they see the hope we have.

We bless others with silent and gracious living.

Jesus tells us in Matthew 5: 14,16, *"You are the light of the world . . . let your light shine before men."* What we are and do affects others more deeply than what we say, just as each grain of sand on a beach will affect the position of all the others. Your influence in another person's life can encourage and help or devalue them.

The waves of spiritual influence going forth from your relationship with the Saviour will impact those around you, making it easier for them to realize their need of salvation. Enthrone Christ in your life, being unafraid of what mortal man can do, so that you can speak freely of the hope that lives in you. Then your life will also play the music of the gospel.

We must continue to bless others with silent and gracious living, loving them with the love of Jesus *"so that your daily life may win the respect of outsiders."* (1 Thess. 4: 12). Let us put away all the hindrances of the world and let us live the music of the gospel so that the whole wide world will hear the most wonderful news of God's love for them.

Prayer: *Grant to me, O God, that my behaviour may show the hope of salvation and the love of Jesus to those around me. Amen*

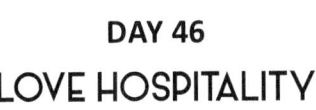

DAY 46
LOVE HOSPITALITY

Hebrews 13:1-2, *"Keep on loving one another as brothers and sisters. Do not forget to show hospitality to strangers, for by so doing some people have shown hospitality to angels without knowing it."* NIV

In our text, Abraham is sitting in the door of his tent, probably nodding off during the heat of the day, when suddenly, three unknown men are standing before him. Even though he may have been feeling exhausted and having a down day, he didn't miss the opportunity to show hospitality and welcome his visitors. Amazingly, we are told that two were angels and the third was the Son of God. It makes one wonder just who we are showing hospitality and kindness to.

In our busy lives, it is very easy to be unaware of the care someone may need. We cannot know unless we ourselves have suffered in a like manner, just how much it can mean for someone to be able to unload their troubles or be invited for a meal. During the great depression in Australia, many families were without the means of survival, and many men just walked the roads with their swags looking for work or food. Hence the name of the Australian swagman came to be. I remember many occasions when a swagman would come to our farm, and even if dad had no work for them, mum would always make them a meal and a cup of tea. Some of them may have been the angles the writer of Hebrews talks about.

God will always bless the hospitable person.

God will always bless the hospitable person who shows a listening ear or comfort to someone in pain and loneliness. We must be careful not to make the excuse of not having enough time because God will always ensure that you still achieve your daily work when you show hospitality. Let us continue to minister to those in need, for we are in turn ministering to our Lord Himself, who said: *"Truly I tell you, whatever you did for one of the least of these brothers and sisters of mine, you did for me."* (Matt.25:40)

Prayer: *Help me, dear Lord, never to miss an opportunity to show hospitality to those in need and to always be prepared to bear with others the burdens they carry. Amen*

DAY 47
SHINING AS STARS

Philippians 2:15-16, *"You may become blameless and pure, "children of God without fault in a warped and crooked generation. Then you will shine among them like stars in the sky as you hold firmly to the word of life"* NIV.

I remember seeing the very first satellite glide across the southern sky as we stood in our front yard of the country farm. As a child, it was not easy to see because of the brightness of the millions and trillions of other stars shining forth as God had created them to do. Today, I have a much greater appreciation of God's heavenly creation.

Our faithfulness to Jesus will set us apart as shining stars.

God created each of His children and brought salvation to each of us to be His shining stars here on earth. In verse 12, Paul tells us to *"work out our salvation."* This happens as we allow the Holy Spirit to work in our lives so we can imitate the life that Christ lived on earth, as we attract others to have the life that we have.

Then in verse 15, he tells us to *"do everything without grumbling or complaining."* How hard that can be for some of us, but as the Holy Spirit works within, we will become *"blameless and pure,"* to shine forth to the people we live among. Our love for other believers and our faithfulness to Jesus will set us apart as shining stars.

Yes, we will often fail, but when the Holy Spirit is alive in us, making us more like Jesus, we will have the qualities of life that will draw others to Christ... *"the fruit of the Spirit is love, joy, peace, forbearance, kindness, goodness, faithfulness, gentleness and self-control"* (Gal.5: 22-23).

Can you look at the night sky and imagine each star as a believer shining for Christ? Each one a star that the Holy Spirit is working through to repel the darkness around them and share the gospel with others for Christ.

Share your light with someone today or ask yourself why is my light dim and what you need to do to make it brighter.

Prayer: *Loving God, fill me with Your Spirit, that I might live for You and that others will come to know You as I shine my light for You. Amen*

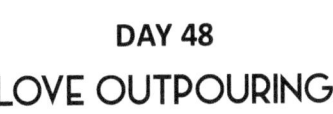

DAY 48
LOVE OUTPOURING

John 7:38, *"Whoever believes in me, as Scripture has said, rivers of living water will flow from within them."* NIV

Some of us wonder if we were filled with the Holy Spirit at our conversion, especially when we see other Christians who seem to be more spiritual and overflowing with goodness and love. The answer is that we must give and bless as we see a need, and we will soon find the Holy Spirit will give us more opportunities. God will give you all the benefits that He can trust you with, to give away to others.

Some years ago, my husband and I came across an Aeolian harp (wind harp) called 'The Singing Ship.' It is constructed on a coastal hill at Emu Park in central Queensland. It is structured in the shape of a harp but with strings of wire and hollow pipes set at different heights and angles. The Aeolian harp is the only stringed instrument played solely in rhythm to the wind. We sat and listened to the beautiful sound flowing from it, as unseen fingers touched it; the breath of heaven's wind flowed over the strings and through the pipes.

> **Let the music of the Spirit flow through you to bless others.**

When the disciples received the Holy Spirit in Acts 2, they didn't just sit around the room holding a holiness meeting; they went out and preached the gospel. Today, there is just as much of the Holy Spirit's presence here in our world as back then; the difference is we do not have the same receptive attitude, and we can be reluctant to let the music of the Spirit flow through us to bless others.

We must give out for the Spirit to flow through us to others. Acts 2: 42-44, tells of the fellowship of the believers, *"They devoted themselves to the apostles' teaching... Everyone was filled with awe, (inspiration)... All the believers were together and had everything in common."* Their joy was characteristic of the Holy Spirit in their lives and resulted in love, joy, peace etc., which is attractive to the unsaved. Are you blessing the lives of others as you are filled with the Holy Spirit flowing through you?

Prayer: *Thank You Lord, that You freely gave Your life for our Salvation. Help me to always be generous in giving of myself to bless others and to help them find forgiveness in You. Amen*

DAY 49

GOD HAS A PLAN

Jeremiah 1:5, *"I formed you… I knew you… I set you apart; I appointed you."* NIV

From the beginning of time God has always had a plan for each of us. When we read about the life of Jeremiah, we come to understand that God didn't call him to a life of success but a life of faithfulness. He felt inferior for the task God asked of him, but in verse 8, God told him, *"Do not be afraid of them, for I am with you and will rescue you."* God gave Jeremiah words to speak and courage and perseverance to carry out what He had commanded him to do.

> **God has created within you all the ability you need for your life work.**

We are prone to say, *'Yes, but that was Jeremiah.'* We are no different to Jeremiah, for he was an ordinary man, just as we are. God's plan for each of us is different, yet necessary in the scheme of things. The path God longs to lead you along is so you will know His power and love in your life.

Are you prepared to seek God and be led by Him? The amazing experience for each of us is that when we walk each day with Jesus, we will find no emergency that He has not made provision for in our nature. We must believe that He will give the courage, longsuffering and grace for each situation.

Over my life, God has taught me many skills that I could not have imagined myself capable of, but it was necessary that I might walk the path and do the work He requires of me. God has created within you, all the ability you will ever need for your life work. Don't fret or be jealous about another's life. Just stay close to and trust Jesus each day so you may know His leading in your life. He doesn't call all of us to be Jeremiahs, but He calls each of us to trust Him in everything and surrender ourselves to Him.

Faithfully do your work each day, as unto God, until He guides you to change tack to do something else. This will bring to your life the secret of blessing and usefulness that is only known to those who walk with the Lord. Prov. 3:5, *"Trust in the Lord with all your heart and lean not on your own understanding… acknowledge Him… and He will make your paths straight."*

Prayer: *Dear Lord, help me to trust You to lead me in the path You have for me. May I be faithful in serving You, no matter how menial my task. Amen.*

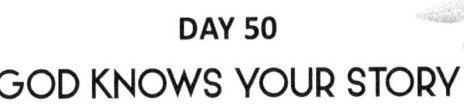

DAY 50
GOD KNOWS YOUR STORY

Psalm 139:1, *"You have searched me, Lord, and you know me."* Gen.8:1, *"God remembered Noah and all the wild animals and the livestock that were with him in the ark."* NIV

How often have you thought God doesn't care? Consider Noah, how he must have felt when he was building the ark, not knowing what a flood was or how he was going to muster two of every kind of animal into the ark, let alone take care of them. I don't think I would have the faith and trust Noah had, but when God even remembered the care needed for all the animals, how much more will He remember us in every circumstance we face? *"Look at the birds of the air; they do not sow or reap or store away in barns, and yet your heavenly Father feeds them. Are you not much more valuable than they?"* (Matt.6:26)

The words of our verse, help us understand the intimacy we can enjoy with Jesus. He knows us better than anyone else, so even the most intimate things of our life, like all our anxious thoughts, confusion, and struggles with temptation; we can bring to Him, knowing He understands how we feel.

> **Our Lord longs for us to trust Him with the seasons of our lives.**

After seven months of being shut in the ark, I wonder just how anxious Noah was, but God knew and allowed the water to recede very quickly so that they could plant their crops and harvest their food at precisely the right moment. Noah trusted that God had everything in hand, he didn't stress or worry about anything. In the very same way, our Lord longs for us to trust Him with the seasons of our lives and every circumstance that concerns us.

Our God waits to be trusted with everything that concerns us. In time, we will look back and see how God has led us, knowing He is always right, always good, and always supplies at precisely the right moment. Let us be careful to guard against thoughts of doubt and distrust and cultivate meek, gentle and pure thoughts as we praise God, who knows us and still loves us. At the right time, just as He said to Noah, *"Go forth,"* He will guide us on our journey to bring glory to His name, as we trust Him to write the story of our life.

Prayer: *Dear Father, strengthen my trust in You so I won't look on the dark clouds that surround me, like what You have withheld, but on what You have given me in Jesus my Saviour. Amen*

DAY 51
GENTLENESS OF SPIRIT

Philippians 4:5, *"Let your gentleness be evident to all. The Lord is near"* NIV.

Gentleness does not mean weakness but rather the strength of the spirit to show a considerable reserve of force. To be gentle shows great strength of character. It is like a father knowing his strength but only applying a gentle touch to his child.

To be gentle shows great strength of character.

We must never forget that the Lord is near and that because of that, we can afford to be gentle, for all things are possible when we trust. When someone lashes out against you, and you want to retaliate, the inbuilt gentleness of God's spirit helps you hold your tongue and have a tolerant spirit, making allowances for the other person. Don't be upset that they have done something to you, but ask God for understanding as to the manner of their behaviour. *"The Lord's servant must not be quarrelsome but must be kind to everyone, able to teach, not resentful"* (2 Tim.2:24).

Gentleness is not a grace that comes easily or by chance to any of us, for we must choose to be gentle and nourish our thoughts until it becomes a natural part of our nature and behaviour. Each time something happens where gentleness is called for, prayerfully resolve to display it by committing the fighting spirit within to the Lord. This is the strength of gentleness.

With gentleness, there must be humility as we deal with the faults and moods of others, always remembering the defects within ourselves that others tolerate. Remember our own sin, but always speak the truth, even though sometimes it is a painful truth, watching against our attitude and tone of voice, so it is well received. These are the qualities that will make us Christ's gentle folk.

Prayer: *Dear Lord, let my behaviour be filled with the grace and gentleness of Christ. Let me so live that Your beauty may be seen in my face as I walk with You and as You guide my steps. Amen*

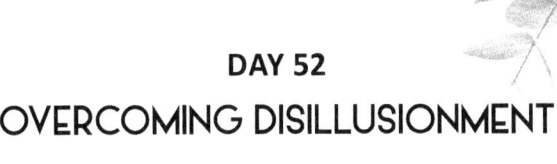

DAY 52
OVERCOMING DISILLUSIONMENT

John 2: 24-25, *"Jesus would not entrust himself to them... for he knew what was in each person."* NIV

In our life with family and friends, it is very easy to be disillusioned or disappointed with each other, which can easily lead to a very negative view or judgement of a person, causing us to have little faith in their sincerity and goodness. The trouble often lies not within the other person but within us, because we are true only to our own ideas of each another. So many of the cruel ideas we have of each other spring from the fact that we are disillusioned with them. Everything about each other must be either delightful and pleasing or mean and horrible, according to our own ideas.

We can even become disillusioned about ourselves, but God hasn't made you His child through the shed blood of Jesus, just to squander His plan for your life. Jesus knows what is in each of us and refuses to be disappointed in the cause of our suffering.

Although we disappoint God, He is never disillusioned with any of us.

In life we who love Jesus need to be careful not to demand another person's perfection. When we do not get what we desire, we become critical and vindictive because we could be demanding something that the person may not be able to give. We must discipline ourselves and not be disillusioned, so we do not become judgemental and unkind to others.

Only Jesus can satisfy our understanding and acceptance of those we love. Our loyalty must be to God first so He can help us accept each other just as we are and where we are. Only then, as we pray to Him, can we be like our Lord and hold no suspicion or bitterness toward another. Our confidence must be in Jesus, knowing that His grace can help anyone have the perfect life that God desires for them, for even though we disappoint Him, He is never disillusioned with any one of us. When we place our trust in our fellow man, we will end in despair of everyone.

Prayer: *Dear Lord, please help me to see the good in others as I know what You can do in their lives as they trust in You. Amen*

DAY 53
GOD CHOSE YOU

Luke 18:31,32, *"Jesus took the Twelve aside and told them, …. The disciples did not understand."* NIV

When Jesus was here on earth, He chose the 12 disciples as his close friends. When He told them in Luke 18 about His death and resurrection, they did not understand, but this did not make them any less his close friends because He understood them and loved them. He knew what they would become.

Have you ever been asked to take on some position in the church for Jesus, and you think it unwise to choose you, because you feel others may have better skills to do the task? This is precisely why He chose you.

Be prepared to let God lead and teach you then He will use you.

Whilst ever we are filled with our own self-sufficiency, God cannot use us in His work, but when we are emptied of self-glorification and are prepared to let God lead and teach us, He will use us in His great work of bringing others to Him. Paul tells us in 2 Corinthians 12:9,10. *"My grace is sufficient for you, for my power is made perfect in weakness… For when I am weak, then I am strong."*

If we are to do the work of God, the most critical issue is that we maintain a good relationship with God. In our Christian life, it is not the work we do that is important but maintaining a close connection to our Heavenly Father, so that He can do His work through us. If we allow evil to pull us away, we need to be quick to put our life back in God's hands.

The one thing that God requires is that we have an unbroken, growing relationship with Jesus. James 4:6-8,10 says, *"God opposes the proud, but gives grace to the humble. Submit yourselves then, to God. Resist the devil, and he will flee from you. Draw near to God, and he will draw near to you. Humble yourselves before the Lord, and he will lift you up."*

Your Heavenly Father has chosen you to do His work here on earth.

Prayer: *Thank You, Father, for wanting to use me in Your plan of Redemption. Help me stay close to You so that my relationship is continually growing, and my faith and trust are stronger each day. Amen*

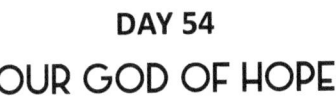

DAY 54
OUR GOD OF HOPE

Romans 15:13, *"May the God of hope fill you with all joy and peace as you trust in him, so that you may overflow with hope by the power of the Holy Spirit"* NIV.

So many people put their hope in things like financial stability or material things, but these can't bring the real hope that only Jesus offers. We all need hope in our lives otherwise we lack any purpose for existence. Hope is something we cannot see, so can we trust it? In life, there are things we trust without seeing them. We trust our insurance company to fix our home when it is damaged in a storm, or we hope that the aroma will fill the kitchen when we bake an apple pie. We can put our hope in these things because they are natural laws.

Even though we cannot see hope, we can understand that it is like the artist of our soul. We trust and have faith in God, and our hope rests on God's faithfulness to us. God cannot deny Himself because God is God. In Numbers 14: 16, Moses argues with God that the Egyptian people would say, *"The Lord was not able to bring these people into the land he promised them on oath."* Moses knew that God must always act worthy of Himself.

> *Our hope rests on God's faithfulness. God cannot deny Himself because God is God.*

True hope comes from our Creator God by trusting in Him even when our circumstances are beyond our control and complicated. Often when we have made a significant decision, we begin to worry and doubt. If we will turn to God's promises and have faith and trust, God will fill us with peace to have hope and belief, which enables us to move forward. *"Everyone who calls on the name of the Lord will be saved"* (Romans 10: 13.)

Claim God's promise today and hope in Him.

Prayer: *Help me, O Lord, to know the Hope of Your calling and the greatness of Your power toward those who believe. Amen.*

DAY 55

HE IS ABLE

2 Corinthians 9:8, *"God is able to make all grace abound to you, so that in all things at all times, having all that you need, you will abound to every good work."* NIV

Abundance is characteristic of our God. Take a walk on a spring morning along any street or through any garden and admire the flowers and foliage God has carpeted our world with. Witness the new foliage breaking forth from the dormant trees and the stunning colours of the flowers in the gardens on your walk, and each day you will see great change as the earth awakes to the sun's warmth.

This abundance is equalled in the heavens above, where the heavens are lit and inlaid with constellations, depth upon depth, answering the beauty of the earth beneath. Halleluiah! What a Creator.

> *Abundance is characteristic of our God. HALLALUIAH!*

But what shall we say of the abundance of His grace, as day by day it always abounds to us so that in everything, we will lack nothing? His peace passes understanding, and His love is beyond our ability to understand. Get a picture of God's greatness in your mind. He holds the ocean in the palm of His hand; He covers the heavens with stars and the seashore with shells.

Psalm 8:4 says, *"What is man that you are mindful of him, and the son of man that you care for him?"* Yes, He is so great, yet so mindful of who you are and what concerns you. He loves you with everlasting love, so much so that He gave His only Son to die in your place to save you from eternal damnation. He will make all grace abound towards you so that you may abound in every good work.

Jesus said, *"I have come that you may have life, and have it to the full"* (John 10:10). As God pours His grace into our lives, we will overflow and abound in good works to others. The more generous we are in giving to others for our dear Saviour's sake, the more we will be filled by our Heavenly Father's grace.

Prayer: *Give me grace, dear Lord, to see your beauty in the commonplaces of everyday life and to feel Your nearness in my life today as I overflow in goodness to others. Amen*

DAY 56
EYES TO SEE

Psalm 119:18, *"Open my eyes that I may see wonderful things in your law."* NIV

Do you know what anamorphic art is? It is basically when you look at an image with a distorted perspective. You will remove the distortion, by bringing the image back to the way you would typically expect to see it. To see it correctly it must be viewed in a certain way meaning that only one person can see it at any time. An anamorphic image appears senseless unless you know how or where to place your eye; only then is the actual image revealed.

Sometimes the Bible can be hard to understand, but when we read the same passage many times, like viewing it from different angles, we find unique and profound truths within its pages. Verse 10 tells us to *"seek God with all our heart,"* and v.11 says, *"I have hidden your word in my heart so that I don't sin against you."* God wants us to feed on His Word, digesting every word so that He can reveal different images (truths) to us, so that we might grow closer to Him.

In Romans 7:7, we read that Paul learnt what coveting meant through studying the Law. When we meditate on God's word (not just read it), sin becomes distasteful, and God's Word excites our hearts to praise Him. Feeding on God's word will transform our lives and give us wisdom and insight as the eyes of our souls are opened to see its true meaning.

> God's Word excites our hearts to praise Him.

Psalm 119:9 says, *"How can a young person stay on the path of purity? By living according to your word."* When we open our eyes to see what God's word says, we will gain new perspectives of His truth. Nobody can achieve growth in Christ unless they often take time to be alone with God reading and meditating on His Word.

Spend time reading the same passage of the Bible every day for a week, read different translations and view it from different perspectives... and see what God reveals to you.

Prayer: *Dear Lord, give us eyes to see the wonderful truths in Your Word. Guide us to connect the different paths from the Bible. Amen*

DAY 57

SIMPLY TRUST

1 Kings 17:15, *"So there was food every day for Elijah and for the woman and her family"* NIV.

The well-known missionary, George Mueller was the director of an orphanage during the 19th century. One morning with his helpers, they had the 300 children seated for breakfast, and together they gave thanks for their food. But there was no food! Mueller had experienced situations like this before and he knew this was just another opportunity to see the hand of God provide. Within minutes, a baker arrived with bread, explaining how he couldn't sleep during the night, so decided to bake bread for the orphanage. Shortly after, the town milkman's cart broke down in front of the orphanage, and not wanting the milk to spoil gave it to George Mueller for the children.

We need to have a clear vision of God as our Provider.

During the pandemic of 2020, many experienced anxiety and self-pity when some essential resources began to become scarce. People panicked and bought excessively. Many also worried about their health, finances and even friendships were strained. We need to be reminded that just as God provided for Elijah in 1 Kings 17 when the widow's flour didn't run out, and in the case of the children in the orphanage, He can do the same today. We need to have a clear vision of God as our Provider.

In Matthew 6: 30-31, Jesus says, *"O you of little faith? Do not worry about what you shall eat or what you shall drink, or what you shall wear. Your heavenly Father knows that you need them."* Before we look for solutions to our problems in life, we must be careful to seek our Heavenly Father first, because it can save us a lot of time, energy and frustration.

Do you genuinely believe that the God you trust will supply all your needs? Philippians 4:19 *"And my God will supply all your needs according to His riches in glory in Christ Jesus".*

Prayer: *Father, please help me to see You as the provider for all my needs. Forgive me for when I have sought to find my own way to my needs before I have come to You. Amen*

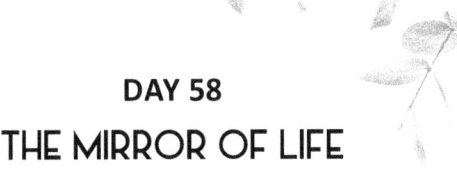

DAY 58
THE MIRROR OF LIFE

James 1:23-24, *"Anyone who listens to the word but does not do what it says is like someone who looks at his face in a mirror and, after looking at himself, goes away and immediately forgets what he looks like."* NIV

In the same way as we look into a mirror and very often are shocked at our appearance, here James uses this analogy to look at how we act out Christ's teaching from His Word. However, looking is not enough, we are to be doers, acting on what God shows us about our spiritual lives.

James in effect is saying that day by day as we live in the world, if we forget to do what God has shown us from His Word it is the same as forgetting what we look like the moment we walk away from the mirror.

We must cease to be hearers who forget and become doers.

If we trust God, we won't settle for just appearing religious. We need to be careful not to just listen to the Word (v.22); otherwise, we can be easily deceived. Obedience to what God says is the proof of our new birth in Christ, which will lead to a changed life, attitude, and conduct, as we reflect the love of Jesus from within. It is the 'doing' that brings blessing to others and us.

As we do what God's Word tells us and live like our Saviour, we will become more like Him. Let us always be alert to the slightest inconsistency between the perfect life of Christ and the life we live each day, because only as we cease to be hearers who forget and become doers that we will make progress in our walk with the Lord. *"But why do you call Me 'Lord, Lord,' and not do the things which I say."* (Luke 6:46).

Is there something God is saying to you about listening, learning, and doing what His Word says so that you can know and experience the blessings He wants to pour into your life?

Prayer: *Dear Lord, help me to love Your Word so that I will live my life by what You say, to bless those around me each day. Amen*

DAY 59
BLESSED BY GOD

Luke 24:50, *"He lifted up His hands and blessed them."* NIV

Jesus blessed His disciples so they could move forward and be fruitful. To bless is what our Heavenly Father does; it is how God sees us, not something that we feel. We are blessed when we acknowledge the Royalty of a Holy God and find peace and contentment in knowing Him.

When we read the beatitudes in Matt. 5:3-12, so often we take them into our subconscious mind with little thought, except thinking that they are amazing but never really allowing them in any way to change our lives. The teaching of the beatitudes is not in proportion to our natural way of looking at things or whether we are rich or poor. They are not how most people would typically live their lives.

Find peace and contentment in knowing Jesus.

By taking them into our soul, accepting them and meditating on them, will cause a tremendous awakening of our spiritual life. To live these statements of Jesus out in our lives will take us on a spiritual journey of hungering and thirsting daily for our life to be more like our Saviour. They are not a set of rules and regulations, but a statement of the life we will be blessed with, and the comfort found in a relationship with Jesus, regardless of our outward circumstances.

As we live out these principles, day by day, there will be an exchange from self-life to a life lived in the Spirit of God. Living in spiritual proximity with God enables us to bless and help others in His Name.

This blessed life can be yours today as you seek a deep spiritual awakening of your soul through the Holy Spirit.

Prayer: *Lord, take my whole life, my heart, my mind and lips and through me, bring blessing to others. Amen.*

DAY 60
JOY ... MY JOY

John 15:11, *"That my joy may be in you and that your joy may be complete."* NIV

Have you ever asked Jesus to fill you with His joy?

Jesus's joy was not what we would call happiness but absolute surrender and self-sacrifice to His Father. It was the joy of going to the cross so that God might have a renewed relationship with us, His children.

True joy is not found in being healthy, successful in business, financial security, or in a perfect relationship, but in an excellent and complete understanding of God. Of having the same communion that Jesus had with Him. *"I have no greater joy than to hear that my children are walking in the truth."* (3 John 1:4)

If we desire the greater joy of perfect and complete understanding of our God, we need to stop trying to control our circumstances. When we try to control everything in our lives, we don't hear that still small voice of the Holy Spirit within. We must surrender our circumstances to our Heavenly Father and stop worrying about them. God wants us to reach a place where the joy of being His witness and proclaiming who Jesus is, becomes as natural as breathing.

> *When we live in Christ, we will not be aware of the blessing we are to others.*

When we find the joy of serving Jesus, rivers of God's living water, compassion, love and encouragement will flow through us to bless others. When we live in Christ, we will not be aware of the blessing we are to others.

Prayer: *Forgive me Lord, for trying to solve everything myself. I desire the joy that only comes when I am fully committed to You. Please help my unbelief. Amen*

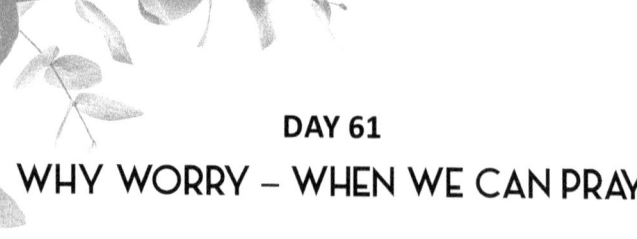

DAY 61
WHY WORRY – WHEN WE CAN PRAY

Lamentations 3:22-24, *"Because of the Lord's great love, we are not consumed, for His compassions never fail. They are new every morning; great is your faithfulness. The Lord is my portion; therefore, I will wait on him."* NIV

Is there any benefit for us, either spiritually, emotionally, or physically, when we worry? The unequivocal answer is NO. Are you one who will worry just because you have nothing to worry about? Sadly, worry has become a way of life for too many but let us stop and think about it. All that worry does for us is waste our time, causes anxiety and stress and robs us of peace and trust.

Not even the birds in the air or the lilies in the fields worry.

In Matthew 6:25,27, Jesus says, *"Do not worry about life... Who of you by worrying can add a single hour to his life?"* Be honest, none of us are exempt from trying to solve our problems through conscious thought, being too fearful of the results, we become too careful or too anxious. Worry can consume us as our mind races, and emotions churn within. Like Jerimiah, we must accept that, God's compassions never fail; our worries will never consume us, if we will wait on Him. Not even the birds or the lilies in the fields worry, and we are more valuable to God than these. He has never failed, and never will, we must learn to hand our worries over and patiently wait.

For years I thought I was doing this, but I would continue to worry, blocking the peace He could give me. To overcome my instinct to worry, I learnt Philippians 4:6-7, by heart and each time I became worried or anxious, I would say it repeatedly as a prayer to my God and Saviour. *"The Lord is near. Do not be anxious about anything, but by prayer and petition, with thanksgiving, present your requests to God. And the peace of God, will guard your hearts and your minds in Christ Jesus."* When you use this verse as your prayer, remember to thank God for the answer He has for you. These verses have been my saving grace on many occasions, and I commend them to you.

Is there a situation in your life that you need to stop worrying about and leave in God's hands today?

Prayer: Dear Father, how great is Your faithfulness and love to me. Help me to leave my worries with You, to know the peace You have promised. Amen

*I know in my heart that man is good.
That what is right will always eventually triumph.
And there's purpose and worth to each and every life.*

Ronald Reagan

*"I cry out to God Most High,
to God who fulfils his purpose for me."*

Psalm 57:1

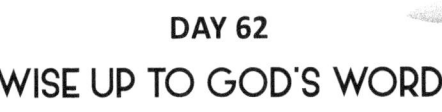

DAY 62
WISE UP TO GOD'S WORD

Proverbs 7:1-2, *"My son, keep my words, and store up my commands within you. . . and you will live, guard my teachings as the apple of your eye."* NIV

Before the 15th century, Scriptures were written by hand, taking 12 months to write one copy, so very few people had a copy, and not many could read. How fortunate and blessed we are; having access to God's Holy Word is an amazing privilege. The problem is, for many of us we find the Bible hard to understand, so instead of persevering, we just don't read it. Even though, to hear our Pastor speak from Scripture helps, very often this is all we rely on to grow our faith.

You say, *"I don't understand it."* Before you can understand, you must read it, and little by little God will reveal His truth to you. In time you will genuinely love reading your Bible. The words God speaks in scripture are to be cherished because God will use them to help and guide us. The Psalmist tells us in Psalm 119:11, *"Thy Word have I hid in my heart that I might not sin against Thee."* As small children at Sunday School, we were given a passage to learn. Being competitive, I always tried to be first to learn it, so I had the pick of the prizes. God knew what He was doing, because over many years, He has brought those chapters to mind, helping me in my walk with Him or enabling me to speak 'scripture' into someone's life. I am very thankful for the chapters I learnt.

> Seek to live according to the wisdom that the Bible teaches.

Another good practice is to journal what you receive from the passage you read, as there is something about the written word that seals what you have read, in your heart. If we are to live for Christ and grow in our relationship with our Heavenly Father, we need to have a passionate love of God's Word. We need to read, meditate, learn, and then fulfil what we read. James 1:22, *"Do not merely listen to the word, and so deceive yourselves. Do what it says."*

As you live according to the wisdom the Bible teaches, you will be like the scribes, the words will go from your mind into your heart so that its words will remain with you forever. Praise and glory to our God.

Prayer: *Thank You Lord, for the Bible and Your words and promises within. Guide me that I will make reading it each day a priority in my life. Amen.*

DAY 63
GOD'S MUCH MORE

2 Chronicles 25:9, *"The Lord can give you so much more"* NIV.

Throughout the Bible, time and again, we come to the words 'much more,' yet we fail to take hold of what God is telling us. Our text comes from the passage where Amaziah, King of Judah, paid the Israelite King a hundred 'talents' of silver (over $200 million US) to hire one hundred thousand of Israel's top fighting men to help Amaziah defeat Edom. A prophet came and told him the Lord didn't want the troops from Israel to fight, as they had turned away from God. When the king asked the man of God, *'what about the silver I have paid?'* The man of God replied, *"The Lord can give you so much more."*

Believe in the God of 'much more than we can imagine.'

Close your eyes and, with spiritual imagination, see God's hand at work in your present situation. See His much more - healing your illness and pain; your anxiety and depression; overcoming your family problems; relieving your grief; or overcoming your addiction. God's heart is to give and to heal. Ephesians 3:20, says *"Now to him who is able to do immeasurably more than all we ask or imagine, according to his power that is at work within us."*

In relationships, we can often be hurt, disappointed or disillusioned. This was my experience in a close relationship. At first, I was hurt and wanted to speak out about how I felt and tell them that they didn't understand; then Jesus showed me in Luke 2:50, *"But they did not understand what he was saying to them."* Because they weren't experiencing my pain, I realized that by saying what I felt, they would not understand anyway. As I sought God in my disappointment, He led me to realize again what He tells us in Matthew 6:25, 33, *"Do not worry about your life… But seek first His kingdom… and all these things* (God's 'much more') *will be given to you as well."*

I didn't have to feel hurt or disappointed because God had so 'much more' for me if I handed it to Him. We must not succumb to despair but trust everything and believe in the God of 'much more than we can imagine'.

Prayer: *O Father God, we praise You for Your Son and Holy Spirt. Praise be to You that in Christ we have everything that will give us fulfilment and joy. Praise be to You forever and forever. Amen*

DAY 64

GUARDING OUR TONGUE

James 3:5-6, *"The tongue is a small part of the body, but it makes great boasts... A world of evil among the parts of the body."* NIV

In the 21st century, we have seen bushfires destroy people's homes and lives. We have been heartbroken as we watch this destruction. One Sunday night in 1666, a single spark from the baker's fire in Pudding Lane started the great London fire that left more than 70,000 people homeless and destroyed 80% of the then city of London.

We react in horror to these events, and yet one of our body's smallest parts can be just as destructive in another person's life. We can do untold damage in a person's life, simply by speaking a harsh or hurtful word (a small spark). At some stage, we have all been on the receiving end of hurtful words and know just how they burn into our souls.

Proverbs 21:23, warns us to guard our tongue so we can stay out of trouble. The only way we can succeed is to continually ask our Father to keep us from the temptation of speaking hurtful and unkind words and fill us with His grace and kindness through the Holy Spirit within us. Each of us should make this a daily practice.

> *Our words can destroy, or we can speak words that build others up.*

Praise God that just as our words can destroy, we can also speak words that build others up. Proverbs 16:24 says, *"Gracious words are a honeycomb, sweet to the soul and healing to the bones."* And in Colossians 4:6, Paul says, *"Let your conversation be always full of grace, seasoned with salt, so that you will know how to answer everyone."*

We have within us the power to stand with hurting people who need encouragement in their walk with Christ, or even to lead them to the cross of Jesus. The question we must all ask is: Do my words put fires out?

Prayer: *Dear Father, please forgive me for the unkind and hurtful words I have spoken. If there is anyone that I need to say sorry to, please show me and give me the courage to apologize. Guard my tongue, that I will only speak words that put fires out and help people grow. Amen.*

DAY 65
SUNFLOWER MOMENTS

Psalm 86:5, *"You, Lord, are forgiving and good, abounding in love to all who call to you"* NIV.

I have just read a post from a friend, telling how she got out of bed needing strength to face the anniversary of her teenage son's accidental death some years ago. He was killed in a sporting accident, and as she grieved, she remembered how he would tell her, *"You're a good old stick,"* and how no longer could she cook his favourite 'Bread and Butter Pudding' for him.

She visited his grave, and as she placed his favourite flower, a Sunflower, on it, she knew that he was enjoying the presence of his Heavenly Father. At that moment she knew she had to make this day count and be meaningful.

Go forward in God, looking for your Sunflower Moments.

Sometimes our grief and troubles seem insurmountable, and like David, we cry out to God. *"Hear me, Lord, and answer me, for I am poor and needy"* (Psalm 86: 1). By the end of her day, my friend was able to see the unexpected bright spots – the Sunflower Moments on a rough day that reminded her of how life, even for the believer, can seem hard and cold. David tells us in verse 15, *"But you, O Lord are a compassionate and gracious God… abounding in love and faithfulness."*

Often, we do not understand God's dealings with us, but in these places, God sends us Sunflowers, an encouraging word, a phone call, coffee with a friend, or a verse of comfort from His Word. These little things move us forward with a lighter step and hope in our loving Heavenly Father. Oh, the joy as God lifts us above our difficulty, for then we can join David and proclaim, *"You are great and do marvellous deeds, you alone are God."* (v.10) If you are in a difficult place in your life, be encouraged, dwell on the words of Psalm 86, and go forward in God's strength, to find your *'Sunflower Moments.'*

I went for a walk in my garden when the day had just begun,
And I noticed that one of my favourite flowers was lifting its head to the sun.
For some moments, I took in its beauty, and it seemed to say to me,
This fragrance, this beauty, belongs to me for God has placed it all there,
But it isn't mine to hold selfishly it's only mine to share.

K. Cameron-Smith

DAY 66
PRAISE BE TO GOD

Psalm 65:1-2, *"Praise awaits you, our God, in Zion... You who answer prayer, to you all people will come"* NIV.

There is nothing like a beautiful sunset to make us stop, take a photo or two or even three and enjoy the beauty of Creation. Why do we react in that way? Is it that like the Psalmist said, *"Praise him, sun and moon; praise him, all you shining stars"* (Psalm 148:3). God's creation is ever praising Him.

Sunrise and sunset always remind me of our lives because our life is our story from beginning to end, a small part of the big story. As we go through life, God brings us closer to Himself, and our story changes. Unlike animals, God has given us more than just instinct. He has given us His Word, which is the story of the beginning and the end, into which our story fits.

In the beginning, there was God the Creator and His Creation. As we come into the world and find our place in the big story, we see Jesus who came to save us, and then He sends His Spirit to dwell within us as we ask forgiveness and trust Him. In our verse, the Psalmist is in fellowship with God, and as he prays and gives praise, it's as though he is calling all creation to wake up and enjoy fellowship with God.

> *God's creation is ever praising Him.*

For many of us, as we live each day, it is as though Nature seems to conceal the glory and beauty of God's Presence, or is it that we don't look for the beauty around us? Then as the sunset of our life unfolds, there is no voice or language that man can detect, but when our hearts are clean, we realize that Christ is the beauty we have searched for. The wonderful reality is that even throughout life, He reveals Himself, *"Blessed are the pure in heart, for they will see God"* (Matt.5:8). Let us look for Him and enjoy His fellowship every day.

Do you enjoy the company of your Heavenly Father each day?

Prayer: *Heavenly Father, help me to sense Your Presence as I trust You each day on my life journey. Amen*

DAY 67

WHY PRAY

Luke 11:1, *"Lord, teach us to pray."* **NIV**

Whilst we look upon prayer as a way of obtaining things for ourselves, God encourages us to pray to know Him better. Our relationship with Christ is nourished through prayer. When we are born again by the blood that Jesus shed for us, we can either starve, or nourish our life with God through prayer. There is no better teacher of prayer than Christ. He alone is the Master and taught His disciples how to intercede for humanity. He taught them by His example, and as they witnessed this subconscious influence upon their lives, they asked Him to teach them to pray.

> *God encourages us to pray so we can get to know Him better.*

Prayer must be natural, as though we were in conversation with a close friend. We need to pray for others before ourselves, remembering to be thankful for the answer to our prayer, even though the answer may not come as requested. Just as a starving child will continue asking until someone gives him food so we must *"pray without ceasing"* if we are to receive.

To have faith in God, means that we know God will be faithful to us. When a person is always considering his health, he will become sick, so when we look at our faith, we will cut the roots which grows faith in us. Look to the character of your Heavenly Father, who will not fail, leaving the ultimate answer to your prayer with God. We have all heard the words *"prayer changes things,"* which is partly true, but sometimes prayer changes us, and then we can change things. Sometimes God says no to our request, purely because He knows that to give what we ask will not be of benefit for us. Sometimes He has to first shape our life in order that we can accept His answer.

When we stand before God, we will have to thank Him for the unanswered as well as answered prayers. Remember, prayer will grow our relationship with Jesus, often not a question of altering things but altering us. Be sure to give your Lord time to teach you how to pray by speaking to Him daily. Shut out the distractions of life and spend quality time with God, and He will bless you.

"Our Father, who art in Heaven, Holy is Your name.
May Your kingdom come, and Your will be done on earth as it is in Heaven."

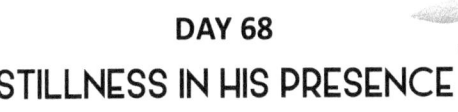

DAY 68
STILLNESS IN HIS PRESENCE

Ezekiel 1:24-25 *"When they stood still, they lowered their wings. Then there came a voice from above the vault over their heads as they stood with lowered wings."* NIV

Our scripture is taken from Ezekiel's vision, as he watched and saw the living creatures with outstretched wings. As they moved their wings there was a roar like rushing water, like the voice of the Almighty, but it was not until they lowered their wings in stillness that Ezekiel heard the voice of God telling him what to prophesy to the people.

How do we get to hear the voice of our Heavenly Father? The secret is that it wasn't until they lowered their wings that God spoke. We have probably all seen a bird after it has had a bath from the rain, sitting perfectly still but it's wings are still fluttering. Here we are told that it was when the fluttering stopped that God spoke. Is this like you and me? We come to Jesus in prayer, but our mind is everywhere, fluttering with other thoughts, everything, except being still in the presence of God.

> *Be still and allow your mind to connect with Jesus.*

This reminds me of a dear friend, who whilst here on earth, would sit with his eyes closed praying regardless of what was happening around him. Suddenly one would see a smile come over his face and you knew that he had entered into the stillness of the presence of his Lord. There was never any rushing or energy wasted, for his spirit knew the calm and peace known only to those who wait in God's presence until they hear from Him.

If you desire to experience the presence of your Lord, then be still, allowing your mind to connect with Jesus, who said, *"My sheep listen to my voice; I know them, and they follow me. I give them eternal life, and they shall never perish; no one will snatch them out of my hand"* (John 10:27,28). It is time to be still and relax your mind to connect with your God.

Prayer: *Lord, help me to be still, just now, to be still, so that You can fill my willing, waiting spirit with Your message for me today. Amen*

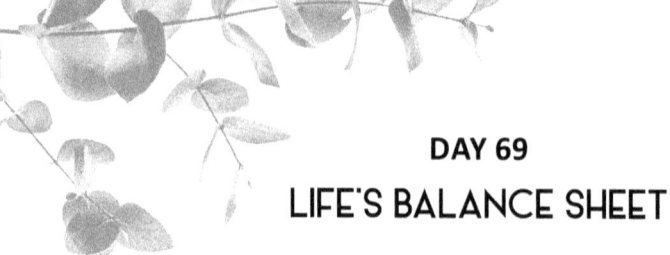

DAY 69
LIFE'S BALANCE SHEET

Exodus 34:2, *"Be ready in the morning... Present yourself to me there on top of the mountain."* NIV

Early morning has been my time for meeting with the Lord. I find the beginning of each day invaluable as God fills me with strength and hope for my day ahead. Having slept, the fatigue of yesterday is gone, and I can go forward to face the day having been blessed and filled with the Spirit. For you, it may be a different time and that is okay. We are all different and many are time poor. Even when I had small children and a husband who started work at 6 am, I would get up before my family to spend time alone with God. I don't say this for any praise but to encourage you to make a specific time to spend with Jesus daily, because I know it will make a difference to your day.

Be encouraged, spend time with Jesus; and be blessed and fulfilled.

This alone time with God will encourage you throughout the day. It is a unique experience when our soul can live in the awareness of Jesus all day. I know you will find this a precious time. When we meet with God and hear His voice through Scripture, He will keep bringing those inspirational words to our hearts, when the baby is sick and crying, when the car won't start, when the kids are late for school, and the thousand other experiences that we have every day. Hear Him say afresh, *"Lo, I am with you always, even unto the end of the world"* (Matt. 28:20), and we will answer with confidence... *"Amen, Lord."*

Why don't we claim God's help in our moments of uncertainty? We lose hope when we allow our lives to plunge into gloom and despair. James 12: 1 tell us, *"Let us throw off everything that hinders, and the sin that so easily entangles."* Remember the tempter will find every excuse to attack you. To reach God's hights for your life, you must deny your own choice and pleasure. I encourage you to start your day on the mountain with your Lord.

From morning till night Lord, I'm busy, is this motion getting me somewhere?
Where am I going Lord? Am I closer to being there? I've
been so busy going, I haven't thought about where.
Of course, I know. I want to know You Lord; and spend more time in prayer.
Unknown

DAY 70
FILLED WITH HEAVEN

Isaiah 6:3, *"Holy, holy, holy is the Lord Almighty; the whole earth is full of his glory."* NIV

King Uzziah started his reign of Judah on a promising note, but unfortunately, it ended badly. In the year of his death Isaiah, the prophet, broken in spirit because of the moral degeneration of God's people, enters the temple where the sacrifice is taking place, and receives a vision of God sitting on the throne. As he becomes aware of the Seraphin worshipping, the earthly life surrounding him fades from sight. Isaiah tells us the Seraphin were above him, and each had six wings, two covered their faces depicting Reverence of God's majesty; two covered their feet, revealing Humility and Modesty; and with two they did fly, showing Obedient Service. *"They were calling to one another: Holy, holy, holy, is the Lord Almighty."* (v.3)

Isaiah was entranced, seeing himself as a sinner. We can only imagine that his response was not unlike our own when we are faced with the reality of being a sinner, revealed to us through Jesus, our Saviour. Isiah heard the call of God and was prepared to go and serve – are you?

> The world is filled with trouble, but it is also filled with God's glory.

Today our world is not unlike that of Isaiah's time. All around us are broken people; caused by drugs, illness, abuse, and immorality, but are we prepared to go in our Saviour's name to bring healing and salvation to our fellow man? We are eager to give care but are afraid to talk of the love and peace we enjoy through our relationship with Jesus. There are countless numbers who have never heard of Jesus and His love for them.

As we worship God let us be humble and like Isaiah, hear the voice that others cannot hear; being aware of a Presence we cannot see and enter into communion with God. Even though the world around us is filled with trouble, it is also filled with God's glory. We must believe in the Lord God, knowing that in Him, we can overcome and share His love with the world.

Prayer: *Lord, sometimes it can be hard to comprehend that Your glory fills every space, but we know that You reign and are filled with love for everyone. Glory and blessing, power and honour belong to You, Lord Jesus. Amen*

DAY 71
FROM STRESS TO STRENGTH

Isaiah 51:1, *"Listen to me, you who pursue righteousness and who seek the Lord: Look to the rock from which you were cut"* NIV.

In his book 'The Angel Inside,' Chris Widener tells the story of a young man who is disheartened and sad. Whilst visiting the city of Florence, he is confronted by an elderly gentleman who asks what he learnt when he visited Michelangelo's statue of David. When he told the gentleman that he had learnt nothing, they went back to the statue, where he helped the young man see through the eyes of Michelangelo and explained how Michelangelo, when he had looked at the piece of granite, saw David inside. His task was to chisel the granite to produce the completed and majestic statue of David.

> God chisels at your life with purpose, by using the trials you face.

For us to become what God made us to be, we, must go through the same process. God must use adversity and suffering to bring us to the place where we are ready to be moulded and polished, fit for His use. God chips away at whatever doesn't belong, sanding away our arrogance, pride and self-will.

In Isaiah 51, we read how God destroyed the wickedness of Satan to develop a people of purpose. When we look back to what Abraham, Jacob, Joseph, David and others went through, we see in each case, God loved them enough to see them as righteous and beloved. One can only imagine how happy Satan must have been when Christ died on the cross, but once more God overcame what was evil and made way for each of us to have victory in Christ, our Saviour. From the death of Stephen came the conversion of Saul. After World War 1, many men of purpose, strength and determination came from men who had experienced stress and soul-destroying trauma to the extreme.

God chisels at your life with purpose, using the suffering and trials you face to prepare you for something more significant that you must face; something that others can't face. God sees the person you can become. We need to trust Jesus and to see stress as something to help us grow and make us stronger, so that God can use us in His world to care for and love others for Him.

Prayer: *Thank You, Father even though we don't always like it, You see what is inside us and what we can be for You. Please use us as you see fit. Amen*

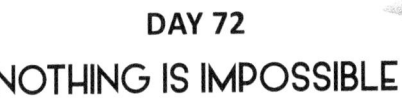

DAY 72
NOTHING IS IMPOSSIBLE

Matt. 14:29,30, *"Then Peter got down out of the boat, walked on the water and came toward Jesus. But when he saw the wind, he was afraid and, beginning to sink, cried out, Lord, save me!"* NIV.

When Peter saw Jesus walking on the water, he probably didn't think about the possibility of sinking but was anxious to be with Him. He stepped out of the boat, looking to Jesus for the strength and courage required to do what on the human level was impossible. Whilst his whole being (spirit and flesh) gazed on the face of Jesus, he walked on the water. All Peter needed to do was to concern himself with looking only to Jesus and trusting Him. Even if the waves had been tenfold the size of the waves God held back for Moses and the children of Israel, Peter did not need to doubt. Immediately he did, he began to fail. Then his focus on Jesus became confused with things that were none of his business.

Like so many of us, his mind began to think of the storm and doubts immediately set in. As intelligent as we are, many of us restrain our thoughts and actions, thinking something is impossible. We fail to move further than the boundaries of our self-imposed limitations and as a result never know what we are capable of when we put our total trust and focus on our Saviour.

> *Know what you are capable of, by trust and focus on your Saviour.*

When the Lord calls you to come, step gently out and don't for one moment look away from Jesus; even if there is danger and difficulties, stay focused. Don't even listen to what common sense tells you when it comes to carrying out what God requires of you. We must *"lift up our eyes unto the hills, from whence comes our help"* (Psalm 121: 1). We must go forward – there is no other way. Only when we leave our comfort zone and step out for Christ can we experience the blessing of the fruits He will give.

> *Is the Red Sea of your life in front of you and no matter what you try to do,*
> *There is no way out, for you cannot go back, your only way is through.*
> *Lord, I will wait because you never fail, You give me strength to go on,*
> *Please walk with me and take my hand for through trust my fear has gone.*
>   Annie Johnson Flint (1866-1932)

DAY 73

ALONE TIME

Matt. 14:23, *"He went up on a mountainside by himself to pray. Later that night, he was there alone."* (NIV)

Jesus felt the need for being alone with His Father, therefore, how much more should you and I feel an urgency to be alone with God? Like Jesus, when we are in communication and interacting with others, we need alone time to recharge our souls with the power of the Holy Spirit. When Jesus was alone with the Father, He realized His destiny was to die for our redemption, a time to understand the frailty of human life and to totally understand dependency on God. If Jesus as the Son of God needed time to be alone with God, how much more do we.

> What a privilege is yours when you can be real and alone with God.

As a child of God, you need to understand the amazing privilege that is yours, when you can be real and alone with God. God has you all alone to Himself, to comfort and bring peace to your soul. Seek out your own private time and place (your Beulah land) for poor is the soul who has no such place.

"When he was alone with his own disciples, he explained everything." (Mark 4: 34) It is when we are alone with God, that He will speak to our soul. If we could only understand just how important alone time with Christ is, we would make time every day for *"God and me."* Imagine yourself as the one remaining human on earth, this would truly be *"God and me."* Oh, the thought to have God all alone to yourself, and to know that God has you all alone to Himself, to whisper His intent for your life.

Be encouraged and make time every day for time alone with God, for nothing else will bring peace and satisfaction like this to your life.

Prayer: *Dear Jesus, please keep prompting me to make time for You each day. Help me not to be tempted to put anything else before You. Amen.*

DAY 74
I CHOOSE JOY!

Nehemiah 8:10, *"The joy of the Lord is your strength."* NIV

Joy is an inner feeling that helps one to endure hardship and connect with meaning and purpose for their life, but it does not come from favourable circumstances; it comes from God. When we live in the very presence of our Lord, being filled with the Holy Spirit, joy is a spiritual quality that we always have. *"I have told you this so that my joy may be in you and that your joy may be complete"* (John 15:11).

We pursue happiness but choose joy. Some weeks ago, I met an elderly lady whose persona was full of joy. It was a pleasure to sit and chat with her as she told me about her life of over 90 years. It was evident that she had lived her life in a deep and meaningful relationship with her Lord. When I asked her for a word of wisdom, and her desire to live as long as possible despite her disability, she didn't hesitate to tell me that it was the joy of the Lord that filled her days with the little kindnesses that came her way.

Joy comes from God, not your favourable circumstances.

The joy she finds in God's presence transforms and regenerates her each day. Paul tells us that joy, peace, forbearance, and kindness are all fruits of the Spirit (Gal.5:22). For my friend, God is her all, and there is no power beside Him, as His joy brings peace and happiness to her life.

For you, it may seem hard work to feel God's spiritual, consistent joy, but the secret is to understand that you have power to control how you think, to accept the joy God wants for you or let your thoughts be those of despair and discouragement. Don't accept or believe you need to feel desperate about anything but look for and accept the joy God wants to express in your life.

As we rejoice in the Lord, joy can unlock a sense of purpose and hope which will release us from our difficult circumstances as we reach out and help others. *"A cheerful heart is good medicine, but a crushed spirit dries up the bones"* (Prov.17:22).

Prayer: *Dear Lord, may I find joy in a deeper relationship with You and as I serve others for You. Amen*

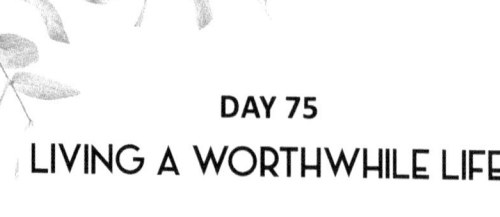

DAY 75
LIVING A WORTHWHILE LIFE

Colossians 3:17, *"Whatever you do – no matter what it is – in word or deed, do everything in the name of the Lord Jesus."* NIV

Throughout our world during the 2020 pandemic, people were without purpose in their life. They lacked motivation to look on the bright side, making the best of each day. Nothing is more disastrous than drifting without any purpose for your life. At times we have to stop and know just where we are at and understand that God has built into each of us a definite purpose for our life. In life, there are things that we cannot change, but we have the inbuilt power of God to change our attitude, which will give purpose to each day.

We have the inbuilt power of God to change our attitude.

Before our birth, God gave purpose to our souls, and the members of our bodies. Psalm: 139:16 *"Your eyes saw my unformed body. All the days ordained for me were written in your book before one of them came to be."* I cannot imagine that our loving Heavenly Father spent so much thought and care on our bodies and had no purpose for our souls. As I look back through my life, there were good and difficult times, but I can see how God has gradually unfolded my life's purpose day by day.

In stressful times, we must go steadily forward, trusting our God for the needed wisdom and strength to face each day. Each morning, say aloud to yourself, *"By God's grace, I will do my best in everything I am called to do today."* Some ideas that I have found helpful are, start each day in God's presence. Make a list of what you want to achieve and cross it out as the day progresses, as this gives you satisfaction in achievement. In a crisis, look for something to keep your mind active, like doing puzzles or reading, avoid watching too many news programmes and don't forget to exercise. These are just some of the many things we can do.

Most importantly, God is working it out, we must commit to Him and know within, *"The Lord will fulfil his purpose, for me; your love, O Lord, endures forever."* (Psalm 138:8) Be encouraged to change your attitude to your situation and seek to find constructive things to do each day.

Prayer: *Thank You, Lord, that despite my situation, You have control of everything and I am thankful. Keep me trusting You every day. Amen*

DAY 76
COMFORT FROM GOD

Jeremiah 29:11, *"For I know the plans I have for you," declares the Lord, "plans to prosper you and not to harm you, plans to give you hope and a future."* NIV

Sometimes, you find yourself captive in a situation. It may be of your own doing, or it may be the cause of someone. With a heavy heart, you begin fretting and planning a way out of an abusive relationship, poverty, addiction or even you have broken the law. You may have asked God's forgiveness, but those close to you, do not understand, and life is hard. Unfortunately, your circumstances have brought you to a place where you feel completely and utterly helpless, like a prison inmate, with no outside contact to someone you trust. You feel more vulnerable than at any other time of your life.

You are not alone. If Jesus is your Saviour, He is there with you to love, care and to protect you. Even though things look bleak, with Jesus, you can 'BE.' - Be the best you can each day where you are and ask for the Lord's help. Like God had a plan for the Israelites, (Jeremiah 29:11) hope in Him and always remember although everything appears to be against you, God is thinking thoughts of peace over you and many of your friends are praying. As you lean on Jesus, you will experience His peace and courage and as you minister for Him, you will find peace in the peace of those you minister to.

> In the peace of those we minister to, we shall find peace.

See the horizon flushed with hope. See the end coming a little closer every day, for there is an allotted time to your present trouble. God will surely visit with you, but in the meantime, you must live a life of constant prayer. *"Then you will call on me and come and pray to me, and I will listen to you. You will seek me and find me when you seek me with all your heart. I will be found by you," declares the Lord."* (v.12-14)

My friend, live in the spirit of prayer and faith and converse with God so that His peace and hope may fill your life despite your circumstances. Jesus has saved you from sin, so he can bring peace in every situation of life.

Prayer: *Thank You Lord, for all your gracious care of me in every situation of life. Help me to believe in Your infinite love and know Your blessing on my life. Amen*

DAY 77

DO NOT FEAR

Isaiah 41:13," *For I am the Lord your God who takes hold of your right hand and says to you, do not fear; I will help you"* NIV.

The song *"Tell Your Heart to Beat Again"* was inspired by a true story of a heart surgeon. After removing and repairing his patient's heart, he gently and carefully placed it back in the chest cavity and began massaging it to help it start beating again. Despite all his efforts, his patient's heart failed to beat. Finally, in desperation, he knelt beside the bed and whispered into the unconscious patient's ear. "Jane," he said, *"this is your surgeon. Your operation was a complete success, and everything went like clockwork. Now can you tell your heart to beat again."* Within a few seconds, her heart began to beat.

Jesus gives us hope regardless of our situation.

Fear is a distressing emotion brought on by the expectation of danger, evil, or pain, and it can be natural or often imagined; a feeling of being afraid. Like Jane in our story, fear can almost cripple us when we fear something like major surgery or even what will happen to us in a broken world. During the 2020 pandemic, it was incredible how many people, including Christians, were living in fear.

A fearful person lacks hope, and even though most of us feel afraid and are scared at some time in our life we too have a capable 'Surgeon' who has mended our hearts and given us hope regardless of our situation. *"When I am afraid, I put my trust in… God, whose word I praise. In God I trust and am not afraid. What can mere mortals do to me"* (Psalm 56:3-4).

When fear comes to us, we must come to our Surgeon, the Lord Jesus, and with His strength and love we can make our hearts beat again with life and courage to go on. In every trial and battle we can know the grace and power of our Heavenly Father, helping us overcome our fear.

What do you need to bring to the Lord so that He can give you peace in your fear?

Prayer: *Lord, hold me safe in the hollow of Your almighty hand, through all the storms and troubles of life and for that I am evermore grateful. Amen.*

DAY 78
MY GOD REIGNS

Psalm 103:19, *"The Lord has established his throne in heaven, and his kingdom rules over all"* NIV.

In the early hours, as my body crumbled with pain, and my soul felt no one cared, I sat upright in my chair and tears began to fall as I cried, *"Oh Lord, I wish my pain would..."* I was going to say, leave me and never come back, but my words were checked, and the sentence would never be finished.

I stopped, for it was as though an angel stood before me holding a key as he said: *'My Master sends His love and asked me to give you this key.'* I asked, *'What is it a key to?'* He replied, *'Your pain.'* Then he was gone. This was too amazing to be real; I could lock away my pain to be free and choose as I wished. I was over my pain, so I took it and locked it away forever. *'Now, what do I choose?'* I asked as I sat in my chair. Yes, I will choose to have no trouble or problems, to always be happy, free to choose the good things in life.

I took the key and turned to unlock the door to my future, but as I did so, my hand began to burn. *'What am I doing?'* I have no idea what is good for me or that I may cause sorrow for myself and others. I thought of all the hurtful and foolish things that may happen, and I felt ashamed. Bowing my head, I asked the Lord to send his angel to take the key back. I did not want it.

We have no idea what is good for us; our safety is in God.

I lifted my head, and the Lord Himself with outstretched arms stood by me. As I handed Him the key, I saw the scars of the nail prints on His hands. How could I have spoken against anything He had brought to my life, for He loved me more than I could understand. Then He took the key and placed it on His girdle. As I looked again, there on His girdle hung all the keys to my life. With gentleness, He asked, *'Do you not know that My Kingdom rules everything.'* I answered, *'Oh Lord forgive me for complaining about my pain or anything that comes to me.'*

As He laid His hand on me, He said, *'My child, your safety is in Me, for I died to save you so that you are free to love, trust, and praise forever.'*

Prayer: *Gentle Jesus, look today upon Your child; help me to stay close to You each day so that my life is filled with love and trust for You. Amen*

DAY 79
GOD IS ENOUGH

Hebrews 13:5, *"Keep your lives free from the love of money and be content with what you have, because God has said, 'Never will I leave you; never will I forsake you.'"* NIV

Are you content with what you have! We never appear satisfied with what we possess. Do you want more money, more influence, or more brains and ability? When we are young, we have great ideas for what we will achieve, and whilst these things are necessary, God says to us, NO! We each have within us a God given power which is awaiting our use. God is all we need. Have you ever explored the resources of your soul?

God will never neglect you, so be content with what you have.

Moses only had a rod, but in God's help, it opened the Red Sea for His people to cross. David had five stones, but with God's help, they brought down the giant Goliath. When we trust our Heavenly Father, He will always help us. I have always been competitive and ambitious, always setting goals to achieve. As life continued, through circumstances of having to give up work, I learnt that when I totally trusted my God, it was enough. In the past years, I have seen God provide for my needs in some amazing ways. I had to accept and be content, only to find out that God provided everything I needed.

Therefore, let us be content, whether we are blessed with plenty or only the basis needs of life. Remember, the most impressive and gracious deeds that have blessed humanity and the world have not been done by wealthy men. Jesus had none of this world's goods, and the disciples didn't even have any substance to give the lame man *"Silver or gold I do not have, but what I do have I give you. In the name of Jesus Christ of Nazareth, walk"* (Acts 3:6).

Money and the things of this world will never make us happy. It is human love and God that is needed to make a difference. So, don't covet what others have, and don't hoard, but give of the riches God fills your life with every day. Be strong and content in Christ, encouraging others each day, saying, *"The Lord is my helper; I will not be afraid"* in life or death, sorrow, or joy.

Heavenly peace, divinest comfort, here by faith in Him to dwell!
For I know, whate'er befall me, Jesus doeth all things well.
Frances J. Crosby, 1875

DAY 80
WHY DOES GOD WAIT

John 11:4,6, *"This sickness will not end in death. No, it is for God's glory so that God's Son may be glorified through it... He stayed where He was two more days"* NIV.

What an experience for Jesus's disciples and friends at Bethany. When Jesus received word that His friend Lazarus was ill, He waited instead of rushing to his assistance. I am sure His disciples asked, *"why does He wait?"* Then, to add more confusion, Jesus returns to Judea. After two days, Jesus announces that Lazarus has died. If you were one of His disciples, would you have thought how inconsiderate, let alone when He said, *"I am glad I was not there, so that you may believe."* The disciples didn't understand the power of Jesus.

As Jesus reaches Bethany, Martha rushes out to meet Him, and I can almost hear her say, *"It's too late. Is this as good as You could do?"* Despite her hurt, Jesus reassures her, *"Your brother will live again."* This happened just before Jesus' crucifixion, and He was trying to tell her that He would bring the gift of life, but Martha still did not understand. Jesus then says, *"Did I not tell you that if you believed, you would see the glory of God?"* When Jesus wept, we believe He was sorrowful and felt compassion for the sisters. Could it have been that He wanted them to understand He was everything they needed. He is all that we need every day. He waits so that He can bring glory to God.

> **We need to understand the power of our God.**

There are many times when we have prayed for something or someone without His immediate intervention. We must understand that as hard as it is, this is a time when we must simply leave everything to God and just trust. I have learnt that when He answers, though often not what I had asked, it has outweighed anything I could have imagined. But importantly, I have learnt that God waits so that there is no doubt in my mind that it was Him, and all glory belongs to Him. God is aware of all things; He has His finger on the pulse of your life, and you can be sure that He will come to save you when the precise moment has arrived.

> *O anxious soul, be still, be strong, for though He lingers, trust, and wait.*
> *Don't doubt, He will not wait too long. Don't fear, He'll not come too late.*
> Unknown

DAY 81
PRUNED FOR GROWTH

John 15:2, *"Every branch that does bear fruit he prunes so that it will be even more fruitful."* NIV

Being a gardener, I thought I knew everything about pruning roses, until a lady in the next street brutally cut her rose bushes back, right down to the graft, leaving them bare of branches or leaves. I asked with curiosity why, and she explained that when she takes every cane off, the graft point absorbs all the nutrients from the roots to become larger and more robust; ultimately producing stronger canes with bigger and better flowers. She prunes this way to make them thrive.

> **Don't allow your spiritual life to die to end up in the fire.**

Jesus explains in John 15 how He is the vine or plant, and our Heavenly Father is the gardener who is always doing divine pruning of our lives to equip us to bear fruit for His Kingdom. He tells us that as the branch must remain part of the vine and feed from it, we also must have continual fellowship with God through Jesus, to bring forth souls for the Kingdom of Heaven. I wondered if Jesus chose pruning imagery to help us understand we will have good times of bearing fruit, but also bad times when we are being pruned of bad habits and hinderances, so we can grow through the Holy Spirit in our lives.

He warns that if we don't work on our relationship with God, we will fail to bear fruit and will grow in our own wilful way, causing us to be cut off and thrown away. *"If you do not remain in me, you are like a branch that is thrown away and withers; such branches are picked up, thrown into the fire and burned"* (v.6). We have a choice; do we draw on God's power, growing to bring forth good fruit, or do we allow our spiritual life to wither and die, only to end up in the fire? This is a scary thought because we will not end up in a good place.

Let us continually draw our spiritual nourishment each day from Jesus, which will result in fruitfulness and bring glory to our Father in Heaven. Remember also that the growth of anything is slow, so keep asking Jesus to make you holy. God always keeps His promise.

Prayer: *Father, help me to keep trusting You, even during the difficult times when You are pruning habits and hindrances from my life. Keep pruning me to gain the growth that will bring forth the beauty of Jesus in me. Amen*

DAY 82
FAITH CAN'T BE SEEN

Hebrews 11:1, *"Now faith is confidence in what we hope for and assurance about what we do not see."* NIV

We hear people say that they have their faith, but just what do they trust in? We all have faith that our car will start, but don't ask us how, as that is the manufacture's responsibility. It is not about us as an individual but about our maker; faith that God will do what He has promised. Faith in God is to believe in the 'faithfulness' of a God who cannot lie and is faithful to His word.

Faith is seeing something happen for us and believing that God sent it. It is not working on our own willpower to believe that something we have asked for will happen, because that makes our willpower our faith and belief. It is not wishful positive thinking. It is none of these things, but the confidence in a God who knows best, who is truth, who displays His creation every day in our lives, and who reveals His visible character through His Son Jesus, our Saviour. *"No one has ever seen God, but the one and only Son, who is himself God."* (John 1:18)

> What we need is more trust to believe in a God who has promised.

We ask for more faith, but what we need is more trust to believe in God who is faithful to what He has promised. It is as though God's promises become prophesy that we can claim as we cooperate with our faithful God. *"The hope of eternal life, which God, who does not lie, promised before the beginning of time."* (Titus 1:2)

Faith is like walking each day in the dark with God, in who *"we live and move and have our being."* We walk with an unseen God and trust in His faithfulness to us.

Prayer: *Father, when I struggle to believe, help me to rely on Your promise of love and care, helping me to understand that You will never leave me or forsake me. Amen*

DAY 83
REJOICING GREATLY

John 15:11, *"I have told you this so that my joy may be in you and that your joy may be complete"* NIV.

Even though joy was the characteristic that Jesus showed throughout His ministry, one must wonder just how He could have spoken or even thought about joy the night before His crucifixion. He speaks of joy from within, like a spring rising from an unknown depth which was foreign to the disciples at that moment. However, He knew His sacrifice was going to create joy for all future generations - a joy which, through the indwelling Holy Spirit, would bring everlasting life to millions of people.

The more joy that flows to others, the happier we will be.

Jesus spoke of His joy because He knew the satisfaction of knowing the joy through fulfilling His Father's Will. As He healed or gave forgiveness, He would often repeat the words *"Take courage"* (Matt.14:27). His joy was in serving His Father, rejoicing greatly in giving himself for others.

When Jesus is our Lord, the Holy Spirit fills us with the same joy that Jesus spoke about, and which filled His life. As He fills us, we are to pass this joy on to those we encounter every day, like those with an addiction, the depressed or have experienced abuse. The more joy that flows from our hearts to others, the more infinitely happy we will be. We must fix in our minds that God is love and that love cannot be contained but must flow out to others.

Let us abide in Christ, with our hearts open to His guidance and love, so that He may speak through us to those who are weary with life. We are to initiate and pass on the love and grace that God has for mankind. Jesus didn't just speak a word, but instead stooped to minister to the needs around Him in a way that joy and happiness were the results.

We must not be well-wishers but well-doers. Lending a listening ear will encourage a lonely and despairing soul, and as we do so, we allow our Lord to work through us, and to fill us with great joy.

Make me a channel of blessing today, make me a channel of blessing, I pray.

James George Deck (1807-1884)

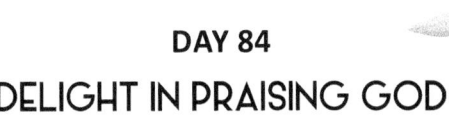

DAY 84
DELIGHT IN PRAISING GOD

Psalm 147:1, *"Praise the Lord. How good it is to sing praises to our God, how pleasant and fitting to praise him!"* NIV.

When we think about praising God, we tend to think about singing, but there are many ways to bring praise and for many things. His creation: the sun, moon and shining stars and the angels praise Him because He spoke and they were created (Psalm 148:1-5). We cannot sing unless our emotions are joyful, which is probably why God's people are encouraged to lift their voices in praise to their God throughout Scripture.

Singing always inspires those who raise their voices and those who hear it. I was born tone-deaf and married a choir conductor, not a good combination. However, over many years, even though I still can't sing in tune, I have gained great joy from my husband's ability to sing and understand music. Today, he is singing in God's choir, but nothing brings me more comfort than listening to music and singing the beloved songs of praise. Thankfully, one day I too will be able to sing praises, in tune, to my God, for *"He (will) put a new song in my mouth"* (Psalm 40:3).

> **Praise comes from a heart in thankfulness.**

Praise comes from a heart of thankfulness for all the goodness of a loving God poured out on His creation every day. Let us delight in praising Him before we eat our meal, when we see the beauty of His creation, for the provision of our everyday needs, for the job He has given us to do, and for our family and friends. There is a never-ending list of things that we can give praise for, and it is a good practice at the end of each day to reflect on all that your Lord has done for you that day and be thankful with a joyful heart. *"Sing to the Lord, for He has done glorious things"* (Isaiah 12:5).

Let us put our hope in God's love for us and, through His strength, delight only in Him, remembering how great and worthy our Lord is of our praise.

Praise to the Lord, the Almighty, the King of creation!
O my soul, praise him, for he is your health and salvation!
Come, all who hear; now to his temple draw near,
join me in glad adoration.

Joachim Neander

PAGE 85
ENCOURAGEMENT DAY

I Thess. 5:14, *"We urge you, brothers and sisters... encourage the disheartened."* NIV

When Jesus came to our earth, He didn't touch down like a visitor from outer space, bringing His own culture with Him. No! He took on himself humanity, to become like us. He was God and man. He felt our sufferings, our frailty, and just what it's like to be disheartened and disillusioned.

Jesus feels our suffering, what it's like to be disheartened and disillusioned.

Think about the emergency workers who are first at the scene of any disaster, showing courage and dedication to their careers. When the World Trade Centre in New York City was attacked in 2001, thousands of people were killed and injured; including more than 400 emergency workers. Also, in the horrific bushfires in Australia, many of our front-line workers fought till they were exhausted to save homes and lives. These men and women encourage the disheartened, but they themselves also need encouragement.

Paul showed us in his letter to the church in Thessalonica that the Christians needed to encourage the disheartened, as the people were going through persecution. He encouraged them to *"always strive to do what is good for each other and for everyone else"* (verse 15).

Jesus has sent you and me into the world to identify with others as He identified with us, becoming vulnerable as He did to encourage others. Life is no different today! We need uplifting, and we also need to uplift those around us, encouraging them when they are disheartened. Jesus is faithful; and will do it through us, for without Him, we can do nothing.

Is there someone who needs your encouragement today?

And the wind of the Spirit blows on my life,
And I stop with a sense of shame,
As the words of Jesus again are heard,
GO AND DO THE SAME.

K. Cameron-Smith

DAY 86
KEPT FOR JESUS

Jude 1, *"Jude, a servant of Jesus Christ, to those who have been called, who are loved in God the Father and kept for Jesus Christ."* NIV

What a powerful thought; we are being kept for Jesus. It is as though a power that originates in the Divine operates through us by the energy of the Holy Spirit. Behind all that we do or choose, behind all the influences that come into our lives, there is the gracious movement of the Holy Spirit keeping us for Christ as He comes to dwell in our mortal bodies. Our soul is being kept for God's Spirit to energize and, our heart is the fountain that His Spirit will flow from to others. He will even use our imagination as we are being kept for the Master's use.

This shows us just how much Christ loves and needs every one of us, and how God will use us for the very purpose we were born to fulfil for Him in the world.

> Ask the Lord to keep you from temptation every day.

Even though the Spirit is keeping us for Christ, let us not take it for granted as there is always the possibility of becoming complacent about our calling. We must therefore keep ourselves living in the love of God. If you love Jesus as your Lord, you must follow Him and learn from Him, growing each day in the Spirit. Always be aware, lest you begin to drift backwards and forget that you are here to be used by God.

There is only One who can keep us from stumbling from within and without. Keep watch and ask the Lord to keep you from temptation every day. You are of more importance than the world in which you live because the Lord needs you to do His work. We are *"kept for Jesus Christ;"* let us always be aware and grateful for our calling.

Christ prayed for you and me, *"My prayer is not that you take them out of the world but that you protect them from the evil one,"* (John 17:15). He prayed for our wellbeing, protection, unity, our joy, and our sanctification. Oh, how He loves us. We surely need to do our part to be kept for Him.

Prayer: *Thank You, Heavenly Father, that You have called us into fellowship with Jesus. Keep us by Your mighty power that through faith we might genuinely serve You. Amen.*

DAY 87
FACING SORROW

John 12:27-28, *"Now my heart is troubled, and what shall I say? 'Father save me from this hour'? No, it was for this very reason I came to his hour. Father, glorify your name"* NIV.

We all know that at some time in our life, we will have to face sorrow and suffering, and we must not ask God to prevent it. As God's children, how are we to face sorrow? Often our first response is to question God, but the one thing we must be careful of, is not to ask God, why?

> *God is refining us to be used to bring comfort to others.*

What God desires us to do is to trust in Him. We must endeavour to preserve the person God created us to be as we face sorrow and suffering so that our life will bring glory to Him. When Jesus faced death on the cross, He came to God with the ultimate prayer of trust. *"My Father, if it is possible, may this cup be taken from me. Yet not as I will, but as you will"* (Matthew 26:39).

Even though we would like to avoid sorrow, we cannot. It comes to each of us, and we must understand that as God's children, we must have an attitude of trust. As we yield to Him, He will bring us through our grief. As hard as it may be, let's rejoice knowing that God is refining us to be used to bring comfort to others.

Sorrow and difficulties come to us to strengthen our faith, develop our character, and develop our love and dependence on God. Our attitude to suffering can give us strength or destroy us. The Christian who has faced great sorrow and suffering will always receive you and help you in your hour of need.

If you can understand yourself as you work through your suffering with Jesus beside you, God will make you an encourager for others.

Prayer: *Dear Lord, as hard as it is when sorrow and difficulties come, please help me, to remember how you faced death for me, and to know that You will help me as I trust. Amen*

DAY 88
MISPLACED CONFIDENCE

Philippians 3:8, *"I consider everything a loss because of the surpassing worth of knowing Christ Jesus my Lord, for whose sake I have lost all things. I consider them garbage, that I may gain Christ"* (NIV).

During my childhood and early adult life, I experienced many setbacks with my health, including poliomyelitis as a child. By age 40, I did not have good health, and, as I aged I knew that it would decrease unless I did something positive. Even with knowledge I had gained from being a nurse, I still did not have the answers, so I asked God to show me what to do.

No answer came quickly, and my health continued to deteriorate until in my early 50s, God revealed other methods that I pursued and where I found help. With my new found knowledge, I thought I had all the answers for everyone else and with my misguided confidence, I wanted to fix everyone. As humans, we tend to cling to our self-made standards and justify everything to ourselves, often lifting ourselves and putting others down.

We tend to cling to our self-made standards.

Paul warned the Philippian church about doing just that. They were putting their confidence in religious performance, and Paul told them that it is far more important to put their trust in the Lord. In verses 3-4, he said, *"If someone else thinks they have reasons to put confidence in the flesh, I have more."* He knew that everything he had achieved was just garbage, compared with knowing Christ and allowing Him to guide and grow him each day.

I had to learn that talking about the benefits I had found did not fit for everyone else and that it was more important for me to have confidence in God and tell others about Jesus. Whilst looking after our health is essential, we don't have to strive to have confidence in these things. Jesus loves us just as we are and gives us the power to become more like Him.

You have to accept the love and peace Jesus offers you and allow Him to guide you. Jesus died for you; He loves you and wants you to trust Him.

What would it look like for you to trust in God and rest in His love for you?

Prayer: *Dear Lord, help me to put my confidence totally in You, trusting you to guide my life in Your way each day. Amen*

DAY 89

A PARENT'S WISH

Ephesians 3:16, *"I pray that out of his glorious riches he may strengthen you with power through his Spirit in your inner being."* NIV

What would you wish for your child? I wonder what your first thought would be. Perhaps good health, success in their career, or a loving and caring spouse. We could go on, for we all have our children's best interest at heart. We want to see them do well in this life, and no matter our desire, somewhere or something falls short of our expectations. Would you wish for your child trials, as well as success, or the ability to feel what those who are hurting and lonely feel. For so many of us today, we can experience disappointment as our children choose to disregard any teaching from God.

There is power in praying God's Word

The greatest thing we can do as parents is to pray daily for our children. For their salvation and commitment to their Lord and for specific needs that they may have. Only in the last few years, God has shown me that the most powerful prayers that I can pray for them is to pray His Scripture over them.

I have found Ephesians 3:14-19 a most profound prayer to pray for my family. Here is a prayer for each one, regardless of their commitment to Jesus or their circumstances. I take these words and make them my prayer each evening.

"Father, may You grant that out of Your glorious riches You may strengthen each of my children (here I name each one) *with power through Your Spirit in their inner being, so that through faith, Christ may dwell and abide in their hearts. And I pray that they will be rooted deep and established securely on God's love. Father grant that they may have power, together with all the Lord's people, to grasp how wide and long and high and deep is the love of Christ. May they know and experience this love that surpasses human knowledge—that they may be filled to the measure of all the fullness of God."*

As I pray, I know that my loved ones are in God's hands, allowing Him to work out His will for each one in His time and for His purpose. I can only tell you about the peace this gives me as I surrender them totally to my God, for no matter my wish for them, the best is that they love Jesus as Lord and Master.

Prayer: *Thank You Lord, for showing me the value of praying Your Words over my family, and for the life of hope both now and forever in Christ Jesus. Amen.*

DAY 90
SPIRITUAL LAZINESS

Hebrews 10:24, *"Let us consider how we may spur (encourage and stimulate) one another on toward love and good deeds."* NIV

Unfortunately, we can all be capable of spiritual laziness, often longing for what we might call spiritual retirement. Oh, yes, we read our Bible, pray for others and attend church, all of which are an essential part of our Christian growth, but some believers want to be comfortable as though they are in retirement.

The writer of Hebrews encourages us to hold fast to the hope we have in Christ without wavering and encourage one another. The encouragement comes from the ministry of the Holy Spirit in our lives. To encourage others takes initiative, the initiative of Christ-realization, not self-realization.

Let's be careful not to just enjoy Jesus for ourselves, as this can be our first step in the wrong direction. We must also not just 'appear to be' spiritually active, looking for recognition, as this is not what God requires of us.

Seek God till Your heart burns for the salvation of others.

We must seek God till our heart burns for the salvation of others. To aim to finish our race well we must persevere in our faith, being obedient to our Lord and endure to the end. Jesus never promoted the idea of retirement. The older we get, the greater joy we will have as we encourage others in their faith. Each day, ask the Lord to lead you to someone who you can help and encourage in the Spirit. Always consider that as Christians, we can never retire. Jesus has called us to a life of total unselfishness, supporting and encouraging each other.

Ephesians 4:2 says, *"Be completely humble and gentle; be patient, bearing with one another in love."*

Prayer: *Dear Lord, please lead me to someone who needs encouragement and help to find Jesus, and please give me the words of scripture to speak into that person's life today. Amen.*

DAY 91

BE READY TO MEET THE KING

Matthew 25:10, *"But while they were on their way to buy the oil, the bridegroom arrived. The virgins who were ready went in with him to the wedding banquet. And the door was shut."* NIV

In this parable, Jesus tells how the virgins lamps went out because they failed to have enough oil. We must maintain our fellowship with Jesus, allowing the Holy Spirit to guide us as we study the Bible and come to God in prayer daily, as well as worshipping with fellow believers. We must keep our relationship with Jesus burning brightly; otherwise, the Evil One will put out our love for our Saviour and on Jesus returns, we will miss being called home to Heaven.

Each of us is responsible for our own relationship with Jesus.

The virgins were foolish and went to sleep. We need to sleep; the sleep of knowing we are secure in Christ and trusting Him each day. Peter slept when he was in prison, Acts 12: 6-7. *"Peter was sleeping between two soldiers, . . . Suddenly an angel of the Lord appeared, . . . He struck Peter on the side and woke him up. "Quick, get up!" he said, and the chains fell off Peter's wrists."* Peter slept because he trusted in Jesus, unlike the virgins who took their salvation for granted.

Their problem was they assumed they could borrow from those who came prepared. Not so, each of us is responsible for our own relationship with Jesus. We can have salvation and assurance of eternal life without money or price, yet we fail to make the choice that will save us. Like the foolish virgins, we will say, *"Lord, Lord,' . . . Then I (Jesus) will tell them plainly, 'I never knew you."* (Matthew 7: 21-23) They thought the bridegroom would recognize them. What a shock it will be for us if He says, *"I never knew you."* Don't make the mistake that these virgins made by not being ready when Jesus returns to this earth to take those who love and trust Him to heaven.

We must ask ourselves: *"Does Jesus know me; am I trusting Him every day? Am I ready for His return?"* Be sure to come today and ask Jesus to forgive your sin, letting Him fill you with the Holy Spirit, and hear Him say, *"Do not fear, for I have redeemed you... you are mine."* (Isiah 43: 1)

Prayer: *Jesus, thank You for dying so that I can have eternal life. Help me to stay close to You so that I will be ready to go when You return. Amen*

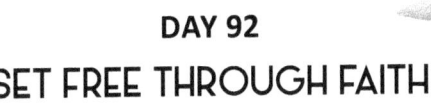

DAY 92
SET FREE THROUGH FAITH

Galatians 3:23-24, *"We were . . . locked up until the faith that was to come would be revealed. Christ came that we might be justified by faith."* NIV

In the Old Testament, the law showed men the holy standard God needed them to live by, helping them see their utter helplessness in the sight of a Holy God, allowing them to see the way of faith. When Christ brought redemption through faith in Jesus our Saviour, humanity was willing and glad to learn God's way through forgiveness rather than being locked in the law.

Moses tried through self-effort, even violence, to bring about the release of the Israelites from Egypt. God locked him in the desert as a shepherd for forty years being prepared and willing to be the person God required to bring the Israelites to the promised land. Paul and Silas, while imprisoned, trusted God through faith to bring deliverance to them. Had John not been sent to the Isle of Patmos, where he was reliant on his faith in God, he would never have seen the glorious vision of the Heavenly Kingdom to come.

> When man and mountain meet, God does amazing things.

Today God still, as it were, locks us up until our faith gives us freedom. Our very natures, circumstances, trials and disappointments will so often keep us looking inward to our own strengths, until eventually, through helplessness, we are willing to come to Christ in trust and leave everything to Him to work out for us. How much pain we would save ourselves if we were not so self-reliant and were willing to bring our problem to the Lord in the first instance.

My brother or sister, are you suffering from some great trouble or disappointment in your life? It can be a hard place when we refuse to come to Christ and leave it to Him. He promised, *"all things God works for the good of those who love him"* (Romans 8:28). Deal with the issue of your life the way God intended you to and know He said, *"Call on me in the day of trouble; I will deliver you"* (Psalm 50:15). God will reveal Himself to you through help and blessing that you would never have known otherwise, for when man and mountain meet, God does amazing things.

Prayer: *Oh Lord, I fail to know Your power in my life. Help me to always come in faith to You, knowing that by the power of Your Spirit within me, I will be blessed beyond my understanding. Amen*

*Look for yourself,
and you will find in the long run only hatred,
loneliness, despair, rage, ruin, and decay.
But look for Christ, and you will find Him,
and with Him everything else thrown in*
C.S. Lewis

*"Jesus answered, "I am the way and the truth and the life.
No one comes to the Father except through me."*
John 14:6

DAY 93
GOD'S PROVISION

Matthew 14:20, *"They all ate and were satisfied, and the disciples picked up twelve basketfuls of broken pieces that were left over."* NIV

The disciples were careful as they handed out the bread and fish that Jesus blessed to ensure there was sufficient. They quickly discovered that the group had all they could eat. We must remember there is no end to God's supply, for, *"God is able to bless you abundantly, so that in all things at all times, having all that you need, you will abound in every good work"* (2 Cor. 9:8).

Even though there was plenty to feed the 5,000, Jesus made sure there was no waste of what was left when he said to the disciples, *"Gather the pieces that are left over. Let nothing be wasted"* (John 6:12). In nature God created what we might think of as rubbish, to take on a new texture for reuse, as even our bodies return to the dust they came from. There is no waste in God's world, neither should there be in our lives each day. We can trust God for our every need but let us be careful to respect His gift and take great care to appreciate it.

> *God wants us to be thankful for his provision and value everything.*

In past generations, even though many people had very little, each household item and garment were cared for in a particular way. People valued things and were thankful for what they had. Today, we have become a throw-away society and take our supply for granted, enjoying so much that is unnecessary, so let us be thankful and careful to care for and value everything.

Before the meal was distributed, Jesus gave thanks to God, *"Looking up to heaven, he gave thanks and broke the loaves, and gave them to the disciples"* (v.19). In many homes today, giving thanks before a meal, is no longer carried out. Jesus set the example for us to follow, and this is one way our children can learn to be thankful instead of expecting everything to be provided. We must appreciate and value God's supply of everything each day. (1 Timothy 6: 8) *"But if we have food and clothing, we will be content with that."* Is there a provision from God that you need to thank Him for?

Prayer: *Teach us, to live in fellowship with You in every circumstance of life, being thankful for everything You provide for us each day. Amen.*

DAY 94

YOU ARE ROYALTY

John 1:12, *"To all who receive Him, to those who believed in His name, He gave the right to become children of God."* NIV

In the British royal family, the closer one is to being the King or Queen, the more the world and the public hear about them. The succession line of the royal family goes on and on, with the result that the one who may be thirtyish or more in the succession line, we don't even know their names. Members of the Royal Family, as well as supporting the King, also carry out important work in public life and charitable service. For instance, The Duke of Kent, 36th in line for succession to the British throne, helps homeless people find shelter and rebuild their lives, yet we never hear about him.

God values each of us the same

Have you ever realized that you are royalty as a child of the King of Kings? Even though, as a child of the King, we may not be in the spotlight, like a great Christian evangelist or Christian teacher, we are still His child, and God values each of us the same!

He considers each of us essential in His kingdom. Important enough to represent Him in the area He has called us to serve, and one day to reign with Him. 2 Timothy 2: 12 says, *"If we endure, we will also reign with Him."* We may not wear an earthly crown, but when we are a child of the King or Glory, we have a vital part to play in His Kingdom.

Rejoice today that God loves you and values you dearly.

Prayer: *Thank You, Jesus, for giving your life for me so that I could be a child of the King of Glory. May I always be faithful in serving you here on earth. Amen*

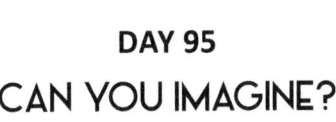

DAY 95

CAN YOU IMAGINE?

Revelation 21:3-4, *"They will be his people, and God himself will be with them and be their God. He will wipe every tear from their eyes. There will be no more death or mourning or crying or pain, for the old order of things has passed away."* NIV

Life today is so busy that we spend little time thinking about life after death. Take the time today, and imagine what this will be like for you, when at last your life here is over and you stand in the presence of our Saviour, the Lord Jesus, with His face there before you.

How will you feel as you see the splendour and glory of the Lamb? Will you stand and stare in awe, or will it make you want to dance or fall on your knees in humility and adoration. Although my family has always laughed about my terrible singing, I tell them that when I get to heaven, I will sing the Hallelujah Chorus, or, will the sheer presence of Jesus and the splendour around me make it impossible to say anything.

Just imagine, no more death, mourning, crying or pain.

The one thing that we do know is that we will forever and forever worship Jesus with countless angels. Revelation 5: 12-13 says, *"In a loud voice they were saying, "Worthy is the Lamb, who was slain, to receive power and wealth and wisdom and strength and honour and glory and praise! "To him who sits on the throne and to the Lamb be praise and honour and glory and power, for ever and ever!"*

Here on earth, we can only imagine what it will be like. The one thing that we need to be certain of is that we will be there, by having a personal relationship with Jesus through asking His forgiveness, and inviting Him into our lives, then living each day here on earth in close communion with Him. Jesus said, *"I am the way and the truth and the life. No one comes to the Father except through me"* (John 14:6). Let each of us pray for the salvation of those we love that they may be there with us.

Prayer: *Even though I can't imagine what it will be like when I look into Your face Lord, I praise You, that Your grace and joy will fill my soul as I bow in Your presence on that wonderful day. Amen*

DAY 96
THE MYSTERY OF LIFE

Job 2:10, *"Shall we accept good from God, and not trouble?"* NIV

Sometimes in life, we wonder what we did to get where we are in the maze. Imagine flying a long distance, falling asleep, everyone disembarking and not noticing you sleeping, the plane is parked, and suddenly you awake in complete darkness. For a moment, you would probably shake your head and then ask yourself, why didn't someone wake me, or how on earth did I end up here? Maybe, you have experienced the total helplessness of finding yourself or a close friend with a terminal disease to which no doctor has the answer.

We must expect bad as well as good in this life.

The questions concerning the mystery of life are, 'Can God make us love Him alone quite apart from His gifts?' and 'Why is evil permitted?' These questions are always with us, as are our unending prayers for the salvation of a loved one. The great Adversary of souls is always trying to find fault with our conduct so that he can accuse us before God. Satan even asked for Peter, *"Simon, Satan has asked to sift all of you as wheat. But I have prayed for you, that your faith may not fail."* (Luke 22:31)

I am sure that Job found himself asking the same questions we ask today. How did I get here? Imagine losing all your children, being poor, and being afflicted with a dreadful disease. Then your wife says, *"Are you still maintaining your integrity? Curse God and die!"* (v.9). Job remembered God and how good He had been, telling his wife that we must expect bad as well as good in this life. Christ never underestimated the power of Satan, and we must, like Job, always remember Christ's faithfulness to us in every situation we face. In the circumstances of life, whether prosperity or helplessness, we must remember that God is our faithful creator who will not give to us more than we can bear. Like Job, we must hold onto our integrity and trust God.

"The greatest thing is to give thanks for everything. He who has learned this knows what it means to live." Albert Schweitzer

Prayer: *Even though my flesh and heart fail me, help me Lord, to give thanks and remember that You are the strength of my heart and will never forget me. Amen.*

DAY 97
GOD'S SPECIAL FORGIVENESS

Luke 11:4, *"Forgive us our sins, for we also forgive everyone who sins against us. And lead us not into temptation"* NIV.

The four moral codes to maintain a high standard of a meaningful life are: Justice in our relationship with others. Caution and discernment in directing our affairs. Strength to bear trouble and sorrow. Temperance in all things. These standards are all good, but there needs to be added to this mix - Forgiveness, which does not come naturally to us as humans.

Forgiveness can be nice words, but true forgiveness requires deep feelings from the heart to forgive and forget, leading to understanding, empathy, and compassion for the one who has hurt us. This is the prerogative of the Christian. When Christ was on earth, He showed us the example we must follow. As He forgave us, we also must forgive. God is unable to forgive a person with an unforgiving spirit. *"But if you do not forgive others their sins, your Father will not forgive your sins"* (Matt. 6:15).

> *God is unable to forgive a person with an unforgiving spirit.*

Are you willing to forgive? Maybe you refuse to forgive someone for *some* hurtful deed done to you. You need to ask, in light of God's word, if your soul is right before God because your love for God is in accord with your love for your fellow man. *"Whoever does not love their brother and sister, whom they have seen, cannot love God, whom they have not seen"* (1 John 4:20). These are not easy words to deal with, but they are God's words, and each of us must determine where we stand. Forgiveness brings God's peace enabling growth and happiness. When we withhold forgiveness, hurt and anger will keep eating away at us and will ultimately harm us more than our offender.

Are you needing to forgive but find it difficult, begin by praying for them saying, *"forgive us."* Ask for forgiveness for yourself and them, for although they have wronged you, you need God's forgiveness. Have the courage to ask for an opportunity to meet them, asking for grace to show love and forgiveness. Believe, and know that God's grace is greater than your needs.

Prayer: *Dear Father, help me to have grace, no matter the circumstance, to be able to forgive because if You are willing to forgive them, I must. Amen*

DAY 98

THE WONDER OF IT ALL

John 3:16, *"For God so loved the world that he gave his one and only Son, that whoever believes in Him shall not perish but have eternal life."* NIV

As you read these words for today, I pray that you will bow your head in worship and praise to God your Saviour. Or, if you do not know Jesus, that God would bless you in your spirit to ask Jesus to be your Saviour, that you too will have a relationship with the God of the Universe.

> *God doesn't always give quantity, but He gives us quality of life.*

When we think of the Universe, our world is so tiny it is almost like a pinhead in the scheme of things. Nevertheless, it is encompassed by the love of God. He loved and still loves our world, for He created it. Just as a mother hen broods over her chicks as she teaches, cares for, and loves them; likewise, our Heavenly Father broods over the chaos in our world and longs to bring peace and love to reign among us.

Because of our sins, God could not look upon us, and yet He loved us and desired a personal relationship with each of us. His love was so great that He sent His only Son to live with us. The only way we could come back to Him was through Jesus's willingness to come and die in our place that in giving our life to Jesus, we could again be reconciled to God our Father. What a price Jesus paid. He could have said no, but thankfully He died willingly. He knew that when He hung on the cross, God would turn His back on Him because a Holy God could not look upon the sin that Jesus bore for us. Imagine the pain Jesus must have felt being rejected by His Father, just for you and me.

Then we are told *"that whoever believes in Jesus shall not perish but have everlasting life."* It is hard to imagine living forever, yet it is within reach of each of us. Our eternal life begins the moment we believe and trust in Jesus. God doesn't always give quantity, but He always gives us quality of life.

Hear the God of the Universe say to you, *"Fear not, for I have redeemed you; I have summoned you by name; you are mine"* Isaiah 43:1.

Prayer: Father God, thank you for what you have done for me. Your love is so great, I freely give you my life afresh to be consecrated to You, my Jesus. Amen

DAY 99
GOD'S COMPELLING LOVE

Galatians 2:20, *"The life which I now live in the flesh, I live by the faith of the Son of God, who loved me and gave Himself for me"* NIV.

I would dare to say that there is not one parent, who reads these words, who has held their new-born baby and wondered if they had the capability to bring up their child. Or maybe you have suffered the loss of a loved one and wondered if the veil between them and you, was thick or thin. Our world is very unstable with no constants at all, and yet we can face each new day with joy because Christ lives.

Each day we can do what we do because the love of Christ compels us. *"For Christ's love compels us, because we are convinced that one died for all, and therefore all died"* (2 Cor. 5: 14). Our faith in Christ, compels us to love Him until we understand that when something happens to us it is as though it happens to Him, whether it be heartache, praise or blame, and for this reason alone we are overshadowed by His personal power within us.

> We can face each new day with joy because Christ lives.

When we abandon ourselves to the love of Christ, we can live in our unstable world through faith, because Christ lives in us, and our hope is for the life we will live with our Saviour in heaven. Praise God that because Jesus lives, each of us can face whatever is our lot tomorrow, with faith and hope in our God.

Prayer: *Thank you Lord Jesus for the confidence You give to me each day to face whatever is before me, with the assurance that You love me and care about me. Amen*

DAY 100
JESUS, OUR HERO!

Mark 16:36, *"Abba, Father," he said, "everything is possible for you. Take this cup from me. Yet not what I will, but what you will."* NIV

Let's picture this scene for a moment. It is the night when Jesus was going to be betrayed, and He knew it! As He walked into the Garden of Gethsemane with his 11 disciples, He told 8 of them to stay and commanded Peter, James and John, who said that they would never leave Him, to come further into the garden with Him. Before He left them to keep watch, He told them He was deeply distressed and troubled (v.33), then leaving them to watch, He went a little further to pray. Twice He returned to find them sleeping, telling them to watch and pray so that they wouldn't be tempted. Why weren't they concerned with what He had told them? We have to ask, *Would we have been any different.*

> When everyone else falls away, Jesus is always there for you.

He was overwhelmed as He fell on the ground, crying to God the Father, as He pleaded to be spared death on the cross. He was so emotionally and spiritually exhausted that He sweated drops of blood, yet He knew the dye was cast, and even though He could have walked away, He cried out, *"Yet not my will, but what You will."* At that moment, He accepted your sin and mine and went to the cross for us. There is every possibility that from where He prayed, He overlooked where He would be tried and the Mount of Calvary.

Jesus, the spotless Son of God, was a sinless genuine man whose very nature is unmeasurable love that will release you from your sin when you trust in Him. Yes, Jesus loves you. There is no more remarkable or graphic demonstration of trust in God than what Jesus showed at Gethsemane.

When He returned to the disciples, they left Him as He was captured and taken alone to be tried. When everyone else falls away, Jesus is always there. He suffered and died alone for you. Trust Him today and allow Him to build in you a Spirit filled character, refined by His discipline and love for you. *"For God so loved the world that he gave his one and only Son, that whoever believes in him shall not perish but have eternal life"* (John 3:16).

Prayer: *Jesus, I owe everything to You for the price paid for my redemption. I give You my life, for Your blood has washed me white as snow.*

DAY 101
GOD'S MASTERPIECE

Ephesians 2:10, *"For we are God's handiwork, created in Christ Jesus to do good works, which God prepared in advance for us to do."* NIV

Psalm 139 is a very personal passages of Scripture. In verse 13, we read, *"You created my inmost being; you knit me together in my mother's womb."* and again in verse 16, *"Your eyes saw my unformed body; all the days ordained for me were written in your book before one of them came to be."* God didn't make any mistakes when He created each one of us. He knows our words before we speak (v4). David proclaimed, *"This knowledge is too wonderful for me"* (v6).

For a gardener, there is nothing quite as rewarding as spending the day pulling up weeds and then standing in awe at the beauty of your garden. Like weeds in the garden, sin takes root in our lives, and we become marred by its effect upon us. Thankfully, God can see past the mess we make of things and loves each of us as though we were the only person for Him to love, as though there was no sin in us.

> We are fearfully and wonderfully made in the image of our God.

When God created you and me, *"He saw all that He had made and it was very good"* (Gen.1:31). We easily forget that we have been made with loving hands, and He is ever active in our lives, weeding out the sin because He loves us unconditionally. Whilst here on earth we will never be perfect, let us not forget that we are God's masterpieces, and He will accept and save us when we confess to Him.

We forget that we've been fearfully and wonderfully made with loving hands in the image of our Heavenly Father. When we forget this, we struggle with low self-worth, wallowing in self-pity and depression. Let us live in the delight of our Lord, who died to redeem each of us, and let each one of us allow these truths to shape the way we live.

Prayer: *Loving Father, please show me the weeds in my life, and strengthen me to be who You made me to be in Christ. Amen*

DAY 102
UNIMAGINABLE BEAUTY

Psalm 91:2, *"I will say of the Lord, "He is my refuge and my fortress, my God, in whom I trust"* NIV.

Our Psalm today speaks of our God being our safe place. When I read, *"He will cover me with His feathers, and under his wings, I will find safety; his faithfulness will be my shield,"* I think of a hen, how she gathers her chicks under her wings for safety. It is said that the mother hen has four calls; when the night is near; for food she has found; for danger, and the call of brooding love. I grew up on a poultry farm and experienced the beauty of hundreds of fluffy chickens gathered closely together under the heat light keeping them warm and safe. God's faithfulness to us is our constant shield and protection, even during worldwide trouble, we can find shelter in Him.

> *God's faithfulness to us is our constant shield and protection.*

God tells each of us to come and find a hiding place in Him. A place where we can find comfort when troubles come our way, when everything is dark and lonely, and we are oppressed on every side. What wonderful security is ours, as we read in verse 15, *"I will be with you in trouble, I will deliver you."* God's faithfulness cannot do anything else but protect us in all our ways.

These promises can only be ours when we choose to accept the care and protection of our loving God. Many of us know we will be in Heaven, but we may have a troubled and complicated life on earth. Our God can help us do better, and tells us, (v. 11) *"He will command his angels to guard you in all your ways."* When troubles come, He will give us the strength to move forward with courage, and as we shelter in Him, we will be kept from passionate temper, pride, hatred, and envy, a few of the sins that easily overtake us each day.

This Psalm gives us a glimpse into everything that is ours in Christ Jesus. Let us praise God for the wonder of His continual care and the unimaginable peace and beauty that is ours through Christ.

> *My life has been touched by Your miracles Lord,*
> *In my little world, I love what you do.*
> *But the greatest miracle of them all*
> *Is that I, through grace, belong to You.*
>
> K. Cameron-Smith

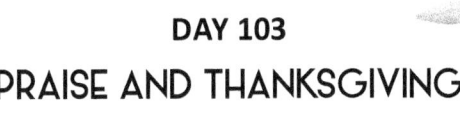

DAY 103
PRAISE AND THANKSGIVING

Psalm 103:1, *"Praise the Lord, O my soul; all my inmost being, praise his holy name"* RSV.

"Praise the Lord," are words that seem to arouse one's soul with all that is within, our voice, hands, mind, and spirit. Truly this calls us to take action to remember the benefits that are ours as children of the living God. In our busy life and world, it is easy to forget the blessings we enjoy, because we look for something more satisfying rather than realising what is already ours.

Learn to live in the presence of the Holy Spirit, and realise that right at this very moment, God is forgiving, healing, redeeming, crowning and satisfying. He is the same yesterday, today, and forever, and it is enough. He is ever longing to show us love beyond our understanding. Because we continually sin, we must constantly ask God's forgiveness, so we are always walking with Jesus. In v.12, we're reminded *"as far as the east is from the west, so far has he removed our transgressions from us."* Praise God!

> *God is the same yesterday, today and forever and it is enough.*

"He heals all your diseases and redeems your life from the pit" (v.3-4). Here the Psalmist is speaking of the diseases of the soul, those things like bad habits, that tend to control the wellbeing of our growth in Christ. He redeems us from our destruction and wastefulness. How great is our God! He then *"crowns us with love and compassion and satisfies our desires with good things."* His power is always at work within our soul to cleanse and restore us to fullness of life in Christ. (Eph. 3: 20). Stop and realize just how blessed you are in Christ as He pours these gifts into your life.

It always amazes me, how a choir conductor amid all the voices singing together, can hear and know the voice that isn't on key. His ear is trained to listen to every voice. So it is with our God, He will miss your voice if you refrain from His praise. Let us together with the Psalmist, *"Praise the Lord, O my soul!"* What do you need to praise God for today?

Prayer: *Let all praise be Yours, dear Lord, for You are ever giving Your choicest gifts to us, Your unworthy children. Accept our thanks and gratitude, which we are unable to express. Amen*

DAY 104
A FATHER'S PRAYER

1 Chronicles 29:19, *"Give my son Solomon the wholehearted devotion to keep your commands, statutes and decrees."* NIV

This prayer of David for his son is truly profound. If every parent were to trust God and pray this prayer for each of their children every day, our world would be a better place. Instead, we so often tell God what we think is best for our children when God knows what is best for every one of us. In verse 10, David commences his prayer by praising, *"Yours, O Lord, is the greatness and power and the glory and the majesty and the splendour, for everything in heaven and earth is Yours."* He continues by exalting God, thanking Him for his goodness and abundance and then completes his prayer by praying for his son.

> **The blessings of God are not merely material things but spiritual.**

David surely knew that life is not without hope when we trust in Jesus. The blessings of God are not merely material things but spiritual. God gave His Son Jesus to die for your sin, because every good thing comes from God. He never wishes that any child on this earth should perish without knowing the blessings He waits to bestow on our children and us.

As parents, we have the privilege of praying for our family and friends. Billy Graham, the great evangelist of the 20th century, was asked, *"Will God continue to answer my prayers for my children after I am gone?"* He replied, *"God honoured Hannah's prayer for her son and he lived all his days for the Lord."* (1 Samuel 1:28) Long after you and I are gone, God will still be at work as He is not limited by time, and many of the things we prayed for will come to pass. *"Before the mountains were born or you brought forth the earth and the world, from everlasting to everlasting you are God"* (Psalm 90:2).

Parents, we don't have to worry; we just need to pray God will give to those we love wholehearted devotion to keep His commandments, giving them the wisdom to seek God every day and have understanding to give their lives to Jesus. Praise be to you, O Lord, that You love to hear our prayers every day.

Prayer: *Heavenly Father, let Your plan be worked out in the lives of my loved ones every day. I bring them to You, O God, to bless them with understanding and wisdom to seek You and know You as Lord of their lives. Amen*

DAY 105

OUR FATHER

Psalm 103:13, *"As a father has compassion on his children, so the Lord has compassion on those who fear him."* NIV

I have very happy memories of my dad. He was quite jovial and as children, he would sing to us while he drove the car, and then the day he walked me down the aisle, he told me I looked beautiful, and he loved me. The concept of being loved and wanted by their father is foreign to many people. Maybe you have not experienced the love of a good father. I lost my dad in an accident when I was just 28, but I am thankful for the happy memories I have of him. In my sadness, though a young, immature Christian, I turned to my Heavenly Father for support and guidance.

Despite our past experiences, God is trustworthy because He knew each of us and loved us before we were even conceived, *"For you created my inmost being; you knit me together in my mother's womb"* (Psalm 139:13). When we love God, we naturally go to Him for help in life's situations. Perhaps you find this difficult and doubt God's love, but as you read your Bible, pray and seek to love Him, your motivation will turn from past hurt to love.

> **He loves us so much that He wants our love.**

No matter who we are, each of us has sinned against God at some point in life. So, why does God still love us despite what we do or who we are? The irony is God doesn't need us, but He loves us so much that He still wants our love. God loves us because He wants to draw us toward what is best for us; that is Himself. He treasures us so much He died so that we could have a home in heaven when we put our trust in Him. He doesn't force us to love Him but instead gives us a choice. Yes, we can have God himself for ourselves. Can you say to God, *"Lord, I truly love You?"*

Do you believe that God loves you as an individual? That He loves you passionately? Do you know Him as your loving Father? It doesn't matter what you have done you can ask His forgiveness and come today and trust Him; because He does indeed love you, for HE IS LOVE.

Prayer: *Dear Lord, please help me to believe that You truly love me and to seek Your love in my life every day. Amen.*

DAY 106
REIGNING IN LIFE

Romans 5:17, *"For if, by the trespass of the one man, death reigned through that one man, how much more will those who receive God's abundant provision of grace and of the gift of righteousness reign in life through the one man, Jesus Christ!"* NIV.

When we think of a person reigning in life, regardless of colour, creed or political persuasion, nearly everyone would immediately think of Queen Elizabeth II, who for almost 70 years reigned as the monarch of the British Commonwealth of Nations. She was renowned for her ability to cope with war, family situations, sorrow, terrorism and political issues with calmness and yet with authority. Throughout her life, she made no apology for the daily comfort she drew from Christ's words and following His example as she exemplified what it meant to be a follower of Jesus in her everyday life.

Only as we receive shall we reign in this life.

As we admire her, let us also avail ourselves of the privilege that is ours during our earthly life, to reign through our Saviour Jesus. We will never understand just how this can be, but we must realize that this blessed life is only possible for those who are born from above through the blood of the risen Lord. By nature, we are born as a living soul, but to reign in life and be born from above, we become a life-giving spirit. It is written: *"The first man Adam became a living being" the last Adam, a life-giving spirit."* (1 Cor.15:45)

For each of us, God has a purpose as we serve Him both on this earth and beyond. There is an abundance of grace awaiting each of us, but we must avail ourselves of it, just as Queen Elizabeth did, by coming to Christ and claiming what God could do through her to meet every situation she faced. Only as we receive shall we reign in this life. To reign in life, we are, in a sense royalty, and that means power as we draw our strength from the Holy Spirit within us. It means victory, *"for we are more than conquerors through Him who loved us."* (Romans 8:37) Because in Christ, we *"always have all sufficiency in all things, we have an abundance for every good work."* (2 Cor. 9:8), enabling us to reign in life and bless others for our Lord.

Prayer: *Thank You Lord, for the trials of life that are ever working for my good, making me partaker of Your abundant grace. As I receive from You, may I reign in this life blessing others for You. Amen.*

DAY 107
GETHSEMANE

Matthew 26:36,38, *"Then Jesus went with his disciples to a place called Gethsemane, and he said to them., My soul is overwhelmed with sorrow to the point of death. Stay here and keep watch with me"* NIV.

Calvary and Gethsemane are unique events but are the gateway to Life for you and me. Each year at Easter, we think about what Jesus went through for our salvation. Ultimately, we will never be able to understand the suffering Jesus bore because it is foreign to our nature but let us never misunderstand the price Jesus paid for our forgiveness. Jesus was God and Man in one. We cannot comprehend how Jesus, the Son of God, sinless and holy, could come and bear our sin as Jesus the Son of Man for our Salvation.

When Jesus came to earth, He came knowing His purpose was to die. He said, *"The Son of Man must suffer many things... and he must be killed and on the third day be raised to life"* (Luke 0:22). As the Son of God, He knew that Satan could not touch Him, but at Gethsemane, He feared that as the Son of Man, He might not get through the onslaught of Satan as He stood alone without God the Father, and that would mean He could not be our Saviour.

> Every one of us, can enter the very presence of God.

At Gethsemane, He handed Himself over to bear the agony and suffering, allowing His body to be broken on the cross for our salvation. The Resurrection of Christ became a triumph for the Son of Man and because of His victory, every one of us, through faith and forgiveness, can enter the very presence of God. Let us give thanks to Jesus every day for what He suffered at Gethsemane.

Prayer: *Lord, please build in me, a Christian character refined by Your discipline and love. Amen*

DAY 108
RESURRECTION POWER

Ephesians 1:18, *"I pray that the eyes of your heart may be enlightened in order that you may know the hope to which he has called you, the riches of his glorious inheritance in his holy people"* NIV.

How many times have you and I bought a new gadget or even furniture and said to ourselves, *"I don't need instructions,"* until halfway through assembly, we discover things are not going right for us, so we decide to look at what the designer told us to do, and with a chuckle from an onlooker we discover we have done it all wrong. Our spiritual life can be just the same, and we need to be continually reminded of God's instructions for us to build a sound spiritual life. We must read God's manual carefully, asking for His wisdom and understanding.

God longs to fill us with nothing less than His power.

In Ephesians 1:18-19, Paul, tries to help the church at Ephesus understand what God can do for them. We may feel weak and wonder if God can do the same for us, but Paul wants us to know the greatness of God's power and the strength of His might that each of us has within us through His Holy Spirit. We need an understanding of God the Father and God the Son, *"in whom are hidden all the treasures of wisdom and knowledge"* (Colossians 2:3). Whilst here on earth, we can know His mighty strength through His Spirit who dwells within each believer so that God meets all our needs (Phill.4:19). By God's grace, we have redemption through the blood of Jesus Christ, *"that we may grasp the depths of the riches of the wisdom and knowledge of our God"* (Romans 11:33). Christ is our hope of glory in the life to come.

This is the 'resurrection power' that every believer can use when they feel burnt-out or hurt; useless or depressed; anxious or totally deflated. Our God longs to fill us with nothing less than His power in every way and everything, and to know the hope we have in Him. Praise be to our God and Father. Don't underestimate God's power within; ask Him to enlighten the eyes of your heart with His important truths today.

Prayer: *Father You sent Your Son to reclaim ruined sinners like us, so that when You return as our Glorious King to take us home to heaven, we will sing together: Hallelujah! What a Saviour.*

DAY 109
BLESS THE LORD

Psalm 103:1, *"Praise the Lord, O my soul; all my inmost being, praise His holy name."* NIV

Let us come and awaken our heart and praise the Lord with our innermost being. When we think about our innermost being, we think of everything that makes us who we are: our vision, hands, mind and spirit. We must praise Him for all His benefit to us, because here and now, our God is ever healing, forgiving, satisfying, and His love and faithfulness are never-ending. As you meditate on these things, be still and let your soul praise Him.

All His benefits; He forgives all your sins. No matter how wretched you have been, Christ died to redeem you and is always willing to forgive you. All you must do is ask. (Verse 3) He heals all the diseases of your soul. All the hurt, anxiety, and the bitterness. He will wash it all away, for He is like a fountain brimming with pitying love, and forgiveness. (Verse 3)

Ephesians 3:20 says, *"Now to him who is able to do immeasurably more than all we ask or imagine, according to the power that is at work within us."* Who is He who redeems your life from the pit of destruction and wastefulness? It is the Almighty Loving Father. And when He has forgiven you, has healed and redeemed you, He will crown you with love and compassion, by the power of the Holy Spirit working in you to create a new you.

Be still and let your soul praise Jesus.

Even after all this, verse 5 says, the Lord satisfies your inner being to grow in grace and knowledge of your Saviour, Jesus, so that your youth is renewed and lifted up like the wings of eagles. You will be restored and transformed in your life for Jesus. It is enough for us to live in the present with our Lord, as we enjoy the benefits of our loving Father. Then as we go about our daily routine and relate to others with the help we have received, we will bless our God.

Prayer: *Holy God, I bless You for all the benefits You give me every day. Without You Lord, I am nothing. I praise You and bless You, Jesus. Amen.*

DAY 110
LINGER AT THE CROSS

Mark 15:34, *"And at three in the afternoon Jesus cried out in a loud voice, "Eloi, Eloi, lama sabachthani!" ("My God, my God, why have you forsaken me!")* NIV.

There never has been or will be, any day like the day Jesus was crucified for the sins of humanity. Jesus stood where no one can stand, between eternal death and eternal life.

> Jesus stood between eternal death and eternal life.

That day, His relationship with His Father was ruptured as He cried out in anguish to God the Father. God abandoned Him because He could not look on the sin of humanity. Let us stand at the cross and realize God the Father wanted our love and trust so much He allowed His precious Son to die for us. Would you or I turn aside and allow our son to die for someone's wrong? Jesus did this for us. In that moment when Jesus cried out, *"It is finished!"* and gave up His spirit for us, the curtain separating the Holy of Holies and outer area of the temple was torn from top to bottom, signifying that Jesus through His death on the Cross had opened the way for everyone to come to Him for forgiveness, and through Him we have access to God the Father.

That day Jesus was forsaken by His Father for you? *"God made him who had no sin to be sin for us, so that in him we might become the righteousness of God"* (2 Cor. 5:21). Linger at the cross and realize afresh how Jesus was humiliated and broken for us. Think how Mary felt as she stood and watched her son die. Hear the centurion who crucified Jesus say, *"Surely this must be the Son of God."* Now see yourself standing there and ask... *"What will I do with Jesus?"* Sin separates you from God, your loving Father, but through forgiveness by Jesus, you can come home to God, who loves you more than you can know. Ask His forgiveness, put your faith and belief in Him and claim Him as your Lord today, giving you assurance of a home in Heaven.

> *At the cross, at the cross where I first saw the light,*
> *And the burden of my heart rolled away,*
> *It was there by faith I received my sight,*
> *And now I am happy all the day!*
>
> Russell Kelso Carter.

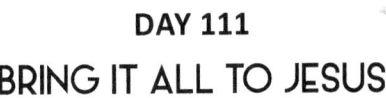

DAY 111
BRING IT ALL TO JESUS

Matthew 14:18, *"Bring them here to me," he said"* NIV.

Are you surrounded by needs at the moment, overwhelmed with problems, difficulties and emergencies? If we could only understand why God has allowed them to come to us, we would find help, blessing and deliverance; for the Holy Spirit longs to help us in all our situations.

When my husband became ill and needed full-time care, I cannot begin to explain some of the situations I found myself in and how the Lord grew me in my dependence on Him and provided everything I needed. Time and again, I would ask (or rather tell) God what was needed, but it was not supplied. Instead, He took me through a spiritual journey of faith and trust until I knew, without doubt, *"My God will meet all your needs according to the riches of his glory in Christ Jesus"* (Phil. 4:19). Yes, even though I knew God's will is best, I had to learn again to let go and allow God to do His work, and the answer always came with the need provided, much better than I had imagined.

We don't give Jesus a chance to work, as we have all the answers.

We must bring all our trials to our loving Heavenly Father, holding them before Him in faith and prayer. Then, we must be still, give thanks and allow Him to begin His work both in us and through us. So often we don't give Jesus a chance to work, as we have all the answers for Him, even when we know in our hearts that His will is best. He will surely do everything to overcome the disaster you are facing, for this is God's opportunity to reveal His grace and glory in your life as you have never known it before. He said, *"Bring them (all your needs) here to me."*

What a privilege is ours – God as our source; His riches our supply; and our Saviour Jesus is the channel through whom we receive all His goodness. Place your needs before Him and see Him richly supply. Draw upon your Jesus in faith, and as you trust and give thanks, be encouraged that He will meet all your needs as He promised.

Prayer: *Thank You, Father, for Your promise to always supply my needs. Please help me to trust You more and be patient to see You work out Your will in my life. Amen*

DAY 112
WHO ARE YOU?

Psalm 39:5, *"Everyone is but a breath, even those who seem secure."* NIV

When you have been on an Internet conversation, did you take a good look at yourself and think, do I really look like that? There were times when I thought I had better get serious about losing weight or having a different hairstyle. Regardless of age, occasionally, it's good to look at ourselves, not so much our outward appearance, but what we look like on our earthly journey and if we're developing into the type of person, we would like to be, as we walk with Jesus.

> It's essential for us to see ourselves from God's perspective.

When we compare ourselves with someone else, we may think of ourselves as being spiritually superior to them, but it's essential for us to see ourselves from God's perspective. Pharoah thought he was great until he saw what God thought of him. *"You are like a lion among the nations; you are like a monster in the seas"* (Ezekiel 32:2). Pharoah was not very impressive at all in God's eyes.

What is important is to know that our Creator has made us in His own image (Genesis 1:27) and that we are becoming the person God wants us to be. When someone looks at you, do they see you, or do they see Christ in you? Let us not be anxious about ourselves, but instead begin to appreciate other people more, and show respect for them simply because they are of value to God.

We cannot change our past, but from today, let each of us prayerfully take hold of God's grace that we have at this moment in time to invest in others and make a difference in their lives. We will find as we treat others with value, we will appreciate more and more our own uniqueness of being held in the love and care of God.

How does the image you have of yourself compare to the vision God has of you?

Prayer: *Jesus, I want to love You more so that Your love and goodness will be what others see in me. Amen*

DAY 113
TURN YOUR ANXIETY INTO CALM

Philippians 4:6, *"Do not be anxious about anything, but in every situation, by prayer and petition, with thanksgiving, present your requests to God."* NIV

Our trials and difficulties may be many or great, but as believers, we must learn to turn to our Heavenly Father, who understands how we feel and is waiting to love and help us. It is the delight of our Lord to always help us and in all circumstances. This is one of my favourite scripture verses and believe me; I dwell on it a lot. When I can't sleep, this is one verse I bring to God, telling Him my troubles, leaving them with Him, thanking Him and praising Him for the peace He has promised, *"And the peace of God, which transcends all understanding, will guard your hearts and your minds in Christ Jesus."* He has promised to guard our hearts and restless minds, which robs us of sleep!

"In every situation," means not just when we have a car accident or lose a loved one. We can live all day long in communion with Jesus, but we often tell Him our problem and then keep being anxious about it. God wants us to bring even the most minor matters, the little things, like a difference of opinion with our partner or friend, our pile of washing, the telephone call we need to make but haven't had time. Whatever makes you anxious in any way, speak to the Lord, and leave it with Him.

> **We tell Him our problem and then keep being anxious about it.**

"By prayer and petition, with thanksgiving." We must wait, and wait, and wait... with earnestness on God. Thank Him for His help, for saving you, for His Holy Word and the Holy Spirit. We have so much to be thankful for. Ephesians 5:20, *"Always giving thanks to God the Father for everything, in the name of our Lord Jesus Christ."* Finally, when we are thankful, then we can stop being anxious as we will receive the blessing of peace our God promised.

Take this verse into your heart, walk humbly in the Spirit, and the result will be, you will glorify God more than you have ever done. *"Let us continually offer to God a sacrifice of praise"* (Hebrews 13:15). A good habit throughout your day is to check that your heart is not anxious about something, and if it is, take care of it and return to a calm state.

Prayer: *Help me, dear Lord, to rejoice always, to pray without ceasing, and always, in everything to give thanks. Amen*

DAY 114

WE MUST DRAW ON GOD'S SUPPLY

Isaiah 12:2, *"Surely God is my salvation; I will trust and not be afraid. The Lord, the Lord himself, is my strength and my defence."* NIV

God offers an unfailing supply each moment of our lives, but we cannot know all that He has for us unless we draw on His love. *"God will meet all your needs according to the riches of his glory in Christ Jesus."* (Phil. 4:19)

For the Israelites, especially at the Feast of Tabernacles, the priests would draw water from the Pool of Siloam and pour it into the temple, to remind them of God's unending supply of water that flowed from the rock in the desert. As it was then, so today, every need of grace, compassion and help from every promise is ours, IF, we have our bucket or pitcher of faith and trust and draw on God's supply.

> *God hears and answers; our part is to believe and received His blessing.*

As a child, I watched my grandfather and dad dig many wells by hand, on the family farm and was always fascinated when they would let down the bucket. Sometimes it would come up empty, simply because they had not dug deep enough, but oh, the smiles on their faces when it came up full of crystal-clear water, and they tasted of its goodness. Our faith is like the bucket given to us that we might drink from the Divine supply. We can be sure that when we come to our Father in the name of Jesus, our God hears and answers; our part then is to have the faith to believe that we have received this blessing and to wait on God's grace to come to us.

Our God is *"the God of all Comfort"* (2 Cor.13:3). He never failed the Israelites or the Apostle Paul, and neither will He fail you or me. He is ever waiting to stoop down from heaven to comfort the heart heavy with grief or wipe the eyes that are red from weeping. Take your bucket and fill it with deep faith and trust in your Lord today that you may praise Him.

Prayer: *Help me to know the riches of Your glorious inheritance, O God, and to know the power towards those who believe that I may live in Your sweet presence each moment of every day. Amen*

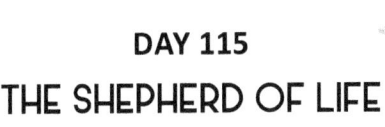

DAY 115

THE SHEPHERD OF LIFE

Psalm 23:1, *"The Lord is my shepherd, I lack nothing"* NIV.

Undoubtedly, this is the most well-known and used chapter of the Bible. It is recited at births and whispered with dying lips. But can you say without a doubt – my Shepherd? The soul can only possess these words when fully surrendered to Jesus. You can only have all of God, and God in all, when you are willing to surrender your all to Him.

At the time when this Psalm was written, the shepherd would lead his sheep from their overnight enclosure. They followed in his footsteps over the rough path. *"Even though I walk through the darkest valley, I will fear no evil, for you are with me"* (verse 4). Whatever rough patches are on your path, always remember that He is leading and will bring you through them because of His great love for you. Just follow in His footsteps as He leads you to *"lie down in green pastures… he leads me beside quiet waters"* (verse 2). As He guides and leads, you will find peace in His presence as He *"restores your soul."*

> **Can you say without a doubt – MY shepherd?**

At the end of each day, the shepherd leads his flock back to the fold for shelter, where he tends to each one with love, giving food and shelter for the night. *"You prepare a table before me in the presence of my enemies. You anoint my head with oil; my cup overflows"* (verse 5). Our Lord always protects and cares for each of His flock, refreshing our thoughts and emotions, which lift us spiritually to praise Him.

"Surely your goodness and love will follow me all the days of my life, and I will dwell in the house of the Lord forever" (verse 6). Oh, the blessing when we will go out no more but abide in His presence forever. Recently, having shown my great grandson that we need to be able to say with confidence that Jesus is MY Shepherd, he went to his father and told him that he wanted to ask Jesus to be his Saviour – his Shepherd. Can you say MY Shepherd with assurance? If not, do so today by asking Jesus to forgive your sin and be your Saviour.

Prayer: *Thank You, Lord, for Your support each day through this troublesome life until my life on earth is over, and I dwell with You forever. Amen*

DAY 116
THE POWER OF STILLNESS

Mark 15:5, *"But Jesus made no reply."* NIV

As Jesus stood condemned before Pilate, He stood in the power of stillness as God's holy silent Lamb. Had He wished, with just one word of rebuke or one look of Divine power, He could have made His accusers fall at His feet, but He let them say and do as they wished.

> *There is a stillness that will allow our God to work for us.*

When we are wrongly accused, we naturally long to retaliate. We so quickly become vindictive, and we stand up for ourselves. Yet, if we can but hold our peace, there is a stillness that will allow our God to work for us. A silence that gives the wisdom to allow God in His unfailing and faithful love to act on our behalf.

Let us beware of taking up our own cause. Instead, we must let our Saviour work through His silent power so that our accuser will remember us like the morning dew, gentle and filled with the sunshine of God's love. *"I tell you, do not resist an evil person"* (Matt. 5:39).

> *Our Jesus had to stand alone,*
> *And feel our hearts like they were stone,*
> *He knew He'd come our souls to save –*
> *That day for us His life He gave,*
> *For us, "He held His peace."*
>
> Unknown

Just as Christ did, when we are insulted, let us allow our Lord to saturate us with a spirit to see the face of Christ in those that we differ with. This attitude of peace and stillness will allow our testimony for Him not to destroy another's life but to save it. Let God be God.

Prayer: *Father, please fill me with Your wisdom that when others come against me, I will be filled with Your peace to see the face of Christ in them. Amen.*

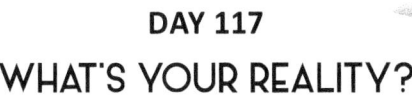

DAY 117
WHAT'S YOUR REALITY?

James 4:13-14, *"You who say, "Today or tomorrow we will go to this or that city, spend a year there, carry on business and make money... Why, you do not even know what will happen tomorrow. What is your life? You are a mist that appears for a little while and then vanishes"* NIV.

Do you go about your day consumed with what you must do, focusing on family, appointments, work and all the other things that make up a typical normal day? The reality is that anyone reading these words may not finish reading or reach the end of today. Most of us give little or no time to consider the all-powerful God who made everything in our world. Instead, we worry over everything and arrive at day's end exhausted. Today is not a typical day, and we are crazy to take it for granted, for today, we may die. Yes we all know this but we live like as if it will never happen.

> Today is not a normal day, and we are crazy if we take it for granted.

Often, we are suddenly confronted with some disease or disorder in our lives, and the first thing we do is start stressing and ask God, *why*. Funny isn't it, how all of a sudden, reality changes, and we see things differently. We believe it is our right to worry and fear. Although we might believe God has control, we are afraid to turn our problems totally over to Him. Philippians 4: 4 tells us to *"rejoice."* Yes, it sounds ridiculous. It doesn't say to rejoice unless your life is in danger. God commands us to *"be anxious about nothing."* When we become consumed by our problems, it is like saying that our worries are more important than God's command to rejoice and be anxious about nothing.

Life is very brief, and we forget that our life is all about God and not us. When we worry and stress, it's like we have forgotten that Jesus has forgiven us. We need to read on, for Paul continues, *"in every situation, by prayer and petition, with thanksgiving, present your requests to God. And the peace of God, which transcends all understanding, will guard your hearts and your minds in Christ Jesus"* (v.6-7). Yes, peace is ours when we rejoice. So, let's get over ourselves and realize our reality is about glorifying God, who created and loves us eternally. Let us rejoice, be glad and give thanks for who we are in Christ.

Prayer: *How can I say thanks for all You have done for me, Lord, except offer You my life afresh and realize that my life is not about me but You, my God. Amen*

DAY 118
VICTORY IN CHRIST

Psalm 44:4, *"You are my King and my God, who decrees victories (commands deliverance) for Jacob"* NIV.

There is no enemy during your growth as a Christian or in your ministry for Christ that Jesus, your Saviour, will not conquer and give you victory over.

God wants us to move forward to face our problems with courage.

We must trust and believe that God has our problems sorted for us because He has promised to give us victory, so do not be afraid of them. Deuteronomy 20:4 *"For the Lord your God is he who goes with you to fight for you against your enemies, to give you the victory."* God wants us to move forward to face them with courage and inspired strength from Him. *"Fear not, for I am with you; don't be afraid."* Unfortunately, we often shrink back and feel unworthy, but this is not what Christ wants for us.

God wants us to claim victory, no matter the circumstance. To hand over the problem to Him requires our total commitment. We must believe and give thanks before we receive victory. Jesus won the victory for you when He died to save you from the enemy and sin, so you share in that triumph that He won.

You are a child of the King of the Universe! You honour God by rightfully claiming what is yours as a member of the Royal Family of the Universe and an heir of the Kingdom of God, not by failing to claim what is yours as His child.

"Claim your share of the Saviour's victory." – F.B. Meyer.

Prayer: *Thank You, Lord, that by Your redeeming blood, I have victory in Your name. I will ever be grateful that You loved me before I knew of Your love for me. Praise You, Jesus, that I will spend eternity with You. Amen.*

DAY 119
PRACTICE GOD'S PRESENCE

Psalm 139:7-10, *"Where can I go from your Spirit? Where can I flee from your presence? If I go up to the heavens, you are there; if I make my bed in the depths, you are there. If I rise on the wings of the dawn, if I settle on the far side of the sea, even there your hand will guide me. Your right hand will hold me fast."* NIV.

We are blessed when constantly aware of God with us 24/7. Every day, we perform some activities more spiritually than others. When we are at church worshipping, teaching children about the Lord, or working with the underprivileged, our persona can be quite different to when we are cooking a meal, working on our car, or just day by day in the workplace. Do you, without conscious awareness, separate your activities into spiritual and regular?

> **We are blessed when we live in constant awareness of God.**

In Leviticus 19:18, God instructs Moses, *"Love your neighbour as yourself."* And in v.11, we read, *"Do not steal,"* then in v.10, *"Do not . . . pick up the grapes that have fallen. Leave them for the poor."* We might ask why God spoke like this, for He spoke both spiritual and non-spiritual words together because that is how He wants us to live all the time. He wants us to understand that all of life is spiritual when we are His beloved and should carry out our activities and speech in a spirit of worship in the presence of our Holy God.

How do we achieve this? - Practicing God's presence is gained when we draw near to Him and draw on His divine resources which are always available to us. Why do we fail to ask for God's help in times of uncertainty when the tempter is near? Nehemiah flashed a prayer to God as he stood before the King, and Abraham's servant asked for God's guidance to choose a wife for his master's son. God is ever-present. Matthew 28:20, *"Lo, I am with you always, even unto the end of the world."* Be encouraged, God is with you. Call on Him in the ordinary, difficult, and spiritual times, worshipping Him, for His ways are perfect.

My life has been touched by Your miracles Lord,
In my little world, I love what you do.
But the greatest miracle of them all, is that I, through grace, belong to You.

K. Cameron-Smith

DAY 120
THE CHRISTIAN EXTRA

Matthew 5:41, *"If anyone forces you to go one mile, go with them two miles."* NIV

Jesus is telling us that when something arises, we must not only do the necessary but also the unnecessary. We continually face emergencies that must be dealt with. As a child of God, Jesus has done a supernatural work in us, which enables us to have strength to do what is required, plus the extra.

Let us be generous in our dealings with our fellow man.

The only thing that affects our enthusiasm to go the extra mile is our personal relationship with Jesus. Is your relationship such that you can say, *"I am here for God to send me where He will."* Your action in a matter, will determine whether you have or haven't entered into the spirit of Christ's ministry.

Let us be generous in our dealings with our fellow man. 2 Corinthians 9:6 says, *"Whoever sows generously will also reap generously."* When something must be done, we need to go beyond the *must*, doing our work with a smile and kindness. Do not just pay your employee, but be thankful for the service rendered. Likewise, do not just do your work to receive payment, but do it with enthusiasm, always being willing to complete your work even if it's past time to finish for the day.

If we are to be disciples of Jesus, we must remember that Jesus said, *"I have chosen you."* As such we must let the Holy Spirit make us the disciple that He wants us to be. God is ever drawing us to Himself by His supernatural grace to make us His, not built by any natural capacity we have.

God does not ask us to do something that is easy for us but to do what we are fit to do by His grace. As His followers, we must be the light in another's life, helping the needy, feeding the hungry, visiting the shut-ins, and as we give out again and again, we will be filled with the measure we give to others. Luke 6:38, *"Give, and it will be given to you... poured into your lap. For with the measure you use, it will be measured to you."*

Prayer: *Dear Lord, help me to be more generous to those around me. Fill me with your perfect love that they may see You and come to You. Amen*

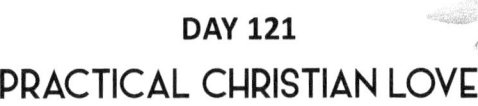

DAY 121
PRACTICAL CHRISTIAN LOVE

Romans 12:10, *"Be devoted to one another in brotherly love. Honour one another above yourselves."* NIV

This passage from Romans 12:9-13, oozes with being committed to loving and caring for our fellow man. Paul tells the Christians in Rome to be joyful in hope, patient in affliction, faithful in prayer, share with those in need and practice hospitality. Here Paul gives practical ways to build relationships whilst caring for others.

The first three are necessary to fit us to show love. The mere knowledge that Jesus will return to take those who love Him to live eternally in heaven gives us great joy to rejoice. God wants us to be patient, silent in our troubles, bringing them to Him in prayer and surrender to Him to sort out for us, and then to pray without ceasing, 1 Thess. 5:17. *"Pray continually, give thanks in all circumstances, for this is God's will for you in Christ Jesus."* We must live our lives in the spirit of prayer. We must come to our God and tell Him everything that is in our heart, all the pleasures and pains that fill our lives, as though we were talking to a dear friend. Prayer is the key to practical Christian love because God's loving kindness will come to meet us and help us.

Prayer is the key to practical Christian love.

Paul tells us to show love to those in need. He does not just mean to give of our substance and time, by listening and showing Christ's love to others, but to also show hospitality. With busy lives, this can be hard to find time for, except with our close friends, but Jesus wants us to open our homes to those who never get asked for a meal and fellowship. I grew up in a home where hospitality was a part of life, seeing love and prayer for people. It is an experience I won't forget, and I have continued to practice in my own home. It is a source of blessing to others whilst bringing great joy to oneself.

The blessings we receive in showing practical Christianity will always far exceed the cost to us. In Matthew 25:40, Jesus said, *"I tell you the truth, whatever you do for one of the least of these brothers of mine, you do for me."* May I encourage you in your love and care of others.

Prayer: *Lord, thank you for the opportunities you give us each day to show your love and care for others. Amen.*

DAY 122
OUR PRIORITY

Matthew 6:33, *"Seek first his kingdom and his righteousness, and all these things will be given to you as well"* NIV.

This would be one of the most serious commands and disciplines of the Christian life. Even those you consider spiritual giants will say: I must live; I must provide food, clothing and a home for my family. When we look at what Jesus is saying in this revolutionary statement, "Seek First," we want to argue for the exact opposite, because the majority of us are more concerned with the physical and material than our relationship with our Heavenly Father.

> *God points out that you will never want or be in need.*

You say, *"How do I live,"* but Jesus reverses the order. When you make your priority the care of your spiritual relationship with your Saviour and never put your care of other things first, God points out that you will never want or be in need. *"Therefore, I tell you, do not worry about your life, what you will eat or drink; or about your body, what you will wear. Is not life more than food, and the body more than clothes?"* (Matt.6:25). Our problem being that we want things other than what we need.

Jesus doesn't say that the person who neglects his physical life will be blessed, but rather, we need to get our priorities in the correct order. If you are careless about what you eat, you will suffer health issues, and God also holds you responsible for keeping your earthly affairs in order.

To get our priorities right, the follower of Jesus must make their relationship with God the dominating factor and, by comparison, to be 'carefully' careless about all other things, for God has promised to take care of us. When we put God first and make our relationship with Him our number one priority, we will see the blessing of God as the Holy Spirit brings harmony to our lives.

Can you hear Jesus saying to you, *"Close your eyes, my child, and say with faith: 'Your will be done Lord, You, take care of it', and I say to you that I will take care of it."*

Prayer: *Lord Jesus, I surrender myself to you. Please take care of everything for me. Amen.*

*"The purpose of life is not to be happy.
It is to be useful, to be honourable, to be compassionate,
to have it make some difference that you have lived and lived well."*
Ralph Waldo Emerson

*"And we know that in all things God works
for the good of those who love him,
who have been called according to his purpose."*
Romans 8:28

DAY 123
UNTIL JESUS CALLS

Colossians 3:23-24, *"Whatever you do, work at it with all your heart… It is the Lord Christ you are serving."* NIV

Jesus told us to let our light shine for Him and not hide it under a bushel. He also tells us to place our light on a stand so it can show the way for others. If a light is covered, the room is dim because it cannot fill the surrounding area with light.

We have all heard of amazing people in high positions whose lights have shone, some for self-gratification and others to lead and guide. Recently I attended the celebration of a life lived for Jesus. He was a man who loved his Lord and served him every day. Coming from a very average background in the early 20th century, he accepted Jesus as his Saviour as a young man, and from then on, never stopped living his life for his Lord.

> **The gate to heaven is not closed, and you don't need a permit.**

He was a man of vision who saw opportunities to bring the gospel to humanity in many different ways. His life was filled with the Holy Spirit, to the extent that every chore was a pleasure, and every person was an opportunity to give care and kindness to, to bring salvation to his fellow man. One could say his enthusiasm and joy for his Lord was unending, and throughout his long life, he showed the way of salvation to many as his light shone for Jesus.

As you read these words, he wants you to know the gate to heaven is not closed, you don't need a permit, and it's accessible through the blood that Jesus shed for your sins. If you have never asked Jesus to be your Saviour, then do so now and enjoy eternal life in heaven with all who love Jesus.

If you have asked Jesus to be your Saviour, then be challenged to let your light shine for Jesus, don't hold back, because your reward will be great. As Jesus himself said in Mark 12:30-31, *"You must love the Lord your God with all your heart, all your soul, all your mind, and all your strength."* Then he added, *"The second is equally important: Love your neighbour as yourself. No other commandment is greater than these."*

Prayer: *Thank You, Jesus, for the great saints, who show us how to live and let our light shine for you each day. Help us to keep shining for You. Amen*

DAY 124
TOO BUSY - THEN WAIT

Isaiah 30:18, *"The Lord longs to be gracious to you; blessed are all who wait for him!"* NIV.

When we have some trouble or sorrow, we tend to look in every direction for a cause, when what we need to do is to look at ourselves and our busyness. Today, we are just too busy, but in being busy, we need to be aware of the subtle danger of never stopping to realize that, in most cases, we can do something about our busyness. Ask yourself, what is essential? How much of what you do is instigated by the Holy Spirit, and how much is poor judgement on your part?

Waiting patiently will bring out grace you were not aware of.

Wherever you have trouble and sorrow, you will also find beautiful space filled with God's comfort and love. As the seasons of the year pass, so does nature and its beauty. When the bulbs that flower in spring and summer reach autumn they gradually appear to die, but they must rest and wait over the cold winter months in the chilled earth to be rejuvenated to flower again when spring arrives. While they are dormant, God is protecting them from the ferocity of winter, which would kill them if they were above the ground.

God is in control of everything and longs to protect you. Behind the clouds, the sun still shines, waiting to peep through when the clouds separate or disperse. God has not forgotten, and He knows you are busy and need a break. When God hides His face, He is waiting a little while so that you will love and trust Him more, and when He answers, the joy will be unspeakable. Isaiah 40: 31, *"They that wait upon the Lord shall renew their strength."*

We must stop letting our ego push us into a life of busyness, being careful to stop praise and flattery being heard above God's voice. God is always trying to get our attention; slow down, so He can bless with blessings that eternity will be too short to utter our praises. Waiting patiently and being still will bring out the grace and hope you were unaware your faith in God could give you.

Prayer: *Jesus, we ask for a more childlike trust to wait patiently, a more faithful spirit to listen, and hear Your still, small voice, so we may be filled with grace and hope in our unbelievable God. Amen*

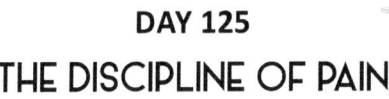

DAY 125
THE DISCIPLINE OF PAIN

Romans 8:18, *"I consider that our present sufferings are not worth comparing with the glory that will be revealed in us"* NIV.

At some stage of life, we all experience emotional or physical pain. We cannot measure pain, and no pain is alike, as each of us must walk our pain path alone. God gives us pain for a purpose and promises to be with us in our pain as we rely on His love to bring Him glory even in our pain.

The apostle Paul lived life with 'a thorn.' Over the centuries, writers have believed that it was physical and possibly had something to do with his eyes. It has always intrigued me that Paul never complained to anyone about his pain, even though three times he asked God to take it away, and each time God told him that His grace was sufficient. *"My grace is sufficient for you, for my power is made perfect in weakness"* (2 Cor.12:9).

> God's grace is at its best when our human weakness is most profound.

It appears Paul was in constant pain, but instead of complaining, that because of it, he could not do what God had asked of him, he bravely claimed the grace of God and did more excellent work through the enabling power of God than he could have done if his life was unhindered by pain. David Ring, an evangelist with cerebral palsy and a great sense of humour, challenges thousands of people with his signature message - *"I have cerebral palsy... What's your problem?"*

Is your pain a mistaken marriage, a failed business, an unfortunate partnership, a physical weakness, disfigurement of your body or face, or another difficult problem that is hard to come to terms with? We must realize that as hard as our problems and disabilities are, they are meant to unite us with God's enabling strength and power. God's grace is there for you, the same sufficient grace given to Paul. It is at its best when our human weakness is most profound. Those who wait on God are often stronger in their weakness than those who enjoy health and vigour. *"Those who hope in the Lord will renew their strength"* (Isaiah 40:31).

Prayer: *Lord, help us to make You our first port of call with the pains and trials of our lives, knowing that regardless, You, have the answer and the grace that will see us through. Amen*

DAY 126
TRUSTING AND GIVING THANKS

Isaiah 12:4, *"Give praise to the Lord, proclaim his name; make known among the nations what he has done."* NIV.

Life for most is not a steady pace but is interrupted from beginning to end with continual change, good and bad. We change homes, careers, schools, and relationships almost too casually. Not all change is our choice because the death of a family member can change our lives forever. For some, the threads of what appears a stable marriage snap, and the whole family suffers, or a longtime friendship ceases simply because the other person's choice is not what we desire. Our financial stability changes through a career change, whether voluntary or involuntary, often leaving us in a difficult position. Any of these issues can bring us to a place where we never wanted to be.

Our God is with us in every difficult situation we face.

Many of these changes affect our lives so much that we long to begin again, vowing not to make the same mistakes, but of course, this is impossible. Mistakes can leave ugly holes in our lives, that we are not proud of. For those of us who belong to the Lord, we can trust and know that our God is a God who takes charge and is with us in every difficult situation that we face. Sometimes, even though we trust Him for eternal life, we can find it very difficult to trust Him for the simple things of life, like the next car payment, finding a new career or home, or any other unexpected change in our lives. Still, when we trust Him, He always takes care of it.

It's easy to give thanks when everything is going well, but we must be grateful in difficult times, such as when we are missing someone who the Lord has taken to be with Him or when we are struggling to make our finances manageable. In our threatened world, where our lives are a continual whirl of good and evil, let us be reassured and remind ourselves every day that we have a God who can deal with all the changes we experience if we will but trust and give thanks to Him. *"I the Lord do not change."* (Malachi 3:6). *"Jesus Christ is the same yesterday, today and forever."* (Hebrews 13:8).

Prayer: *Father God, I thank You that You never change, and every day You are there to help me through life's problems. Thank You, that Your unending grace and goodness never fail. Amen*

DAY 127
OUR GREAT PROVIDER

John 6:5-6, *"Jesus said to Philip, "Where shall we buy bread for these people to eat?" He asked this only to test him."* NIV

When He spoke to Philip, He did not say 'you' but included himself in the feeding of the people. We are told that He wanted to test Philip, just like at times He tests us because He wants to perform a miracle for us, to help us understand that we need to always go and seek His help first. He wants us to consider each circumstance of our life as a matter not just for Him or just for us but for Him and us together. *"I am the vine; you are the branches. If you remain in me and I in you, you will bear much fruit; apart from me you can do nothing"* (John 15:5).

Here we see two groups of people, the crowd and disciples, who needed to know who Jesus was, and He wanted to reveal this to both groups through this miracle. The crowd, on the whole, saw Jesus as 'a Jesus of convenience,' able to provide their needs and heal their illnesses, but in their hearts, there was little change in realising that He was the long-awaited Messiah. That day Jesus intended to convict them to discover who He really was.

> Jeus is not limited by our resources to supply our needs.

Then there were the disciples, from whom He singled out Philip, as He wanted to put his trust in Jesus to provide for their physical needs. Optimistic Andrew remembers the boy with the loaves and fishes but doubts whether Jesus could stretch it to feed so many. As well as the crowd and the disciples, there was the small boy who was willing to give his meal as a gift to Jesus. The Lord increased it to such an extent that all were fed. Is it not always the way that when we give our gift to Jesus, He will do amazing things with it?

Often, when faced with an emergency, we calculate our means. We forget that Jesus is the great I AM, not a Jesus of convenience. He will take the simplest things in our lives and make excellent use of them to bring glory to His name and bless others. He is not limited by our resources to supply our needs, but He will cleanse and grow us spiritually if we will put our lives in His hands. He will use the simplest gift to bring salvation to many others.

Prayer: *Take my life, and let it be consecrated, Lord, to Thee. Lord, I come humbly and give myself to You that You might use me as You wish. Amen*

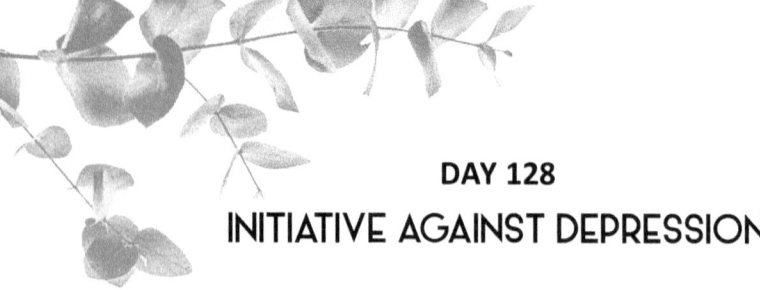

DAY 128

INITIATIVE AGAINST DEPRESSION

I Kings 19:5, *"He (Elijah) lay down under the bush and fell asleep. All at once an angel touched him and said, "Get up and eat."* NIV

We are all capable of depression, so let us guard against the thought that it won't happen to us. Usually, depression points to an event, like a marriage breakup, job loss, or some major issue in life. Fortunately, many of us bounce back, but when our bounce back techniques fail, our situation advances beyond having the blues to our total persona changing to having no interest in anything, often leading to weight gain, sleep disorders, fatigue, moodiness, and even thoughts of death. We are powerless and fall into depression.

Be brave enough to call out to God in your weakness.

Can you relate to any of these symptoms. Take heart because this is exactly what Elijah was experiencing, as we read in v.4, *"He prayed that he might die. "I have had enough, Lord," he said. "Take my life"* (Take time to read 1 Kings Ch.19). Depression is apt to turn us away from the ordinary things of life, but like Elijah, be brave and call out to God in your weakness, for He will inspire you to do the most natural things, like the thing that the angel told to Elijah, *"Get up and eat."*

As we "get up" and do the natural things of life, we will find Jesus there with us. Inspiration comes this way as initiative against depression. Be inspired to do the next thing and then the next for God, and experience fulfilment and satisfaction because you are doing it for the King of Kings and not yourself. That next thing may be something as simple as preparing a nice dinner for your family or speaking positively to someone in your workplace. If you don't do something to overcome your situation, you will likely fall deeper into depression. When the Spirit of God fills you with inspiration to do the thing, then as you do it, the depression will dissipate gradually. Immediately we obey, get up and 'do,' we will enter a higher plane of life in Christ.

What can you do right now to help yourself overcome your depression?

Call out to your God today and be filled with His inspiration to 'do' for Him.

Prayer: *Dear Lord, I am desperate and need Your inspiration. Help me see what I need to do so I can know Your healing in my life. Amen.*

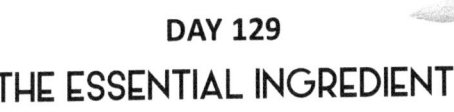

DAY 129
THE ESSENTIAL INGREDIENT

Matthew 8:13, *"Then Jesus said to the centurion, "Go! Let it be done just as you believed it would." And his servant was healed at that moment."* NIV

In reading the whole of Matthew 8, you will quickly understand just what the essential ingredient is. Faith that believes. On two different occasions, Jesus commends the man with leprosy (v.3) and the centurion (v.13) for their believing faith. Then, He speaks rather sternly to the disciples when they thought they would drown (v.26), telling them their faith was unbelieving. Most of us, fall into the boat with the disciples. We come to our Heavenly Father and ask for some needed blessing, whilst all the time, we wonder if we will receive just what we have requested. Our faith fails us, and we say God didn't want us to have the blessing we had asked for.

The leper's faith was so strong he knew that he could be healed if Jesus was willing. Jesus is always willing when we truly believe in His power to heal and provide for us. Jesus praised the centurion for his great faith, in fact Jesus didn't even go to his home, instead healing his servant the very moment the centurion believed.

He will do better for us than we could imagine.

Only when we can genuinely believe without any doubt will we receive. Let us be careful that Jesus doesn't say to you and me, *"Oh, you of little faith, why are you so afraid?"* (v.26). We must expect and not be amazed at what God will do for us. *"Truly I tell you, if you have faith as small as a mustard seed, you can say to this mountain, 'Move from here to there,' and it will move. Nothing will be impossible for you."* (Matt. 17:20)

Having been drawn to our Lord, entrusting our soul, our destiny, our hope, yes, our very life to His care, and inwardly knowing the peace that only our loving Heavenly Father can give, we can know that He will do better for us than we could possibly imagine. This is faith, the essential ingredient to receive all God has for us.

Prayer: *Lord, increase my faith. Help me to be like a child who expects to receive what You offer. From today on, may I have a new sense of Your presence and power Lord, through Your Spirit within me. Amen*

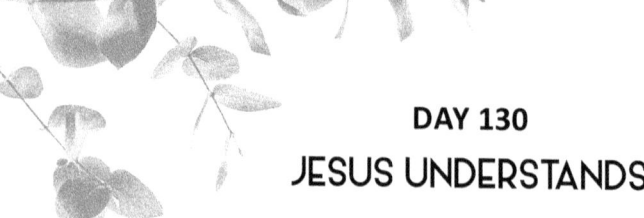

DAY 130
JESUS UNDERSTANDS

Luke 15:13, *"Not long after that, the younger son got together all he had, set off for a distant country and there squandered his wealth in wild living."* NIV

In the story of the prodigal son, we find different aspects. The father who loved both his sons; the son who ran away; and the son who was faithful. It's a story in which Jesus has a lot to say to each of us. Like the younger son who wanted his share, today we see many young people and children running away from their families and homes, because they feel their parents don't understand them or their world. The parents worry about them and what is to happen to them without guidance. You may be the parent of such a child, for whom you have given everything to help them grow up to become a decent citizen, and daily you struggle with the nagging feeling of, *"What did I do wrong."*

> **Trust and be diligent in prayer, that God can do His work.**

Your child may be experiencing the consequences of a life of drugs, gambling, pornography, or crime. Often, they are children who have straight A's in their education, and feeling all prayed out, you ask God why this is happening. Let's remember that no one is exempt from these things and know that Jesus doesn't look for someone to blame. *"Neither this man nor his parents sinned,"* said Jesus, *"but this happened so that the works of God might be displayed in him"* (John 9:3).

What are we to do, when a sister turns her back on her loving parents, who weep just to hear from her, or when a young man sends you a text message to say help me, for I have become addicted to gambling? When the prodigal son came home to ask forgiveness, the loving father says, *"Quick! Bring the best robe and put it on him. Put a ring on his finger and sandals on his feet."* Our Heavenly Father wants us to come to Him, having hope as we pray for the Holy Spirit to intervene in our child's life to bring reconciliation.

We must trust and be diligent in prayer, praying over our children each day, words inspired by the Spirit, so He can do His work. *"Now to him who is able to do immeasurably more than all we ask or imagine, . . . to him be glory . . . in Christ Jesus throughout all generations, for ever and ever! Amen* (Eph.3: 20-21).

Prayer: *Dear Lord, let Your Spirit invade the lives of our children who have turned away from You, and they will hear Your voice and obey. Amen*

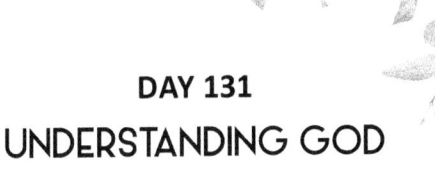

DAY 131

UNDERSTANDING GOD

Psalm 107:43, *"Let the one who is wise heed these things and ponder the loving deeds of the Lord."* NIV

There are many ways to understand God and His loving kindness. The way to increase our knowledge of our infinite loving God will be gained by reading and studying His Word. What the law is to the world, God's Word reveals our moral and spiritual law. You say, *"I read but do not understand it."* At age 20, my ability to understand what I read was very poor. Thankfully I decided to persevere, asking God to help me understand what He wanted to teach me from His Word. *"All things are possible to him who believes"* (Mark 9:23). Start today and experience the joy God will bring you as you read your Bible.

We understand our Lord through meditation. Oh, that we would learn to be silent in God's presence so that the Holy Spirit can concentrate our thoughts on the Father's love that loved before we were born and will love us for all eternity, showing sacrifice of the utmost intensity for us, as Jesus shed his blood for you and me at Calvary. We also understand the love of God through empathy. As we sacrifice for others, listening to their hurts, and loving in the name of Jesus, we will experience the pulse of His love for humanity.

> **God's Word reveals our moral and spiritual law.**

We must give thanks and praise for God's loving kindness to us. We're quick to pray, asking for our needs, but do we stop and give thanks for all the blessings of God we enjoy daily, like creation and the air we breathe? *"give thanks to the Lord for His goodness, and for His wonderful works to the children of men."* (v.15) How often do you wake at night, your mind overcome with a problem, you try to pray, but it's cold and mechanical. You get up, still feeling down, then you praise and thank God for all He has done in your life, dwelling on His power and majesty. It is as though the soul is instantly thawed, the horizon is clear, and your heart can sing with the angels proclaiming, *"Hallelujah to the King of Kings."* These practices will transport us into the Divine Presence Chamber of our God, to experience joy, gladness, and the loving kindness of our Heavenly Father.

Prayer: *Father, thank you for Your unfailing love. You have loved us from the beginning and to all eternity. Continue to enfold us in Your arms. Amen*

DAY 132
DO WHAT YOU CAN

Mark 14:8, *"She did what she could. She poured perfume on my body beforehand to prepare for my burial."* NIV

In these verses (3-9), Mark tells the story of Mary pouring expensive oil over Jesus's body as He feasted with His disciples. The disciples were confused because, in those days, a person dying a criminal's death would not be anointed, so they could not understand why she had done this to Jesus; but Mary did a beautiful thing for Jesus. She was motivated by her love for Him, and He corrected the disciples' attitude by celebrating what she had done.

> **We must respond not for praise but as an act of worship to our Lord**

Very often, we are more concerned about what someone else is doing than about our own personal ministry in seeking to give what we can to help someone else. What we do may seem very little, like offering to take a neighbour's child to drop off at school, or it could be as much as putting yourself out to help someone by providing for their daily needs. Whatever it is, when we, as God's children see the need, we must respond not for praise but as an act of worship to our Lord, who gave His life for us.

The oil Mary used to anoint Jesus, the disciples saw as waste, and sometimes our love and worship of our Lord can express itself in ways others find uncomfortable. We must always let our worship represent a sincere outpouring of love to the only one who is worthy of all glory and praise.

Is there something you can do today to show your love for Jesus?

> *Brother, Let Me Be Your Servant*
> *Let Me Be as Christ to You*
> *Pray That I May Have the Grace*
> *To Let You Be My Servant, too.*
>
> Richard Gillard

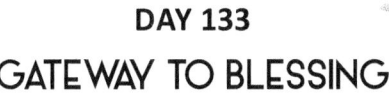

DAY 133
GATEWAY TO BLESSING

Psalm 23:4,5, *"Even though I walk through the valley... I will fear no evil, for you (Jesus) are with me... You anoint me with oil (blessings)... my cup (life) overflows"* NIV.

Have you been four-wheel driving through a valley? You motor along the muddy road, through creeks, down almost impassable gullies and through potholes. You look ahead to the beautiful mountains on either side or up in front. Even though my husband always loved these excursions, I was never at ease, just longing for our journey to reach the mountain and climb up, leaving the disasters of the valley behind.

Psalm 23 talks about the many valleys we pass through in life. It may be you are presently in a valley of a bad relationship; intense pain; a job or business collapse; or even trying to overcome an addiction. As we travel through the valleys with Jesus as our Saviour, we need not fear because even though we live in the natural world, the fact is that our trust is in our supernatural God.

All the forces of evil cannot stop God's blessing in your life.

Sometimes things happen without any explanation, and we wonder where God is in it all. When you are in a valley, He is your partner, so keep praising Him and moving forward while doing good and caring for others. He is with you, be encouraged, and even the unexplainable will pass, as He takes your hand to lead you to victory. As you move forward with Jesus, you will find the valley fading, and your thoughts and emotions will be healed by the blessings God will bring into your life.

We need the valleys in life to experience the supernatural power of the Holy Spirit as we climb to a deeper relationship with God. This experience will cause our life to overflow with God's love as we care and love others. All the forces of evil cannot stop God's blessing in your life. When we climb to the summit of the mountain, we appreciate the problems we have come through because our trust in our Father will be the greater for our experience. It is He who guides and protects and then anoints us with blessings. Let us together bring all the praise and glory to God.

Prayer: *Lead me, gently lead me Jesus, through the valleys of life to experience the supernatural power of the Holy Spirit in my life. Amen*

DAY 134
PURPOSE AND PERSPECTIVE

Philippians 1:20, 21, *"Now as always Christ will be exalted in my body... For to me, to live is Christ and to die is gain."* NIV

Even though we are aware that we will die to this world, when we are young or middle age we give little or no thought to it. This is because we see our earthly life with goals ahead and death appears as something far off. This is why when someone young is taken from this life, some experience deeper grief than when an older person passes. . . What is the purpose of your life?

Our death in this life is not the end.

Our goals, family values, work achievements and life skills are an important part of life. If you are young, you probably have some goals, like being the best person you can at home or your workplace. In middle age, we look forward to taking things a little easier, but as the years of life roll by and we quickly become seniors, we realize that we have fewer days ahead than behind us, and our perspective of life takes a significant shift.

Paul realized life did not revolve around him. His purpose was to glorify Christ through his life. He knew that his life on earth was not just about gaining eternal life but that everything he was and did would bring glory to God. Life is about God, not about us. To live for God's glory is to live for the salvation of humanity. This was Paul's purpose in life, although, I am sure he also had earthly goals, but his priority was that his life would bring glory to God.

The greatest joy and fulfilment we can know is that our lives bring glory to God. Don't allow your circumstances to overwhelm you, but see your priority as being Christ's servant, bringing the gospel to millions who are perishing. Like Paul, when in prison, we must stay focused on God, even through the problems of our life. Realise our death is not the end but the beginning of the true glory of Christ. Our time is in God's hands, and until then, we must continue sharing the gospel. Even when we have lost those dearest to us, let us fix our eyes on Christ, and don't become weary. Hebrews 10:15, *"Through Jesus, . . . let us continually offer to God a sacrifice of praise... And do not forget to do good and to share with others, for . . . God is pleased."*

In your spirit, know that Christ is Lord, fearing not what man can do.
If someone asks, then reply, about the hope that lives in you.

DAY 135
FAITH AND FEELINGS

Romans 5:1, *"Therefore, since we have been justified through faith, we have peace with God through our Lord Jesus Christ."* NIV

We have all heard of the analogy about a chair. The fact is that the chair exists and is waiting to be sat on, but until we have the faith to believe that it won't collapse, we will never know the feeling of comfort we can receive when we are seated.

When it comes to our Christian life, for so many of us, we want the feeling first, but our feelings are affected by our moods or our health and are very deceptive. On the other hand, our faith will naturally bear fruit in our feelings. It is our belief in the Lord, that will give us the joy we desire. *"Even though you do not see him now, you believe in him and are filled with an inexpressible and glorious joy."* (1 Peter 1:8)

The lack of feeling does not always indicate the lack of faith.

All of us have had times when we laid awake stressed over some issue in our lives. Until we take time to hand our problem over to Jesus and leave it there, we can never know the love, joy and peace the Holy Spirit longs to bring us. The blessing of the feeling God gives is the effect of the Spirit's work in our heart. The lack of feeling does not indicate we lack faith, for sometimes our mood stops us from distinguishing between love and the emotion of love or between peace and a sense of peace. God's Word tells us that we must leave everything with Him if we would know His peace (Philippians 4:7).

We must stop struggling and believe in His will for our lives. When you seek feeling, you miss it. Realize that you must have faith to believe that God is in control. Learn to live for Christ regardless of feelings and, in His time, you will have all you require. Let us live in the stillness of the Holy Spirit's presence, and through His promises, have faith to believe in His will for our lives.

"God is in every tomorrow, so I live for today.
Certain of finding at sunrise, guidance and strength all the way;
Power for all my weakness and hope for all my pain,
Comfort for my sorrow, with sunshine and joy after rain."

Laura A. Barter Snow

DAY 136
GOD DELIVERS

Matthew 6:13, *"Lead us not into temptation, but deliver us from the evil one"* NIV.

When Jesus tells us to pray, *"Lead us not into temptation,"* we must realize how important this should be in daily life. The Spirit led Jesus into the desert so He could be tempted. We may well ask, why would God send Him to be tempted, but God allowed His temptation to be like ours, but in His case, He did not sin. Knowing Jesus went down the road of temptation that we tread gives us hope, because even though He is the Son of God, He was also the Son of Man. Our mortal nature links us to Jesus, who has gone through the same ordeals faced daily by every human on planet earth. Temptation comes in different ways, being why it is so important to ask for our Lord's help each day to give us the strength not to yield to the sin it brings to our lives.

Hear Him say, 'I am your help in temptation.'

We think of temptation as gambling, doing drugs, and immorality, but it comes to the sick and the healthy; the successful businessmen and the student; the mother and the father; the rich and poor; even to the pastor, as well as each person in the church. Sometimes we forget that to not do what we should, is just as much a sin in God's sight as doing the wrong thing! No life, no matter how guarded, is not exposed to temptation, so we must pray this prayer as one, saying – *"us."*

Remember it is our loving Father that we come to with this prayer, for He made us and knows us better than we know ourselves. He loves with faithfulness and is always there to say, *"I am with you always, to the very end of the age"* (Matt.28:20). Listen with your heart and hear Him say, *'I am your help in temptation. I can carry you through, so stay by My side, look into My face, cease to trust in your strength and surrender yourself completely to Me that I may lead you to freedom.'* Be of good cheer, for a crown awaits each of us which Jesus will give everyone who is faithful to Him. As you face temptation, seek Jesus knowing He wants you to overcome.

Prayer: *Lord, be my strength, and forbid that I should yield to evil. Please help me to overcome evil with good. Amen.*

DAY 137
GOD'S REVELATION IN NATURE

Psalm 19:1, *"The heavens declare the glory of God; the skies proclaim the work of his hands"* NIV.

The poet Blake wrote: *"When the morning sun ascends the eastern sky, you may behold only a light-yellow disc, whereas I shall see and hear the infinite multitude of the heavenly host, crying, Holy, Holy, Holy!"* God reveals Himself through His creation as well as through Scripture. Everyone, has heard Nature speak to them at some stage of life, even though there is no voice. I feel sure we would look at life with a more negative attitude if, each morning there was no bird song, for they herald a new day, every day, without fail.

Creation is God's testimony of His power and majesty to humanity. *"He has not left himself without testimony: He has shown kindness by giving you rain from heaven and crops in their seasons; he provides you with plenty of food and fills your hearts with joy"* (Acts 14:17). Unfortunately for most, sin has affected our perception of the majesty of God's creation, to the extent that we notice little and take for granted what is happening in nature.

> God reveals Himself through His creation and through Scripture.

The Lord will speak to you as much as to any other if you ask Him to restore your soul and open your eyes to see His creation in a new way. We must listen to God's voice speaking within us, through creation and scripture, by being still and allowing the Holy Spirit to teach us the deep things of God, things to revive our souls. *"The law of the Lord is perfect, refreshing the soul"* (verse 7).

David didn't know anything of salvation through the death and resurrection of Jesus, but still he saw the glory of God in the starry sky and the provision and preservation of life around him as he obeyed the law given to Moses. *"The precepts* (commands) *of the Lord are right, giving joy to the heart. The commands of the Lord are radiant, giving light to the eyes"* (verse 8).

We must love the Word of God, for in Proverbs 4, we are told to pay attention to scripture, for it is our life. Let us proclaim with David, *"May these words of my mouth and this meditation of my heart be pleasing in your sight, Lord, my Rock and my Redeemer"* (verse 14).

Prayer: *Lord, show me Your way, that I may understand and obey Your commands and walk in the light of You, Lord, each day. Amen.*

DAY 138
KEEP TRUSTING

Luke 24:21, *"But we had hoped (trusted) that he was the one who was going to redeem Israel"* NIV.

Have you ever prayed and hoped that God would answer your prayer the way you felt best? Maybe someone close to you passed away when you had asked for healing, and you find yourself saying, *"I trusted."* It's easy to trust our Lord when everything is perfect, and we worship Him with our brothers and sisters in Christ, as did the disciples who trusted that Jesus would redeem Israel. As they walked the road to Emmaus, we find them grieving Jesus's crucifixion and saying, *"we trusted."* They had lost their trust and felt everything was over for them.

We need to keep trusting so we do not grow cold.

It would have been a different scene if they had said, *"Even though everything is against all hope, and our trust seemed pointless, we will not give up but will keep trusting."* I imagine that if this had been the case when Jesus came alongside them, they would have recognized Him through eyes of faith, but instead, Jesus had to say to them (verse 25), *"How foolish you are, and how slow to believe"*. We must beware of the danger of having trusted in the past and failing to trust our future to our Lord. *"Trust in the Lord with all your heart and lean not on your own understanding; in all your ways submit to him, and he will make your paths straight"* (Proverbs 3:5-6).

We can afford to lose everything, but never our faith in our Heavenly Father, whom we can trust with our very lives. We need to keep trusting so that we do not grow cold, and endure to the end as Christ's return draws closer every day. Let's be careful never to put our trust in the past tense – *"We trusted."* Let us always be able to say, *"I am trusting."*

Prayer: *Thank You Lord, for Your grace that saved me. May I always have the courage to say with faith, 'I am trusting You' every day. Amen*

DAY 139
IS GOD'S WILL YOUR WILL

1 Thess. 4:3, *"It is God's will that you should be sanctified."* NIV

It is always God's will that as His child, you should be set apart for His divine purpose, but the question remains, is it your will? Are you willing to let God do in you all that was made possible by His death for you on the cross? If you cannot answer this question, ask God to make you willing. Let the Holy Spirit change you so that Jesus's life will be evident in how you conduct your life.

Be aware of saying, *"I am willing to be set apart; nothing in my hands I bring,"* for it is not a transaction. There is nothing you can do, but through faith and trust, the work of the Holy Spirit will be revealed in your life.

Our attitude must be a life of total humility to Jesus, a life without proud holiness as we are nothing save through the blood shed on Calvary. We must live in the amazing realization that the love of God commended itself to us in that while we cared nothing about Him, He died to complete everything for our salvation. Romans 5:8, *"But God demonstrates his own love for us in this: While we were still sinners, Christ died for us."*

> Our attitude must be a life of total humility for Jesus.

To be sanctified (set apart for a divine purpose) makes you one with Jesus Christ and, in Him one with God. God has given us the right to carry the message of reconciliation to all within our reach. The evidence of the Cross in us is our obedience, service and prayer, with an outcome of thanks and adoration. God will bring about His divine purpose in our lives because of the Cross of Jesus. You are sanctified that you might carry the ministry of reconciliation to others.

This is God's will for you... but is it your will?

Prayer: *O Lord, forgive what I have been; dedicate me for Your divine purpose and order what I shall be in Jesus. Amen*

DAY 140
CUSHION OF PEACE

Philippians 4:7, *"And the peace of God, which transcends all understanding, will guard your hearts and your minds in Christ Jesus"* NIV.

A submarine being tested, had to remain submerged under the sea for several hours. On return, the captain was asked how a terrible storm had affected the sub during the time they had been submerged. The captain looking surprised, remarked that they were unaware of any storm as they had been deep enough below the turbulence caused, and the sub had rested in what is known to sailors as the *'cushion of the sea.'* This part of the sea is never stirred, and why when the seabed is dragged, anything that lies there is never destroyed and remains intact, even after hundreds of years.

Christ wants us filled with trust and hope that gives His deep peace.

When we think of peace, we think of outer peace, like our health improves, our business gets better, or for our marriage to change. We want life to return to a peaceful situation. The peace that our Heavenly Father offers transcends all understanding and is like the cushion of the sea, lying deep down in God's love so it is not reached or disturbed by external trouble. This peace is opposite to what we often ask for, when we want the disturbances and problems around us to end because we just want to get on with life.

If we could ask Jesus, He would tell us that this kind of peace is an illusion. The peace that Jesus offers is profound as we trust Him that all will be well, despite the turbulence of life about us. Jesus spoke to his disciples of peace in John 14:27, *"My peace I give you. I do not give to you as the world gives. Do not let your hearts be troubled and do not be afraid."*

Christ wants us to be filled with His strength to live in a broken world, with trust and hope that alone gives His deep peace, like the 'cushion of the sea.' A place of comfort and strength for our soul, giving us hope to carry on and live for Him. Trust Him today and know His deep peace.

Far, far away, the roar of passion dies,
And loving thoughts rise calm and peacefully,
And no rude storm, how fierce around us flies,
Disturbs the soul that dwells, O Lord, in Thee.

Harriet Beecher Stowe.

DAY 141
A NEW DAY

Isaiah 26:9, *"My soul yearns for you in the night; in the morning my spirit longs for you."* NIV

The night can be long and lonely, and sometimes our mind seems to race with anxiousness, fear, doubt, and uncertainty. We often find sleep difficult or pain more severe in the loneliness of the night.

But the morning comes. Yes! God is faithful; the morning always comes and brings a new day of hope and possibility, for you and me. God's sun heralds in the new day like a great multitude of angles proclaiming His glory and majesty. We must learn again to stand in awe and praise as God's created sun splits the eastern sky. We must be thankful that again we have the opportunity to awaken to do what God has called us to do, no matter how lowly our task.

The amazing thing is, that even on cloudy, rainy, and dismal days, the sun still heralds in the new day even when we can't see it. Likewise, even when we are lonely and afraid, God's love and care are there for each of us, and it is up to us to acknowledge and accept it.

> **The morning brings a new day of hope and possibility.**

God has given this day for you to rejoice and be glad in, so it is up to each of us to make that conscious choice to say with determination, YES – I will be glad and rejoice in this day.

God is still Sovereign, and yes, your day will unfold as God has planned, so regardless of what may eventuate, just remember to rejoice and be glad.

Prayer: *Thank You Lord, for each new day you give me. Your beautiful creation is glorious every day. Please help me to live for you today.*

DAY 142
PASSIONATE PRAYER

James 5:17, *"Elijah was a human being, even as we are. He prayed earnestly."* NIV

When we read that Elijah was a man with the same passions as us, we know that, like him, we often sit down and complain and don't believe. But when things came to the crunch, Elijah prayed earnestly. It was not by his passion but by his prayer. How many of us are passionate about something, but when it comes to praying for someone or something, we focus for a couple of days or weeks. We quickly forget to pray as a new object or person needs our prayer. Like Elijah, our answer will only come through prayer.

Our achievement will be through prayer.

Elijah refused to obtain the results he wanted through his energy or work but committed to praying. We must do likewise and learn to secure through God results that most try to achieve through the energy of their nature. As we pray, the Holy Spirit can work.

Be convinced that as adults, we are ultimately responsible for the spiritual condition of our children, family, and nation. We need to grow up spiritually, pray more, and learn what it means to be forbearing, developing the discipline of spiritual perseverance to pray earnestly as we intercede for the souls around us, our governments and our world. You and I are the spiritual standard for the next generation; we must not let ourselves get in the way but must pray without ceasing. What is your family learning from you about earnest prayer?

Let us not grow apathetic in the responsibility that God has called us to. *"I know your deeds, that you are neither cold nor hot. I wish you were either one or the other! So, because you are lukewarm—neither hot nor cold—I am about to spit you out of my mouth."* (Rev. 3:15-16)

Prayer: *Lord, kindle a flame within my heart that I will not be lukewarm but will know the power of prayer as I intercede for others. Amen.*

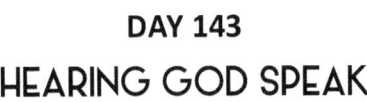

DAY 143
HEARING GOD SPEAK

John 10:5, *"They will never follow a stranger; in fact, they will run away from him because they do not recognize a stranger's voice."* NIV

So many people imagine that God only speaks to those who are holy or what we would call perfect spiritual Christians, but who can determine who is better than another. That is something that only God knows, and God can choose to speak to anyone. It would be unusual to hear God speak in an audible voice, although that can happen, but more often than not it is something within, as though you have had a stamp put on your heart and you just know. Our part is to learn how to hear when God speaks.

In the time of Jesus and today, the care of the sheep was the work of the young shepherds. Each night the sheep from many different flocks are penned together, and each morning the shepherd leads them out by calling them, and they recognize the voice of their shepherd. We could liken it to a group of young children playing together, and suddenly one cries; that child's mother instantly knows that it is her child and rushes to see what is wrong. They know the voice of the shepherd, and the shepherd knows them.

To hear God speak; meditate and be still in His presence.

God is Sovereign and can speak to anyone through the Holy Spirit, as He spoke to Ballam through the donkey (Numbers 22:21-39). When God speaks, it is something the Holy Spirit makes you aware of, and maybe not what you would normally expect, but it will be in accord with the truth of God. When God speaks to us, it will never be self-gratifying, bitter, or filled with fear. These are the things of the Enemy. So how do we know that it is God speaking within?

The most important thing is to listen, for if you fail in listening, you will never hear, and to hear God speak, we need to meditate on His Word and be still in His presence. When God speaks, you will feel a sense of His presence, and be inspired. Be careful of boredom, which will keep you constantly busy, often with your cell phone on social media... or just doing things, because always being busy can hinder you from hearing God.

Prayer: *Lord, help me always to be still before You so that I will hear You when You speak and know Your voice. Amen*

DAY 144
TRIUMPH OVER DEATH

Rev. 1:18, *"I am the Living one; I was dead, and behold I am alive forever and ever! And I hold the keys of death and Hades"* NIV.

In his address in Acts 2, Peter proclaimed that death couldn't keep its hold on Jesus. God raised Him from the dead, but, through all that Christ suffered nothing could rob Him of His love for every man, woman and child. Even those who were responsible for His death, He loved. Oh! how great that gift was!

> **Jesus robbed death of its terror and fear for the believer.**

He died to show us that when we are children of the Lord, we will be raised from death to eternal life. When He died, He robbed death of terror and fear for the believer.

We need not be afraid of the mystery of death. It is merely a gateway into life in heaven with our Lord. As the spirit within us cannot die (Ecclesiastes 12:7), we will still have the same personality but a different environment. There will be the same voices and fellowship that we enjoy here on earth. For those who believe, to die is to 'gain' (Philippians 1:21). Jesus will welcome us into the company of our loved ones who have gone before. Let us not fear the loneliness of death because even though humanly speaking, in one sense we are alone, in another, our Saviour is there to take our hand and lead us through the valley to the promised land. Not for one moment can death separate us from God's love.

Jesus died alone when He bore our sins, as God turned away because He could not look on sin. What a terrible experience Jesus went through just because His love for His Father and us was so great.

What we call death is really only 'sleep' for those who believe, and because of this, we need not fear what is beyond our earthly life. When most of us come to death, our physical body is worn out and exhausted, but we awake with fresh energy where we are presented faultless and with exceeding joy to our Saviour to the glory of God. Praise God.

Prayer: *Praise You Jesus for dying for humanity so that we do not have to fear death when we put our trust in You. Praise You that we can look forward with hope to an eternity of joy and peace with You. Amen*

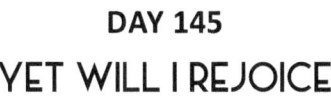

DAY 145
YET WILL I REJOICE

Hebrews 3:17,18, *"Though the fig tree does not blossom… though the olive crop fails and the fields produce no food… though there are no sheep in the pen and no cattle in the stalls; yet I will rejoice in the Lord, I will be joyful in God my Saviour."* NIV

Habakkuk, the prophet, was filled with fear because he knew Babylon would invade Israel, so he dwelt on what God had done for the people of Israel in the past and was able to say with courage, *"Yet, I will rejoice in the Lord."*

Throughout life, we all face devastating situations where we feel there is no way out. We have businesses that fail, loved ones pass away, close friendships unravel, or it may be something like a divorce or serious illness. All these issues take a toll on our lives. I often think of the mothers who said goodbye to their young sons as they went to fight in the first and second World Wars. I cannot imagine the pain they must have felt when they received the news that their loved ones would never return home.

> **Something powerful happens when we speak God's Word aloud with confidence and courage.**

When we fear and are overwhelmed, we need to remember that God is always with us and will not forget us. Psalm 46:1 tells us, *"Be still and know that I am God."* We need to ask God for the courage to face our situation during these very stressful times in life. We need to have faith in God, and as we trust Him, He will give us the strength and courage to work through our devastating situation.

Take courage as Habakkuk did; speak God's Word aloud and claim His comfort. *"The Sovereign Lord is my strength, He makes my feet like the feet of a deer, He enables me to go on the heights"* (v.19). Something powerful happens when we dare to speak God's Word aloud with confidence and courage. We must learn to rest in the sufficiency of our loving Heavenly Father.

Prayer: Thank You God, for the courage and strength You give us when we struggle with our life situations. Please help us to believe and trust the sufficiency of your grace. Amen.

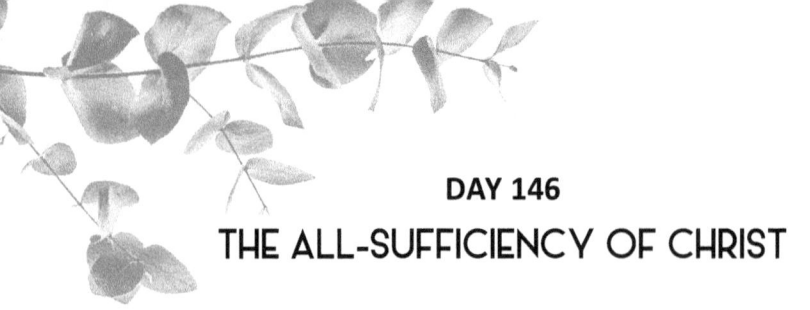

DAY 146
THE ALL-SUFFICIENCY OF CHRIST

Isaiah 33:21-22, *"The Lord will be our Mighty One... The Lord is our king; it is he who will save us."* NIV.

These words can only speak of our Saviour, who is the Creator and Lord of this world. His are the glories of the Cross, victory over Death and Hell, of the Ascension and Pentecost. He reigns forever and will judge each person who has ever lived on this earth with justice.

> **When everyone went to their home, Jesus had nowhere to lay His head.**

As we look around and compare our lot in life with others, sometimes we complain and become discouraged that we do not have what they do, but this Glorious Saviour is ever willing and eager to be the supplier of all our needs. Maybe some people that you have known since childhood have all that you have ever desired; a good position, a beautiful home, lots of friends, good health and more, whilst all this time you have lived from pay to pay with little savings, or you have led a lonely life with few friends, the bare necessities of life your only portion, and a sense of anxiety has tormented you.

But you are not alone in this, for when everyone went to their home, Jesus had nowhere to lay His head and, like Jacob, probably used a stone for a pillow. *"Foxes have dens and birds have nests, but the Son of Man has no place to lay his head"* (Luke 9:58). Some of the greatest saints, like Mother Teresa, have lived from hand to mouth in order that they might help others. Our Lord uses our trials and the needs of life to bring to our awareness what He is prepared to be and do for us.

Jesus is the complement of our lives, no matter how imperfect and ineffective we may be. He is able and willing to compensate for all our deficiencies. Philippians 4:19, *"God will meet all your needs according to the riches of his glory in Christ Jesus"*. Let the Saviour of this world display His all sufficiency in your life as you love Him and trust Him to lead you through life on this earth and then reign with Him above.

Prayer: *Be to me Lord, a place of peace and sufficiency for all my needs, helping me to understand that Your will is sufficient for me. Amen.*

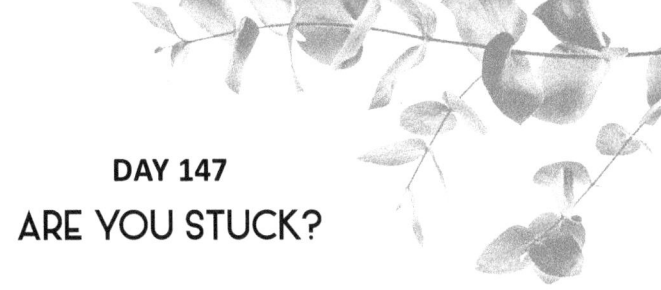

DAY 147
ARE YOU STUCK?

John 5:6-8, *"Do you want to get well?"* . . . *"While I am trying to get in, someone else goes down ahead of me."* Then Jesus said to him, *"Get up! Pick up your mat and walk."* NIV

Are you stuck and can't move forward like the man beside the Pool of Bethesda? Even though you're a believer, you maybe are stuck spiritually, financially or within your marriage. This man Jesus spoke to at the Pool of Bethesda had been there for 38 years, a long time doing nothing.

The first thing Jesus asked was, *"Do you want to get well?"* When you're stuck, you must want to become unstuck. Many want to change, but inside we have learned to be complacent and enjoy being stuck. It is something that we use to get others attention. Do you really want to be well, free from your addiction, financial problems or have a better marriage? If you really want to change and grow spiritually, you must decide that enough is enough. To become unstuck, we must stop making excuses. The evangelist Billy Sunday once said, *"An excuse is just a reason stuffed with a lie."* It's easy to blame someone else for something you should not have or should have done. By blaming and finding excuses, you will only get stuck further.

> **If you really want change, you must decide that enough is enough.**

Then Jesus said, *"Get up!"* The man had to stand up on the inside before he could physically stand up. In other words, he had to decide to stop blaming and have faith in Jesus. Like him, if we are to see change, we must have faith and trust Jesus. He is enough. Is there something your Lord has asked you to do, but because you have seen it as too hard, you have put it aside and remained stuck?

James 1:22, *"Do not merely listen to the word, and so deceive yourselves. Do what it says."* Let us remember Jesus loves us dearly and wants us to obey His Word, so we can grow spiritually and overcome our problems. Like this man, nothing is impossible for the one who believes.

> *"Simply trusting every day, trusting through a stormy way.*
> *Even when my faith is small, trusting Jesus, that is all."*
>
> Edgar Page – 1876

DAY 148
BECOME WISE AND MATURE

Hebrews 5:14, *"Solid food is for the mature, who by constant use have trained themselves to distinguish good from evil."* NIV

Like the people the writer of Hebrews wrote to, many of us don't want to use our energy to grow spiritually; we are content with baby food. Have you been a believer some time, but know little more than when you first believed? To become mature Christians, we must feed on and digest the promises and truth of God's Word. Only from scripture will we gain the maturity God longs us to have in Christ. When we fail to love and study God's Word, we will be confused by the knowledge of others, often becoming misguided as children do. Surely this is why we have so few wise people today, because we listen to others instead of listening to the Holy Spirit within us.

> **When we fail to study God's Word, we will be tossed about by the knowledge of others.**

Whilst God can speak through the words of others, if this is all we depend on for our growth, we will never have a personal grasp of what God wants to say to us from His Word. No relationship can be one-sided or just one day per week. We must seek to know Christ in a more profound way every day. *"Do your best to present yourself to God as one approved, a worker who does not need to be ashamed and who correctly handles the word of truth"* (2 Tim. 2:15). To truly understand God's Word, we must be the workmen ourselves.

Instead of expecting our pastor to do it all for us, we must be responsible for our own growth. As you read the Bible, the Holy Spirit will speak the truth you require to help you grow in your relationship with God. We need to read, digest, meditate, and memorise it because only then will we grow and understand God's Word. God wants us to grow and not remain spiritually immature. *"Reach unity in the faith and in the knowledge of the Son of God and become mature, attaining to the whole measure of the fullness of Christ"* (Eph. 4:13). Do you need to start studying your Bible for yourself?

> *And he walks with me, and he talks with me*
> *And he tells me I am his own.*
> *And the joy we share as we tarry there.*
> *None other has ever known.*
>
> C. Austin Miles (1868–1946)

DAY 149
SHOWING KINDNESS

Luke 7:13, *"When the Lord saw her, His heart went out to her."* NIV

In Luke 7:11-17, we read this wonderful example of our Lord helping the widow. When Jesus saw the widow following behind the coffin of her dead son, kindness naturally flowed from Him, and He said, *"Don't cry."* This is a touching story of Jesus stepping forward and showing compassion by touching the coffin; then speaking to her son, he sat up and began to walk. Jesus knew that not only did she grieve for her son, but she probably depended on him for financial support. The very essence of God in Christ is to do good.

> A moment of kindness can change someone's life.

When our heart is in tune with the Holy Spirit, things like goodness and kindness flow from us to others, but when we live our life for self, we justify everything we do to bring ourselves pleasure. Our goal as a follower of Christ is to grow more like Him and to imitate His life on earth. Friend, we must get back to asking God to change us to show more love and compassion.

In Ephesians 4:31-32, Paul says, *"Be kind and compassionate to one another, forgiving one another, just as God also forgave you in Christ."* Jesus wants us to take our kindness to the next level and even to show kindness to our enemy. When we live our life for Christ, we will be moved to show compassion and care for others.

We often don't realize how a moment of kindness can change someone's life. One night at a youth meeting, a young Christian girl felt the Holy Spirit touch her to show encouragement to another girl. A small act, we might say, but only God knows how that girl cherished the kindness shown to her, giving her hope where there was sadness. *"One kind word can change someone's entire day"* (Charles Spurgeon).

Kindness to others shows evidence of a heart that genuinely cares for others. What are you doing to put more kindness into our world?

Prayer: *Dear Lord, please give me the opportunity to show Your love and kindness to someone today. Help me never do so just to receive something in return but out of devotion and love for You, Jesus. Amen*

DAY 150
FAITHFUL FRIEND AND HELPER

Hebrews 5:8-9, *"Son though he was, he learned obedience from what he suffered and, once made perfect, he became the source of eternal salvation for all who obey him"* NIV.

Why is it that when we find ourselves in a dark place, we are always tempted to find a way out without trusting Jesus to help us? We go to our friends, often accepting advice that is not what God would have for us. In Isaiah 50:11, we are warned, these things are not God's way, and we will *"lie down in torment."*

> **Jesus has walked your road, and He knows all the pitfalls of your situation.**

When Jesus ascended into heaven and was crowned with glory, He sent the Holy Spirit to be our faithful friend and helper. Let us remember, Jesus understands every temptation common to man. He has walked your road and knows the pitfalls of your situation. When Christ died, He became the 'Salvation' of anyone who would obey Him.

In the human world, an engineer knows that exact obedience is essential to the working of any machine or the building of any structure; otherwise, there is failure. This same essential obedience is necessary in the spiritual realm. When you want to get yourselves out of your dark place, only obedience to your Lord and His dealings with you will suffice. Be careful not to meddle in God's dealings lest you frustrate God's work of grace in your life. Just commit your situation to Him, and in His perfect time, He will send His angel to give you the strength to obey and know deliverance.

Because Jesus learned these things by experience, He has been made perfect to bring eternal salvation to every soul of man. You can force a rosebud to open, but you will spoil the flower. Leave it all to Jesus... hands off... Your will Lord, not mine. *"Call on me in the day of trouble; I will deliver you"* (Psalm 50:15).

Prayer: *Thank You Lord, that I can come to You because You know each step of this difficult path of my life. Please help me to obey Your promptings, for I need Your help. Amen.*

DAY 151
GOD'S MIRACLE BOOK

2 Timothy 3:16, *"All Scripture is God-breathed and is useful for teaching, rebuking, correcting and training in righteousness."* NIV

The Bible is God's miracle book, filled with promises to humanity. The writing of the Bible is a miracle when we consider it was written in three different languages, on three different continents by over forty authors, over a period of 1,600 years. They were men from all walks of life, very poor to kings, yet it fits together from Genesis to Revelations, many books confirming the truth of others. A true miracle because it's one book by one author, God the Holy Spirit, who inspired and breathed His words into hearts and minds of the writers. Filled with God's love for humanity, it tells us who we are, why we're here and how to live. *"If you hold to my teaching, you are really my disciples. Then you will know the truth, and the truth will set you free"* (John 8:31-32).

Today it's easy to become distracted by work and a busy life, but God wants us to live by the truth of His Word so we will know the true happiness He longs to give each of us. Many false teachers change the scriptures to blend with their thinking. As believers we must learn the truth of the Bible by allowing the Holy Spirit to help us understand what God is saying to us.

> Do not become distracted by the things of this life.

Today we have so much access to the Bible, but it's not how many Bibles or about technology, but about whether we allow its words to guide and impact our lives. It's the Bible that gives us the wisdom to know that we need a Saviour and to come to Jesus for the forgiveness of our sins. In the Bible, Jesus tells us He knows about every problem you have and how you can overcome it through trust in Him. It tells us, through the life Jesus lived, how to live that we might receive great benefits and blessings from Him. Many books inspire, but only the Holy Spirit can transform our life to prepare us for the coming again of Jesus when we shall be with God for eternity. Search the Bible and let it guide you, that your life may bring glory to God. *"My son, if you accept my words and store up my commands within you, . . . then you will understand . . . and find the knowledge of God"* (Proverbs 2:1,5).

Prayer: *Thank You Lord, for the Bible. Give me inspiration to read, study and apply the truths You have shared in its pages. Amen*

DAY 152
DYING MEANS LIVING

Philippians 3:8, *"I consider everything a loss because of the surpassing worth of knowing Christ Jesus my Lord, for whose sake I have lost all things. I consider them garbage, that I may gain Christ."* NIV

When Paul experienced the presence of the Lord on the road to Damascus, his life was turned around. At that moment, he saw Jesus, high and lifted upon the cross for his sins, learning his way of life was going against the redeeming grace of God. We must remember Paul was a Jew, having learnt from the Pharisees the words of the then Scriptures. From that hour, he was aware of God's power and forgetting his past life, became ambitious to bring others to salvation in Christ Jesus. Philippians 3:12-14 says, *"Not that I have already obtained all this, or have already arrived at my goal… I press on toward the goal to win the prize for which God has called me heavenward in Christ Jesus."* As great an Apostle as Paul was, he never felt he had obtained his highest calling, always looking forward to greater intimacy with God.

> *Always look forward to greater intimacy with God.*

If this is the life we desire, how can we achieve our ideal? To achieve true life in Christ, we must die to self. Like Paul, we must change our thinking of who we are to who we want to be in our life. We are called to conform to the image of Christ. To achieve this, we must be more 'in fellowship' with Christ and regularly worship God in His sanctuary. We must crucify our desires and habits, both sinful and innocent, if they interfere with our spiritual growth, as we are changed into the likeness of Christ through the power of the Spirit.

Just as the farmer or gardener plants a seed into the darkness and solitude of the earth so that it can be nourished and germinate into some tree or plant that can bear fruit, so we, if we are to bear fruit for the King of Creation, we must bury our nature with Christ so we can be the beautiful person God intends us to be. From time spent with God, we can rise to have abundant life.

Dying to self and living for and in Christ must be the goal of every child of God.

Prayer: *Thank You Father, for Your never-ending grace that you pour out on me each day. Please teach and guide me, so that I may bear much fruit for Your Kingdom. Amen*

DAY 153
WITHOUT FEAR

Matthew 8:26, *"He replied, "You of little faith, why are you so afraid?"* NIV

Had anyone of us been in that boat with the disciples, I'm pretty sure we too would have been fearful. These experienced fishermen knew how to manage their craft in a storm, but although they had the needed experience, the storm was too great for them.

Do you have confidence in God? Is it not true that, like the disciples, we trust God up to a certain point, and then we chicken out and become increasingly fearful? When something devastating happens, we often completely forget to come to God. It is as though we feel He is asleep, and we lose our confidence in the God of the Universe.

> *Resting in God's grace, a oneness that will give great joy to Him.*

Yes, like the disciples, our faith hardly exists. How easily we hurt our Saviour; his heart must ache, for He is always faithful to us. *"If we are faithless, He remains faithful, for He cannot deny Himself"* (2 Timothy 2:13). As we go through life, and while everything is smooth sailing, we claim faith and trust in Jesus, but the moment a crisis arises, we instantly reveal who we really rely on. If we genuinely love and trust God, we can be at breaking point and not lose confidence knowing that He will come through for us. *"In all these things we are more than conquerors through him who loved us."* (Romans 8:37)

As we grow in our relationship with our Heavenly Father (sanctification), we can reach a point where we are resting in God's grace, a oneness that will give great joy to Him. May each of us strive to reach the peace of oneness with Christ? *"Because of the Lord's great love, we are not consumed, for his compassions never fail. They are new every morning; great is your faithfulness."* (Lamentations 3:22-23)

Prayer: *Thank You Father, that we can trust Your faithfulness to us in every crisis of our lives. Amen*

*You were made by God and for God,
and until you understand that
life will never make sense.*

Rick Warren

*"Great are your purposes and mighty are your deeds.
Your eyes are open to the ways of all mankind
you reward each person according to their conduct
and as their deeds deserve."*
Jeremiah 32:19

DAY 154
TODAY COULD BE THE DAY

1 Thessalonians 4:16, *"For the Lord himself will come down from heaven, with a loud command, with the voice of the archangel and with the trumpet call of God."* NIV

Before Jesus ascension to the right hand of God the Father, He told His disciples He would return to take them to the home He had prepared for them. *"I go to prepare a place for you. And if I go and prepare a place for you, I will come again and receive you to Myself; that where I am, there you may be also"* (John 14:3). When He returns, everyone who is alive will be instantly aware regardless of where you live in the world because His return will be personal, visible, and glorious. He has said to be ready, to watch and pray for that day, but are you ready, or are you living life to please yourself?

> His return will be personal, visible, and glorious.

There was a poem called, *'If Jesus came to your house,'* which was basically saying, if Jesus knocked on your door today, would you change some things before you felt at ease to let Him in? For instance, would you be happy to let Him see the books and magazines you read, or the TV programmes you watch? Would you continue going to the places you go, and would you have to make an effort to attend church? Would you be anxious about your friends turning up knowing what they would say or do, and would you have to control your temper and the quarrelling that goes on in your family now?

The Bible tells us to *"Take heed to yourselves, lest your hearts be weighed down with... cares of this life, and that Day comes on you unexpectedly"* (Luke 21:34-36). Jesus is coming back because He wants to spend time with you. Many people who have accepted Christ as Saviour don't honestly believe that He is really coming back. He wants us to enjoy life with Him in Heaven without tears, pain, or suffering. Knowing this, what would keep you from accepting Him as Saviour and putting Him first in your life by changing your daily living habits so you are prepared should Jesus return today? What could be more important than saying, *"I want to live for Jesus so I can live with Him forever?"*

Prayer: *Thank You, Jesus, for the truth that You will come again to take us to be with You eternally. Even though we do not know whether it will be in the morning, noon, or evening, it will be a wonderful day that we can look forward to with hope. Amen*

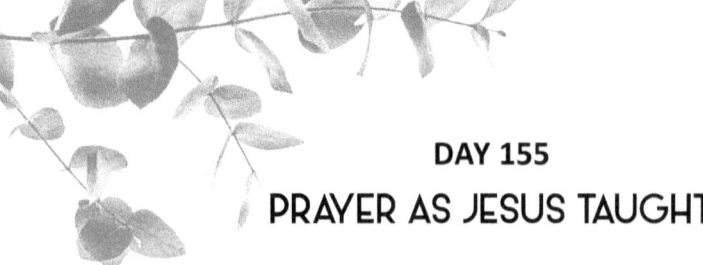

DAY 155
PRAYER AS JESUS TAUGHT

1 Thess. 5:17, *"Pray continually."* NIV

The way we think about prayer is based on the concept we hold. Prayer is a conversation and an encounter with God, and through prayer, we bring heaven into the ordinary day, which changes the concept we hold in our minds.

Through prayer, we bring heaven into the ordinary day.

When we think of the breath we breathe and the blood flowing in our hearts, we think of these as natural occurrences within us. Prayer also is a natural inbuilt happening, for we believe when God created us, He placed in us a desire to communicate with Him. Just as our blood and breath flow without conscious thought, when we love Jesus as our Saviour, His Spirit is ever keeping us in communion with God, without any thought on our part. Our life with Jesus must be a continual prayer till we find our way from duty to delight. Beware of anything that would block a sudden prayer. Prayer is not dependent on place, time, or occasion. A prayer like Stephen's in Acts 7: 59, *"While they were stoning him, Stephen prayed, "Lord Jesus, receive my spirit . . . Lord, do not hold this sin against them."* Form the delight of letting your heart rise to God anytime in prayer, meditation, or praise.

Amazingly, Jesus never mentioned unanswered prayer because He knew that prayer is always answered. When you pray, pray with certainty, having no thought of the times when God didn't seem to answer. *"For everyone who asks, receives."* (Matt.7:8) Don't reply, but! for God always answers us, not sometimes, but every time, even though the answer may not be the way we desire. Ask yourself – Do I expect God to answer?

Our danger is we want to make Jesus's supernatural answer fit into what we ask for. If it were only common sense, there would be no need to hear His words or pray continually. Strive to come to a place of speaking with God continually, trusting Him every moment of every day, to enjoy the intimacy that your loving Heavenly Father will bring you.

Prayer: *Lord Jesus, please come to dwell in my heart, that being rooted and established in love, I may have power, together with all Your holy people, to grasp how wide, long, high, and deep is the love of Christ. Amen*

DAY 156
SHARING THE LOVE

Colossians 4:3, *"Pray . . . that God may open a door for our message, so that we may proclaim the mystery of Christ."* NIV

In Colossians chapter 4, Paul tells the church to *"devote yourselves to prayer, being watchful and thankful."* Have you ever prayed for an opportunity to share with someone you know, how much God loves them?

Back in the late 1950's Evangelist Billy Graham came to a nearby city to preach the gospel. I especially remember my dad's enthusiasm as the time approached, taking counselling lessons by correspondence and talking to people who lived around our farm about the opportunity to hear Billy Graham. Every night my parents went to the crusade, and one rainy night, dad asked a neighbour if he would like to go. That night our neighbour gave his life to Jesus, the following night he took his wife, who also came to faith in Christ. This couple spent much time praying for and speaking to others about their newfound faith. From that rainy night, they became the backbone of a new group of believers who formed the first Christian church in the district. We need to pray for the opportunity to share God's love each day.

We need to pray for opportunities to share God's love each day.

Paul also tells us to *"Be wise in the way you act toward outsiders; making the most of every opportunity"* (v.5). Every day, there are opportunities to care for, listen to, and encourage others. We must be wise and gain understanding as we present God's word of Salvation.

Sometimes we can feel very uncomfortable, and in verse 6, Paul says," *Let your conversation be always full of grace, seasoned with salt, so that you may know how to give the right response."* When we pray and genuinely care, we can be sure that God will give the right response through His Spirit within us. So don't be afraid; pray, care and listen, and then share by telling your own story. When you speak up for Jesus, the rewards of changed lives will fill you with joy in the Lord.

Prayer: *Jesus, help me to look for opportunities to pray for someone and as you open the door, help me to speak boldly for You by sharing Your love with them. Amen*

DAY 157
DON'T BE SHORTSIGHTED

Romans 8:18, *"I consider that our present sufferings are not worth comparing with the glory that will be revealed in us"* NIV.

There are times in everyone's life when we suffer and struggle. Maybe it has been the death of your partner or child; it could be the loss of your business or job, sickness, or poverty. Each time I hear about the struggles someone is facing, I think of the story about the emperor moth as he struggled to release his huge body from the cocoon which had held him in captivity many months, and how a human observer thinking he was helping, cut the last confining fibres to enable the moth to release himself without any further stress. The observer waited for the shrivelled wings of the moth to expand to reveal the moth's perfect splendour, but in vain, the tenderness shown had proved the ruination of the moth.

> **Your loving Heavenly Father will bring you through your suffering.**

In Romans 5: 3-4, Paul tells us, *"We know that suffering produces perseverance; perseverance, character; and character, hope."* Looking back there were many stresses and struggles; some even being brought about by my own decisions. However, I now see how my Heavenly Father has used them to shape the person I have become, enabling me to understand other people better, allowing me to help them as they go through some of the same struggles of life that I have experienced, and even giving me words of wisdom for many.

Oh, how short sighted we are. In our eagerness to help, we forget that others need to go through the pain and groans of suffering to perfect the life God wants for them. Because our God loves with holy love, He allows our sufferings so that we can be partakers of His holiness. He never spares us our pain and crying because He makes us perfect through them, having His glorious end in view.

My friend, be encouraged because your loving Heavenly Father will bring you through your suffering. Just look up and trust Him, as He works out His perfect will within your life.

Prayer: *Abba, Father, thank you for your love and concern for me when I am suffering the pain of human life that's beyond my understanding. Thank You for the hope I have, as You perfect in me, the person only You can see. Amen*

DAY 158
THE PARADOX OF HEAVEN

Psalm 55:6, *"I said, "Oh, that I had the wings of a dove! I would fly away and be at rest"* NIV.

I am sure that like myself, there have been times in your life when you have felt sorry for yourself, when you are weary, just wanting to forget the troubles and burdens you are facing and run away and hide so that your life will not be affected in any way. However, the reality is that God allows us to have crushing burdens, as they can give us wings when we bring them to our Lord and ask for His help to cope. *"Cast your cares on the Lord and he will sustain you"* (v.22).

God knew your capacity to bear the burden before He sent it to you, for He saw your need to know and understand more of His love. When you can no longer take the constant strain do not fear, because it is in the fear that you will be crushed. Like the frail little plant that can wilt and die under the heat of the sun or choose to drink in the sunshine and rain to grow and blossom, so it is that we can lay down and cringe beneath our load of life or accept the power from God to rise above it. We lack the faith of the little plant that simply trusts the Creator to provide. Our faith grows as we exercise trust in impossible circumstances.

> *It is in the fear that you will be crushed.*

If you turn back, instead of facing your situation with God's help, it is then that your fear will multiply. Climb up, oh child of God, for life cannot crush you unless you stay where you are. The key to God's power is found in obedience to His Word, which will lift you on wings like an eagle to be alone and at peace, secure and at rest in Christ. Matt.11:28 says, *"Come to me, all you who are weary and burdened, and I will give you rest."*

What are you facing today that you need to hand over to your Heavenly Father and know His peace?

Prayer: *Forgive me Lord, for I am weak and weary. I give my burden to You and ask You to lift my spirit to a higher level to know Your unfailing love for me today. Amen*

DAY 159
NOT SOME, BUT ALL

Romans 8:28, *"We know that in all things God works for the good of those who love him"* NIV.

How much do we understand of what the Apostle Paul means? He does not say *"some things; most things; or happy things,"* but he certainly says, *"ALL things."* When we think of all things, it can be from the smallest to the most incredible thing we imagine, from the most unimportant daily trifle to the outstanding achievements of life.

> **God works all things (good or bad) for His purpose chosen for you.**

The Apostle Paul then goes on to say *"work"* – yes, all things are working; not *have worked* or *will work,* right now, God is working behind the scenes to bring about His great plan for our lives. Then, our amazing God melds everything *"together"* to give a beautiful blend in our life. Yes, *"all things working together,"* right here and now. What is the music that uplifts and inspires you? There are many different notes, each of which has no meaning alone, but when the composer moves those separate notes around with pauses and rests, they all come together to bring a beautiful, uplifting tune.

I am pretty sure Joseph often wondered why his brothers sold him into slavery or why, he was thrown into prison, when he had done no wrong. It was not by chance, for after years of suffering, God brought him before Pharaoh's throne to become 'Second in Command' in all of Egypt. Throughout his ordeals, Joseph trusted God, and God worked all things (good and bad) together for the good purpose He had chosen for him. (Read Joseph's story in Genesis 37-42).

Jesus replied to His disciples, *"You do not realize now what I am doing, but later you will understand"* (John 13:7). Even if we had to face a thousand trials, it would not be the 999th that would work the good for us, but the next one.

Prayer: *Thank You Lord, for you see everything that will happen in my life; You desire only untold love for me, and Your hand is always upon me and filling me with the riches of Your grace. Thank you, Lord, that You are working it out for me. Amen.*

DAY 160
THE TREE OF LIFE

Rev. 22:14, *"Blessed are they that wash their robes, that they may have right to the tree of life."* RSV

The condition of partaking of the Tree of Life is that we are washed by the blood of Jesus. Let us be thankful and stop focusing so much on trying to be suitable by keeping the commandments, which for each of us is an impossible task as we are conscious of our sin each day, as our own desires tempt us. Thankfully, we can wash our robes daily by asking Jesus's forgiveness so we can continue to come and partake of the Tree of Life as we eat of its fruit for our every need. Whatever each passing experience of our human life may require, it will be met out of the fullness of the Divine supply of sufficient grace as we fellowship with our Lord.

In verse 2, John refers to the Tree of Life yielding the food we require for that month, and in verse 19, we read that each of us has a distinct part in this tree. The Tree of Life is first mentioned in the book of Genesis, where it symbolises the fact that Adam and Eve were to centre their lives in God. As we also centre our lives in Jesus and allow our spirits to be nurtured, the Holy Spirit will always be our source of eternal life and blessing.

> *God will always be our source of eternal life and blessing.*

Having learnt of its monthly yield, this emphasises that each season of our human life will be met from the Divine supply? January days, as we resolve to build a better relationship with our Saviour. February days, as we bear the storms of life and call on the help of our Lord. The days of mid-life when we are filled with the flowers brought about by the warmth and light of our close fellowship with Jesus. September days, when we bear fruit for the kingdom, and December days of sickness and or age, when we feel the Father's gentle arms around us. Whatever season of your life you are presently in, let Him lead you through all the varying experiences and phases, allowing you an opportunity to learn the blessing of a close relationship with your Saviour. Jesus is the complement of your every need.

Prayer: *Give me grace dear Lord, to come to You each day for cleansing, and that in all the various circumstances of my life, may I live in close relationship with You and bring glory to Your Holy name. Amen.*

DAY 161
TIME TO REVIEW

Psalm 39:5, *"Everyone is but a breath, even those who seem secure."* NIV

No matter your age, we all know that we have but a breath between this life and the next. Therefore, it is good practice occasionally to review our lives, where we have been and where we are going in our journey. We must ask ourselves, have we achieved our goals and are we becoming the person we want to be.

We can't change things in the past, but we can change how we view each day we have.

Today many have become too careful, too anxious, or too fearful of our life outcomes, and we consider that when Paul told us to be careful about nothing, it is just impractical for our day and age. You must be honest and know the truth about yourself, remembering not to under-rate yourself but realize afresh that God created you *"just a little lower than the angels."* Do you honestly believe this? No matter what you look like on the outside, you are an image bearer of God. As His creation, you reflect His glory - or do you?

Whatever we think at this time in our lives, the more important question is whether we are becoming the person God wants us to be. Jesus told us, *"Do not worry about your life... Is not life more than food, and the body more than clothes"* (Matt.6:25). He also told us not to worry about tomorrow because we know, tomorrow may not even come our way. We need to make the most of the opportunities each day to live holy lives, speak words of encouragement into our families' and friends' lives, help someone in need, live for Jesus in our workplace, and most importantly, to glorify God in everything we do.

We cannot change anything we have done, but we can change how we view each day we have, remembering to make wise use of time because our life is but a fleeting breath. From now on, prayerfully and resolutely take hold of God's grace and seek His will for your life every day. We have this moment in time, so let's make the most of it. You cannot save time, but you can invest it wisely for your God.

Prayer: *Dear Lord, thank you for the hours of this day. Let me not miss the opportunities You give me to share Your love and care with others and live my life today so that all I do will bring glory to Your Holy name. Amen*

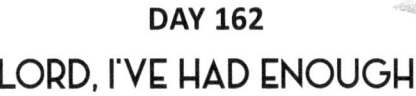

DAY 162
LORD, I'VE HAD ENOUGH

1 Kings 19:4, *"He came to a broom bush, sat down under it and prayed that he might die. "I have had enough, Lord," he said. "Take my life; I am no better than my ancestors."* (NIV)

I doubt anyone reading this would have had to face 450 leaders of an opposing religion; call down fire from heaven; pray for rain till storm clouds appeared, or have a queen threaten their life. Poor Elijah was in a state of discouragement when he ran away, sat down under the bush, and told the Lord that he had, 'had enough'.

What does your day consist of, cranky children, hostile teenagers, a dissatisfied and grumbling spouse, or a demanding and complaining boss? When we face such a day, we feel we can relate to how Elijah must have felt. How often do you say to yourself or anyone listening, *"I've had enough?"* At such a time, we need to follow the Lord's prescription for discouragement that He gave to Elijah. In 1 Kings 19:5, we read, *"He lay down... and fell asleep"*. Even though sometimes, we cannot avoid a poor night's sleep, we should, as much as possible, get a good night's rest. When we don't have rest, our temper is too often too short.

> **Spend some quiet time with the Lord each day for the ability to cope.**

Then the angel appeared and told him to *"Get up and eat"* (1 Kings 19:5). Good nourishment gives us the strength to cope with the problems of our day. In verse 12, God spoke to Elijah in a gentle whisper. There is no getting around it; no matter how busy you are, you must spend some quiet time with the Lord every day to cope with whatever happens.

If we only give priority to these simple daily rules, we will find God guiding our lives through the trials we face, just as Elijah did in verse 19. Let us follow God's prescription for discouragement so that we are able to regain control of ourselves and our emotions.

Prayer: *Lord, please help me to always remember to come to You when trouble strikes so that I don't become discouraged and can reach out to help others. Amen*

DAY 163
VICTORY IN JESUS

1 Samuel 14:6, *"Nothing can hinder the Lord from saving, whether by many or by few."* NIV

King Saul had no weapons and just 600 men about to fight the Philistines, who were equipped with every benefit they required to win the battle against the Israelites. However, without Saul's knowledge, his son Jonathan and his armour bearer decided to show themselves to the Philistines. They believed if the Philistines called them to climb up the cliff to their camp, God would give the Philistines into the hands of the Israelites (1 Samuel 13 and 14).

> *When things are falling apart, God is making them fall into place.*

How unlike us this battle is. When something happens, like a problem in our job or our marriage, like the Philistines, we gather our resources and are ready to do battle, without any thought where our success lies. When something happens, be careful that your resources don't take your eyes off your Saviour. God is the source of accomplishment, and He will fight for us.

God's kingdom operates on faith, and the loyalty God requires of us will often not make sense. Faith is not about how much we trust God but how much God trusts us to be obedient to what He has asked of us. Our obedience needs to be like Noah's, who obeyed God, without any idea what he was doing, and God honoured his obedience. Believing unto faith takes action, and when things seem to be falling apart, God is making them fall into place.

God's glory requires weakness from us. When Paul pleaded with God to take away the thorn, the Lord said to him, *"My grace is sufficient for you, for my power is made perfect in weakness"* (2 Cor.12:9). God's glory is strong when we are weak and without resources. Like the Israelites, we must surrender our resources (weapons) to see the victory that only God can give. Jonathan and his armour bearer believed that God would deliver the Israelites, so without weapons, they overtook the men at the outpost, and the whole Philistine army fled. What resources do you need to give to Jesus, so He can give you victory?

Prayer: *Lord, help me to always look to and believe in You as the source of all my needs. Strengthen my obedience to You so I will not hesitate when You require something of me. Amen*

DAY 164
DANGER ZONE

2 Samuel 11:1, *"In the spring, at the time when kings go off to war... David remained in Jerusalem"* NIV.

David had gone from being a shepherd to the most powerful king known. He had enjoyed success after success and survived the many hazards, to reach the pinnacle of his reign. Instead of leading his people into war, he became complacent, ignoring the danger zone of rising to the top. In a weak moment, he allowed himself to be deceived and committed adultery with the beautiful Bathsheba.

To cover for his sin, he had to eventually put his trusted and loyal soldier, Uriah, Bathsheba's husband, in a position in the army where he was killed. We are like David when, we knowingly do something that is wrong, and we continue to lie as we try to cover our sin, or worse still, we involve others. All this time, we are digging a deeper hole and a tangled web that is harder to overcome. I say this, knowing how hard it can be, because after 25 years the Lord convicted me of something I had done in a responsible position in a firm. I shed many tears and anxious moments before I had courage to go back to management and put it right.

> Do not linger in a danger zone, or your sinful heart will betray you.

Fortunately for David, God still loved him and was willing to forgive him for the wrong he had done. David cried out to God, *"Wash away all my iniquity and cleanse me from my sin"* (Psalm 51:2). Our Lord Jesus specializes in miracle cures and is always willing to forgive us, regardless of what we have done when we come to Him in repentance and a broken spirit.

As David found out, it never pays to linger in a danger zone, or our sinful hearts will surely betray us. It can be hard to stay grounded when people say you're special, but we must. We can celebrate our accomplishments when we achieve success, but we must keep moving forward, lest we become complacent and fall into the danger zone and sin like David did. Every day we must ask our Lord to guard our hearts and steps.

Prayer: *Father, when I am successful in life, help me to acknowledge Your guiding hand on me and bring all the praise to You, lest I fall away. Amen*

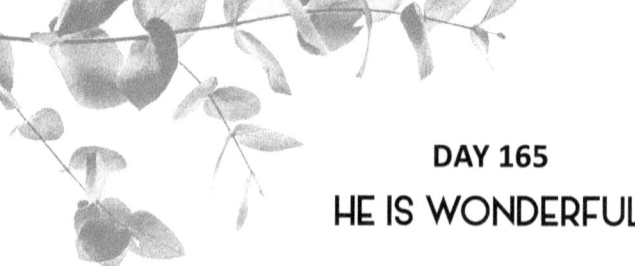

DAY 165
HE IS WONDERFUL

Romans 5:8, *"God demonstrates his own love for us in this: While we were still sinners, Christ died for us."* NIV

As a small child I remember singing, *"Jesus loves me, this I know, for the Bible tells me so."* Even if you didn't grow up in a Christian home or didn't go to church, most children knew the words of this age-old chorus. Today, can you say, *"I know Jesus loves me."* The Bible tells us, even when we are sinners, God loves us so much that Christ, the Son of the God of the Universe, came and died for each of us.

> God doesn't need us because He has everything except our love.

The Lord loves you so much that He will send His angels to help your heart to know and sing, *"Jesus loves me."* He loves us even when we are unlovely, when we feel lonely and unhappy, and He wants us to accept His love in Christ so we can replace feeling lonely and sad with being content in every situation of life because we are so filled with His love and peace; we can rejoice.

Do you know this glorious life which can give daily victory over sin? It is not just that Jesus came, but that the cross made the difference when He willingly died and took our sins upon Himself so that we might have new life in Christ. Ask Jesus to forgive you of all the sin in your life, and experience His love being sent down to fill you with new life through His Spirit. Isaiah 54:10 says, *"Though the mountains be shaken and the hills be removed, yet my unfailing love for you will not be shaken nor my covenant of peace be removed,"* says the Lord, who has compassion on you."

Ironically, God does not need us because He has everything, that is, except our love. He desperately wants our love, and we desperately need Him even though, most of the time, we think we don't. Accept His gift and know the wonder of His love today. As night falls upon your life and you depart this world, you can rest in peace and say with the saints above, *"I know Jesus is mine, and He is wonderful."*

Prayer: *Dear Lord, nothing in the world can compare with the wonderful love you demonstrated when you came and died that we might know You. Please forgive my sin and fill me today with Your incredible love. Amen*

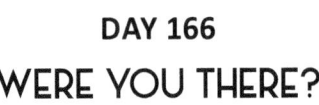

DAY 166
WERE YOU THERE?

Job 38:4-5, *"Where were you when I laid the earth's foundation? Tell me, if you understand. Who marked off its dimensions?"* NIV.

There is probably no one who reads these words who has not been amazed at the wonder of creation. We cannot explain the universe or the millions of other mysteries that we encounter every day. Each planet is influenced by the others, and then there is light and darkness, storms and sunshine in the exact order to make every creature on the earth grow and multiply. Why, just today, as I sat with my great grandchildren eating our lunch, we watched some ants, come and carry the large crumbs we had dropped; how did they know we had dropped them?

As Job sat brooding over his problems, God seemed to draw close to him and point out that man is surrounded by mysteries he cannot solve. Every day, often without any thought of our Creator, we use them all and have made them serve our purposes. Let us not be surprised if we discover similar mysteries in God's dealings with us. Our God uses the same power He used to create our world in His daily care of us. After God spoke to Job of man's smallness compared to Himself, Job replies, *"Surely I spoke of things I did not understand, things too wonderful for me to know"* (Job 42:3).

> **Man is surrounded by mysteries he cannot solve.**

In life, there are many times when we say to God, why? Why did my spouse die, why did I get sexually abused, and why did so many people die in war? There is no end to our whys, but our Almighty God does not have to answer our questions by constantly telling us about His dealings with our lives. *"For as the heavens are higher than the earth, so are my ways higher than your ways, and my thoughts than your thoughts"* (Isaiah 55:9). We must understand that God, who sees the future, is behind all the mysteries of our lives. Our Father's heart is longing for us to trust Him. It is as though He says to each of us, *you cannot understand, but you are dear to Me; trust Me, and "let not your heart be troubled."*

Prayer: *Lord, my mind grows tired if I try to understand the many mysteries of life. Help me to believe in Your unchanging love for me and to trust where I cannot see or understand. Amen*

DAY 167
TREASURED MOMENTS

Ecclesiastes 3:1,11, *"There is a time for everything and a season for every activity under heaven... He has made everything beautiful in its time. He has also set eternity in the hearts of men."* NIV

Let us not be impatient in life, because God has given each of us time to do all we must do. You must have time to eat, sleep, work, weep, love, a time for friendship, and, most importantly, time to meditate on God and His Word. There will always be enough time. When we make haste, we tend to make errors, and so we achieve no more than if we had taken time to do our task at normal pace.

> We will never be completely satisfied with the things of time or sense.

Consider God's creation. He made the sun, the moon and the stars. We never see the sun or moon rise or set one-millionth of a second too soon or too late. Everything in God's creation is ordered, and everything will end at the time God has planned.

Throughout life, I had many different occupations, and I often wondered why I had done so many different things. Now, looking back, I understand God's leading in my life and His purpose for each skill. Yes, there is a right time for everything in our lives if we let Him lead us.

In verse 11, the writer tells us, *"God has set eternity in the hearts of men."* With the finite capacity of our minds, we will never be completely satisfied with the things of time or sense. There is a season for everything, and the trials of this life will pass, and be replaced with beauty.

Everyone has a void in their life that needs filling. God has placed within each of us an inbuilt instinct to seek and find God, but we often seek to fill that void in our life with everything except God. Yes, He has given us time to spend with Him; we just must organize ourselves better. Make Jesus, the Lord of your life, coming into communion with Him each day so that He can continually fill that void within with His joy and peace.

Prayer: *Thank you, loving Father, for watching over all the seasons of my life. Help me to trust in You and enjoy the life you have given me. Amen.*

DAY 168
NO APOLOGIES

Ecclesiastes 2:24, *"A person can do nothing better than to... find satisfaction in their own toil. This too, I see, is from the hand of God."* NIV

Even before Adam and Eve sinned, God appointed work as a necessity of life, but if we are to find the satisfaction that God intended, we must do our work each day as though it was for our Heavenly Father. *"Whatever you do, work at it with all your heart, as working for the Lord, not for human masters."* (Coll.3:23) Our problem is we forget that as Christians, Jesus is our master, and if we could see Him there with us, our work ethic would be very different.

We all have days when everything goes wrong, and we feel as though our calling is a sentence. However, let us remember that just as coal is made through heat within the earth burning the great forests of yesteryear; likewise, spiritual force is stored in the depths of our very beings.

There are days when we feel our work is a disaster.

Through pain and suffering we never understand, we are able to help others through their pain and issues of life.

There are also days when our work is a disaster. This can happen when we have to do menial work, when we have been educated in a profession. Things like doing housework; meeting the needs of grumpy customers, demanding bosses, or coping with rude or impolite co-workers. All these things can make us forget our calling to work for the Lord.

I have always found that whether it was just doing the washing or holding a responsible leadership position, the greatest satisfaction one can feel is to come to the end of the day tired but knowing you have worked hard and well to the very best of your ability. Paul tells us in Coll.3:24, *"You know that you will receive an inheritance from the Lord as a reward."*

Do you find satisfaction and joy in serving your Lord everyday as you use your ability through your work to help others? Remember, it is not what you do but how you do it that is important, and in that you will find satisfaction.

Prayer: *Thank You Lord, for giving me skills to use in my life. What You have given me, let me use to help others. Help me to like who I am and what I do each day and to do everything as unto You. Amen.*

DAY 169
BUILDING BRIDGES

Ephesians 4:4,6. *"There is one body and one Spirit, just as you were called to one hope when you were called; one God and Father of all, who is over all and through all and in all."* NIV

Nothing excites Satan more than seeing disharmony within the church. Like the church at Ephesus, we are people of diverse temperaments, personalities, likes and dislikes, but God's plan is to unite us together for His glory. As God's children, we must live in harmony, so the world knows who Jesus is. This takes the supernatural work of the Holy Spirit, firstly in each of us and also in the church. Paul urges us *"to live a life that is worthy of the calling we have received."* We must be humble, not having a high opinion of self, and know who we are, compared with Christ's life. When we have an accurate opinion of ourselves, we respect other people by being kind and understanding.

> We are to be tolerant of those who disagree with us.

We must be gentle, able to keep ourselves under control which is the strength of gentleness. Jesus said, *"I am gentle and humble in heart."* (Matt. 5:5) Gentle people display a strength of character; not being easily hurt or worried if someone does something wrong to them. Paul says we must be patient and persevere when everything is against us, and never seek revenge. We are to bear our cross with love. Every effort must be made to have peace and to be tolerant with those who disagree with us, being patient with another person's faults. We must love one another even when someone has done something wrong. *"I pray that you, will be rooted and established in love."* (Eph. 3:17)

God wants us to have these qualities of the Spirit, to produce maturity in our faith. The lack of individual maturity in the Spirit, will be the instrument that will drive a wedge between us to prevent us maintaining unity in Christ and being able to show those around us who Jesus really is in our lives. Each of us must be responsible if harmony is to be maintained.

"Finally, all of you, have unity of mind, sympathy, brotherly love, a tender heart, and a humble mind" (1 Peter 3:8). How committed are you to this challenge that is only possible through Christ?

Prayer: *Heavenly Father, even though it seems impossible, please help me to live my life in harmony with others, that Your name may be glorified. Amen.*

DAY 170
BATTLE VICTORY

Romans 6:4,10-11, *"We were… buried with Him. For by the death He died, He died to sin (ending His relation to it) … and the life He lives, He is living to God – in unbroken fellowship with Him. Even so consider yourselves also dead to sin and your relation to it broken, but (that you are) alive to God – living in unbroken fellowship with Him… in Christ Jesus"* NIV.

During World War 2, Japanese military leaders dispatched Hiroo Onoda to a remote island in the Philippines to spy on Allied Forces. When the war ended and hostilities ceased, Onoda remained in the jungle, still believing the war was raging. No one could convince him otherwise. It wasn't until 1974, when his commanding officer travelled to the Philippines, convincing him the war was over, that Onoda knew the reality of peace.

Often, we make the same mistake. When Jesus died for our sins and rose again, He took our sins in His body, which were buried with Him so you and I can live in unbroken fellowship with our Heavenly Father.

> *We can live in unbroken fellowship with our Heavenly Father*

Unfortunately, we often continue to yield to temptation, listening to lies and failing to fully trust Jesus. When Jesus took our sins, it is as though we were "buried with Him," which means we no longer have to be overpowered by the temptations of life because we can choose to live and obey God through the power of Christ's victory over sin. Are you tempted to believe that sin still holds power over your life? Don't be like Onoda and go on living enslaved to the wrong belief. Walk today in newness of life in Christ, knowing that although temptation still comes your way, you are forgiven and can live out your life in the power of Christ's victory.

As a believer, you will never have total deliverance from sin whilst on earth; in fact, you will continue to sin even though you are mostly unaware of it. However, what has been destroyed by the blood of Christ is the mastery of sin over all believers.

Prayer: *Thank You Jesus, for winning the battle for me. Please help me to live each day in the victory of the resurrection of You, my Saviour. Amen*

DAY 171

LIVING WATER

Jeremiah 2:13, *"My people have committed two sins: They have forsaken me, the spring of living water, and have dug their own cisterns, broken cisterns that cannot hold water."* NIV

In the cycle of history, hard times have developed strength within humanity that were otherwise not known, which in turn produces good times, which as humans, we find things more manageable and so develop weak people. Today, are we vulnerable people with a sense of security who need to know what hard times are about? We may think differently, but it is proven that hard times bring us things we value.

Boredom can cause us to take responsibility for our lives.

Many Christians today are like people in Jeremiah's time who sought to support life on things of the world that give pleasure for a time. Sound familiar, seeking something else to bring us happiness? For Christians, our life is like crossing a desert where we are looking for the next oasis with living water to sustain us, when we already have Jesus's living water. Living water is alive, flowing, crystal clear water springing from beneath the earth, and dead water is collected and stored in wells or tanks, to become stagnant and stale.

When Jesus spoke to the Samaritan woman at the well, he said to her, *"If you knew the gift of God and who it is that asks you for a drink, you would have asked him and he would have given you living water"* (John 4: 10). He was referring to her having the living Holy Spirit within her life, but she did not get it, until He told her about her life, and she realized Jesus was the Messiah. She was seeking happiness in the things of this world, like many today, who pursue the latest technology or product that will give satisfaction. We don't like to be bored, yet boredom can cause us to take responsibility for our lives.

Being thirsty is not God's plan for you. If you want meaning in life, you must go back to the living water that Jesus offers and take the Holy Spirit into your soul allowing Him to bubble within to find the meaning you so desire.

Prayer: *Lord, forgive me for seeking my happiness apart from You. Fill me afresh with the living Holy Spirit that I may be guided to experience all You desire for me. Amen*

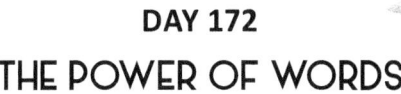

DAY 172
THE POWER OF WORDS

James 3:9, *"With the tongue we praise our Lord and Father, and with it we curse human beings, who have been made in God's likeness."* NIV

In James 3, we learn about how powerful our tongue is. Although just a tiny part of the body, it has great power to praise or destroy both others and ourselves. Once we speak, we cannot take back what we said, although, we sometimes wish we had never said degrading or hurtful words to someone.

When the Children of Israel were thirsty, God told Moses to strike the rock and fresh water would flow. (Exodus 17:6). The second time they needed water, God told Moses to speak to the rock (Numbers 20:8), but Moses struck the rock twice before water came, and because He did not do as God had asked neither he nor Aaron would enter the Promised Land (v.12). In the Bible, Jesus tells us to speak to the mountain (our trials). Jesus always used words to heal, not to hurt, and He wants us to use our words to bless others.

Our tongue reveals the wisdom that is inside us.

Our tongue reveals our wisdom, which comes from God. It can protect our integrity being a good guard, or destroy us by speaking unsavoury things that reveals who we are. With the tongue we praise our Lord and Father, and with it we curse human beings who have been made in the likeness of God.

James refers to the rudder of a ship, how, though small, can guide the ship wherever the captain wants to go (v.4). With Jesus as Captain, we must allow Him to guide in what we say by being aware of the voice of His Spirit within. When we control what we say, we can control our lives, so be quick to listen but slow to speak because our words can destroy us. *"Everyone should be quick to listen, slow to speak and slow to become angry"* (James 1:19).

When you say bad things about someone, you are also speaking against yourself. Let us endeavour to speak healing positive words, and good spiritual words over ourselves and others because we have the power to bring change in others' lives through the blessings we speak over them and ourselves. Are there words in your vocabulary that you need to change?

Prayer: *Lord, help me to pause before I speak, to be aware of what You would have me say that my words will always praise Your name. Amen*

DAY 173

I CAN'T - I CAN

1 Corinthians 10:13, *"No temptation has overtaken you except what is common to mankind. And God is faithful; he will not let you be tempted beyond what you can bear. But when you are tempted, he will also provide a way out so that you can endure it."* NIV

Among the prolific words we speak are *"I can't."* I can't help but hate him for what he did to me; I can't quit my addiction; I can't forgive and forget. It almost sounds as though it's a law we must obey. Think about the most powerful law of nature – the law of gravity, the force that pulls everything down to earth. Continually saying and believing that we can't, makes us prisoners to the downward pull of defeat. Not only are we ground bound, but sin bound. This is what our enemy wants us to do, to be and to feel.

The word can't is not part of what God wants for you.

What's pulling you down to defeat? What is it you feel you can't overcome? The Lord wants you to realize that can't is not part of what He wants for you. When you received Jesus as Saviour, He sent the Holy Spirit to fill your life with the strength and power of Almighty God. In Christ, and by the power of the Holy Spirit within, He has made it possible for you to replace the I can't with, *"I can do all this through him who gives me strength"* (Philippians 4: 13).

Think how a large aircraft defies the law of gravity. It almost seems impossible how it is achieved, but we know that it is done by using a higher law, the law of motion, where four major forces; lift, weight, thrust and drag, acting on the aircraft, give the ability for flight. If humanity can achieve this incredible feat of flying an aircraft, how much can Christ do for you if you will only let Him?

Ask God through the Spirit to help and heal you so you will no longer be 'sin' bound and defeated. By faith, give yourself over to the control of the Spirit, who will infuse you with strength so you are no longer captive to 'I can't.' *"The law of the Spirit who gives life has set you free from the law of sin and death."* (Rom.8:2) - When the Spirit sets you free, you are free indeed.

Take my will Lord and make it Yours;
It shall be no longer mine
Take me and I will be, ever, only, all for Thee.

Frances Ridley Havergal 1853

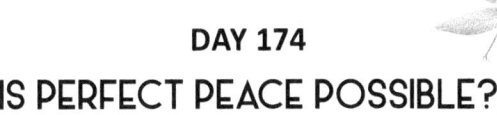

DAY 174
IS PERFECT PEACE POSSIBLE?

Isaiah 26:2," You *will keep in perfect peace those whose minds are steadfast, because they trust in you"* NIV.

There are few things in our world today that are perfect, yet God tells us that He will keep us in perfect peace if we trust Him daily with our lives. So, why do we find it difficult to trust God? Are we afraid our lives won't work out unless we control them ourselves? When we think about it, we trust God to control the universe, the very existence of everything in life as we know it, so why is it complex and challenging for our Heavenly Father to be able to manage what you are worried or anxious about and manage your life for you.

Anxiety and worry come from confused thoughts of our mind and what we think is our strength. What we think about can change us, our relationships and our world. This is why God told us to fix our minds on things above and to stop thinking about earthly things (Coll.3:2). When we get lazy in our thinking, it is then that our emotions take control, and we act out the way we feel.

> **Fix your mind on things above and stop thinking about earthly things.**

We will not experience peace when our thoughts are in the grey zone. We can all change our thinking and choose to believe in God's almighty wisdom. In life our minds are continually bombarded with thoughts, from which we must decide what are best for our life. *"As a man thinketh, so is he!"* If we controlled our thoughts, so we only thought of true things that are of good report, we would experience a tremendous change in our lives and experience God's perfect peace. *"Brothers and sisters, whatever is true, whatever is noble, whatever is right, whatever is pure, whatever is lovely, whatever is admirable—if anything is excellent or praiseworthy - think about such things"* (Phil. 4:8).

Realize that as a believer, Christ is your life, not the world. He is in you, so be careful that nothing like wrong thinking hinders His indwelling Spirit as you trust Him for His perfect peace. *"And the peace of God, which transcends all understanding, will guard your hearts and your minds in Christ Jesus.* "(Phil. 4:7).

Prayer: *Thank You Lord, that Your promises never fail, they are always true, and we can trust You for the peace you have promised. Amen*

DAY 175
PRAISING THE LORD

Numbers 21:16-17, *"The Lord said to Moses, "Gather the people together and I will give them water. Then Israel sang this song: "Spring up, O well! Sing about it"* NIV.

They sang a strange song in a strange place. The Israelites travelling the desert, were dying of thirst, without sign of water anywhere. God told Moses to gather the people in circles and start digging into the dry dusty sand, whilst singing, *"Spring up, O well."* We read in Numbers that as they sang, there was a gurgling sound, and the water bubbled and rushed into a flowing stream which filled the well to overflowing.

Give praise even during your worst circumstance.

What a beautiful picture of the river of blessing we can experience each day, if we will only reach out to the Lord and praise Him even during our worst circumstances. The water flowed because they called to God in faith and gave praise before they experienced anything. It is easy to praise God for something when we see the answer come, but the Lord wants our faith to call on Him and give praise first. *"Do not be anxious about anything, but in every situation, by prayer and petition, with thanksgiving, present your requests to God"* (Phil. 4: 6). Our praise will bring God's blessings even if our prayer has been with little faith.

Last week, having asked my family to dinner, I discovered I had no potatoes. God knew my need because that afternoon, when walking with a neighbour, she offered me her surplus potatoes. God knew my need and blessed me, saving me a trip to the shop. When we live in a spirit of praise recognizing God's unfailing faithfulness, we will see His little miracles happen each day.

Nothing pleases God like praise. When we give praise for God's love and care before the answer comes, it is a true test of our faith. Do you thank God for His daily blessings, which are more than you realize? Praise God for the good things as well as the trials, which are blessings in disguise. Be encouraged to praise Him in advance for the things you have not yet seen come to fruition.

Count your many blessings, name them one by one,
And it will surprise you what the lord has done.

Johnson Oatman, Jr.

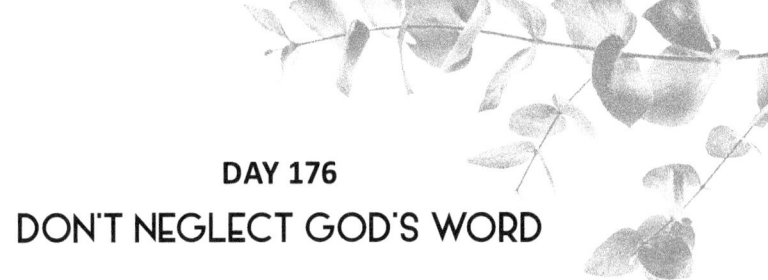

DAY 176
DON'T NEGLECT GOD'S WORD

2 Timothy 3:16, *"All Scripture is God-breathed and is useful for teaching, rebuking, correcting and training in righteousness."* NIV

The Bible gives us spiritual insight into what life with Christ can be like. It is the Christian's roadmap to daily living. We intend to read it, but fail in carrying it out. Theodore Roosevelt once said, *"A thorough knowledge of the Bible is worth more than a college education."* What makes us want to read magazines and novels or watch movies more than read what God has to say to us? Are we being deceived into thinking we have heard it all before?

Psalm 27:8 says, *"My heart says of you, "Seek his face!" Your face, Lord, I will seek."* My dad loved fishing, and as children, we were blessed to eat delicious fresh fish regularly. However, my mum didn't debone it and even as children that was something we were aware of. Did we try to eat the bones. No, we learnt to know just where they were, and we put them aside to enjoy the lovely fish flesh. This is something like us when we start reading our Bible each day. At first, we will not understand everything. Put it aside and go on to enjoy what is easy for you to absorb spiritually. Given time, the Holy Spirit will bring meaning to the words you have put aside and bless you in your learning. Evangelist Billy Graham said, *"The very practice of reading [the Bible] will have a purifying effect upon your mind and heart. Let nothing take the place of this daily exercise."*

Let nothing take the place of this daily exercise.

To start, read it aloud because it is like God's voice speaking His Holy Word back to you. More importantly, don't neglect His Word, for He has many things that He wants to tell you, and He can't do that when your Bible is closed and collecting dust. Even though it might be a struggle at first, you will find the more you read, the more you will enjoy it, without even being aware God is nourishing your body, soul and spirit through His words of Scripture. Look up to God and ask Him to reveal what He wants you to learn each day. *"Every word of God proves true; he is a shield to those who take refuge in him"* (Proverbs 30:5).

Prayer: *Lord, give me a burning desire to read Your Word daily. Please speak to me and teach me the things You want me to learn so that I may come to love Your Bible more and more. Amen*

DAY 177
NEVER TOO OLD

Galatians 6:9, *"Let us not become weary in doing good, for at the proper time we will reap a harvest if we do not give up."* NIV

We underestimate our value in God's great work. Great results are often achieved not by groups but through the self-sacrifice and devotion of one person. God can do the unbelievable with word spoken, or a deed done.

In the 21st century, amongst all the demands of our personal lives, we are quite happy to lend a helping hand to a neighbour, which is very important in the Kingdom of God. However, we will find an excuse to help our church family where people are hurting and discouraged spiritually. We feel we are not good enough to teach children or take a home group, but the amazing thing is we will be blessed by God when we are prepared to become involved in His work.

> We will be blessed by God when we become involved.

Throughout history, there has been many people who have taken their 'small' talent and, with God's help, have done great things for God within His church. An elderly friend was astounded when her Youth Pastor asked her to become a Youth Leader. What was he thinking? As she thought about it, God showed her that she had life experiences and knowledge she could hand on to these young people. As she took up the challenge, God worked in her life to not only be a Youth Leader but grow her deeper in relationship with Him. Such are the experiences we can have when we give our whole life to our Lord.

With modern technology, even those confined to their homes can reach out with a scripture or word of encouragement to those weighed down or suffering. We must remember that we do everything for the glory of our Heavenly Father. Colossians 3:17 says, *"And whatever you do, in word or deed, do everything in the name of the Lord Jesus, giving thanks to God the Father through him."* On the day we stand before Jesus, we will recognise the help of each other. Till then, we remember God's promise, *"Let us not grow weary while doing good, for in due season we shall reap if we do not lose heart."*

Prayer: *Thank You Lord, for all those who have willingly given their time to share the gospel with people like me so that others might come to know You as their Saviour and Lord. Amen*

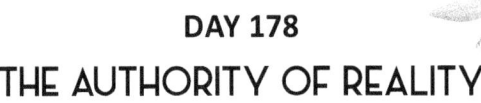

DAY 178
THE AUTHORITY OF REALITY

James 4:8, *"Come near to God and he will come near to you"* NIV.

The moment we draw close to God is when we truly begin to live, and everything until that time just becomes existence. Think back to when you were first confronted with sin in your life, and a Saviour willing to die to bring you into relationship with the God of the Universe. Nothing else mattered except your need as you opened your heart to Jesus. In that moment, you began to live.

Our Lord is always waiting for us to come to Him. He never fails to hear us when we cry to Him. Whenever the truth of God is brought into our soul, we must act on it, if we are to continually grow spiritually and have unbroken fellowship with our Heavenly Father. The weakest saint who hears God's voice within and acts is free the moment they act, with all the power of God available to them.

To go back is the costliest mistake we can make in our spiritual growth.

Often after we come to God and confess we are wrong, we go back again to where we were. Time after time the Lord brings some sin to our awareness, but we keep going back to the same sin, until we realize we have no right to go back. This can be, the costliest mistake we make, causing us physical and emotional pain as we break through, but breakthrough we must if we are to reach the potential God has for us.

When Jesus says, *"Come to Me,"* we can be sure He will guide us through our own self-imposed limitations, and the moment we willingly step over the line, the supernatural power of God will instantly invade our lives. When we say yes to Christ and cling to Him, the power of the world, the flesh and the devil are paralysed, not by our act, but because of God's redemptive power over evil. What is the Lord asking of you that will bring your life to new heights for HIm?

Prayer: *Lord, help me understand how much You want to help me overcome everything that would keep me from a better relationship with You. Give me the courage to come with it to You today. I give it to You, Jesus and ask for Your help. Thank You Lord, that You want to help me. Amen.*

DAY 179

I TRUST IN GOD

Philippians 4:19, *"And my God will meet all your needs according to the riches of his glory in Christ Jesus"* NIV.

As Christians, we look to Jesus as to how we should live our lives, and the one quality of Christ that stands out is, He completely trusted in His Father. Even when hungry, He refused to make stones into bread; or eat anything until His Father sent the angels to minister to Him.

Each day, He is watching over you.

Trusting God gives us clearness of vision as He supplies all that we need, and we don't have to worry about wanting more of anything. When we serve two masters, our judgement becomes distorted, and we make mistakes, but when we trust God, we can be sure He will take care of everything about our life because of His unending love for us. *"And my God will meet all your needs according to the riches of his glory in Christ Jesus"* (1 Peter 5:7). Our God is not stingy in His provision, for every day, we see the beauty of the rose. He cares that the eagle soars above the earth and the flowers bloom, because He wants us enjoying the beauty of His creation.

God can be trusted, even when like Daniel, we find ourselves in the lion's den of trials or the battlefield of life, imprisoned by guilt, depression, substance abuse, mental, or physical illness. Even when we want to put the blame for our mistake back on Him, He still loves and cares so much we can trust Him. *"So do not fear, for I am with you; do not be dismayed... I will strengthen you and help you"* (Isaiah 41:10).

Our Lord is willingly to guard and guide us through life if we will allow Him. As His child, you are adopted into His family, and surely this amazing grace shows a special love on His part. He takes care of the spiritual and the physical, caring for you until He leads you home to live forever with Him. No matter how uncomfortable your life is, keep trusting Jesus, He is watching over you.

Prayer: *Thank You Lord, that You are more than father or mother to those who trust You. You love us with a tenderness that never fails us or becomes weary with our downfalls. Surround us with Your guiding care each day. Amen.*

DAY 180

PURE GOLD

Isaiah 53:7, *"He was oppressed and afflicted, yet he did not open his mouth."* NIV

How much grace does it require to bear a misunderstanding or receive unkind and unjust judgement? Nothing will test one's attitude and character more than false accusation. How we cope in situations will prove whether we take on the attitude and nature of our Lord to be pure gold or just electroplated. The way we cope with handling our trials is the way we can know the blessings that await us. Are you strong of character, like David in 2 Samuel 16: 11-12? *"My son, my own flesh and blood, is trying to kill me... Leave him alone; let him curse... It may be that the Lord will look upon my misery and restore to me his covenant blessing instead of his curse today."*

> We can only aspire to pure gold when we allow Jesus to change us within.

You may say, *"I am not holy, nor ever likely to be, so how can I turn the other cheek and ignore incorrect judgement and bullying, which will leave me in despair."* Jesus is your regenerator, if you are his beloved child, He can put His own holiness into you through the Holy Spirit. *"Be holy, because I am holy"* (1 Peter 1:16.).

Our part is to accept God's will for us through the blood of the Cross. Until we are struck by our need for salvation, God cannot impart the Holy Spirit into us to give us the same character as Jesus. As we allow Him to change our disposition, we can aspire to pure gold when we are ridiculed. Only God's grace will get us through these situations of life.

Blessed are you who have the character of Holy God. Believe that such a life is attainable by all who allow God to lead and control them through His Spirit.

> *I stand amazed in the presence of Jesus the Nazarene,*
> *And wonder how He could love me, a sinner condemned, unclean.*
> *How marvellous, how wonderful*
> *Is my Saviour's love for me.*
>
> Charles H. Gabriel 1905

DAY 181

THE HOLY SPIRIT WITHIN

Romans 8:9, *"You, however, are not in the realm of the flesh but are in the realm of the Spirit, if indeed the Spirit of God lives in you. And if anyone does not have the Spirit of Christ, they do not belong to Christ."* NIV

How can you be sure that you are a son or daughter of the Lord God? In 1 John 3:1, the apostle clearly tells us that if we are children of God, we shall be content to be unknown by the world and often viewed as being of little worth. Even the Lord was despised by the world, and we must be careful that the things of this world no longer have appeal to us.

> *We are all guilty at times of failure.*

At all times, we must be aware and sensitive to the leading of the Holy Spirit within us. In Acts 8:26-40, we read the account about Phillip, who, without hesitating, left the revival that was taking place in Samaria and at the leading of the Holy Spirit, went to the desert so the Ethiopian statesman might be saved. Are you obedient when the Lord asks you to teach children about Jesus or go and pray with someone who is sick or bereaved, or do you find some excuse not to go? We are all guilty at times of failure when prompted by the Holy Spirit.

John tells us we must love our brothers and sisters in Christ, although we are all very different and often complex, but we must come to love them as ourselves. We begin by loving them with strength from the Holy Spirit to lead us through different phases of self-sacrifice until we can love them in the Spirit. Always be careful not to speak ill of another but to pray for them.

In our Christian walk, if we have offended or failed to love, we must be aware of our sin and come to Jesus for forgiveness and cleansing. It was once said, if a pig and a sheep fell into the same muddy pit, one would wallow in it, whilst the other would never rest until it was free and clean again. Let us become increasingly conscious of the indwelling Holy Spirit and live in the light of the love of God, continually being cleansed by the Lord.

Prayer: *In the name of Jesus, my Saviour, and by the power of the Holy Spirit within me, dear Lord, help me to keep focused on You, loving my Your children and keeping myself untainted from the world around me. Amen*

DAY 182
OUR GOD OF COMFORT

Psalm 121:2, *"My help comes from the Lord, the Maker of heaven and earth"* NIV.

When David wrote this Psalm, I wonder if he felt like we often do, alone and lonely. He probably had deep feelings of uncertainty, as it is believed that he wrote it during a time of battle. He could certainly never have known how much God would use these words to bring our focus back to the only one who never leaves us and is always there to hear our cry for help. Our blessed Jesus.

I first learnt this Psalm as a little child, and knowing it by heart, it is one passage of Scripture that God has used time and again to comfort me. They are words of deep meaning and can be prayed as a beautiful prayer of worship to our Saviour.

When we worship our God, we look up with adoration to His holiness, His greatness, His majesty, His power, His love and His glory, for He alone is Creator and Saviour. When we realize that as His children, *"our help comes from the Lord, the Maker of Heaven and Earth,"* we genuinely come with thankful hearts for the death He died to bring salvation to our lost souls.

> Jesus never leaves us and is always there to hear our cry for help.

Oh! the joy of being reminded again that He never slumbers, that He watches over us and will keep us from all harm. He brings calm and peace to one's soul that can only come from a loving Heavenly Father.

Take time to reread these beautiful words in Psalm 121, meditate on the love of a Holy God within them, and worship your Saviour today. May you be blessed with God's peace and comfort both now and forever more.

Prayer: *Holy God, I bow in awe that You would love me so much that You sent Your Son that I might know Your comfort and peace in my life each day. Thank You Father, I give You my life so that You might use me in Your service. Amen*

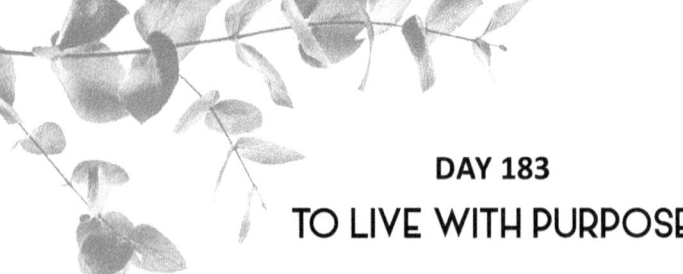

DAY 183
TO LIVE WITH PURPOSE

Romans 12:11,12, *"Never be lacking in zeal, but keep your spiritual fervour, serving the Lord. Be joyful in hope, patient in affliction, faithful in prayer."* NIV

Some days, we get up with little enthusiasm for what our day holds. We may be in pain or not excited with our work for that day. For whatever reason, we just can't get it together to live each day with the intention and passion that Paul speaks of in our verse. In 1 Corinthians 10:31, Paul tells the Christians in Corinth, *"Whatever you do, do it all for the glory of God."* Being joyful, patient, and faithful calls for being steadfast in our walk with God. Sometimes we forget the early Christians were no different; in fact, in many cases, their daily experiences were often those of persecution, so what is our excuse?

A life without faithful prayer can become a life without hope.

We are to be joyful in the hope and assurance of a home in heaven. We are to come to God for patience in the trials we face every day, but importantly, we must be faithful in prayer. Prayer is our weapon against spiritual warfare, and as we faithfully pray every day, we will experience joy and patience that only comes from our Saviour. Even when things are going well, we must continue praying because a life without faithful continuous prayer can soon become a life without hope and patience.

Even if time poor, offer a prayer to God before you get out of bed; spend a few seconds as a family as you say grace and ask God's blessing and guidance on your lives for the day; pray when in a line of traffic or enroute to work; pray while you work at home. There are many times in a day when we can pray. Think about it, there is no excuse for us not to faithfully pray every day.

As we speak with our treasured and faithful Saviour, Jesus, our most mundane moments gain meaning, finding joy in hope and patience in trial. When we spend time with God, we will be lifted in spirit and grateful to our Heavenly Father for His faithfulness. Let us be faithful to Him and pray without ceasing.

Prayer: *Forgive me, Jesus, for rushing into my day without any thought that you are interested in me and my issues in life. Help me not to miss my communion in prayer with you every day. Amen*

*Efforts and courage are not enough
without purpose and direction.*
John F. Kennedy

*"Many are the plans in a person's heart,
but it is the Lord's purpose that prevails."*
Proverbs 19:21

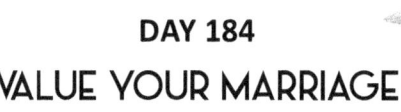

DAY 184
VALUE YOUR MARRIAGE

1 Corinthians 13:7, *"Love always protects, always trusts, always hopes, always perseveres."* NIV

Our most complex relationship is our marriage, and having a perfect marriage is a tall order. Prior to marriage, we often fantasise about how wonderful it will be, when suddenly the reality of our fantasy becomes just that, a fantasy. None of us are perfect, as the world only contains imperfect people. God's word says a lot about marriage and how we play our part to bring about a healthy relationship.

Both partners have needs and weaknesses, and God places us together so we can encourage and support each other. Likewise, both have qualities to bring to the marriage to build a strong relationship. As you connect with your partner, love and understanding helps them overcome their weaknesses, being a healing force to bring love, acceptance, safety, and intimacy. Both must feel valued, safe, and loved. God wants each to respect the other and speaks of this in 1 Peter 3:1-7. Jesus longs to breathe the fragrance of perfect love into your marriage. This is what we long for but often miss because each constantly seeks to get more than to give. When both are inspired by love that makes the other the centre of thought, tenderness, and care, love for each other will bloom through all the years.

> Someone must be first to say sorry, so let it be you.

Show respect by being polite to each other and your children. *"Do not let any unwholesome talk come out of your mouths, but only what is helpful for building others up"* (Eph.4:29). Never let romance leave your marriage. Tell each other, 'I love you,' daily and go on a date. When you have issues, try to understand the other's point of view, committing your differences to God to work out for you. Most importantly, always forgive. Someone must be first to say sorry, so let it be you. Very quickly, differences will be forgotten as you hug and make up. *"Be kind to each other, tender-hearted, forgiving each other, as God in Christ forgave you."* Let God guide you by reading His word and praying together daily to bring blessing and understanding that you desire.

Prayer: Thank You Lord, for my spouse. Help me to bring to my marriage the qualities that will increase our love for each other and build each other up. Amen

DAY 185

THE KEYS OF THE KINGDOM

Matthew 16:19, *"I will give you the keys of the kingdom of heaven; and whatever you forbid – that is, declare to be improper and unlawful – on earth must be already forbidden in heaven; and whatever you permit on earth – declare lawful – must be what is already permitted in heaven."* NIV

In the ancient world, when a person came to seek the counsel of a king, a servant similar to a butler today, would assist the seeker in reaching the king.

> *Your Heavenly Father will bring to you those who need your help.*

Christ spoke these words to Peter, but in a sense, they were told to every disciple of the Lord. He has given each of us a similar responsibility to unlock the door of Faith, Hope and Love in another person's soul. In Matthew, He gave the authority to His disciples to represent Him, and as they lived with Christ, they learnt the skills He used in connecting and helping people understand how to live in the Kingdom of God. As you walk daily in the presence of the Holy Spirit, your Heavenly Father will bring to you those who need your help.

You may know someone who is carrying a burden of sin and guilt, and as you try to connect with this person, Christ will come alongside you to give you the ability to cheer and encourage them, and through your words and actions unlock the door of the dark cell in their life. Your actions will manifest the true meaning of the keys of the Kingdom. Maybe there is a child who has been abused or someone suspected of evil things that are untrue, who God needs you to encourage or support. In each case Christ will send us His true power, to work in His vineyard. Proverbs 19:17. *"He who is kind to the poor lends to the Lord, and he will reward him for what he has done."*

We must always be looking for the opportunity to humbly serve Christ. When our life is lived, in constant fellowship with Christ our Saviour, we have the power to set lives free that are bound by the issues of their life. Above all, we must endeavour to point the burdened soul to Christ our Lord.

Prayer: *Lord Jesus, thank you that You break the power of sin; You set the prisoner free; Your blood can make the foulest clean; Your blood avails for me. Amen*

DAY 186
EXCLUSIVE JESUS

Matthew 11:28, *"Come to me, all you who are weary and burdened, and I will give you rest"* NIV.

What stops us from coming to our Lord and handing everything to Him? Do we feel humiliated to be told to come to Jesus? If we really want to know how real our relationship with Jesus is, then test yourself with the question; am I prepared to do what He asks of me if I come to Him with my problem? If you have the tiniest doubt that God may ask something big of you that you think you can't do... it holds you back.

"Come to me." When you hear these words within your being, you are aware of something that has happened in you and your need to come. A friend, who is the most loving and caring mother, always saw fault in her husband even though he was a good man. No matter how often she sought counselling and knew what to do, she failed to do it because it meant that there had to be change within her if things were to improve. As a Christian, she knew God's love and grace, yet she would fail to take her situation to Christ because she was unwilling to take that final step.

> The Holy Spirit cannot move a problem unless you willingly let Him.

In this way, we can hurt ourselves when all the time we know the Holy Spirit will give the needed grace and show us what we must do with the problem that is preventing the peace we desire. The Holy Spirit cannot move the problem unless you are willing to let Him. The rest of our soul when we hand our problem over, is most desirable as it affects our spiritual, emotional and physical health. Don't walk away from God again! Jesus has been patient with you and stands with outstretched arms. Think of the rest and peace Jesus offers as He says to you... *"Come to Me."*

> *Thank You, Lord, that you accepted me*
> *Though guilty and stained, You, died on a tree*
> *loving so much that You even called me*
> *Lord Jesus, I come; I come to Thee.*
>
> Unknown

DAY 187

BOLD FAITH

Joshua 1:7-9, *"Be strong and very courageous. Be careful to obey all the law my servant Moses gave you, do not turn from it to the right or to the left, that you may be successful wherever you go. 8. Do not let this Book of the Law depart from your mouth; meditate on it day and night, so that you may be careful to do everything written in it... 9. Do not be discouraged, for the Lord you God will be with you wherever you go."* NIV

After having been blessed by Moses with the spirit of wisdom (Deut. 34:9), Joshua is commanded by the Lord to cross the Jordan river and take control of the promised land. Joshua was already very courageous, but he needed bold faith to carry out the task before him.

> We can allow fear to poison our life, or we can fear the power of the God we serve.

Do you remember learning to drive? At first you were probably fearful, but as you mastered the art, you reached the stage where you didn't need conscious thought about when to brake etc. Instead, you could listen to your favourite music, enabling you to have both conscious and subconscious thoughts simultaneously. Then the time comes when something happens, like being cut off or in an accident. Immediately we feel angry or scared, and fear takes over. Fear poisons everything and makes us overreact.

In Prov. 9:10, we are told, *"The fear of the Lord is the beginning of wisdom."* We have two choices, we can allow fear to poison our mind, or like Joshua, we can fear the power of the God we serve. It is the fear God uses to give us courage to face our foes, as it excites our faith to know that we don't need to worry every day about everything that will happen. The fear of the Lord will bring us peace with God.

Your boldness, peace in God and faith in hard times to stay calm regardless of things happening around you gives power, for others to cope and say, *"I want what you have; I want to follow Jesus."* A person of bold faith is what God has called you to be, not a person of fear.

Prayer: *Father God, thank you that I can trust You in hard times to give me the courage and wisdom to not be afraid but to have the bold faith you can empower me with through your Holy Spirit. Amen*

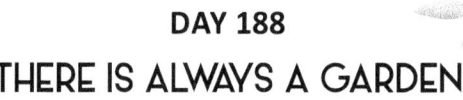

DAY 188
THERE IS ALWAYS A GARDEN

Psalm 6:4,6. *"Deliver me; save me because of your unfailing love. I am worn out from my groaning"* NIV.

At any stage of our life, as we reflect on the overwhelming pressures of our age, often, it would appear as though God is indifferent to our suffering. Sometimes it takes trouble for us to be honest with ourselves. I imagine that when David wrote this Psalm, he was probably at his deepest place and cried out to God in anguish.

Amid all the anguish of everyday, nature continues to pursue her unbroken routine of succession regardless of our sorrow. God is ever present in the order of His creation, producing a new day and new flowers to bloom and brighten the world, just as you can be eternally sure and dare to believe that He never leaves the melting pot of your life. Even though you cannot see Him, He is there to embrace and comfort you.

> **He never leaves the melting pot of your life.**

For most, there is a time each year when our thoughts turn to one who, for whatever reason has passed from this life. If you are in a sad, dark place, remember there is a garden, for when we come to the Christ of the Cross and remain in His presence, then the garden of our character will arise, having been watered by the tears of our Lord. Isaiah 58:11 says, *"The Lord will guide you always... You will be like a well-watered garden, like a spring whose waters never fail."*

When we walk with Jesus through the dark places of life, He will produce rare and beautiful flowers within our character to light the way for others. If you are lonely, suffering, or troubled, talk about it to God and you will find that the Lord Jesus will walk in the paths of your garden in the cool of the day, just as He did so long ago in the Garden of Eden.

Prayer: *Near your heart Father God, we will find the comfort only You can give. Thank You that we can experience the very presence of our Saviour Jesus as You hold us through all our sorrows close to Your heart. Amen.*

DAY 189
SIMPLICITY OF THE TRUTH

Micah 6:8, *"He has shown you, O mortal, what is good. And what does the Lord require of you? To act justly and to love mercy and to walk humbly with your God."* (NIV)

The political outlook was dark to extreme at the time of the Prophet Micah, and he felt the country needed a revival of faith. Upon enquiry of God, he received the answer that God required something more spiritual. Micah's words diffuse all our noble deeds, in our daily running around endeavouring to do what may please our God. Consider this verse and think, what can you bring to the Lord of the Universe that could impress Him, or what will be the heritage and teaching you leave your family?

> *Children accept things at face value when as adults we struggle.*

The beauty of this verse is its simplicity. It covers all 10 Commandments, the Golden Rule and even the Sermon on the Mount.

To act justly... Even small children know justice as they share their toys, or if one receives a lolly, all do. As adults, let us follow their example.

To love mercy... Children love kindness when shown to them, and we know that special feeling when we kiss a baby. Do not try to love mercy until you have shown it, but dare to step out showing kindness and do good even for the unlovely. James 1:27 says, *"Religion that God our Father accepts as pure and faultless is this: to look after orphans and widows in their distress and to keep oneself from being polluted by the world."*

Walk humbly... Children are even good at walking humbly because there is not much they do that offends God so badly that they need to put it right. As adults, we must be careful not to run ahead of God but walk hand in hand with Him each day in humble living and giving all the glory to Him.

Why do children accept things at face value when as adults we struggle? What do we do when we have tried and failed? Let's understand that Our Heavenly Father always forgives, always shows us compassion and casts our sins into the depths of the sea. He delights in showing us mercy, so let us go forward by the power of His indwelling Holy Spirit, to show justice, to love mercy, and walk humbly with our God.

Prayer: *Dear Lord, please give me the grace to act justly, to love mercy and to walk humbly with You, my God. Amen*

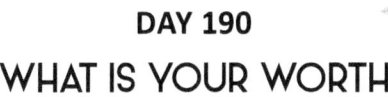

DAY 190
WHAT IS YOUR WORTH

Ecclesiastes 2:26, *"To the person who pleases him, God gives wisdom, knowledge and happiness, but to the sinner he gives the task of gathering and storing up wealth to hand it over to the one who pleases God. This too is meaningless, a chasing after the wind"* NIV.

Leaving a legacy to your family involves far more than what you leave of monetary value. The teacher tells us in Ecclesiastes that these things will pass away. We hear about what someone was worth when they died, as though it is a status symbol, however, over the years, I have seen families torn apart when one person thinks they should have received what was left to another family member. You may well ask if it was all worth it.

A lasting legacy is written on the hearts of those we love to be of value to your descendants forever. The greatest gift we can leave behind is to have guided our loved ones to know Jesus as Saviour. When our children are young, they probably don't see faith as important, but the value of a Godly heritage gives substance to their lives as they come to realize how important the prayers of godly parents have influenced their values over the years.

> We should tell our family how God has worked in our lives.

As I look back at life, especially the things I did that I am not proud of, I can certainly say I really value the prayers of my parents, for it was probably only their prayers that kept me from making many mistakes in life. We should ask ourselves, *"What is the legacy I am building for my family?"* Is it superficial like money, real estate etc., or is it faith in God, wisdom, and a good work ethic etc., which are things of lasting value that will endure forever?

One day, your grandchildren will ask you about your faith and what a blessing to tell them about what God has done for you. We should tell our family often about how God has worked in our lives, perhaps by writing a journal or story of your Christian life. Encourage your family to read God's word and write notes in the margin that remind them of how God spoke through His word.

Prayer: *Help me, Lord, to see the value of leaving a good example of faith and wisdom for my family. Amen*

DAY 191
AWAITING MY NEW HOME

2 Corinthians 5:1, *"For we know that if the earthly tent we live in is destroyed, we have a building from God, an eternal house in heaven, not built by human hands."* NIV

As tenant of the house (my body), which I have occupied for over seventy years, I am aware the owner will provide little or nothing more for repairs. In some ways, I welcome this notice because although everything is still pleasant, and my garden blooms each spring, evidence of decay shows the house is no longer good enough to dwell in, so I am getting ready to move, to leave my body.

We shall be like Him, and we shall see Him as He is.

Once that decision is settled in our mind, it is amazing how our thoughts turn to our prospective home, consulting with the builder and reading descriptions of its other dwellers. Jesus' description tells us that it is beautiful beyond our understanding. He also tells us to invest there, we must suffer the loss of every earthly thing ever owned and rejoice in what some might refer to as a sacrifice. Many have gone to live there, telling me to come and join them later. I saw their smiling faces as they passed on, and even though I can make new investments here, my answer is always, *"I am getting ready to move."*

Jesus talked many times about 'going to the Father' and preparing a home for those who love Him. John 14: 2, *"My Father's house has many rooms; if that were not so, would I have told you, that I am going there to prepare a place for you".* We, who belong to Christ are going to the Father, where the difficulties and disappointments of this earthly life are no more. He is ever leading us on to the home He has prepared for us.

Whilst we are here, we cannot understand what it will be like, though we know that we shall be like Him, and we shall see Him as He is. God is working in us and for us, for this very purpose. Praise be to our Lord and God.

> *Let us go singing, then, and not go sighing;*
> *When we are sure our time is in His hand,*
> *Why should we weep, and fear, and call it dying?*
> *When it's only flitting to a better land.*
>
> Unknown

DAY 192
JUST BELIEVE

John 11:25, *"I am the resurrection and the life. He who believes in me will live, even though he dies"* NIV.

When Jesus was met by Martha, she was suffering and confused over the loss of her brother Lazarus and in her confusion, she said, *"if you had been here, my brother would not have died."* (v.21). It was almost like saying, *'Where have you been?'* *'Do you really care?'* or *'Is this as good as you could do?'* When Jesus assured her that her brother would live again, she still didn't grasp what Jesus meant. He turned to her and told her, *"I am the resurrection and the life, ... Do you believe this?"* (v.25) It was as though He was trying to help her understand that life is all about Him.

Still today, so many of us or our friends and relatives have heard Him say, *"He who believes in me will live, even though he dies; and whoever lives and believes in me will never die. Do you believe this?"* (v.25). What do you believe right now as you read these words from the one who died to give you life? Jesus is saying to you today, *'I have what you need.'* Life for everyone on this planet is all about Jesus, yet so often because we want to have control, we turn away. When you are prepared to put Him first, to believe and trust Him, you too, can live even though you have to die bodily. For each of us, even though our body will die, our spirit never dies. Your spirit is what makes you who you are, and when life on earth shall end, your spirit will live on. Where?

> You can live even though you must die bodily.

In John 14:6. Jesus again says, *"I am the way and the truth and the life."* He told his disciples that He would go and prepare a place for them called heaven, where they could live forever with Him. Are you sure you will reside in heaven? If you are unsure or have never believed that Jesus is the way and that He loves you so much He died to save you from eternal death, then trust Him today. Give your life to Him, so you are sure of a home in heaven.

Prayer: *Jesus, I acknowledge that I have sinned and believe that You died to save me. Please forgive me my sin and help me to trust You and live for You each day. Amen*

DAY 193
NOTHING TO DREDGE UP

Micah 7:19, *"You will tread our sins underfoot and hurl all our iniquities into the depths of the sea"* NIV.

The Mariana Trench, located in the western Pacific Ocean, is the deepest oceanic trench on Earth. The maximum known depth is 10,984 metres (36,037 ft). Corrie Ten Boom, a holocaust survivor, held a mental picture of the forgiveness of her sin being cast by Jesus into the deepest sea and that God had put up a sign saying, 'No fishing allowed.'

When God forgives, we are totally forgiven.

Many believers fail to grasp just what Jesus has done for us when we accept Him as our Saviour. *"If we confess our sins, he is faithful and just and will forgive us our sins and purify us from all unrighteousness"* (1 John 1:9). At the close of Micah's message from God to the Children of Israel; God says that He will cast all our sins into the depths of the sea. Like Corrie Ten Boom, our sins are as it were in the depths of the sea, never to be dredged up.

When God forgives, we are totally forgiven, and He doesn't want us to keep dredging up the past sins of our life that we are ashamed of; instead, we must accept His grace and follow Him with the freedom of knowing that we are truly forgiven. *"Those who believe will find full redemption"* (Psalm 103:7).

If we allow ourselves to think of the thoughts of shame and failure for our past sins, we can't serve God wholeheartedly because we keep allowing Satan to pull our past into our minds. If you find these feelings haunting you, ask Jesus to help you fully grasp the truth of His forgiveness and the new life He has given you, by continually bringing God's compassionate and faithful love into focus. Put the false belief that God can't possibly forgive you for the sins that you have committed behind you, and allow His forgiveness to set you free. God loves you and will never give up on you.

Prayer: *Dear God, You sent Your Son Jesus to save me from my sins. Please help me live with the freedom of knowing I am fully forgiven. Amen*

DAY 194
WAIT WITH PATIENCE

Psalm 37:7, *"Be still before the Lord and wait patiently for him."* NIV

Often, I sit on my veranda and watch the little finches as they go about their family needs. If I am to observe and understand them, I have to be very still and patient, not even moving my eyes as they are watching me more intently than I am watching them. To be completely still and composed takes immeasurable strength in any given situation. To be still is what our Father requires of us, if we would see the power of His Spirit working in our life to eliminate our fretting and anxiety. The Psalmist has shown us the way to inner tranquillity in our hearts.

Firstly, you must **trust**, in the Lord (v3), knowing He is always faithful, expecting great things from Jesus, your Guide and Friend. As you trust, you are to **delight** (v4) in God's way of thinking and looking at things. When you do, you will lose your desire for the things of this world and your focus will change to a greater desire for the things of eternity. Your God is a giving God and will give you Himself. As He fills your life, the desires of your heart will be satisfied by His abiding love for you. **Commit** your way to the Lord. (V5) Give Him total responsibility for your life for He is God of your minor issues as well as the major crises in your life. You must always be looking to Jesus because only He can see over the hedge or round the corner, and He will help you know the way to go without any anxiety or fretting.

> Delight in God's way of thinking and looking at things.

As you remain still and wait patiently, you will hear His whisper in your heart despite the noise of the world around you. An excellent place to start learning to keep silent is to remain in God's presence for a few minutes when you have finished praying, or quietly sitting and letting the words of Scripture sink deeply into your soul.

When we are willing to trust and commit, *"we know that in all things God works for the good of those who love Him..."* (Rom. 8:28) Think about how you can be still and silent before God.

Prayer: *Lord, please help me to have the patience and discipline to learn to be still so that I can hear Your voice within my heart. Amen*

DAY 195
REAL CHRISTIANITY

Matthew 5:13, *"You are the salt of the earth. But if the salt loses its saltiness, how can it be made salty again?"* NIV

Following Jesus is not easy and is not a list of rules, but rather the quality of a blessed life described in the Beatitudes (Matthew 5). Jesus took His disciples aside to teach them what it means to be a Spirit filled follower of Him. Salt was used to stop foods decaying and for adding flavour, so Christ wants us to help prevent further decay in our world whilst bringing the sweetness of His love to those around us.

Sow seeds of reconciliation with one another.

These verses teach us what it is to have a blessed life of wholeness, joy and comfort that comes from a close relationship with Jesus. - We are blessed when we are **_poor in spirit_**, i.e., showing humility before a holy God as we recognize our desperate need of Him (v.3). - Just as Jesus grieved for humanity, so we must **_mourn_** for others, being deeply touched by their suffering that they might come to Christ (v.4). - We need to be **_meek_**, demonstrating self-control by always being gentle and kind (v.5). - As we **_hunger_** for a deeper relationship with our Saviour, we will be filled with goodness and purity of heart for ourselves and others (v.6). - An essential quality of true Christianity is to be **_merciful_** by showing compassionate love to those who struggle and fail (v.7). - Let us always be **_pure in heart_** i.e., being single-minded in our love and devotion to Jesus (v.8). - Being **_peacemakers_** by sharing the peace that only Jesus can give and working to sow seeds of reconciliation with one another (v.9). - Lastly, we must be prepared to be **_persecuted_** for our Lord, as we are kind to those who misuse us, and as we are willing to suffer for the love of Jesus (v.10).

As we allow the Holy Spirit to live in us and change us, we will be filled with these qualities that will attract others to want to know our Lord. Being obedient to the life Jesus wants for us will allow others' lives to be brighter, and we will indeed be the "salt of the earth."

Prayer: *Lord, mould me to be filled with these qualities in my life, that I will flavour the lives of others to be blessed with knowing you as their Saviour. Amen*

DAY 196

HEROS

Matthew 25:40, *"Whatever you did for one of the least of these brothers of Mine, you did it for Me."* NIV

As a carer, one can feel totally alone, helpless and frustrated because you continually give, and keep giving. Having been my husband's carer for eight years, I understand the demands can strip you down to the very lowest. However, caregiving is a divine appointment with God.

Every day for 30 years, a mum combs his hair and dresses him, then his dad brushes his teeth. It's the same routine every day, and life would seem so unfair, but deep in his heart, even though sometimes their son can't express it, he thanks God because of his parent's care. They are his heroes. Psalm 121:1-2 says, *"I lift my eyes to the hills – where does my help come from? My help comes from the Lord, the Maker of heaven and earth."*

A caregiver displays God's great love and care for His children.

There is the little child who needs a home, and God brings parents who are broken hearted from being unable to conceive, to give love and care to the child. They become the ones to soothe the crying and make the child's life worthwhile. They provide care and love to make a difference in the child's life. John 15:12-13 says, *"My command is this: Love each other as I have loved you. Greater love has no one than this, that one lay down his life for his friends."*

Caregivers are truly heroes, giving their lives to bring life to someone they love. They give us insight into the great love and care that Jesus had for each of us when He came to this earth to become the greatest hero and carer of all time. John 3:16, *"For God so loved the world that he gave his one and only Son, that whoever believes in him shall not perish but have eternal life."*

Do you know Jesus as your caregiver? Is He your hero? Come today and thank Him for giving His life so that you may live and know His love.

Prayer: *Gentle Jesus, thank you for dying for me, for loving and caring for me every day. Bless and comfort those who care for others, and lift the load each feels. Amen.*

DAY 197

FINISH WELL

Philippians 3:13-14, *"But one thing I do: Forgetting what is behind... I press on toward the goal to win the prize for which God has called me heavenward in Christ Jesus."* NIV

We need to look at Paul, who forgot what had happened to him and moved forward with confidence that he would finish his missionary journey well. In our day and age, most do not finish well; it is fight or flight, both being easier than finishing well. As part of the church of Jesus, we must continually work on ourselves so in ministry and relationships, we can do what is required with grace and love.

Do what is required of you with grace and love.

In the book of Judges, we read the account of Samson the Nazarene. As a Nazarene, he vowed not to drink anything alcoholic, not to cut his hair, or go near anything unclean, such as a corpse. Unfortunately, he broke everything in the vow he had taken, the final straw being when he told Delilah, a pretty Philistinian girl, that his strength was in his long hair, which we know she cut off. Had he given up his relationship with Delilah, he would not have been humiliated. He knew that he had to overcome for God, and in the end, he said to God, *"Sovereign Lord, remember me"* (Judges 16: 28). God enabled him to finish well as he gave his life to save his people.

Sometimes God wants us to leave or break away from something that may be hindering our relationship with Him. We have His power to help us overcome, but if we compromise, we lose God's power within, even though like Samson, God still loves us and remembers us. Whatever time you have on this earth, God has given you enough to finish well.

Never believe that wrong will triumph, and never think that God has forgotten you. Leave your past behind and press on to a brighter future in Christ. Now is the time to decide and stop riding the fence. *"Press on toward the goal to win the prize for which God has called you heavenward in Christ Jesus."*

Prayer: *Dear Lord, help me to keep my eyes focused on You and Your will for my life so that I can press on to win the prize for which You have called me. Amen.*

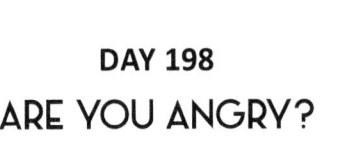

DAY 198
ARE YOU ANGRY?

Psalm 37:8-9, *"Refrain from anger and turn from wrath... it leads to evil... hope in the Lord."* NIV

Most of us, at some time become angry about something, but then worse still, for many, their anger leads to outrage. When this happens, our anger gets out of control, and we lose all control of our emotions, or we could say we lose our temper. You say, *"I have to stand up for myself"* in this situation, but that's when we say or do things that we don't intend to or mean.

Who wins? Certainly not the person you have lost it with, as they have been hurt by the things you have said or done. On the other hand, most times, you will feel remorseful and become angry with yourself for losing control. Even though you might tell the other person you are sorry, deep within them, the hurt you caused will take time to heal, especially in close relationships like marriage. In Ephesians 5:26, Paul warns us to be careful not to sin when we are angry, and Proverbs 14:17 tells us, *"A quick tempered man does foolish things."*

If you tend to lose your temper, what are you doing about it?

So, what's the answer? Today's verse, clearly tells us to, *"hope in the Lord."* If you tend to lose your temper, what are you currently doing about your problem? At the moment when you lose control, you probably don't consider the Lord or what He has said. On another level, as you feel your anger rising, simply walk away from the situation and find a quiet place. Then ask Jesus to take control of your anger, asking for the calmness of His Spirit to fill your heart and mind. Surrender yourself and the situation to God because this fulfils what He wants you to do.

We all learn by our mistakes, and if we genuinely want the Holy Spirit to control us in this area, we will bring it to Jesus each day, asking for the Holy Spirit to keep our anger under control and thanking Him that we have the peace of knowing Him.

Prayer: *Dear Lord, I am putting my hope in You. I surrender my life and my problem to you. Please help me to come to You daily until my anger is controlled by You, Jesus. Amen*

DAY 199
THE WEARINESS OF LIFE

Jeremiah 6:16, *"Where the good way is, walk in it, and you will find rest for your souls"* NIV.

Because of busyness of life, sometimes we feel drained of strength, unable to endure, and have no energy left. In other words, we are weary of life, filled with impatience, intolerance and find no pleasure in our lives.

> *Throughout the seasons of our lives, weariness comes to us all.*

Throughout the seasons of our lives, these times come to us all. As students, there is the constant pressure of study and assignments, which can cause escapism to substance abuse; or we face the pressures of long work hours and providing for family needs. There is the busy taxi mum who feels the day will never end; the tensions of bringing up teenagers in our modern world, and just when all seems good, often we lose a partner or dear friend and experience the pain of sadness and loneliness.

Is this where you are, not only in your physical body but your emotions and spirit feel crushed? As Christians, we are not immune to weariness, but the difference is that we can come to Jesus, at any time, and through His Word and prayer, we can find rest and refreshment. Even in our business, just a few moments alone with God can make the difference to our day. *"Come with me by yourselves to a quiet place and get some rest"* (Mark 6:31). The rest our Lord gives is real and is ours for the asking.

> *I need You every hour most gracious Lord, no tender voice like Yours can peace afford. I need Thee every hour in joy or pain, come quickly and abide or life is vain. I need You; O I need You, every hour I need You. O bless me now, my Saviour as I come to Thee*
>
> Annie Hawks – 1835

These words express Annie's need each day with the care of three children. She experienced the Lord's nearness. Take these words to heart, knowing that God can do more than we ask of Him to bring comfort in our moments of weariness.

Prayer: *Thank You Jesus, that You are always ready to hear and give peace and joy to my soul. Amen*

DAY 200
SO FAR, SO GOOD

1 Samuel 7:12, *"Thus far the Lord has helped us"* NIV.

I gain great satisfaction whenever I look down a long avenue of trees. As I look to the far end, the trees appear very small, and the leaves and branches mat together to form the beginning of the avenue, growing larger and more significant as my eyes draw level to where I stand. So too, with life, looking back to the green branches of God's love and mercy overshadowing us down the avenue of our life. Let us look up and see the many birds in the branches, singing songs of blessings received so far in life.

The tree trunks are like the strong pillars of God's faithfulness that have borne us up in our struggles. Has your Lord led you through poverty, through wealth, through sickness or health, through service in some far away country or given assistance at home? Through difficulties, trials, triumph and prayer, let us give thanks for all the ways our Lord has led us to where we stand today.

We still have time to grow closer to our Lord.

But this also points us forward because it means that we are not yet at the end, and there's still more temptation, more trials, more joys, more success and victories, more strength and struggles, and more sickness, then old age, and finally the end of life ahead for us all.

Praise God, it is not over yet, for we still have time to grow closer to our Lord, as we grow more in likeness to Him. We can experience more of God's glory, more fullness of the Spirit, more peace, more courage and more grateful confidence that He has led us thus far and will be with us all our days. Joshua 1:9. *"Be strong and courageous. Do not be afraid; do not be discouraged, for the Lord your God will be with you wherever you go."*

> *"He who has helped you thus far*
> *Will help you all your journey through.*
> *And give you daily cause to raise*
> *New Hallelujahs to His praise."*
>
> Unknown.

"AND AGAIN, THEY SHOUTED "HALLELUJAH!" (Rev.19:3)

DAY 201

THE FATHER'S JOY

Matthew 3:17, *"This is my Son, whom I love; with him I am well pleased"* NIV.

When John baptised Jesus, God was filled with so much joy that He spoke aloud. *"This is my Son, whom I love; with him I am well pleased."* In Mark's gospel, God says, *"You are my Son."* Matthew and Mark both reveal there was great joy and affection, affirming God's love for His only Son, our Saviour, Jesus Christ.

God's love and grace for you are beyond understanding.

For many of us, we long to feel loved by our earthly father. It is as though there is a big hole within our hearts and emotions, often never getting any better; and sadly, today often leads some to suicide. For others, because of achievement, they long for public affirmation in front of other people, just like God bestowed on Jesus. When Jesus was baptised, He had not begun His ministry, which meant that God's affirmation and joy had nothing to do with achievement. He was accepted and approved by God before His ministry had even commenced.

Today some of us will do anything to receive acceptance and affirmation when Jesus has already done everything for us to be accepted and affirmed by our Heavenly Father. God has chosen you to be His beloved child, and His love and grace for you are beyond understanding, no matter how frail or weak you are or what you have or have not done. God in 'Jesus' is unconditional love and is always there to pick you up and carry you forward.

You are accepted and loved by your Heavenly Father, and nothing will give your Lord greater joy than for you to stop condemning yourself. Romans 8:1 says, *"Therefore, there is now no condemnation for those who are in Christ Jesus."* There is no greater love than the love of Jesus, who died to save you. Trust and accept God's free gift of love and eternal life given through the blood Jesus shed for you.

Prayer: *Dear Heavenly Father, thank You for sending Jesus to die so that I might know your love and grace. Thank You that now You are my Father too. Amen.*

DAY 202
LISTEN FOR THE CHECKS

1 Kings 19:12, *"After the earthquake came a fire, but the Lord was not in the fire. And after the fire came a gentle whisper."* NIV

The reason many of us do not understand the ways of God is we don't give heed to His gentle checks and restraints. We must listen for His still small voice. In life, it is easy to miss a still small voice but when we listen, we will feel it in our soul.

Elijah had fled from Jezebel in fear of his life. He sat down under a tree and told the Lord he wanted to die. After an angel fed him, he went to Horeb, and God spoke to him. There was a mighty wind, an earthquake, then a fire, but God did not speak through these elements. It was in the gentle breeze that Elijah heard the whisper, as he listened intently, he heard God's words.

If we fail to respond and believe, He will eventually cease to speak.

Often God impresses something on our hearts and minds that we ignore. In my experience that small whisper, if listened to, will become a growing noise within as His love makes it very clear what He wants of me. God's voice is for the ear of the one who loves Him, as the one who loves will always hear. When our God whispers in love, if we fail to respond and believe, then He will eventually cease speaking. He is love, and we must be constantly alert, if we want to know Him and hear His voice, or we may miss what He has to say.

When you're in conversation, give heed when your conscience prompts, refrain or reword what you want to say. We must give heed when a course of action seems right and suddenly a suggestion comes to our spirit. Listen, even if God's plan seems senseless to us. We must learn to be still, listen for God's whisper, wait on Him, and He will form a plan about everything in our heart, to bring peace of mind. How often have you been amazed at how God has brought His will to pass in your life? *"In all things God works for the good of those who love Him"* (Rom.8:28). Our part is to listen, obey, and trust God.

> *When we walk with the Lord in the light of His Word,*
> *what a glory He sheds on our way.*
> *When we do His good will, He abides with us still,*
> *with all who will trust and obey.*
>
> John H. Sammis 1887

DAY 203
DISCIPLE OR APOSTLE

2 Chron. 16: 9, *"For the eyes of the Lord range throughout the earth to strengthen those whose hearts are fully committed to Him."* NIV

In Luke 6:13, we read that *"Jesus called His disciples unto Him, and then He chose twelve, who He named apostles."* These twelve young men followed Jesus everywhere, learning about Him and the salvation He was to offer humanity. He taught them about the divine order of everything He had created until their spiritual strength and trust was sufficient to send them out to form the Christian church, teaching others to also become disciples.

> There is no limit to what God will do through you to glorifying Him.

To become an apostle of Christ, we must understand God's way of life. As we grow closer to Jesus, we are called to serve Him as the original apostles did. Our Lord didn't choose us for a life of comfort and enjoyment, but through our witness, He can bring salvation to many. God seeks out men and women, who desire a deeper life with Him. Someone who will trust Him and follow Him for all He desires to do through them. There is no limit to what God will do through you when you are totally committed to giving all the glory to Him.

Today, many Christians find they get pleasure reading novels, going to the movies, or spending hours on the Web. By contrast, we spend little time reading the Scriptures. I often think how we would react if suddenly Jesus came in real life to visit with us, would you be embarrassed at the mess around you; would you have to turn off the movie you were watching, hoping He hadn't seen, or would you have to rush about to pick up questionable magazines and replace them with your Bible - if you could find it. If we could only grasp the blessings, we can experience from our God by delving into His Word and learning from Him, we would come to know what an infinitely loving God we serve.

The only way to become an extraordinary Christian, is to walk in the Holy Spirit each waking hour, to be one who Christ would call an apostle.

Prayer: *Most Holy Lord, give me a teachable heart; that I will desire to sit at Your feet each day and learn from You. Choose me Lord, teach me and then send me to where You would have me serve You. Amen.*

DAY 204

AT YOUR WITS' END

Psalm 107:27-28, *"They were at their wits' end. Then they cried out to the Lord in their trouble, and he brought them out of their distress"* NIV.

> *Are you wondering which way to turn, as you stand with a furrowed brow?*
> *You just can't face what's before you, for the burden is too much right now.*
> *It's like the whole world is against you, and you're facing your problem alone,*
> *But remember that where you're standing, God's help and power are shown.*
>
> Antoinette Wilson

Words express exactly where we find ourselves so often. Are you at your 'Wit's End' right now, and wondering which way to turn? Are you standing there because of intense pain or sorrow; a relationship breakup; an employment issue; abuse, or a drug related problem? You are not alone, so don't feel discouraged. Often, when we reach this place in our life, we are so worried and confused that we forget to look for our Saviour when He is standing right beside us wanting to help *"Let the one who is wise heed these things and ponder the loving deeds of the Lord"* (verse 43).

> **Be wise and leave your problem with Jesus.**

Be wise and stop right where you are. Listen, and you will hear your Lord say, *"My child, when you are in much spiritual and emotional need, turn to me and say, 'Lord, please take care of it for me.' Close your eyes and rest in me. You pray to me for what you desire, like you were telling the doctor how to treat you, but I say, do not act this way, but pray as I taught you, saying, "Hallowed be Thy Name; Thy will be done on Earth as it is in Heaven." My child, if you truly want my will to be done, it is like saying to Me, 'Lord, you take care of it for me.' When you ask Me to take care of it, I will resolve your most difficult problem."*

It is when we are prepared to totally surrender ourselves to the Lord and leave our problems totally with Him, right there; when you are at your Wit's End, that we will have the peace we desire and be able to say, *"Give thanks to the Lord, for He is good; His love endures forever"* (Psalm 107:1).

Prayer: *Dear Father, thank You that You love with everlasting love. Lord, I surrender myself afresh to You that I may know the joy and peace of obedience to You. Amen*

DAY 205
INDEBTED TO CHRIST

1 Corinthians 7:23, *"You were bought at a price; do not become slaves of human beings"* NIV.

Throughout Paul's life, he was overwhelmed with a sense of being indebted to Jesus, living each day in the presence of the Holy Spirit as he expressed what God placed in his life. As Christ's followers, do we feel that Jesus is our spiritual creditor, always being ready to listen and do what He says?

> We will only know His blessing when we take hold of His power within.

Is your life so filled with the Spirit that when He speaks into your heart, you feel it an honour as a child of God to allow your life to be of value in the great work of redeeming the lost? If God told you to do something that didn't make any sense, what do you do? Do you obey your common sense, or knowing you are indebted to Christ, you risk everything and do what He says?

Consider Abraham when God told him to sacrifice his son, although he had previously been told a great nation would be born of him. Common sense would certainly have said, *'This contradicts what God has already said.'* However, Abraham obeyed God, despite his common sense screaming within him not to. His trust in God was greater than his doubt. What would you or I do under similar circumstances, and would our indebtedness to our Saviour keep us trusting in His almighty power regardless of what He had asked of us?

The very moment we step into spiritual obedience and do what our Saviour asks, risking everything that we hold as common sense, we will immediately know in our hearts that our God is with us. We must trust in our Lord, and when He asks the unnatural, we will only know His blessing when we take hold of His power within and step forward for what we know is from our God. To be indebted to God is to bank your faith in the character of a loving God. *"Still another said, "I will follow you, Lord; but first let me go back and say goodbye to my family"* (Luke 9:61).

Prayer: *Without You, Lord, I am nothing. Give me the strength and courage to always obey, even when it is against all that speaks common sense or is foreign to my thinking. Amen*

DAY 206
CONTENTMENT

Philippians 4:11, *"I have learned to be content whatever the circumstances."* NIV.

When Paul wrote these words to the church at Philippi, he was in a dungeon with no comfort, yet needing nothing. For our part, this really takes some understanding as we like our comforts and our things around us. Paul is speaking about being so blessed by God that circumstances and things are irrelevant to the comfort Jesus gives to the person who is totally committed to Him.

Being blessed begins and ends with recognising just who Jesus is and finding true contentment in Him. It is the ability to see the good in everyone and everything, and thereby inheriting God's creation totally.

The comfort Jesus gives is beyond our understanding.

Jesus told us, *"Blessed are those who hunger and thirst for righteousness, for they will be filled"* (Matt.5:6). When we hunger and thirst to be more like Christ and more fitted for His Kingdom, we can be sure that we will receive a blessed state of mind and contentment in Christ. The wonderful realization is that this blessed contentment is available to every one of us if it represents the true purpose of our life; we have the assurance that *"Never will I leave you; never will I forsake you"* (Hebrews 13:5).

From the contented heart will flow the harvest of the blessedness of Christian qualities that we find in Galatians 5:22-23, *"But the fruit of the Spirit is love, joy, peace, forbearance, kindness, goodness, faithfulness, gentleness and self-control. Against such things there is no law."* May you find the peace and contentment of a well-balanced Christian character that is yours in Christ.

> *Hallelujah! I have found him*
> *Who my soul so long has craved!*
> *Jesus satisfies my longings,*
> *Through His blood I now am saved.*
>
> Clara Tear Williams

DAY 207
BEAUTIFULLY DRESSED

Isaiah 52:1, *"Awake, awake, Zion, clothe yourself with strength! Put on your garments of splendour."*

Romans 13: 11-12, *"The hour has already come for you to wake up from your slumber... let us put aside the deeds of darkness and put on the armour of light."* NIV

Each day we go out into the arena of life, where we don't always find it easy to live out the character of Jesus. As we go to whatever our task may be, God tells us to put on, or in other words, to live in the strength and might of our Lord. We cannot buy strength of spirit or generate it through prayer or resolutions; we must put it on.

> *When the Spirit dwells within, the beauty of the Father is seen in us.*

He waits to fill you with the power and wisdom of the Holy Spirit, so don't simply pray for God to keep and help you, but instead, accept the strength that is yours in Christ. Psalm 27:1 says, *"The Lord is the stronghold of my life, of whom shall I be afraid?"*

Put on your beautiful garments. Each day, we are to clothe ourselves by not only doing the right deeds but we must do them in a beautiful way. When we speak the truth, speak it in love; when we give help, do it with grace and joy. Yes, we must cultivate the beauty of our life in Christ in everything we do by showing compassion, kindness, humility, meekness and generosity. When the Spirit dwells within us, the beauty of the Father must be seen in us. Our problem is that no matter how we try, we cannot fashion beautiful garments from our own nature. Christ has prepared them for each of us, and they must be woven into our souls through our deep relationship with Jesus each day.

Make a new start today. Wake up out of your slumber, put off the works of evil that hold you and replace them with the beautiful garments prepared for you in Jesus Christ, the armour of Light.

Prayer: *Lord of all power, I come, trusting in Your strength and infinite goodness. I ask You for the strength to put off the things that hinder me and for the grace to put on Your garments of love and compassion. Please help me, dear Lord, to let Your Spirit guide and control my life to reflect Your beauty each day. Amen*

DAY 208
UNBOUNDED GRACE

Isaiah 44:22,23. *"I have swept away your offenses like a cloud, your sins like the morning mist... Sing for joy, O heavens, for the Lord has done this"* NIV.

When we read the Old Testament, we are amazed at how many times God's people rebelled and disobeyed and how many times, because of His great love and compassion, God reached out to them with unbounded grace and mercy. Time after time, He forgave them and redeemed them. He swept away their offenses like a cloud. Then to top everything off, every time this happened, the heavens sang for joy as Almighty God displayed his glory for Israel.

When I read this, I have this picture in my mind of the whole heavens above filled with God's angels singing praises to the Creator. It is truly amazing and wonderful when we stop and meditate on the fact that the God of the Universe loves each of us, more than we can possibly imagine. Yes, our loving Father will do no less for each of us with our sins and blunders than He did for the Children of Israel.

God's love is so great for you that He redeems the most painful places in your soul.

God's love is so great for you and me that He redeems the most painful places in our souls – even those we have tried to hide for so long. There is no wound that He can't heal; no broken heart that He can't comfort; no need that He can't supply; and no soul; not one of us, that He won't forgive. Jesus alone can mend our hurting souls.

Do not feel guilty any longer. Bring your burden to Jesus today and ask His forgiveness, then be assured that He has redeemed and values you. Jesus said, *"I tell you, there is rejoicing in the presence of the angels of God over one sinner who repents"* (Luke 15:10). The angels of Heaven are rejoicing and praising the God of the Universe because Jesus, in His forgiveness has won the victory.

Prayer: *Dear Jesus, there are so many things I will do differently with your help! Please forgive me and heal me of my blunders. Thank you for your great love and mercy for me and all humanity. Amen*

DAY 209
GOD IS IN CONTROL

Matthew 7:11, *"If you, then, though you are evil, know how to give good gifts to your children, how much more will your Father in heaven give good gifts to those who ask him!"* NIV.

We have all experienced the excitement of purchasing a gift for someone, knowing it is what they want. The real excitement comes when we see their face light up, and hear their cry of delight. That is a special moment. Can you imagine God's joy when we thank Him, for He gives abundantly more than we can ask?

God is my Father; He loves me, so why should I worry.

In life, not everything that happens is just what we ask for or want, and sometimes terrible things can happen to us, but we need to understand that God didn't make it happen. We need to get our minds around the fact, God is here for us. His only desire is to be with us, to help and love us. Once we can understand this fact, then when difficulties happen, it becomes as easy as breathing to remember; my loving Father knows all about it.

Once, you would probably have gone to this friend or that pastor seeking an answer, but now with understanding as a child of God, He is in divine control of your life, you can go at once to Him. God's principle is always – God is my Father; He loves me, so why should I worry. When difficulties come into our lives, we must trust Him, even when we think he is an unloving Father. Nothing happens for us without God's will being behind it, so we can rest in Him with confidence that all will be well, even when it appears otherwise. We must remember that *"your Father in heaven gives good things to those who ask Him!"*

Remember that when we pray, we must have the attitude of mind which will make asking the perfectly natural thing to do. *"Ask, and it shall be given you"* (Matt; 7:7). It has been my experience that I have not always received what I asked for, only to learn later that had God given what I asked, I would have not been able to cope with what I felt best for me. He always provides what we need, not necessarily what we think we need.

Prayer: *Thank You Lord, that I can trust You to give me the best gift for every need that I may have in life. Amen*

DAY 210
THINK DIFFERENTLY

Romans 12:2, *"Do not conform to the pattern of this world, but be transformed (changed) by the renewing of your mind."* NIV

Over the years as I have had more contact with other nationalities, I have come to understand that we are all shaped by the culture of the country where we grew up. Understanding the culture of our ancestors is important for us all and essential to hand on to our children.

There is another more critical culture that moulds our lives in such a way that, as a believer, it can be hard to break away from. Paul refers to this as the culture of our sinful world, which influences and often changes us without us noticing anything different. We must be vigilant every day, making sure that the unquestioned assumptions of our world today are not affecting our spiritual life.

> Ensure that the world's assumptions are not influencing your spiritual life.

Our verse tells us to be transformed or changed. Jesus tells us to *"Remain in me, as I also remain in you"* (John 15:4). He also said in v.7, *"If you remain in me and my words remain in you."* This is within reach of each of us, for when Jesus asks that His words remain in us, He can mean nothing else than that we should often (daily) read, reflect and bring them to mind. As we dwell on His words, the Holy Spirit will renew our minds, resulting in change in our actions.

As followers of Christ our goal must be true maturity in Christ by allowing the Holy Spirit to change us from passively taking on the ways of our world and allowing the world's thinking to engulf us. We must actively follow God's way by learning to understand *"His good, pleasing and perfect will"* (v. 2) until our lives reflect the Glory of our Lord.

Prayer: *Dear Lord, may my soul thirst for when my life will reflect Your Glory. Until then, keep me diligent in dwelling on Your Word, that I might change by renewing my mind. Amen*

DAY 211
EARNEST PRAYER

Acts 12:5, *"Peter was kept in prison, but the church was earnestly praying to God for him."* NIV

Praying earnestly for Peter's release, sounds like an impossible situation, as he is in prison, possibly awaiting execution. They were praying and believed that if anyone could bring Peter back to them, it would be Jesus. Even though they prayed earnestly, they didn't believe it when Peter was miraculously released and came to them. (Verse 15)

> *Most of us in severe circumstances often panic and forget to pray.*

Are we any different? There are times in our lives when something drastic happens, like your little child is rushed to hospital with a raging fever or having a seizure. I remember when our son was very small, the car wheel accidentally passed over his arm, flattening it like paper. We were so frantic we didn't think to pray. Most of us in similar circumstances panic and forget to pray, but God is with us and we are like those who prayed for Peter, when God does answer, we can't believe it.

When we pray in these situations, our prayer is focused and passionate as we come to God, pouring out our soul in earnest prayer as though saying, *"Please God, hear me; I need You."* We don't say to God that we would like Him to answer our prayer, no; we plead with expectation to God for His intervention. *"Elijah was a human being, even as we are. He prayed earnestly that it would not rain, and it did not rain on the land for three and a half years."* (James 5:17). He prayed with expectation and believed.

You may be asked to pray for the salvation of someone. Do you give up after a few days or weeks, or do you continue praying, maybe for years, until the person accepts Christ as Saviour? 1 Thess.5:16-18 says we must *"Rejoice always, pray continually, give thanks in all circumstances; for this is God's will for you in Christ Jesus."* Let us continue in earnest prayer for those who need Christ as Saviour. When we pray earnestly, endlessly and expectantly, God moves, and we see our prayers answered as souls are saved.

Prayer: *Thank You Lord, that You are more eager to hear our prayer than we are to pray. Please help us always remember to pray earnestly for others so they may be saved. Amen*

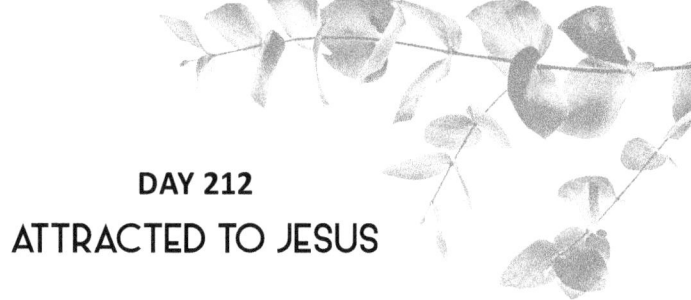

DAY 212
ATTRACTED TO JESUS

Mark 1:37, *"They exclaimed: "Everyone is looking for you!"* NIV

There is no part of our lives here on earth that Jesus is not waiting and willing to share. Through all our relationships and circumstances, regardless of how horrible or nasty, as well as the good times, He waits to breathe His perfect love into our lives if we let Him. We all need the love He offers freely to us, but too many miss it.

Why do our marriages fail, our children turn to the world, or our circumstances seem to be always against us? Could it be that we seek to get more than to give? In our relationships, and especially our marriages, if we made the other person the centre of our thought and care, we would see significant change.

Humility and pride are opposite sides of the same coin.

If we allowed God's love to shine through our actions, our children would be attracted to Jesus like a sunflower to the sun. We must be careful of the example we show so that it will not turn them away. When we rightly present Christ's love, our lives will draw others to want the life we live. Too often, we feel superior to others and are quite willing to live a good moral and respectable life because it suits us, but when it comes to following Jesus and His teaching, we turn away.

So, what made Jesus popular? It was His humility that attracted the people to Him. Today, we admire His ideals and teaching but turn away because we love ourselves more than we love Jesus, *"For everyone who exalts himself will be humbled, and he who humbles himself will be exalted"* (Luke 14:11), reminding us, humility and pride are opposite sides of the same coin. The Bible compares humility to meekness, selflessness, and gentleness, not just to think about the welfare of others, but as Jesus did, to associate ourselves with them. *"He has told you, O man, what is good; and what does the Lord require of you but to do justice, and to love kindness, and to walk humbly with your God"* (Micah 6:8). What does God require of you that will make a difference in the life of someone today?

Prayer: *Help me, dear Lord, to live my life more for You so that those I love and have contact with will see You in the way I live and not me. Amen*

DAY 213

OUR WORLD

Genesis 2:15, *"The Lord God took the man and put him in the Garden of Eden to work it and take care of it."* NIV

Growing up on a farm, each day I saw my mum and dad delight in carrying out the work required to bring food to others. It was a hard life, but a wonderful life that I wouldn't exchange for anything. Memories flood my mind of having to rise before the sun to help catch chickens so they could be immunised against disease or helping to pick pineapples on a hot summer's day. At the time I probably thought, why me? But now I understand the benefits I learned in caring for the animals and plants God had created.

> *If Jesus were beside you, would you hear Him say, "Well done."*

In Genesis 1:27, we read, *"God created man in his own image."* Our God is the great Creator and is ever working in the spiritual realm for the benefit of His creation. Being created in His image gives us an inbuilt sense to also want to create, work and care for our world. Just like the Lord God put Adam and Eve in the Garden of Eden to care for it, He wants us to love and care for His creation today.

We are not all called to care for the land, but each of us has been called to our own individual work or profession. What you do is essential, but much more important is how you do it. We need to be aware that we work as unto God, and must each ask: *Am I putting my best into my work? Is my work ethic such that if Jesus were beside me, I would hear Him say, "Well done,"* or are we clocking off early or coming in late?

Most importantly, as our God loved you and me so much that He sent Jesus to die for our sins, we owe our allegiance to Him. He has called us to care for each other, to encourage, support and love one another for Him. Galatians 6:10. *"So then, while we have opportunity, let us do good to all people, and especially to those who are of the household of the faith."* What work has God given you today? Reflect on God's wise and loving care of us and our world, thanking Him for calling you to work for Him, bringing glory to Him today in your work.

Prayer: *Thank You, Father, for giving us the honour and joy of caring for Your creation. Help me to show your care and love to my fellow man. Amen*

DAY 214
VISION THROUGH PURITY

Matthew 5:8, *"Blessed are the pure in heart, for they will see God"* NIV.

When we accept Jesus as Saviour and ask His forgiveness, He cleanses us from sin, the dross in our life, but this does not necessarily mean that we are pure. We must ask ourselves what purity of heart really means and how does this allow us to see God. We are all aware of the saying "pure gold," which we use to describe something made of only one ingredient. From this, we understand that a pure heart is nothing but 100% Jesus. Just as gold is heated so that the impurities come to the top to be lifted away and give 100% purity, we also have to grow in righteousness.

Even though we may aim at doing God's will, if we are honest with ourselves, we often allow other things like wealth, success, material objects or entertainment attract our hearts, often without being aware that it has happened. If the spiritual radiance of our life with God is being impaired even to a small degree, we must leave everything and get it right, remembering that the vision of God for us depends on the purity of our hearts.

> It is in our hearts that we see and know God.

First and foremost, we must see our goal in 1 Timothy 1:5 *"The goal of this command is love, which comes from a pure heart and a good conscience and a sincere faith."* God will make us pure by His sovereign grace as we keep our hearts right with Him because it is in our hearts that we see and know God in Christ. When we understand, to see and know God comes to our hearts through the words of our Lord in Scripture, we will have the purity that enables us to see and have deep fellowship with Him. To maintain a strong personal relationship with Jesus, there will be some things we must put aside from doing, thinking or touching.

Let us each aim to proclaim with Lord Alfred Tennyson, "My strength is as the strength of ten, because my heart is pure."

Prayer: *Dear Lord, give me eyes to see You and a heart to hear Your voice, that You will become more real to me than anyone or anything on this earth. Amen.*

*We are here to be excited from youth to old age,
To have an insatiable curiosity about the world . . . .
And every person is born for a purpose.
Everyone has a God given potential, in essence, built into them,
And if we are to live life to its fullest,
We must realize that potential.*

Norman Vincent Peale

*"But I have raised you up for this very purpose,
that I might show you my power and that my
name might be proclaimed in all the earth."*
Exodus 9:16

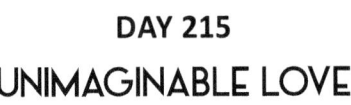

DAY 215
UNIMAGINABLE LOVE

Ephesians 3:17-18, *"That Christ may dwell in your hearts through faith. And I pray that you, being rooted and established in love, may have power, together with all the Lord's holy people, to grasp how wide and long and high and deep is the love of Christ."* NIV

When we stop and meditate on the dimensions of the love of Christ, it is beyond our human understanding. It is as wide as the east is from the west – how far is that! Paul tells us in Romans 3:16, *"For God so loved the world that he gave his one and only Son."* The length: There is no beginning date, and God's love is forever; it is unchangeable and is in this moment! Its' height is as high as heaven is above the earth. How high - the infinity of space. Its' depth: Only Christ descended to the depths of the bottomless pit, taking our sins with Him. It is wonderful to know that however low you fall or how terrible your situation is, God's arms of love are beneath you to lift you up.

No matter how we try, we cannot understand the greatness of God's love, but it is ours to enjoy. Time has shown the best way to know Christ's love is to show it. As you reach out to others, Christ's love in you will become wider, longer, deeper and higher, and you will know the love of Christ within like never before. 1 John 4:11-12, *"Since God so loved us, we also ought to love one another... If we love one another, God lives in us and his love is made complete in us."*

> **We will never understand God's love, but it is ours to enjoy.**

Is there someone you feel you cannot love? You must distinguish between the emotion of love, which is feeling, and different to the love of Christ flowing from you. You probably won't feel love initially, but you must be willing to let Christ's love flow to them as you reach out to them. Is this too much to ask in light of God's love for you? Know that God's love is at work within you by the power of His Spirit, and He will enable you to love beyond understanding. 1 John 4:21 says, *"He has given us this command: Anyone who loves God must also love their brother and sister."* Divine Love is always there and is for everyone. *"To Him be glory, throughout all generations, for ever and ever. Amen."*

Love divine, all loves excelling,
joy of Heaven to Earth come down.
Fix in us Your humble dwelling,
all Your faithful mercies crown.

Charles Wesley 1747

DAY 216
THE ROAD TO SUCCESS

Psalm 25:1, *"Who then, are those who fear the Lord? He will instruct them in the ways they should choose."* NIV

This Psalm describes a person who has learned the road to success but has not always found it easy. As he faces enemies from without and within, he realizes the road to success is to be found by walking in companionship and friendship with God. When God is our refuge, we are, as it were, hiding in Him, being aware of His presence with us 24/7. For us, this doesn't mean that we think about Him from time to time, but that our whole life is filled with Him.

Don't rob yourself any longer of the marvellous companionship of God.

A child's conscience is always aware of their parent's presence, and when something happens to the child, the parent is there to care for and protect them. When we live and move in the continual presence of our God, we will look at everything as God sees it and act accordingly.

When God is our refuge, *"God is our refuge and strength, an ever-present help in trouble"* (Psalm 46:1), nothing can get at us unless it comes through Christ our Saviour. No care, no problem, no anxiety. This is why Jesus emphasized how worry can take us out of God's presence.

We must look to the Lord for help (v.1), knowing that it is Him we need to trust (v.2,3) and wait patiently on Him in prayer (v.4,5); then we will find our refuge in our God, who will put His shield around us against all the attacks of evil. Don't rob yourself any longer of the marvellous companionship of God. *"His soul shall dwell at ease"* (v.13). Nothing can come to you through God's shield around you unless He has sent it to strengthen your trust in Him.

Prayer: *Thank You Lord, for being my refuge and help in trouble. Please remind me constantly to keep close to You so I can know the peace You want to give me. Amen*

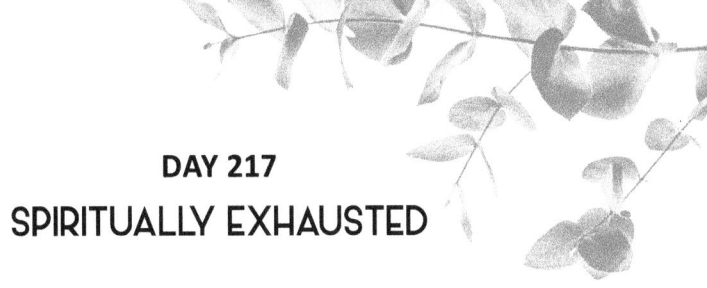

DAY 217
SPIRITUALLY EXHAUSTED

Isaiah 40:28, *"Do you not know? The Lord is the everlasting God... He will not grow tired or weary."* NIV

We all know what it is like to feel exhausted, as we are literally sapped of strength and energy and feel worn out. Exhaustion happens when we don't look after our own physical needs, and our natural physical instinct being to take food and rest to renew our strength.

When Jesus told Peter to "feed my sheep," He didn't give him anything to feed them with because Peter needed to learn to first be nourished by feeding on God before he could do what Jesus asked of him.

We must draw our strength from Jesus, who never grows tired or weary.

At this moment in your life is there someone draining you of your spiritual and physical strength? If you are to continue to help them spiritually, then you need to draw your spiritual strength from your Heavenly Father. Like Peter, before we can help others, we must learn to draw our strength direct from Jesus, who never grows tired or weary.

As we disciple others for Jesus, we must draw from Jesus until the one we are helping spiritually, learns for themselves to be nourished through faith and trust in Jesus. We can only be the best for our Heavenly Father as we draw our spiritual strength from Him each day through reading His word and prayer. Let us claim God's promise, *"Those who hope in the Lord will renew their strength"* (verse 31).

If you are depleted of your spiritual and physical strength, then say to the Lord – *"Oh Lord, I am so exhausted."* Spend time in the presence of Jesus today and draw on His strength, remembering God's words, *"For I am the Lord your God who takes hold of your right hand and says to you, do not fear; I will help you"* (Isaiah 41: 13).

Prayer: *Lord, you know how I so often fail to come and be renewed by the strength of Your Spirit. May Your grace and mercy come to my aid so that I may reach out to help others to trust and have faith in You. Amen*

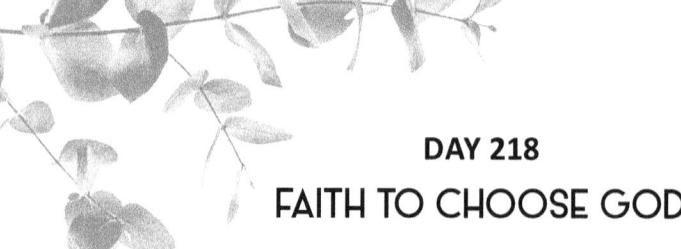

DAY 218
FAITH TO CHOOSE GOD

2 Corinthians 5:7, *"For we live by faith, not by sight."* NIV

Unlike Satan and sometimes ourselves, we want to feel and say that we have faith; however, God wants us to face facts, not feelings. When Christ died to save us, His perfect work was complete; the facts about Jesus Christ and his promises were there for us.

God will give you the feeling of peace only when He sees that you trust Him.

When we are prepared to face these precious facts and believe that God can do as He has promised, then and only then will He take care of our feelings. God doesn't give us a feeling of love or encouragement, so that we can trust Him, nor does He give us feelings so that we have the assurance that we have already trusted Him.

If you are hurting, depressed, lonely or in pain, you must understand that God will give you the feeling of peace or being loved only when He knows that apart from how you feel, you trust Him.

We must believe in His Word and rely on His faithfulness to His promise, regardless of how we may feel. Until then, the feelings cannot be ours. When we're prepared to trust our Lord, whether we feel His blessing or not, He will give us peace and love beyond our understanding, in His time and as His love sees best for our individual life.

We must believe God's facts regardless, and apart from our feelings because our feelings are as uncertain as shifting sand. God's truths will never change; they are as certain as Jesus Christ Himself, who *"is the same yesterday and today and forever."* (Hebrews 13:8)

When darkness veils His lovely face
I rest on His unchanging grace;
In every high and stormy gale,
My anchor holds within the veil.

Edward Mote 1834

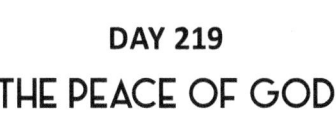

DAY 219
THE PEACE OF GOD

John 16:33, *"In me you may have peace. In this world you will have trouble. But take heart! I have overcome the world"* NIV.

Being blessed is totally different to being happy. When Paul was in prison, I am pretty sure that he was anything but comfortable and happy, and yet he was greatly blessed with the peace that only comes to those who love Jesus as Saviour. As he wrote the letter to the Philippian church he spoke of God's peace being a blessing of divine aid or protection. *"The peace of God, which transcends all understanding, will guard your hearts and your minds in Christ Jesus"* (Phil.4:7). God's peace comes from within through the work of the Holy Spirit in our lives.

Niccolò Paganini was a world-renowned violinist of the early 19th century. Just before he went on stage to play at a concert, he discovered that his favourite violin had been stolen and replaced with just an ordinary, everyday one. For some minutes, he was devastated, but then it came to him that the instrument was secondary, and if he played from his heart, his music would be just as good as expected. He walked onto the stage and proclaimed, *"Ladies and gentlemen, today I will show you that the music is not in the instrument, but it comes from the soul."* That day he showed that the music for each of us must come from within our souls.

> God's peace is like a blessing of divine aid or protection.

Paul showed this peace to the other prisoners and jailer, as he experienced the blessing of God's divine aid in giving him peace, to reveal to all present and to the whole world that the music of the soul is not dependent on conditions, or things, or feelings, but on our relationship with our Saviour.

Is your soul filled with the music of the blessed peace of God? Come to Jesus today, for He loves you and longs to give you His peace to fill your heart, despite your circumstances.

Prayer: *Peace, peace! Wonderful peace, coming down from the Father above. May Your peace Lord, always sweep over my soul so that I may experience the full extent of Your love. Amen*

DAY 220
PRAISE AND WORSHIP

John 4:24, *"God is spirit, and his worshipers must worship in Spirit and in truth"* NIV.

When we look at defining what worship is, we find the meaning of reverence, adoration, or to bring homage, but true worship is both a doing and an attitude of the heart. It is coming to a Holy God in an act of praise and adoration for who He is and for His worth to those who love Him. *"To offer your bodies as a living sacrifice, holy and pleasing to God... this is your true and proper worship"* (Romans 12:1. NIV).

> Worship is to give God His true worth, offering yourself to Him as a living sacrifice.

Today we see some churches producing magnificent worship services, which are pleasing to our eyes and ears, but unless it touches the spirit of the worshipers, it is of little value. Unfortunately, sometimes great words are produced that have little or no effect on a person's soul. Our worship, as Christians, must come from a heart relationship of love to our Heavenly Father.

For different people, worship can take various forms. Whilst we traditionally think of worship as singing praises to God, it can also come from meditation on a passage of scripture. For example, Psalm 100:1 says, *"Shout for joy to the Lord, all the earth."* The whole of Psalm 100 makes one want to respond to God's grace and goodness. Worship may also come in response to the moving testimony of someone, where we will give praise and thanks to God.

Whilst I enjoy praising God in singing, my worship often comes during my quiet time with my Father, often through scripture, prayer, creation, or even a poem. Regardless of how you worship, the importance is to give God His true worth, offering yourself to Him as a living sacrifice, and praising Him for the blessings He pours out on your life.

> O worship the Lord in the beauty of holiness.
> Bow down before him, his glory proclaim;
> with gold of obedience, and incense of lowliness,
> kneel and adore him: the Lord is his name.
>
> John S. B. Monsell

DAY 221
SHUT THE DOOR

Matthew 6:6, *"When you pray, go into your room, close the door and pray to your Father who is unseen."* NIV

Jesus is speaking about a time each day, when we pray with deliberate effort of our will, because in our busy lives it's easy to say, *'I will do it later.'* We can pray at anytime and anywhere, which is true, but Jesus speaks about a secret place (a room or special place) and says close the door. Jesus showed this example to his disciples when He went away alone to pray to His Father in secret.

When He speaks about shutting the door, He knows the first conflict we face in our quiet time is our wandering thoughts. He wants us to shut out the world from our minds and speak to Him in secret. We need to discipline our minds and concentrate on our time in the presence of a Holy God.

In His secret place, God speaks intimately through the Spirit

In our special place, we need to respect and trust our Father who loves to hear from us. We are comforted in knowing that there is no problem we have that He cannot solve. Coming in this manner, we experience the presence of the Holy Spirit within, for He sees, not as the world sees or even as we see ourselves. He sees us in secret, being still in His presence, and speaks intimately through the Spirit.

He listens to our requests, rejoicing when they are in accord with His will, as sometimes He will answer with something more appropriate and better for us. If our problem remains, He will give us strength and grace to overcome in His name. When we come in faith and trust, we come with the highest attribute of prayer, for faith is the quiet assurance of things not yet seen. Hebrews 11:1. *"Now faith is the assurance of things hoped for, the conviction of things not seen."*

When we start our day in the secret presence of God, our life will be stamped with an awareness that only speaks of God being with us throughout the day.

Prayer: *Lift me into the love and purity of Your presence. Help me to be deliberate in having a special time with You every day so I grow in faith and love for You. Amen.*

DAY 222
LESS OF ME

Matthew 5:3, *"Blessed are the poor in spirit, for theirs is the kingdom of heaven."* NIV

This verse seems to say blessed are those who are sad and discouraged, but if we replace the words *'poor in spirit'* with *'being humble,'* we can understand more of what Jesus meant. Today, a lot of emphasis is placed on our strength of will and beauty of character, the outward things that are noticed, but John the Baptist makes it very clear that we have to choose to allow Jesus to become greater and us to become less. (John 3:30)

> *Love Him more than yourself, lest pride should enter your soul.*

We must recognize our sin, spiritual poverty in light of what Jesus did to save us. This is the first beatitude making it obvious that we need to see ourselves as totally dependent on God's grace to save us and having no strength of will to save ourselves.

We are spiritually poor, and in recognising this, we are blessed as we yield to Him. Only through our poverty of spirit can the Holy Spirit flow through us to reveal the true character of Jesus in blessing others. When Jesus becomes more and us less, we will become unaware of our influence on those around us. *"If you love me, keep my commands"* (John 14:15). We must love Him more than ourselves and keep watch lest pride should enter our souls.

Who has influenced your life? You will realize that it was not those who talked about what they did but those who did not have the remotest thought of influencing you. Let us beware lest we become conscious of our good works as we will lose the natural beauty of the character of Jesus within us.

Have you faced your own need of Christ? Do you realize that you are spiritually poor and need God's forgiveness? Turn to Christ in humility and faith, not allowing pride or anything to get in the way, and He will bless and save you.

More about Jesus would I know, More of His grace to others show.
More of His saving fulness see.
More of His love who died for me.

Eliza Edmunds Hewitt (1851-1920)

DAY 223
GOD'S CHALLENGE

Isaiah 6:8, *"Then I heard the voice of the Lord saying, "Whom shall I send? And who will go for us?"* NIV

From the midst of heaven comes the call, *"Who will go for us?"* Throughout history many have heard the call, but surely God's call is to each who love Jesus. It reminds us of Jesus' commission to the disciples to go and preach the Gospel.

Some have sung songs of the saints of God who were patient, brave, and true,
They toiled and fought and lived and died, for the Lord they loved and knew;
They were all of them saints of God; and I mean,
With God's help, to be one too.

K. Cameron-Smith

Look for the opportunity each day to speak for Jesus.

In God's service, there is no time we cease to be His or pass from His eye. We are at His disposal to speak, be kind, compassionate, and encourage those who need His help. He knows us, and there is no hardship, for he understands both the needs of others and our needs. Look for opportunity each day to live and speak for Jesus, so others have the opportunity of knowing Him as Saviour. The wonder is, He takes us into partnership with Himself to save souls. *"He said, "I am the light of the world. Whoever follows me will never walk in darkness, but will have the light of life."* (John 8:12)

Many folks have come, and some have gone,
For the story is not yet told,
There's you and me, and there's God you see,
To gather lots more to the fold.
The people who as yet still need to be reached,
Who will hear and believe when the Gospel is preached,
There's work for us all, from the greatest to the least,
And we all have a job to do.

K. Cameron-Smith

Who is there that you could share the Gospel with today?

Prayer: *I give you my life Lord. Use me even this day to speak for You. Amen*

DAY 224

NEW LIFE

1 Cor. 1:18, *"The message of the cross is foolishness to those who are perishing, but to us who are being saved it is the power of God"* NIV.

Like most mothers about to have their first baby, I well remember reading books on childbirth but no matter pre-natal classes and everything else, none of us can imagine the experience of what it will be like. Looking back now, I had no idea what my body would go through or what I would experience.

Salvation only makes sense to those who experienced it.

In 1 Corinthians, Paul writes about our birth into the family of God. He tells us that salvation is found in the cross and that we are saved through forgiveness of sin and belief and trust in Christ. Many Jews, Greeks and Gentiles were looking for redemption through an influential political leader, so the gospel Paul preached seemed foolishness to the majority. God chose to surprise everyone by bringing salvation so that it would only make sense to those who experienced it.

God often does the unimaginable, and even though Christ's death on the cross was shameful, it was also the foundation of power and wisdom. Over the years, there have been many times when I wished I could help someone understand the simplicity of the gospel. I have often prayed that God would open a person's heart to understand just how they can have eternal life through forgiveness and trust. However, I have learned that I cannot give another person what I have; I can only make them desire to have what I have.

If we are to attract our relatives and friends to our Lord, they have to desire to have the life we live each day. For this attraction to happen you and I must continually grow in our trust and faith and leave everything else to our Heavenly Father. When we trust and let our lives shine for Him, He will answer our prayers for others. Matthew 5:*16 "Let your light so shine before men, that they may see your good deeds (lifestyle) and praise your Father in heaven."*

Prayer: *Dear God, thank You for surprising us every day with Your wisdom and grace. Help me to live today so that others will know You too. Amen.*

DAY 225
HE LIVES - SO I LIVE

Revelation 1:18, *"I am the Living One; I was dead, and now look, I am alive for ever and ever!"* NIV.

At times of sorrow, we come face to face with our mortality, but let us also learn the lesson of immortality given to each of us through the death of Jesus when He conquered death once and for all. Let us reread Paul's words, *"For me, to live is Christ and to die is gain"* (Phil. 1:21).

Listen and hear the everlasting praise to our immortal God again, as we hear the bird song, singers as they sing of it and poets proclaiming the joy of eternal life in Christ. It is told and retold, yet often we fail to take hold of it. Sorrowing weary soul, hear it again until hope rises to conviction, and conviction to the absolute certainty of the knowledge that Christ died and rose again to redeem you from death to life everlasting.

> *Christ died and rose again to redeem you from death to life everlasting.*

When Jesus is Lord of your life, you can know that though you face death, you can go with Christ's love in your heart and your faith in an immortal God that will bring radiance to your face as you trust Him to bear you on to a better life forever and ever. Do not fear the uncertainty of death but see it with sure hope as the door to eternal life with Jesus, your Lord and Saviour.

Prayer: *Praise You Lord, that You overcame death, took our sin and have given us new life in Christ. Amen.*

DAY 226
A LIVING TEMPLE

1 Peter 2:9, *"But you are a chosen people, a royal priesthood, a holy nation, God's special possession, that you may declare the praises of him who called you out of darkness into his wonderful light."* NIV

As God's people, each of us is a living temple. You and I bring heaven to those who don't know Christ as Saviour because the Holy Spirit dwells in us. We reflect heaven and Christ to others, or do we? When Christ comes to live in us as His home, He has to do some renovations in our lives. He takes from us the walls we have built up around ourselves, and yes, it often hurts because He wants to not just live in a house but a palace.

> You bring heaven to those who don't know Christ as their Saviour.

We all have many hang-ups we don't want to part with, but as we minister for the Lord, He will replace the habits and attitudes with compassion and love. Remember that while on earth, we can never be perfect. Peter was writing to Christians, suffering for their faith and reminding them of how Jesus suffered to save them. He tells them that God will get them through, that they are living stones, and likewise so are we today. As a living stone, when we are in the world, our lives will have a ripple effect on all around us, which will help them to see God as He really is.

You are the temple of the Holy Spirit. In other words, is your very being so filled with the Spirit of God, that every time you bless someone by praying for them or laying your hands on them, it is as though Christ touched and blessed them. How incredible is your calling that your hands are the hands of Christ.

Your purpose as a living temple is to *"declare the praises of Him who called you out of darkness into His wonderful light."* God has called you holy, and with His presence inside you, He will produce the impossible through you. 1 Peter 2:6 says, *"The one who trusts in him will never be put to shame."* Why would you settle for anything less than to do the right thing?

Prayer: *Thank You Lord, for calling me out of darkness into your marvellous light. Change my life to be more like You so that I might be Your light in the world around me. Amen*

DAY 227

YOUR LIFE PASSION

1 Timothy 6:10-11, *"The love of money is the root of all kinds of evil... But you, man of God, flee from all this, and pursue righteousness, godliness, faith, love, endurance, and gentleness."* NIV

Many people measure their success solely by 'the bottom line' – the money and assets they have accumulated to their wealth. They spend their lives in pursuit of money. When you look at your small children, do you think about what or who they will become?

Paul tells us in 1 Timothy 6:9, that when we want to be rich and follow that goal, we will fall into temptation. Sometimes because of our desire, we make foolish and harmful decisions that plunge us into ruin and destruction. Whilst there is nothing wrong with having money as it is our means of exchange and provision, we must be careful not to prioritise it to become more important than anything in our lives.

> *Pursue righteousness, godliness, faith, love, endurance, and gentleness.*

Many seem to always be looking for a larger house, a better car or a bigger bank balance, even though we brought nothing into the world and can't take anything from it. This is a dangerous passion that we should flee from and realize that God has far better in store for us than money can buy. If we have food and clothing, and trust our Lord to provide all our needs, He will never fail us (1 Tim. 6:7-8).

Besides all our needs, our loving Father has breathed into each of us the very breath of life, and He reminds us in verse 6, that *"godliness with contentment is great gain."* We need to pursue righteousness, godliness, faith, love, endurance, and gentleness. As we follow these traits, God will mature our lives to find deep satisfaction even without a lot of money. How can you better learn to be contented?

Prayer: *Dear Father, You, have blessed me with so much every day. Help me always to be thankful for what I have and always to flee from the desire to have more money. Amen*

DAY 228
LOST OPPORTUNITIES

Matthew 26:46, *"Rise! Let us go!"*

Hebrews 12:17, *"Afterward... when he wanted to inherit this blessing, he was rejected. Even though he sought the blessing with tears, he could not change what he had done"* NIV.

Here we have two examples of lost opportunities. Firstly, the disciples went to sleep, realizing too late that because they had not kept watch, Jesus was about to be betrayed. On the other hand, in the Old Testament, Esau let his brother have his father's blessing because he craved what would satisfy his need in the moment. In both cases, there was no way to repair their mistakes because the 'die' was cast, and they had no peace within because they had missed their opportunity.

Now is your time of hope, a fresh beginning, and a new opportunity.

Let us beware, as this kind of disappointment is not foreign to any of us, for once our decision is made there is no going back, and the opportunity may never come our way again. We must be careful that in choosing to please ourselves, we may affect our own life and the lives of others. Whilst we have all experienced lost opportunities, we must remember that God's forgiveness waits for all, as there is always hope and the opportunity for us to repent.

It is difficult to move forward, if we allow ourselves to stress and be desperate about our error. The opportunity the disciples missed was beyond our understanding, yet Jesus forgave them and said to them, *"Rise! Let us go!"* Right in this moment is your time of hope, a fresh beginning, and a new opportunity. Jesus offers you a new chance to rise up and find the strength to do your very best to serve Him. Set yourself to follow His leading with all your heart and never let your past failure destroy your new beginning. *"Because of the Lord's great love, we are not consumed, for his compassions never fail"* (Lam.3:22).

Prayer: *Lord, let us always serve You with cheerfulness and gladness of heart, delighting ourselves in Your opportunities to rejoice in doing Your work. Amen*

DAY 229
THE COMPLETENESS OF CHRIST

Colossians 2:10, *"In Christ you have been brought to fullness."* NIV

For centuries many have believed their destiny is controlled by when they are born. For believers, we are free in Jesus Christ, we are not bound to the stars holding the answers for us or that we must find 'our other half' or 'soul mate' to be complete.

These beliefs are not truth because what is told to us mostly doesn't come to pass, or someone we know who is married can still feel incomplete, maybe they haven't been able to have children or feel an emptiness within. Paul tells us in v.8 to be careful we don't allow hollow philosophies of this world to take hold of us but rather know our completeness is in Christ.

Jesus doesn't just forgive us and set us free from death, but He completes us by filling our souls with the Holy Spirit. This means that when we have Jesus, we don't need to seek our identity and self-worth in things of this world, for we are no longer incomplete and helpless without a destiny. Indeed, we must guard against the evils of worldly philosophies and false religions.

> *Don't allow philosophies of this world to take hold of you.*

Let us look inward to our needs of insecurity, moodiness, fearfulness and dependency, instead of looking for the approval of others. Unless we bring ourselves to Christ for His help to release us, these things can imprison us just as much as astrology or false religions. Even though marriage is wonderful, it can't make us whole, for only Jesus can do that!

Jesus is head over every power and authority and more powerful than anything in this world that can imprison us. Instead of expecting a person, career, or anything else to complete us, we must constantly remind ourselves that we are complete in Christ and not in anyone or anything else. Let us accept God's invitation to fill us and complete us daily, coming to Him and saying, *"Thank you for giving me fullness in You."* Have you sought spiritual completeness through people instead of God?

Prayer: *Thank You Lord, for making me complete through Your death on the cross, and for Your forgiveness and infilling of my soul with the Holy Spirit. Amen*

DAY 230
GOD KNOWS BEST

Romans 8:28, *"We know that for those who love God all things work together for good, for those who are called according to his purpose"* NIV.

There are times in life, even though we're God's children, that we must suffer. Mary and Martha both said, *"Lord, if you had been here, my brother would not have died"* (John 11: 32). They couldn't understand why Jesus allowed sorrow to fill their lives when He could have come immediately to save Lazarus. Jesus had one answer: *"You may not understand; but I tell you if you believe, you will see."*

Abraham couldn't understand when God asked him to sacrifice his son, but he trusted that God was in control. Joseph likewise didn't understand God's reason for his brother's cruelty and then long years of imprisonment, but he trusted and saw the glory of God in it all. You may be going through grief or sorrow, finding it difficult to understand why God allowed your dear one to pass away. Or you don't understand why your friend took their own life; why you must suffer pain, or why your little child was born with a genetic disorder.

God gave us the Holy Spirit to comfort us in our weakest moments.

Even though it is difficult to understand God's leading of you along this path in life, or why the blessing you need is delayed, we know, *"The Spirit helps us in our weakness... The Spirit intercedes for us in accordance with God's will"* (Romans 8:26-27). God gave us the Holy Spirit to comfort us in our weakness. When we cannot express our overwhelming sorrow, we can cling to our Comforter, who groans before God's throne with words that we cannot speak.

We do not have to understand God's ways and He doesn't expect us to. Just like our own child may not understand us, but is prepared to believe, we must do the same, knowing that someday, we will see God's glory in all things, including the things we don't understand at this moment.

Thank You Lord, for the peace that you give,
For it flows o'er my life every day
In the joys and the sorrows, You have taught me to live
All is well in my life today.

Unknown

DAY 231

BLESSED IN THE WORD

Psalm 1:1-2, *"Blessed is the man who does not walk in the counsel of the wicked… But his delight is in the law of the Lord, and on his law, he meditates day and night."* NIV

When we are blessed, we are happy, and this will be so when we love the words and commands of our God. If we obey God's Word, the beginning will be a blessed life, and the end will be hallelujah to the King of Kings.

In obeying the words of God, we look after the soil of our heart, for there will be depth, moral purpose, and an earnest desire to grow in our faith and trust Jesus. Our hearts will be nourished by God's leading and His will for our lives. Hebrews 4:12, *"For the word of God is living and active… It judges the thoughts and attitudes of the heart."* Without the food we receive for our soul from reading and reflecting on what God's Word speaks into our lives, we will be like the seed planted in rocky ground, where even though we have accepted Jesus as Saviour, our shallow nature will live on its own impulses, impressions, intuitions, instincts, and its surroundings.

> The secret of happiness is to be found in knowing God.

These negatives need to be the things that drive us to the positives of reading and studying scripture each day. We must feed our life in Christ from the deep springs available through the word of God. Reading and studying scripture will move us steadily forward in God's love as He leads us deeper into His secrets and mighty truths, becoming closer to our Lord and living out more of His nature in our daily lives.

Which does your life resemble? Is your life being fed from the deep springs of God's word, or is it being frittered away being influenced by your own instincts and surroundings?

Prayer: *Lord Jesus, open to me the treasures from Your Word, so my soul will be continually enriched, and that I may abound in every good word and work, to Your glory. Amen.*

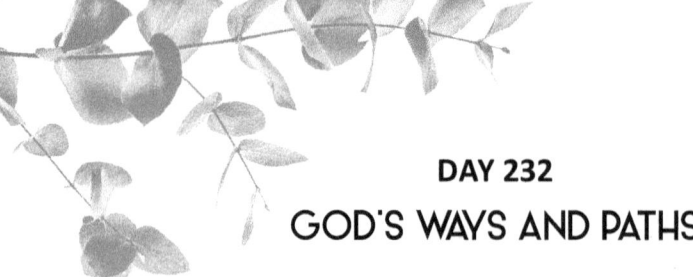

DAY 232
GOD'S WAYS AND PATHS

Psalm 25:4, *"Show me your ways, Lord, teach me your paths."*

Micah 4:2, *"He will teach us his ways, so that we may walk in his paths."* NIV

When it comes to life on earth, what is the difference between a way and a path? A way is broad and filled with everything of this life, while a path is very narrow, unfrequented and can be lonely. What a comfort to know that Jesus is with us on the way and the path, and each has meaning and teaching for us.

God always comes on time for those who faithfully trust Him.

God's ways are those great principles that form life here on earth and on which He acts. The principles of Creation, Providence, Revelation, Human history and finally, Judgement. These are things that the average person takes for granted, but in knowing them, we will know our God in the process. When Moses prayed, *"Teach me your ways so I may know you and continue to find favour with you"* (Exodus 33:13), God answered his prayer, making His ways known to Moses; but to the Children of Israel, God only made known His acts. To know God, we need to know His ways.

This era in time, many believe may be the last days of history. It is essential for each of us who are God's children to know the ways of God because only then can we enter His rest. *"Their hearts are always going astray, and they have not known my ways"* (Heb.3:10). In knowing God's ways, we can look at our troubled world with peace, for we know God is gathering those who walk in His ways to eternal life with Him.

When we read about narrow paths, we understand them to be our Saviour's dealings with us individually. Often, through illness, care of others and loneliness, we can be isolated from the daily contact with other believers. Still, we can be assured of God walking with us on the lonely path we travel. God is faithful and always comes on time for those who faithfully trust Him. All of God's paths are filled with mercy, peace, and grace to help us in our time of need.

Let God teach you His ways as you walk the pathway of your life with Him.

Prayer: *Lord, lead me down the paths of my life, that I may learn of Your way, and experience Your love and grace each day. Amen*

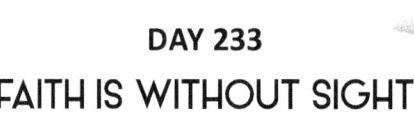

DAY 233
FAITH IS WITHOUT SIGHT

Hebrews 11:8, *"By faith Abraham, . . . obeyed and went, even though he did not know where he was going."* NIV

We can reason when we can see, but when we cannot see and yet believe, then that is faith. *"Without faith it is impossible to please God, because anyone who comes to Him must believe that He exists."* (Hebrews 11: 6.) Think of Captain Cook, who believed that there must be a large land mass in the southern hemisphere. He set out across the sea with only the heavens to chart his course not knowing where he was going. Imagine sailing in what we today call a large yacht? Day after day, month after month, without sight of land, and all the time believing there to be a land to be found. Like Abraham, he believed with faith long before he saw any result.

Is your course through life being measured by your Captain – your Creator? Cook sailed by the heavens not the world around him, and we must do the same. Faith looks ahead in anticipation and hope of reaching the heavenlies. Many of us want to see our way through life before we will start a new venture, but if we could see ahead, would we trust God? We need faith to believe that no matter what we encounter, our Father will see us through our trials, for often in the midnight hour, He will give us endurance to succeed.

> We hold the key, but we must unlock God's storehouse of blessings.

The attributes of Christian growth (faith, hope, and love) cannot be picked from trees like fruit. Our first step of faith turns the key to the powerhouse of God's unending love and care for us. Each of us holds the key, but we must use it to unlock God's storehouse of blessings. God helps not only those who can help themselves but also those who cannot help themselves. We can depend on Him every time. We must have the faith and trust of Abraham as we allow God to steer our course, not losing an opportunity by our own deliberation. Trust and obey; there's no other way.

> *My hope is built on nothing less,*
> *than Jesus' blood and righteousness.*
> *I dare not trust the sweetest frame,*
> *but wholly lean on Jesus' name.*
>
> Edward Mote

DAY 234

SURRENDER

John 17:4, *"I have brought you glory on earth by finishing the work you gave me to do"* NIV.

Jesus spoke these words in His prayer to God shortly before He was arrested. He had completed His work and brought glory to God through surrender to Him. Similarly, when we speak of surrender to God, it is a conscious decision of our will to give God authority over our life. Of all the decisive moments in life, the greatest we ever face is the surrender of our will. We like to maintain control, and God doesn't make or entreat us but waits until we are ready to surrender our will to Him.

> *The greatest decisive moment we face is the surrender of our will.*

Jesus said in Matthew 11:28-29, *"Come to me, all you who are weary and burdened, and I will give you rest. Take my yoke upon you and learn from me, for I am gentle and humble in heart."* As we walk with Jesus and grow spiritually, we surrender voluntarily to Him, asking Him for deliverance.

There is a deeper surrender He desires. He said, *"Whosoever will come after Me, let him deny himself, and take up his cross, and follow Me"* (Matt.16:24). In effect, He is saying, give up the right of yourself to Me. Jesus desires that we surrender our souls and our personality to Him so that we may know His rest and peace. The remainder of life will then reflect that surrender, as we reflect Jesus, never needing to 'suppose' anything.

From then, as we live daily in His presence and are filled with His Spirit, we no longer need to worry about anything because Christ is sufficient for all our needs. Upon surrender to Christ, our whole life is unbroken communion with our God. Have you surrendered your will to your Father that this unbroken communion can be yours today?

> *My Jesus, I love you, I know You are mine.*
> *For You all the pleasures of sin I resign.*
> *My greatest Redeemer, my Saviour art thou,*
> *If ever I loved You, my Jesus it's now.*
>
> William R. Featherston 1864

DAY 235
HAPPY DAYS

Nehemiah 8:12, *"Then all the people went away to eat and drink, to send portions of food and to celebrate with great joy, because they now understood the words that had been made known to them"* NIV.

When we can look on the bright side of life, we feel happy and optimistic. In these moments, we experience something of God's divine purpose of eternal gladness. If we could look at everything as God sees it, our temperament would change to bring us better health, happiness, and new meaning to life. This is the happy temperament that Nehemiah and Ezra felt when they said, *"The joy of the Lord is our strength"* (v.10). The very same that God wants for each of us.

The Jews were in great sorrow, having returned to Jerusalem to find the city destroyed. They took their problem to God and set about to rebuild the wall. When you have a problem, bring it to God, for He sees and feels your tears and hurts and will comfort you openly.

It's how we do what we do that matters.

When they finished the wall, they were filled with great joy and met together to hear Ezra read the Word of God. There is something about completed work done to the very best of our ability, that brings a sense of satisfaction. This is God's way of blessing us; even when your work is washing, cleaning, or mowing the grass. This inner feeling as you admire your work is something we can all feel, remembering that it's not what we do but our attitude to what we do that matters.

They also listened to Ezra read God's Word aloud. It has been my experience to really connect with God's Word when I read it aloud. If you do not understand the Bible when you read it, I encourage you to read aloud, and the Lord will reveal His Word in a new way. Charles Spurgeon said, *"If you want to hear God speak, read His word aloud."* When you spend time reading your Bible each day, you will find God applying its truth till you rejoice and are no longer sad.

Prayer: Thank You Lord, for giving me eyes to see the importance of doing all things well and a heart to love Your Word. Help me to understand and be happy each day. Amen

DAY 236
NOTHING IS ORDINARY

Romans 12:2, *"Do not conform to the pattern of this world, but be transformed by the renewing of your mind."* NIV

Every day is different, filled with opportunities God gives us. Imagine if every day had nothing significant happen to make it stand out from any other day. Today is different and is an extraordinary day. If you woke up this morning, you have a new day of opportunities, but my friend, will you take advantage of what God has given you, or will you at the end of the day feel worthless, ordinary and disappointed?

> God's heart aches because we don't trust His power within us.

In the 17th century, Christopher Wren was commissioned to rebuild a cathedral after the great London fire. He approached three bricklayers and asked what they were doing; the first said, *"I'm laying bricks to get paid,"* the second said, *"I'm building a wall,"* and the third said, *"I'm building a cathedral for God."* Let us be careful of our attitude and how we live each day. *"Be very careful, then, how you live—not as unwise but as wise"* (Eph.5:15). To experience all God has, we need to charge our minds and plug into the power of the Holy Spirit. Today is a new day, different from any other you have lived, so start by spending time in prayer.

Transform your life; renew your mind today to a miraculous mindset. Choose to rejoice in the Lord. Don't live in the past; live for the blessings God has for you today. We often hear about managing time, but we can't control time, so we must use it wisely and manage ourselves by having a right mindset. Get rid of the mindset of stress, worry and anxiety by living in the presence of God and seeing good in everyone. Let's open our minds to see God with us all the time and be grateful for His power through the Holy Spirit.

We have 365 days a year to live in God's presence. It is God who grows us and provides for our needs. *"Wait on the Lord: be of good courage, and he shall strengthen your heart"* (Psalm 27:14). God's greatest heartache is that we don't trust His power within us. Change your mindset from mundane to miraculous today, and experience all God has for you.

Prayer: *Lord, help me to experience You at the beginning of each day so that every day will be miraculous as I see Your hand at work in my life. Amen*

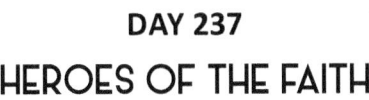

DAY 237
HEROES OF THE FAITH

Hebrews 6:12, *"Imitate those who through faith and patience inherit what has been promised."* NIV

Some of us do not desire to advance our knowledge of God. We might go to church, say a prayer, or read a passage of Scripture, but whilst this is better than nothing, we can never know the same blessing as those who *"hunger and thirst after righteousness."*

When we read the Book of Hebrews and look at the heroes of faith, like Abraham, Moses, David, and others, we will see that through their faith and patience, God always kept His promises. They trusted the Lord, staying close to Him every day and allowing Him to guide them through impossible circumstances. I ask myself, would I or could I have had the faith and patience through their impossible circumstances until I saw God's promise come true?

He will bring you forth like pure gold.

The blacksmiths of yesteryear tempered steel, first heating it, hammering it, and then suddenly plunging it into cold water to see if it would be of use or would break under pressure. If this happened, the blacksmith cast it aside as junk. If we are to know God's blessing when the fire is hottest, stand still, for as surely as He brought the heroes of faith through every circumstance, in like manner He will bring you forth like pure gold, for saints only come from a place of suffering. Allow Him to temper your life like steel so you will not break under pressure.

We need to long for the knowledge and awareness of God so we can say with the heroes of faith, *"The Lord is at hand!"* Let us hunger and thirst to know the Lord more every day, allowing Him to discipline us as we press on to His high calling for each of us. Do you spend time each day getting to know your Saviour better?

Prayer: *Lord, give me a hunger to know you more profoundly every day. Strengthen my faith so that I can stand the trials of this life and live with You eternally. Amen.*

DAY 238
OUR TESTIMONY

Matthew 10:32, *"Whoever acknowledges me before others, I will also acknowledge before my Father in heaven."* NIV

Christ's aim is to see salvation and peace for every human on earth. As believers, nothing is more thrilling that can draw us closer to Jesus than to share our personal experience of Christ with others. In God's mission to save the world, more have come to Christ through the personal testimony of a friend than all the great evangelists that have ever existed. Therefore, let us be careful not to fail our Saviour in sharing our testimony or hide the truth in our hearts that we have been given to share with others.

> We avoid sharing our experience of Christ with others.

When Andrew found the Messiah, he couldn't wait to share the good news with his brother Peter. *"The first thing Andrew did was to find his brother Simon and tell him, "We have found the Messiah" (that is, the Christ)"* (John 1:41). The great blessing that Peter brought to the early church, in part, can be attributed to Andrew. Let us begin to pray and share with others.

Our friends expect us to share our thoughts and experiences with them, and yet we avoid sharing our experience of Christ. It may be just a few words, but the Holy Spirit can show them their need for the Saviour. Our testimony is invaluable to the salvation of others. It may be something as simple as someone speaking to you about death, being afraid to die or asking why you don't appear to get stressed.

The great evangelist D.L. Moody aimed to speak to someone every day about the Saviour. What a revival would break out if each of us were to do the same, always being careful not to refer to religion in our conversation but to let our light shine before humanity. *"Let your light shine before others, that they may see your good deeds and glorify your Father in heaven."* (Matt.5:16). Have you shared the love of the Lord with your friends? Ask the Spirit to speak His words through you.

Prayer: *Dear Lord, don't let me miss an opportunity to let my light shine for You, that Your Holy Spirit might work through me to bring salvation to those I live and mix with every day. Amen*

DAY 239
MAKE EVERY EFFORT

2 Peter 1:5-8, *"Make every effort to add to your faith goodness... knowledge... self-control... perseverance... Godliness... mutual affection... love. For if you possess these qualities... they will keep you from being ineffective and unproductive in your knowledge of our Lord Jesus Christ."* NIV

God, by His glory and goodness, has given each believer divine power when He called us to be His children. He moved first, and now wants us to be partakers of His divine nature. We only have one life to live, and once each moment has passed, it will not return, so let us value every moment and live it with diligence, learning to grow each day in God's grace and live for Him.

By His Spirit, God has instilled in us the desire to live more like Him. Unfortunately, too many live a life of idleness. God calls us to live a life of diligence, making every effort to add daily to our lives, GOODNESS (moral excellence); KNOWLEDGE through reading and studying His Word; SELF-CONTROL, through being master of our nature; PERSEVERANCE, despite the adversities of life; GODLINESS, where our behaviour reflects God's character; BROTHERLY KINDNESS, through thoughtful consideration of others; and LOVE, seeking to build up and encourage others. These qualities of life will protect us from idleness and an ineffective life.

> *Put aside idleness and live an active, fulfilled life for God.*

"But whoever does not have them is near-sighted and blind, forgetting that they have been cleansed from their past sins" (V.9). If we want to have a fulfilled life, we must deny our personal choices, wills, and pleasures to reach the best life we can have for ourselves and others. Our greatest motivation to be faithful to Jesus will come when we understand everything that Jesus did for us. Our strength and joy will increase as His Spirit empowers us to put aside idleness and live an active fulfilled life for God.

How are you growing more like the person God wants you to be, and what can you do today to help yourself live a more fulfilled life for Jesus?

Prayer: *Loving God, please help me to live a fulfilled and diligent life for You in every way. Thank You for Your Spirit, who enables me to have the power to change. Amen*

DAY 240
WE ARE LOVED

John 11:6, *"When he heard that Lazarus was sick, he stayed where he was two more days."* NIV

It is clear at the beginning of this beautiful chapter of Scripture that Jesus loved Mary, Martha, and Lazarus, for He had stayed in their home on many occasions. The two sisters reacted no differently to how we would today. They immediately sent for Jesus, their dear friend, for they never doubted He would hurry to come and save Lazarus from death. They felt just as you or I would if a family member was near death and a close friend delayed in coming. Like them, we wouldn't understand why.

Without trials, there would be no trust, no faith, or no patience in life.

At the heart of this story, was Jesus's love. Today, at the heart of God's dealings with us, regardless of how painful our situation, we must trust our lives to God's unfailing and unmerited love. If a close friend or relative has a bad accident the waiting seems so long, as I experienced recently when I wanted to be with a close relative who was in a severe accident.

Jesus waited, not because He didn't love them, but because He did. His infinite love kept Him from hurrying to their home to help in their grief and sorrow. When Jesus arrived, Lazarus had been in the tomb four days, during which time the body had started to decay, and Mary objected to Jesus wanting the stone rolled away. This happened not long before Jesus's crucifixion, occurring this way so God's Son might be glorified (v.4), and they would believe that Jesus was the Messiah (v. 15). We can never know how much of our trust and faith can be attributed to the suffering and pain of life, for Jesus uses trials to develop trust, confidence, and patience in us.

I am the resurrection, and the life: he that believeth in Me, though he were dead, yet shall he live: And whosoever liveth and believeth in Me shall never die" (John 11:25-26). Jesus then asked Martha if she believed, and she answered, *"Yes, Lord, I believe that you are the Christ, the Son of God."* Do you believe Jesus is the resurrection and life, and He loves you and died to save you...?

Prayer: *Thank You Lord, that nothing can ever change Your love for us. We are loved, even though we live in challenging times on earth. Amen*

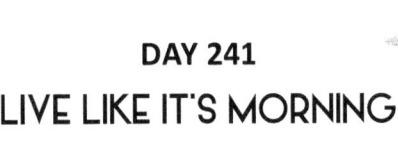

DAY 241
LIVE LIKE IT'S MORNING

Ephesians 5:8,10, *"For you were once darkness, but now you are light in the Lord. Live as children of light... and find out what pleases the Lord."* NIV

Imagine being in an elevator with other people. Suddenly it stops because of a power failure, and you are plunged into total darkness. Everyone gets anxious, and they all start talking at once. Suddenly amid the panic, you pull out your mobile phone and flash on the light. What a difference that light makes as you all wait for the power to come on. People talk pleasantly to each other, tell jokes, you even make friends and connect.

We are told that we are the light, not just like the light. Like the phone draws power from its battery, so we draw power from Jesus, our Saviour. As God's light in the world, we are told to find out what pleases the Lord, like calming fear and lifting the spirit of those who are suffering, but always making sure our light is turned on for all to see and be attracted to.

> Even when the world around us is like midnight, we are to live like it is morning,

When anyone is groping in darkness, trying to find their way, what do they want? They want direction, and you and I, as believers, must be the light that can help them find the path they seek. To be God's light, we must pursue what is good, right, and truthful, keeping our spiritual battery fully charged through Jesus, our source of power.

As Christ's followers, even when the world around us is like midnight, we are called to live like it is morning, although it may sometimes bring scorn on us. Let us offer ourselves as a fragrant offering in His service. *"Follow God's example, therefore, as dearly loved children and walk in the way of love, just as Christ loved us and gave himself up for us as a fragrant offering and sacrifice to God"* (Ephesians 5:1-2).

Prayer: *Thank You Lord, for a new day. Fill me with Your Spirit and power to let my light shine for You, showing Your beauty and love to those I meet every day. Amen.*

DAY 242
USE YOUR MONEY WISELY

2 Corinthians 9:7, *"Each of you should give what you have decided in your heart to give, not reluctantly or under compulsion, for God loves a cheerful giver."* NIV

Money and how we obtain it is a gift from God. *"Wealth and honour come from you; you are the ruler of all things"* (1 Chron.29:12). These words were spoken by King David, who, because he honoured God, went from being a humble shepherd to becoming the King of Israel.

> As we give ourselves to Christ, we will always have enough money.

We say we work hard for our money, and rightly so, but we forget it is God who gives us the strength to work. He keeps our positions for us and gives us the ability each day to carry out our work. Many of us can testify to God leading our lives through the positions we have held, and God has always provided for our needs. Even though you may not have been wealthy, you can say, *"I have never gone without anything I needed, and always had more than enough."*

God expects us to provide for our families and not squander our money on gambling, excessive alcohol or drugs etc. *"Anyone who does not provide for their relatives, and especially for their own household, has denied the faith and is worse than an unbeliever"* (1 Tim.5:8). It is also right to maintain a certain amount of capital to increase our business. When a man uses his money wisely, taking only what he requires as a legitimate profit, and then pays his employees a share of the extra, he is doing something more excellent than if he sold everything and distributed a small amount to a vast number of people.

We need to guard against the love of money by giving a certain amount to God's work. It can be easy to pay all our bills and then give God what is left over, but when His blessings come, we need to first set aside the amount decided, and then use the rest for our needs. As we give ourselves entirely to Christ, we can then decide what to give to God's work, and it will be no surprise that you always have enough, for God is no man's debtor. *"Who has ever given to God, that God should repay them?"* (Romans 11:35)

Prayer: *Lord, teach me how to 'gain' by giving and to 'find' by losing, according to Your word. Amen*

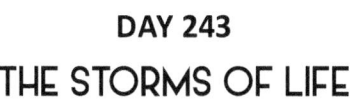

DAY 243
THE STORMS OF LIFE

Job 23:10, *"But he knows the way that I take; when he has tested me, I will come forth as gold."* NIV

The problems that Job was called to face seem impossible to most of us today as we enjoy the comforts of life. Job had all the comforts of life when God allowed Satan to attack him. God knew that Job's faith in his Heavenly Father would help him face and overcome the storms that Satan would bring into his life. Our faith grows amid storms when we cling to Christ as Job did.

God is faithful, but we must believe in the power of Almighty God and trust Him to bring the unseen into plain view. Only then will the impossible become possible because faith and trust deal with supernatural power. It is in the storms of our lives that there is conflict in the spiritual world around us between good and evil, and it is in such a conflict our faith, finds soil in which to grow.

It is in the storms of our lives that our faith finds soil to grow in.

I love giant eucalyptus trees standing alone in a paddock providing shelter for cattle. They are often gnarled and twisted because they have had to stand firm against the elements of climate and have endured the storms of nature. So, in the spiritual world, when we have to face our problems, we must remember to stand alongside Jesus and trust Him as He leads us along our path of suffering, sorrow or conflict until we become *"more than conquerors through him who loved us. "*(Romans 8:37).

In the middle of your storm you must go on. God is there to meet with you, to dry your tears, heal your wounds, and provide your need as He whispers His secrets that will help you come through with insurmountable faith that all the demons of hell flee from. You will be able to say with Paul, *"For I am convinced that neither death nor life, neither angels nor demons, neither the present nor the future, nor any powers, neither height nor depth, nor anything else in all creation, will be able to separate us from the love of God that is in Christ Jesus our Lord."* (Romans 8:38-39)

Prayer: *Lord, give me the faith of Job so that I never doubt that You can help me in every circumstance of my life. Amen*

DAY 244
LOVE RESTORES

John 21:16, *"Jesus said, "Simon son of John, do you love me?" He answered, "Yes, Lord, you know that I love you"* NIV.

Have you been pretending to be leading a devoted Christian life when in fact, you have failed in your relationship with Jesus? We must look within ourselves, as Peter had to, if we are to answer to our Lord. Many of us who call ourselves God's beloved, allow some secret sin to eat at the heart of our love for our Saviour. When Satan tempts us, we try to justify ourselves to our conscience, or we allow our unsaved friends to influence us to be involved in the pleasures of this world that we know will lead us away from Christ.

> *Our Lord restore us, with infinite love and compassion.*

These influences remind me of termites. They enter our home often through a very tiny hole or crack and begin eating at the very structure that holds the house together. The homeowner is totally unaware of the damage they are doing until something drastic happens to the construction of the house. Then they have a significant cost to fix the problem to rid the house of these invaders. Any new buyer of their home is then always suspicious of purchasing.

How like us. When we fail, there is always a cost, and we are despised by those around us who never seem to believe in total restoration. We may know of someone who has incurred shame or disgrace, and seen their lives destroyed by unforgiveness of others. But as in Peter's case, our Lord stoops to restore us, the outcast, with infinite love and compassion. Jesus always loves and always restores. *"Return to the Lord... I will heal their waywardness and love them freely, for my anger has turned away from them."* (Hosea 14: 2,4)

God knew underneath Peter's denial there was devoted love, and He didn't hesitate to ask Him to care for His flock. God's love and touch in our lives, can restore us to Him regardless of our sins. The one thing that Christ asks is that we follow Him. If you have been wayward, return today to Jesus because He wants to forgive and love you, restoring you to fullness of life. This is Redemption.

Prayer: *Dear Lord, forgive us our sins, for we would be Yours; help us to stay close to You so that we don't go our own way. Amen.*

*People go on chasing goals,
To prove something doesn't have to be proved:
they're already worthwhile.*
Spencer Johnson, M.D.

"*In him we were also chosen, having been predestined
according to the plan of him who works out everything
in conformity with the purpose of his will.*"
Ephesians 1:11

DAY 245
STILL AND SAFE

Psalm 91:1, *"Whoever dwells in the shelter of the Most High will rest in the shadow of the Almighty"* NIV.

I love trees, and there is something about a large spreading tree that seems to invite me to want to sit and rest in its shade. When I consider this verse, I receive a mental picture of being overshadowed by the Lord, and just relaxing and being still in the shadow of His love and care.

When busy, we feel accepted, important, and in control, because busyness helps us put aside our troubles and heartaches for a time. Often, we stay active because inwardly, we doubt that God can handle things for us without our help.

> In times of disturbance, we need to surrender to rest and realize our frailty.

In times of disturbance what we need is to surrender ourselves to rest and realize our frailty. The Psalmist tells us in v.9-11, *"If you say, "The Lord is my refuge," no harm will overtake you... For he will command his angels concerning you to guard you in all your ways."* Oh! What security is ours if we just rest and remain in God's presence?

Your path ahead may be long, uncertain, and overwhelming, but His love surrounds you. He hears you and stays with you, both now and forever. His faithfulness is ever sure. Read this encouraging Psalm every day for the next month, and your life will be changed through this song of faith. In Him is your dwelling place. Under His wings, you will find refuge, even among all your troubles.

Do you need to stop today and realize your frailty in the light of the love Jesus has for you?

Prayer: *Dear Lord, thank you for overshadowing me with your unfailing love. Please guide me and keep me close to you. Amen*

DAY 246
FAITH, REGARDLESS OF CIRCUMSTANCES

Psalm 106:12,13, *"Then they believed his promises and sang his praise. But they soon forgot what he had done and did not wait for his counsel."* NIV

Have you wondered how Moses coped with the unbelief and impatience of the Children of Israel as he led them out of Egypt. In Hebrews 11:27, we are told, *"he persevered because he saw him who is invisible."* Unfortunately for the Israelites, they only had faith when the circumstances surrounding their lives were favourable, but fortunately, Moses's faith enabled him to endure and plead before God on their behalf.

> As children of God, we need to believe first so that we can see.

Today many believers live intermittent Christian lives because circumstances surrounding them occupy their minds instead of being focused and centred on God. Like the Israelites, we are largely governed by circumstances and the things that appeal to our senses instead of having faith in our eternal God. Each day, we need to see God at work in our lives in everything that concerns us. Nothing is too small for His concern when we totally trust our lives to Him.

Like the Children of Israel, we fail to believe without seeing. It wasn't until they saw God work, that they believed. Remember how terrified they were for their lives as they stood on the banks of the Red Sea with the Egyptians in hot pursuit. They doubted until God opened the way, - *"then they believed."*

We have all heard the world say, *"seeing is believing,"* but as children of God, we need to believe first to see. Jesus said in John 21:29, *"blessed are those who have not seen and yet have believed."* Every invention known to man was a 'seeing' in the inventor's mind before it became something of substance.

St. Augustine said, *"Faith is to believe in what we do not see, and the reward of this faith is to see what we believe."* Do you believe and trust God no matter your circumstances or only when they are favourable? God sees the beginning and the end. We are to have faith and believe, then we shall see.

Prayer: *Spirit of the Living God, breathe into me faith to trust and to always believe and in all the circumstances of my life. Amen*

DAY 247
OUR DESTINY

1 John 3:2-3, *"We know that when he appears, we shall be like him, for we shall see him as he is. Everyone who has this hope in him purifies himself, just as He is pure."* NIV

We are forgiven and reborn through the blood of Jesus, to do good work that God has prepared for us, that we may partake of our highest calling to be like Jesus. In reaching our destiny, as Paul tells the Ephesians, *"Then we will no longer be immature like children. We won't be tossed and blown about by every wind of new teaching. We will not be influenced when people try to trick us with clever lies, that sound like the truth. Instead, we will speak the truth in love, growing in every way more and more like Christ, who is the head of his body, the church"* (Eph. 4: 14-15).

To be like Christ compels us to anchor ourselves to Him, bearing His name and bringing the truth to our fellow man. We must not be content to stand still but must grow in grace, patience, humility, spirituality and have a heavenly disposition of mind. All these qualities are only obtained through total commitment to Jesus, allowing the Holy Spirit to lead and guide our lives.

To be like Him is the destiny of every born-again Christian.

Here on earth, we can only imagine what it will be like to see Christ face to face, to be with Him in unbroken fellowship and to be like Him, - the destiny of every born-again Christian. We try to understand our future life, what our resurrection body will be like, how we will converse or what ministry we will have. For us to try to understand these things is akin to an unborn baby trying to understand what it is like to live in the world.

Meanwhile, we must continue to grow knowing that it will be enough to be like Jesus and to see Him face to face. Revelation 3:21, *"The one who conquers, I will grant him to sit with me on my throne, as I also conquered and sat down with my Father on his throne."* What an amazing destiny awaits us. Praise and glory to our Lord and Saviour, Jesus Christ.

Prayer: *Almighty God, how great is Your love for me that You sent Your only son to die for my redemption, to have a destiny that You alone can give. Praise and thanks be to You, my Jesus. Amen*

DAY 248
WHOSE SLAVE, ARE YOU?

Romans 6:16, *"Don't you know that when you offer yourselves to someone as obedient slaves, you are slaves of the one you obey."* NIV

I had a friend who though a Christian, had a habit that controlled him. Amazingly from the night he accepted Jesus as Saviour he had no desire for his habit anymore. Time passed, and I noted that whenever he had a crisis in life, he would return to his habit, give it up and return to it again the next time a crisis was faced.

> **Human power can't break the stronghold of something that enslaves us.**

The secret of being Christ's slave is obedience. When we yield to any desire that dominates either our soul or mind, we become a slave to ourselves. We say it's easy and okay because we can rid ourselves of our habit or addiction instantly, but when it comes to the test, like my friend, time and time again, we obey our desire once more. Without knowing the consequence, even a child will yield to selfishness, or a teenager will lust for anything attractive like money, or drugs.

Without total obedience to Jesus, these things can own them for life, often turning into more threatening situations. No human power can break the stronghold of something that has enslaved us. The only power that can help you, is the power of the redeeming grace of Christ through the Holy Spirit within you. Humble yourself before Jesus and seek His help to deliver you from being a slave to yourself. *"But now that you have been set free from sin and have become slaves of God, the benefit you reap leads to holiness, and the result is eternal life."* (Rom. 6.22)

Total commitment to Christ, is the only answer to breaking any self-indulged habit. We must remember that we are Christs by right, and only when we live our life with Him do we have perfect freedom. What you must ask yourself is, "Whose slave am I?"

Prayer: *Dear Jesus, I come and commit myself totally to You, to be Your slave and live each day aware of Your power within, to overcome being a slave to myself. Amen*

DAY 249
COMFORT IN GRIEF

Psalm 116:3, *"The cords of death entangled me... I was overcome by trouble and sorrow"* NIV.

When deep sorrow fills the soul of a partner, a close relative or friend, or a parent who has lost a child, it can be very difficult to minister to them. When a person is enveloped by grief, they can move into an empty and lonely world.

I remember comforting the mother of a teenage son, who was grieving deeply. Her son had been in a terrible accident. Sitting beside this dear Christian friend, I was lost for words. She talked, I listened, and we cried as she explained the whole awful experience and what she was feeling. We hugged and shared a time of prayer, then I came away wondering if I had been of any use at all. That day, I learnt that I did not have the answer for her grief, as I had not lost a child. Also, I realized just how important it is to listen when someone is grieving.

> The Lord is the only one who can dry our tears and comfort our soul.

The psalmist said, *"I called on the name of the Lord "O Lord, save me!"* (Psalm 116:4). The Lord is the only one who can truly dry our tears and comfort our souls when we grieve deeply. Isaiah 53: 4 says, *"Surely he took up our infirmities (sickness and grief) and carried our sorrow."* Jesus carried our sins, and still, He grieves for our life to be committed to Him.

The Word of God gives us proper perspective and hope, which is the very thing we can easily lose when we are overcome by grief or stress. We need to take comfort in knowing, *"God is faithful; He will not let you be tempted beyond what you can bear"* (1 Corinthians 10:13). The wonderful comfort is that death can never conquer those who die in Christ.

God is in control, and by trusting in the God of all comfort, we can heal, and together, with the psalmist say, *"O Lord, truly I am your servant; you have freed me from my chains... Praise the Lord!"* (Psalm 116: 16,19.). We have the assurance that one day we will be with them again if we are a believer in Christ and know Him as our Saviour.

Prayer: *Be with me Lord, for every day I need you. I need the strength to face whatever this day may bring. Please help me to overcome my grief. Amen*

DAY 250
SPRING IN THE HEART

Isaiah 35:1, *"The desert and the parched land will be glad; the wilderness will rejoice and blossom, like the crocus."* NIV

Just as the crocus plant waits on a barren hill, for the right time to spring forth in bloom, the very thought of God's presence will give hope of spring ahead for us. Three things will bring a sense of spring to our souls.

God's presence brings peace. During times of winter, those times of illness, depression, anxiety, defeat and sorrow, we are sure and know that God is near to fill us with His love and compassion.

> *Without hope, there is no life – Hope is victorious over despair.*

The optimism of boundless hope. Spring is the herald of hope. As I write these words, I am sitting on a hill of my forbear's settlement in Australia, looking out on drought impoverished land as it waits for rain. The farmers of our vast land always live, hoping that summer will bring the required rains to grow grass to feed the cattle and sheep, and grow the crops. Without hope, there is no life. As spring is victorious over winter, so hope is victorious over despair. Psalm 119:114, *"You are my hiding place and my shield; I hope in your word."*

The ingredient of love. Spring has always been and will always be a time of love. Love rules in the bush and the field as reproduction continues to clothe our earth. The birds build nests, animals reproduce, and even in our human world, spring is a popular time for weddings and births. We will know the excitement of spring as each day we trust in the love of Jesus for us.

We need to cherish the presence of God in every season of life, regardless of circumstances. We must hope in the boundless provision of God, conscious and thankful for love flowing into our lives and those we love. Our lives are not altogether what our circumstances are, for we can have everything the world offers but lack the joy of spring that comes to those who love God, or we can lack all the pleasures of this life but know the joy of being redeemed.

Do you give in to despair, or will you watch in hope as Micah did? *"But as for me, I watch in hope for the Lord"* (Micah 7:7).

Prayer: *Dear Father, may my life reflect spring to those around me as I put my trust in You and not in the things of this world. Amen.*

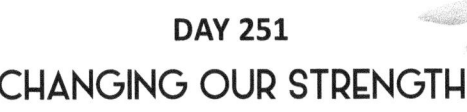

DAY 251
CHANGING OUR STRENGTH

Isaiah 40:31, *"Those who hope in the Lord will renew their strength. They will soar on wings like eagles; they will run and not grow weary; they will walk and not be faint."* NIV

At some stages in life, we can feel burdened and lose the will to go on. We feel the strain of life and want to give up. Our problems can come from many sources like finances, employment, family relationships, our partner, illness and we could go on to include anything that makes us feel defeated. There were times I felt like taking the easy way out of a situation by not being prepared to overcome the problem facing me, and so many times, I have returned to this verse for encouragement.

We can't alter our environment, but if we can just change our courage, and our power to endure, we are assured of victory. It always puzzled me why Isaiah talked of soaring, then running and lastly, walking when I felt it should be the other way around. The inevitable order is so, because firstly we need the courage and strength of the eagle to lift us to soar above our problems. Then, as we continue to renew our strength and we hope in the Lord, endurance kicks in, and we can begin to run and not grow weary. Lastly, with our courage and strength renewed and having gained the endurance that comes from God, we can walk in the power of God with hope and the assurance of victory.

> When we alter our courage and power to endure, then we are assured of victory.

Let us understand there is no burden, if we bear it with strength and endurance, that we will not have victory over, but first, we must claim the promise – *"Those who hope in the Lord will renew their strength."* Once we make that first step of hope in our Lord, we can be sure that our strength will be changed by God, and then the blessing to hear Him say in Isaiah 41:10, *"Do not fear, for I am with you; do not be anxious, for I am your God."* God's sustaining grace is sufficient.

Prayer: *You know Lord, how often I fail to maintain a balance in my life. Thank You that Your grace is boundless, and your faithfulness is unending. Strengthen me to walk each day with You that I will finish my life with joy and peace. Amen.*

DAY 252
THANKFUL IN ALL THINGS

1 Thessalonians 5:18, *"Give thanks in all circumstances, for this is God's will for you."* NIV

How can we be thankful when the plumbing is broken and no one is available to fix it, when we are being bullied at work or school or when our marriage is falling apart. Being thankful and contented in these and many other situations of life doesn't come easily, especially when the issue is outside our control.

> *God wants to be involved with us in our everyday problems.*

We can quickly become angry with those who caused our problem and even at times with God. Our attitude and mood changes, affecting our ability to have wisdom or understanding in the situation, and we can hurt those who don't deserve it. Let's stop and see what God's Word says because He is in control and wants to work through our circumstances with us. Romans 8: 28 tells us, *"In all things God works for the good of those who love him,"* and in 1 Cor. 10: 13 we read, *"Every test that you have experienced is the kind that normally comes to people."* Our God is the God of comfort and of the impossible.

God wants to be involved in our everyday problems. Nothing is too big or too small for Him. Tell God everything in your heart, unload on Him, your pain and pleasures, just as you would a close friend. He wants to hear about your troubles so He can comfort you. Tell Him your desires that He may guide you. Talk to Him about your temptations so He can shield you from them, being totally open and honest, for His desire is to love and heal.

Problems with our relationships, work, finances or even the little everyday inconveniences concern our Heavenly Father. God's love is not determined by our circumstances. His love is steadfast. Stop, and give thanks for everything to do with your life, knowing He cares for you.

Prayer: *Thank You Lord, that I can always depend on Your love and care in every circumstance. Thank You that You understand and affirm that You will guide and undertake all of my life. Amen*

DAY 253
KEEP LOVING

Exodus 31:11,14, *"Moses sought the favour of the Lord his God. "O Lord," he said, "why should your anger burn against your people…" Then the Lord relented and did not bring the disaster He had threatened."* NIV

Moses spent a long time on the mountain with God when he received the ten commandments. Meanwhile, the Israelite people had become impatient with waiting, so they took all their gold jewellery and had Aaron melt it to make a golden calf for them to worship. When I read this, I wondered how fickle these people were, yet unfortunately, we are often no different. The moment we become discouraged or frustrated about something, we take ill-advised action. Today, we see people becoming depressed, often taking their own lives as they fail to find help.

When God wanted to punish the Israelites, Moses went again to God and pleaded on their behalf, even though they wanted to stone him. In verse 22, we find Moses angry at Aaron for listening to the people, but Moses goes to the Lord again and pleads that the Lord forgive their sins. (v. 32) As we think about how Moses was prepared to put his life at risk to save his people, we are reminded how Jesus laid down His life for our sin.

We need to smile and be tough minded but tender-hearted.

We can choose to be like Moses and the other Prophets and plead for forgiveness of those we know and love, or we can choose to be like Jonah, who, when asked by God to go to the people of Nineveh, decided to run away and didn't care about them.

We must love our enemies and plead for their salvation, bring our loved ones to the throne of God every day and, denying ourselves, become obedient to our calling in Christ. As we serve others, we will know God's blessing. In Matthew 5:13, Jesus said, *"You are the salt of the earth."* If we lose our saltiness, we are no longer any good. In these days, when people are hurting mentally, we need to smile, be tough minded but tender-hearted.

Prayer: *Dear Lord, help me to love others for You, even when hate comes from them. Help me to find the satisfaction of serving You by helping others. Amen*

DAY 254
ALWAYS ACCEPTABLE

Galatians 3:3, *"After beginning by means of the Spirit, are you now trying to finish by means of the flesh?"* NIV

As we look back on each day we sometimes wonder just where we are and where Jesus has been in our lives that day. We know we have done things that make us fall short, like losing our temper, speaking unkind words, not being the spouse, parent or sibling we should be, or not listening when a friend needs help. We vow to do better tomorrow, but that is not the right approach. We cannot earn God's grace.

God's grace is free to all who believe.

In the first few verses of Galatians 3, Paul tells us that God continually fills us with His Spirit and works through us and we are always acceptable in God's eyes. We have done nothing to deserve His acceptance, yet we are clothed in righteousness, through the blood of Jesus and our trust in Him.

Abraham twice put Sarah's life at risk to save his own. In Genesis 12, he told Pharaoh that she was his sister, and then in Genesis 20:1-18, he again claimed her to be his sister. Like us, he just didn't learn; yet in Galatians 3:6, we read, *"He believed God, and it was credited to him as righteousness."*

Even if we distance ourselves from our Heavenly Father, hindering God's purpose for us, He can still use us because His ability does not depend on our good behaviour. God is always willing to work through us by His Spirit within us. We are saved and each day we need to choose to grow in His grace, not work for it. God's grace is free to all who believe.

Prayer: *Thank You Lord, that despite my failures, You still choose to use me because Your grace is sufficient for all my needs. Amen*

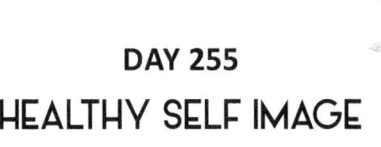

DAY 255
HEALTHY SELF IMAGE

Genesis 1:27, *"God created man in his own image, in the image of God he created him."* NIV

We are created in God's image. Stop and think what an incredible reality that is. We are distinguished from any other created beings. If we could recreate the perfect qualities through imagination to make us, we would find there would be a faint hint of the Creator. Your present self-image has been formed from past experiences. When we come across someone who seems superior, we under-rate ourselves, but psychologists tell us, this type of person often feels insecure and inferior, and their apparent superiority is just a cover.

We tend to cling to promotions, new clothes, awards, success, and many other things to give a feeling of a better self-image. These things are only temporary and will never fill the void in us. Your self-esteem does not come from what you do or own, but the understanding that you are a child of a loving Heavenly Father. When you grasp this, your appreciation of everyone else will help you realize that we are all equal in the sight of God.

> **The greatest self-image improver is to reach out to others.**

You must aim to find your authentic self, to make an accurate evaluation of just who you are. In Hebrews 2:7, we read, *"You made him a little lower than the angels; and crowned him with glory and honour."* If you believe in an all-wise, all-powerful Creator God, then you will understand that God is interested in you and only wants the best for you.

If we picture ourselves as a fear-haunted nobody, we must get rid of it and hold our heads high. We are not pathetic victims who need sympathy, but in God's eyes, each is someone through whom He can do great work. He sees us as someone full of love and laughter desiring to serve Him, so we must picture ourselves imparting help to others and start living our life God's way, thinking less and less about ourselves. The greatest self-image improver is to reach out to others. When our self-image is submerged, God's image shows. What is important, is not how people see you, but that they see Jesus in you.

Prayer: *Heavenly Father, help me to hold a steady picture in my mind of how You see me and to know that I am important to You every day, as your child. Amen.*

DAY 256
LET CHANGE OCCUR

Galatians 5:22-23, *"The fruit of the Spirit is love, joy, peace, forbearance, kindness, goodness, faithfulness, gentleness and self-control. Against such things there is no law."* NIV

Self-control for each of us is probably one of the hardest things to master, especially when we become Christians. Maybe, you have had some bad habits, like a wrong mindset or a terrible attitude, not to mention addictions, and deep inside even though you want to live like Jesus, you find time and again that you do not have the will or the ability to change. Maybe you have sought help or read self-help books, but the difficulty to overcome is still there. We have to move from living for ourselves to living life like Jesus and being filled with His Spirit.

> We must shift our focus from effort to surrender, living in submission and trust in Jesus rather than in self.

The wonderful news is that God knows just how you feel, and He alone has the remedy. *"Live in the Spirit, and you will not gratify the desires of the flesh."* (v.16). Even Paul knew what it was like to have conflict between the flesh and the spirit, and this is why he constantly reminded the early Christians to allow the Spirit to lead them. It sounds simple, but we must shift our focus from effort to surrender, living each moment in submission and trust in Jesus rather than in ourselves.

Each day we must submit to the Holy Spirit so that by His grace, He will gradually be able to produce love, joy, peace, forbearance, kindness, goodness, faithfulness, gentleness, and self-control in our lives. These are the qualities of life to be desired and we achieve as we allow the Spirit to lead us.

Are you ready to let change occur in your life? You can change because the Spirit of God lives in you. As you surrender to Him, He will produce His likeness in you.

Prayer: *Lord, please fill me with Your power to change and grow to be like You. I surrender myself to You; please take care of my life so that I might grow in Your grace. Amen*

DAY 257

FAINT NOT

Psalm 27:13, *"I had fainted, unless I had believed to see the goodness of the Lord"* KJV.

Sometimes in life we are called to lift our spirit above that feeling of, - *I can't do this any longer... or what can I do.* A friend struggled in her marriage for over 50 years, with her husband becoming irritable and very controlling, and as a result, she was feeling trapped. She said, *"I know God tells me not to faint, but what can I do if that is exactly what is happening to me."*

You may find yourself in a similar circumstance, where everything pushes you down, and you feel like you are fainting under the load. When you physically faint, you cannot do anything, and in your weakness, you collapse to the ground or on the shoulder of someone. You cease being yourself; you become still and must put your trust totally in another person.

Your trust will lift your shattered life to bring peace.

When we feel we are fainting due to sorrow or a relationship, it is then that our Heavenly Father wants us to lean hard on Him as He says, *"Be still and know that I am God."* For all of us, there comes a time when our life on earth draws to a close; the physical suffering and weakness prevent us from doing anything apart from lying still in God's arms and simply trusting Him to carry us home.

That is all your God asks of you regardless of the circumstance. Just be still, lean on Him, trusting Him for guidance, and you will find that the peace, born from conflict, is not like the hush before the storm but rather, the serenity and quiet that follows it. It is your trust that will lift your shattered life to bring confidence, safety and peace as you bow at the feet of Jesus.

My heart was sinking beneath the wave,
Of deepening stress and raging grief;
It seemed to me that none could save,
And nothing could bring my soul relief,
But He arose, I saw His face,
Then came a calm, filled with His grace.

Unknown

DAY 258
EXALT OUR GOD

Psalm 46:10, *"Be still, and know that I am god; I will be exalted among the nations, I will be exalted in the earth"* NIV.

One of our great joys is the worship of our God. Each of us has different ways of worshipping, but in every instance, we enter into the calmness of spirit where our soul reflects, as in a mirror, the majesty and glory of the Lord. When we exalt or highly praise the Lord, something happens in our soul that is very special. Some worship in song, some in reading and meditation of God's Word, or for others it may be a quiet place where we can be still as we reflect on the greatness of God.

Our God is perfect; let us exalt Him.

Going outside after dark and sitting still while looking into the heavens above, makes me realize just how awesome our Creator is and He loves us more than we can imagine. The Hebrew word 'still' means to cease striving. God wants us to come and worship Him in a spirit of praise with an inner stillness, so we do not miss that quiet voice of God's Spirit within us. In these moments, we will experience the power to deal with life's problems. When we are tense or stressed, the spiritual forces of the Holy God cannot work in our lives for our benefit.

Being still helps us meditate on God's many attributes, of always being faithful, always eternal, is all-knowing, just, unchangeable, gracious, holy, merciful, long-suffering, impartial and infinite. Our God is perfect so let us exalt Him. Yes, life on this earth can be unpredictable, and there are countless things we will never understand, but we have peace that God knows all and still loves us deeply.

Knowing this enables me to "be still" – I can be at peace and worship Him for who He is. Make time today to be still and know your God. Psalm 46: 1,7. *"God is our refuge and strength, an ever-present help in trouble. The Lord Almighty is with us."*

O worship the King,
All glorious above,
And gratefully sing,
His power and His love.

Robert Grant 1833.

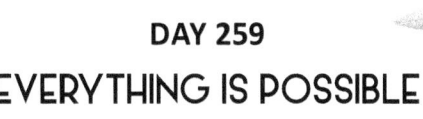

DAY 259
EVERYTHING IS POSSIBLE

Matthew 17:20, *"Nothing will be impossible for you."* NIV

The mustard seed is the smallest of seeds, but Jesus says that even if our faith is only that small, and we are willing to trust Him, the impossible becomes possible as we lead a life believing His promises and find truth and peace in each one.

It is possible- to have deep peace in every situation of life if we will come humbly and give everything that concerns us into His hands. *"Cast your cares on the Lord and he will sustain you; he will never let the righteous be shaken"* (Psalm 55: 22).

> **It is possible– to have deep peace in every situation of life.**

It is possible- to see with joy the will of God in everything, even the sorrows of life. *"He has promised to rescue us from the hand of our enemies, and to enable us to serve him without fear"* (Luke 1: 74-75).

It is possible- to become strong within by taking refuge in God's divine power through His indwelling Holy Spirit and be filled with the attributes that once were not part of our nature. *"But the fruit of the Spirit is love, joy, peace, forbearance, kindness, goodness, faithfulness, gentleness and self-control. Against such things there is no law"* (Gal. 5: 22-23).

It is possible- to have evil thoughts in our minds changed and cleansed to have pure and holy ideals. *"Therefore, if anyone is in Christ, the new creation has come. The old has gone, the new is here"* (2 Cor. 5:17).

If you allow the seed of God's truth in your heart to grow through the power of the Holy Spirit, you can have as much of God as you desire. Trust and reckon on His faithfulness to you. Christ has put the key of God's treasure in your hand to take as much as you want of Him. Whose fault is it if you allow yourself only a small portion of the riches God makes available to you?

Prayer: *Dear Lord, increase my faith to take hold of all You offer of Yourself to me. Give me this hour a sense of the power available to me through Your Spirit. Amen.*

DAY 260
SPIRITUAL SAINTS

Philippians 3:10, *"I want to know Christ and the power of His resurrection."* NIV

The spirit filled Christian never believes circumstances to be coincidence but that everything within the domain of their life is determined by the indwelling Holy Spirit. Their life is about knowing Jesus more profoundly every day!

> **We will never be perfect this side of heaven.**

Everything they do, whether work, play, or serving Jesus, is to enthrone Christ in their life and to bring the glory to God. When Jesus was here on earth, He knew His relationship to His Father even in the menial everyday tasks. The night before Jesus died, at the Passover feast with His disciples, *"He got up from the meal, took off his outer clothing, and wrapped a towel around his waist. After that, he poured water into a basin and began to wash his disciples' feet, drying them with the towel that was wrapped around him"* (John 13: 4-5). Very often in Christian service, we take the initiative purely because something must be done without realizing Jesus' part in the action.

We often forget that when we accept Jesus as Saviour, we become a saint of God even though we are still vulnerable to sin, and we will never be perfect this side of heaven. We are not here to realize ourselves but to realize and know Jesus. We must endeavour to be a spiritual saint, with our aim being *"to know Christ and the power of His resurrection."*

We must take our example from Paul, *"Forgetting the things which are behind,* (we can't change the past) *and straining toward what is ahead* (the future is available). *I press on toward the goal"* (Philippians 3: 13-14). Do you know Christ just where you are in your walk with Him?

Prayer: *Take my life Lord and let me be committed to realizing You every day and in everything I do. Amen.*

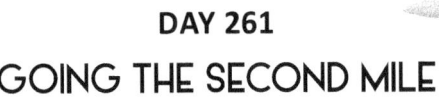

DAY 261
GOING THE SECOND MILE

Matthew 25:40, *"I tell you the truth, whatever you did for one of the least of these brothers of mine, you did for me."* NIV

Jesus identified with those who were hungry and homeless, the outcasts and those who were suffering. He told us to minister to these people as if we were ministering to Jesus himself. When we show compassion, sympathy, and kindness to others, He accepts it as being done to Him.

These words of Jesus remind me of a young friend who saw the need of a teenager and took her into her home, teaching her the skills of life that she had been deprived of in an abusive family situation. The teenager flourished under loving care and came to a place of giving her heart to the Lord. The personal ministry shown by my friend was no small cost to her own life, but in doing so, she was ministering to her Lord at the same time.

> When we show compassion, God accepts it as being done to Him.

We have all heard the saying; *give a man a fish, and you feed him for a day; teach a man to fish, and you feed him for a lifetime.* We must always be aware of those who need help, remembering that their outstretched hand is the hand of Christ. At the same time, we must also be mindful to help wisely so we don't encourage anyone to become lazy and careless.

In our scripture passage, Jesus tells how those who see a need and don't respond will be told to depart to eternal punishment. We must ask for the grace of the Holy Spirit to see and do the work of our God. When we reach out to others, our Lord will see it as payment to Himself.

Is there someone who needs your help today?

Prayer: *Dear God, help us not to be self-centred. May we always remember that our best and happiest life, is lived when we help others through their sorrows and trials. Amen.*

DAY 262
TRUST OR TROUBLE

John 20:29, *"Blessed are those who have not seen and yet have believed"* NIV.

Every day we allow ourselves to become burdened with things that surround and concern us, like relationships, work, sickness, and bad habits, to name a few. God also places unseen things in our lives that are steps to overcome and encourage us to climb to a higher level of trust and faith.

We don't need to fear but to trust God.

Remember Peter when he wanted to walk on water. To do so, he had to get out of the boat and walk, despite the fear he probably felt. He needed to trust more than be afraid. One of these emotions had to become greater, for it is the greater that will always win. Or take a little bird as it learns to fly. At first, it gets tangled in bushes, and unless it trusts the natural God given power within its wings to soar, it will never experience the joy of full flight but will stay entangled in the difficulties it sees around itself.

God has to bring you to see that you can't have the joy, peace and happiness that He has for your life while you continue to focus on your problems and rely on your own strength. Without losing his faith, Abraham saw his own body as dead and trusted God to give him many descendants. He had to look away from himself and trust God completely. Only then, he experienced God's promise to him.

God is always trying to show us precisely the same thing. We must learn to trust and surrender fully to Him if we are to experience the results, He longs us to have. It is then that His Spirit will become real, and we will know that we don't need to fear but to trust. *"God is my salvation; I will trust and not be afraid. The Lord, the Lord himself, is my strength and my defence, he has become my salvation"* (Isaiah 12:2).

Prayer: *Lord, help me believe in Your Word before I see or know what You desire for my life. Please help me to trust until I can understand. Amen.*

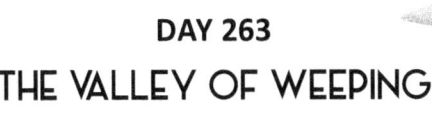

DAY 263
THE VALLEY OF WEEPING

Psalm 84:5-6, *"Blessed are those whose strength is in you, as they pass through the Valley of Baka* (weeping), *they make it a place of springs"* NIV.

It is possible that there wasn't any such place as Baka, but that it refers to the balsam tree that weeps resin. I experienced just such a thing happening after lightning struck the ground near six magnificent fox tail palms. At first, the palms seemed not affected, then a few days later, they started to weep their sap through their trunks, caused by the intense heat of the lightning flash. The sap had boiled inside the palms, and they eventually died, their pain being too great to bear.

For those of us who trust and worship God, we can expect at some stage of life to have to pass through great stress and grief, but as we bear the sorrows of this life, we can experience the incredible comfort that only comes from our Heavenly Father. This Psalm speaks of people whose strength is in the Lord and who long for the presence of their God. They *"cry out for the living God"* (v. 2). They put their trust in *"the Lord Almighty"* (v. 12).

> *Our valley of weeping will be an experience of the Lord's faithfulness.*

When night descends on the garden of our soul, and everything seems closed to our grief filled life and we weep, we must let the dew of heaven fall on our lives and trust God to bring us out of the valley. When we depend on Jesus in our time of despair and grief, our valley of weeping will become an experience of the Lord's faithfulness like we have never before known. *"My grace is sufficient for you, for my power is made perfect in weakness"* (2 Cor. 12:9).

> *When we pass through our valley of weeping;*
> *We can be certain our God will sustain.*
> *He'll be there to comfort and lift us*
> *Through all our sorrow and pain.*
> *Thank you, dear Lord, that we are assured of Your sustaining grace. Amen.*

DAY 264
THE PROMISE BOX

Psalm 119:49, *"Remember your word to your servant, for you have given me hope."* NIV

As a small child, when other Christians visited our home, after prayer together, each person present would take a promise from a special promise box and read it aloud. Most Christian homes had a 'promise box' in their living room in those days, and each day a promise would be taken from the box and claimed in the name of Jesus. Maybe today, we could reinstate this practise, by each day taking a promise from God's Word for our life.

> **The promise excites faith, which relies on fulfilment of the promise.**

Our faith and God's promises are closely linked, for the promise from God excites our faith, and faith relies on the fulfilment of the promise. 1 Chron. 17: 23,24 says, *"Do as you promised, so that it will be established and that your name will be great forever."* David came with bold faith and asked, knowing God would not be unfaithful to His promise. Our mistake is that we ask for things that have not been promised. We must be sure we ask according to what God promised in His word, for every promise carries a message for us.

"His divine power has given us everything we need for a Godly life." (2 Peter 1:3). Everything we need is already available to us in Jesus, but we must claim – His Precious Promises. Our God wants us to be filled with His very nature, a wonderful promise we struggle to comprehend.

We never need to be anxious when we come with a promise to God, for His everlasting faithfulness gives faith to believe in the fulfilment of the promise. For us, it's possible to accomplish every Precious Promise through our trust in His faithfulness. Every promise in the Bible is built on God's justice and holiness, preventing Him from deception, and His goodness preventing Him from forgetting His promise. Find God's promise for your need today and come to Him and claim it for your own!

Standing on the promises of Christ my King
Through eternal ages let his praises ring
Glory in the highest, I will shout and sing
Standing on the promises of God.

Russell Kelsa Carter – 1886

265 DAY
LIVING SACRIFICES

Romans 12:1-2, *"Therefore, I urge you, brothers and sisters, in view of God's mercy, to offer your bodies as a living sacrifice, holy and pleasing to God; this is your true and proper worship. Do not conform to the pattern of this world, but be transformed by the renewing of your mind. Then you will be able to test and approve what God's will is; His good, pleasing and perfect will."* (NIV)

Life can be a real challenge as we endeavour to live a life of sacrifice for God, and maybe this is why Paul doesn't command us but instead shows us the urgency to do so as an act of worship. To be able to live this way, we must allow Jesus to be the master of our lives, and that is only possible as we meditate on God's word each day, allowing the Holy Spirit to guide and help us. It is impossible to make progress to such a high calling without walking each day in the Holy Spirit. When we try to grow spiritually in any other way we conform to this world's patterns and methods of spiritual living.

You may ask, *"Why do I need to be completely given over to God? What is the benefit for me?"* God wants us to be holy and pleasing to Him, and without conforming to a life lived for Jesus, we cannot please Him. It doesn't matter how good we feel about ourselves or how much others approve of us; we will never have the happiness and maturity we can know without the daily renewal of our mind in the Word of God. Paul knew as humans; we need a constant daily reminder as we struggle to live God's way. The more we live in the light and walk in the Spirit, the more love and mercy will fill our lives and overflow to others.

> We need to renew our minds as we struggle to live God's way.

Today, there is an urgency to live this way. We need to understand that we please God when we renew our minds through His words, so let us live our lives as a sacrificial act of worship the way God wants us to, by being transformed daily.

Prayer: *Lord, forgive me for going my own way. Please help me to renew my mind each day through the words of Scripture and follow You in every way. Amen*

DAY 266
THE GIFT OF PRAYER

2 Corinthians 1:10 -11, *"On him we have set our hope that He will continue to deliver us, as you help us by your prayers."* NIV

I have always felt for those who have gone to foreign countries to bring salvation to the unsaved. We read or are told of the difficulties and persecution they face as they continue to work and speak the love of Jesus into the lives of those they live with. Alone, with no family or friends to talk to, I am sure there are days when they wonder, *'are people still praying for us.'* Paul tells us in 2 Corinthians 1, how the hardships and pressure they faced were beyond their ability to endure, to the point where they felt the sentence of death. It was their hope in God, and the prayers of the Christians of the church in Corinth that delivered them.

> *Praying for someone is one of the best ways to show love.*

It is wonderful to experience God working out His will in the lives of our family and friends, through prayers we prayed. During many years of married life, I can think of times when my husband and I differed in our opinion of things, yet as I prayed about our situation, God slowly brought us together on the same page where we could move forward in total agreement. God uses our prayers to accomplish His purposes in the lives of our families, friends and church. Galatians 6:2 *"Carry each other's burdens, and in this way, you will fulfil the law of Christ."* I am sure we can all think of times when we knew that our prayers were not in vain, and that God was moving in the lives of those we prayed for.

Praying for someone is the best way to show love because when we pray for them, we open the door for the help only God can provide. When we pray, we love them in His strength. Never be afraid to ask a person if they would like you to pray for them, as most people are happy for you to do this, and then God can work in their life to bring them salvation and blessing. God's love through your prayer is the greatest love of all.

Prayer: *Almighty God, thank you for the gift of prayer and the way You use it to accomplish Your purposes. Help me to always be faithful in praying for others. Amen*

DAY 267
THE SECRET OF GOD'S PRESENCE

Psalm 119:151, *"You are near, Lord, and all your commands are true."* NIV

As believers, we know God is always with us. Our world displays proof our God is near at hand. Every tree is covered with foliage in spring, and baby birds take flight from the nest, revealing to us our Heavenly Father's almighty presence. But are we always aware of it? We can go hours, even weeks and not notice or see God's hand in everything around us. We can even spend time at church or in prayer, and it's as though He is just a name, a tradition or dream of someone who lived in days long gone.

The story is told how Brother Lawrence, though a simple cook, never lost a sense of the presence of God, when preparing food for his fellow clergy or as he took a walk and noticed new shoots on the trees, he said to himself *"surely God is present."* David felt this also about everything around him, when he spoke of dwelling in the Lord's house all the days of his life. He saw God present everywhere and knew God's peace and power. (Psalm 27: 4-5)

We can know His peace in our troubles.

Jesus said, *"I have told you these things, so that in me you may have peace. In this world you will have trouble. But take heart... I have overcome the world"* (John 16:33). When we abide in Christ and understand that He is in us, we can know His peace in our troubles. Just as Moses saw God's power in a simple burning bush, we can also experience God's power as we enjoy the gentle breeze that cools the air, or in the daily chores we perform for our family. When we constantly commune with Jesus, we will know He is present with us every moment of the day. Realize that He is in you, and you are in Him. Hear God's words in 1 John 4:13 *"This is how we know that we live in him and he in us: He has given us of his Spirit."*

I woke up today with the rise of the sun; so many things just had to be done–
If I miss my prayer time today, my Father in heaven will know anyway.
I cannot; I will not; I'll get it right now, and before heaven's throne my
heart I will bow – It's evening now, and each task is complete.
Was it my own work, some kind of feat?
Or was it some kind of miracle…?

K. Cameron-Smith.

DAY 268
GOD'S IMAGE BEARER

2 Corinthians 3:18, *"And we, who with unveiled faces all reflecting the Lord's glory, are being transformed into His likeness."* NIV

As image bearers of Jesus, let us beware, of how much Christ wants us to be careful not to neutralize the purpose we were born for. We must keep ourselves living and moving in God's love every day to avoid becoming sidetracked. As we surrender to God, the Holy Spirit will transform us into the likeness of Christ our Saviour to reflect the glory of the Lord.

> **The Lord needs each of us to project His image to the world.**

He can use any one of us if we are willing to be the Lord's servant. Many years ago, I was privileged to sit and have coffee with now well-known evangelist Nick Vujicic. He was just a young man at that time, seeking to know God's will for his life. He surrendered his life totally to Christ's service despite being born handicapped. Today through speaking at rallies and using technology, it is estimated that over one million people have come to salvation through his ministry in the last 20 years.

Exodus 34:29, reads, *"Moses was not aware that his face was radiant because he had spoken with the Lord."* Moses had remained so long in the presence of God that God's glory transformed him. Despite Nick's rare physical disorder, he too, allowed God to change him and use him to bring many people to salvation. He is indeed an image bearer of his Heavenly Father.

The Lord needs each of us to project His image to the world. If, like Nick, we conduct our lives in the power of God's transforming grace, we will reflect Jesus, who died to save us all. Knowing you are God's 'image-bearer,' ask yourself; does my reflection of the Lord's glory help others see his love and care?

Prayer: *Thank You Father, for making me in Your image. Help me to reflect Your glory so that others may love You as their Saviour. Amen*

DAY 269
JESUS INTERCEEDS

Hebrews 4:14,16, *"Therefore, since we have a great high priest who has gone through the heavens, let us then approach the throne of grace with confidence, so that we may receive mercy and find grace to help us in our time of need."* NIV

Without Jesus, our prayers falter. As our Saviour, He is our helper and intercessor when we pray. His ministry throughout the centuries and today is intercession before the throne of God on our behalf.

My prayers are often far from perfect as I bring them to my Heavenly Father. As my friend and Saviour, Jesus takes my imperfect prayers, cleanses them of defects, corrects the faults and then claims their answer from His Father, my Father, according to His will.

Wait patiently, give thanks, and rejoice.

Friend, look up; your Saviour as Intercessor has already claimed your answer. Do not disappoint Him, give thanks for His answer. The moment you lose your trust and give up on His answer could be when victory is on its way. He has gone to God's inner chamber with your prayer in His hands, and the Spirit is awaiting your trust that He may whisper to your heart from the throne of God.

Sometimes we despair at the length of time that elapses, but we fail to remember that God knows best. Often, He must change our hearts so that we can rejoice and praise Him when the answer comes. Wait patiently, give thanks, and rejoice, for it is already done. Prov. 3:5-6, *"Trust in the Lord with all your heart and lean not on your own understanding; in all your ways acknowledge Him, and he will make your paths straight."*

Prayer: *Jesus, my Saviour and friend, thank You for bringing my prayers to the throne of Almighty God on my behalf. Help me to be patient as I await Your answer in Your perfect time. Amen*

DAY 270
ARE YOU SHORTSIGHTED?

Luke 19:9-10, *"Today salvation has come to this house. . . . . For the Son of Man came to seek and to save the lost."* NIV

When Jesus was on earth, He reached out to touch lepers and eat with outsiders and sinners. In our passage, we read how He reached out to Zacchaeus, a wealthy man who was the chief of tax collectors. A man probably hated by the people of Jericho, but Jesus put aside all dignity to speak with Zacchaeus and make him feel like someone special when He said, *"I must stay at your house today."* (V.5)

> **People want to feel accepted before they want to believe.**

Can you imagine how Zacchaeus felt? Something like you or I would feel if the King of England came to our home for coffee. He felt a sense of belonging, a sense that he mattered to the Master, and that made all the difference to his understanding and view of Jesus from that moment. He immediately repented and gave to those he had stolen from, and Jesus said, *"Today, salvation has come to this house."*

Let us be careful that our hunger for status doesn't stop us from seeing Christ as our true source of satisfaction. Our pride will blind us from seeing Him as Wonderful Counsellor, or the Prince of Peace in our anxiety. As a proud, rich, and anxious man these things prevented Zacchaeus from knowing Jesus, but when Jesus reached out to him, it changed everything.

There is incredible power in belonging, and the enemy uses this to reach and draw those within our circle away from Jesus, through those involved in this world reaching them first. People like to feel accepted before they want to believe, and we must reach them by making them feel important and wanted.

Let us reach out to those in our lives who are our untouchables and make them the centre of our attention so they will feel a sense of belonging and want the salvation that Jesus offers.

Prayer: *Dear Father, help me put aside all pride and dignity and reach out to those around me so that they may feel a sense of belonging and come to know You as Saviour and Lord. Amen*

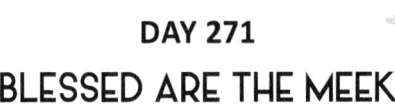

DAY 271
BLESSED ARE THE MEEK

Matthew 5:5, *"Blessed are the meek, for they will inherit the earth."* NIV

According to Luther, the meek man is a sweet-tempered man. Meekness and lowliness are two aspects of the same disposition, one toward man and the other toward God. Even though we are all born with a unique personality, we are not by nature meek, and must learn to be submissive at the feet of our Saviour, whilst being self-controlled and gentle when hurt by others.

Have you ever wondered why Jesus didn't fight back when He suffered? The true Biblical meaning of meekness is strength under control. Meekness is not weakness but strength, coming from a position of power with the intention of producing a positive effect on others. Jesus showed meekness toward His Father by being submissive to His calling and meekness to man by showing His willingness to be loving and gentle in spirit. He entrusted Himself to God and did not consider Himself of great importance. Surely, if anyone had a reason to boast, it was Christ as Saviour of the world.

Meekness is not weakness; it is strength.

Jesus also said that the meek would inherit the earth. There is a sense in which a person with a gentle and tender spirit sees beauty in the world of nature and man, that is hidden from the arrogant and proud. A millionaire may own a treasured painting which he is proud of simply because of its value, while someone he employs sees the beauty in the painting and feels inspired when they look upon it. Who really owns it? So it is that the meek inherit the beauty of God's creation.

True meekness comes from a close, committed relationship with God. Paul in Ephesians 4:2 says, *"Be completely humble and gentle; be patient, bearing with one another in love."* We must ask Jesus to control our proud, boastful nature through the Holy Spirit, asking Him to live, think and speak through us each day. As we live for Him, we need to allow the Spirit to take our envy, pride, anger, covertness, and malice and fill us with humility, to do a menial task for anyone.

Prayer: *Enable me, O God, to walk in humility, take from me all uncleanness, foolish talking, covetousness, bitterness, and anger. Make me meek as Jesus was, helping me to make peace, to heal the irritation of others. Amen.*

DAY 272
KEEP THE END IN FOCUS

Philippians 1:6, *"He who began a good work in you will carry it on to completion until the day of Christ Jesus."* NIV.

We all love hearing a child tell us what they want to be when they grow up. A doctor, a firefighter, a movie star, or even a missionary. Often as a parent, we can see traits in a child and feel that we know just what they will do well at. When Paul looked at the Philippian church, he saw a group of believers whom he loved and prayed for. He was confident they would continue to grow in their faith, believing that Jesus, who began the good work in them would continue it to completion.

Our faith requires spiritual energy and a fixed purpose to grow.

For each of us who believe, to continue in our faith requires spiritual energy and a fixed purpose to grow every day. If we allow the circumstances of life to control us, we will sink down under the power of evil. We have a natural desire to sin or can choose spiritual life in Christ in which we can rise and overcome the power of the tempter.

To do this requires spiritual energy, which Paul refers to in v.11, *"filled with the fruit of righteousness that comes through Jesus Christ."* The spiritual power in Christ is always available to us, but just as we must make the effort to turn on the electrical switch in our home to receive power, so we must make the effort to seek the infilling power of the Holy Spirit.

Where are you in the story of your life? Are you sinking under temptation, or are you growing each day in the strength of the Holy Spirit? It is a matter of choosing, believing, abiding and steadily walking each day with Jesus to be filled with the Spirit of God. Move forward to the glory and praise of God.

Prayer: *Jesus, You are in charge of my life, but I must make it happen. I surrender my life to you, asking for Your help to keep me trusting. Amen*

DAY 273
THE MINISTRY OF PRAYER

Romans 15:30, *"I urge you, . . . to join me in my struggle by praying to God for me."* NIV

It is impossible to live the Christian life through our own strength and goodness. Even the Apostle Paul found he constantly needed his fellow Christians to pray for him because it is only through God's strength that we can know courage, and by His power can know His goodness in helping us day by day.

Do you struggle with life in general and your ability to function daily? Life today is hectic, yet Paul often found himself in much worse situations than we experience, ending up in prison and being abused and persecuted for the work of bringing salvation to the unsaved. Naturally, he prayed for himself, but he also asked the churches he visited to pray for him. These churches became Paul's partners in ministry. Paul needed this prayer support because he knew the unbelievable power that prayer can bring as our Father moves through the Holy Spirit to answer the prayers of the saints. Before Jesus died, He prayed for His disciples, *"Holy Father, protect them by the power of your name."* (John 17:11)

> **Nothing is quite like knowing that others are praying for you.**

We all experience times when we feel alone in our pain, sorrow, or relationships, needing the support and prayers of others to feel the healing touch of our Saviour. Our prayer must be specific and come from our hearts rather than a repetition of words; only then will we experience God's strength within as we pray. When we intercede and agonize before God for others, it can be difficult to express ourselves, but God always understands.

If you need prayer do not be afraid to ask for it, as nothing is quite like knowing that others are praying for you as you feel God's loving arms around you. Put your confidence in God, and believe as you pray for others and yourself. You can become a prayer worrier today.

Prayer: *Loving God, thank you that we can pray for each other, and the assurance that You hear me and care for me and others that I pray for day by day. Amen*

DAY 274

FIRST, "GO"

Matthew 5:23,24, *"Therefore, if you are offering your gift at the altar and there remember that your brother or sister has something against you, leave your gift there in front of the altar. First go and be reconciled to them; then come and offer your gift."* NIV

In our walk with Jesus, the one thing we must be aware of is we can always have greater depth in our relationship with Jesus. This is not suddenly accomplished but rather a steady process. As part of the growth process, Jesus tells us to go and be reunited with our brother.

Truth is necessary in all our dealings with God.

There is a difference between memory and recollection. Memory is when we remember to do some task whereas recollection is the readiness, be it good or bad we can recall some memory from our past. In the quietness of time spent in God's presence, there can be a moment of quickened recollection as the Holy Spirit suggests something from our past that must be put right before we can move forward in our relationship with Him. If you have anything you are holding back from God, be sure the Holy Spirit will make you conscious of it as you grow in Him.

We must get along with our fellow man as the first step in acceptance by God. What is it your brother has against you? Is it that you lost your temper with someone, or because of hurt, hatred has resulted? Perhaps you have done something that you know needs to be corrected, or did you fail in helping when a need was before you?

Truth is necessary in dealing with God, and we must never disregard a conviction. If the Spirit brings something to mind, we know that He is wanting it put right. Within each of us, is a stubbornness to put it right because of the humiliation it may cause us, but God says, go and be reconciled first and then come to Me. If we want to be a disciple of Jesus, we must suffer humiliation by going to our brother or sister and putting it right. Is the Holy Spirit convicting you of something you need to put right with someone?

Prayer: *O Lord, give me a broken and contrite heart, help me to have the courage, despite humiliation, to put things right, that I might know Your forgiveness and peace. Amen*

DAY 275
WILL GOD ANSWER MY PRAYER

John 15:7, *"If you remain in me and my words remain in you, ask whatever you wish, and it will be given to you."* NIV

Jesus expected His Father to answer His prayers, and He taught his disciples (and us) in this scripture that we can obtain answers through prayer. When Jesus prayed, everything He asked for was to bring glory to His Father. You may know someone who lives to bring glory to God, which often seems to elude many of us. Like Jesus, our prayers that receive answers must be for the glory of God.

In this verse, God has promised, *"Ask whatever you wish and it will be given you. V8 This is to God's glory; that you bear much fruit."* From this, we see these verses are not a promise to answer every prayer we utter but that God will respond to our longing for personal growth in our spiritual life.

> Our spiritual growth takes time, so don't give up.

The fruit we are to bear is: *"The fruit of the spirit is love, joy, peace, longsuffering, kindness, goodness, faithfulness, gentleness, self-control. Against such there is no law."* (Galatians 5: 22-23) Are there any of these qualities that you need to ask the Spirit to help you achieve in your life?

Just like human growth, our spiritual growth takes time, so don't give up, keep on asking God to make you holy, in His time and at His pace, *"it will be done for you."* As we remain in God through prayer and study of His Word, He will begin to satisfy us, and we will find ourselves praising our Heavenly Father for the answers we receive.

Prayer: *Dear Lord, thank You for always hearing and answering my prayer. Please help me to keep praying, even when nothing seems right to me.*

*The purpose of human life is to serve,
and to show compassion and the will to help others.*
Albert Schweitzer

*" For we are God's handiwork, created in
Christ Jesus to do good works,
which God prepared in advance for us to do."*
Ephesians 2:10

DAY 276
GOD'S BLESSINGS

Isaiah 30:18, *"The Lord longs to be gracious to you; He rises to show you compassion. For the Lord is a God of justice. Blessed are all who wait for him!"* NIV

We can sometimes think of ourselves being here for God because of His death on the cross for our sins. More wonderful still is to visualize God waiting to pour out His blessings on us. For every believer, He has glorious purposes and blessings beyond anything we can imagine. In our human state, we ask, *'How is it, if He waits to be gracious that even after I come to Him and plead, He does not give the help I need but waits even longer?'*

Pause... and think of how He waited until his disciples were desperate, having exhausted every avenue before He released Peter from prison to them.

> *God's delays are never neglectful or unkind.*

Listen for His voice as He whispers: *"My grace is sufficient for you, for My power is made perfect in weakness"* 2 Corinthians 12:9. How often we misinterpret God's dealings with us? We ask and do not receive, and we conclude that He is strangely neglectful when all the time, He knows when we are spiritually ready to receive His blessing.

God's delays are never neglectful or unkind. His blessing will come at such a time so that we will have no doubt it came from Him. At such a time, our hearts will lift in praise, and the blessing will be doubly precious. Be assured that He will not delay one hour too long, surrender your situation to your loving Heavenly Father and wait expectantly but patiently.

Prayer: *Dear Father, forgive me when I rush ahead of You and tell You what I need and when I need it. Please give me the strength to be patient and wait for Your perfect time.*

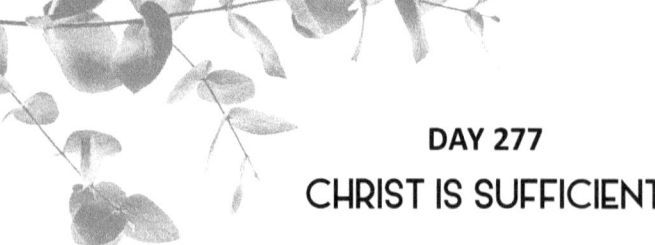

DAY 277
CHRIST IS SUFFICIENT

Revelation 1:8, *"I am the Alpha and the Omega,"* says the Lord God, *"who is, and who was, and who is to come... the Almighty."* NIV

As God's children, from the beginning of life until our death, there will be nothing that can touch us, that our Almighty loving Father will not supply the strength and grace to sustain us. Jesus is the only one who can sustain us in times of loneliness and sorrow. Most of us have experienced these emotions in life, and we know the sufficiency of Jesus comes as we depend on the fullness of Jesus in our lives. One may have a guide on an Alpine climb, but only as you experience his ability to cross ravines and glaciers that you can genuinely trust his ability and knowledge as a guide. So, it is only when we face loneliness or sorrow, we find in Jesus the complement of our need.

> **Our loving Father will always supply strength and grace to sustain us.**

In Eccles.7:3, we read, *"Sorrow is better than laughter, because sober reflection is good for the heart."* (NET.) When we sorrow, it can be God's way to reveal our very nature to us. It makes us think deeply, long and soberly about who we really are. Often God uses sorrow to help us to see other's troubles in a new light and be able to help them through their difficulty. Remember that God often has to break us to make us anew. *"Blessed are those who mourn, for they will be comforted"* (Matt. 5:4).

When John was in a lonely state, imprisoned on Patmos, God sent His angel to reveal His intention for His world (v17). When we are lonely, nearly always we will cry out to God for help. At a time like this, we can be confident of His nearness and comfort; Paul explains in Philippians 4:5-7, *"The Lord is near. Do not be anxious about anything... present your requests to God. And the peace of God, which transcends all understanding, will guard your hearts and your minds in Christ Jesus."* Yes, Jesus is first and last in our lives when we trust and love Him in our sorrow or loneliness. Let's stop for a moment and join with the heavenly host worshipping the Lord.

"Holy, holy, holy is the Lord God Almighty, who was, and is, and is to come."

Prayer: *Dear Lord, thank You that You are the Alpha and Omega of my life, Grant that I may always know Your abiding comfort. Amen.*

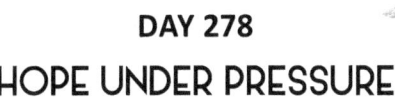

DAY 278
HOPE UNDER PRESSURE

2 Corinthians 1:8-9, *"We were under great pressure, far beyond our ability to endure, so that we despaired of life itself... But this happened that we might not rely on ourselves but on God."* NIV

Have you heard of the frog who immediately jumps free when dropped into boiling water. However, if you put him in lukewarm water and then gradually bring the water to the boil, the frog doesn't notice until it's too late. Let us beware to think and value our lives when under pressure, lest we fall into the same trap as the frog.

When David fled into exile because of the rebellion of his son Absalom, although under extreme pressure, still he encouraged himself, *"Why, my soul, are you downcast? Why so disturbed within me? Put your hope in God"* (Psalm 42:5). Amid the disappointment and pressures we face, there is always hope in God as we come to Him. Even if the pressure is of our own making, often bringing not only ourselves but our loved ones to complete misery, we can turn to God, who is full of kindness, and will always forgive us.

> Hope in God, even when you lose all hope in yourself.

After facing great trials in life with help from our loving God, it is like we have a new beginning. The pressure helps us to understand the hardships others face, enabling us to help and sympathize with them in a new and helpful way. We know God never changes and is there for us in everything we face.

Even when you have lost all hope in yourself, your friends, and circumstances, know that you can always hope in God. Trials and hard places are needed to drive us to trust and hope in God. When we come to Jesus in repentance, He will forgive, and we can put the past behind us, facing the present and future with God, who is ever willing to be our All-in-all. Then, like David, we will be able to say, *"Yet I will praise Him."*

Prayer: *Dear Father, teach us to trust Your love, which will lead us safely to the home You have prepared for us. Amen*

DAY 279
THE SCARS OF LIFE

Isaiah 53:5, *"He was pierced for our transgressions… and by his wounds we are healed."* NIV

We all have a mental picture of what and who we are, and it is greatly affected by the scars we have borne. Everything that has happened, our mistakes and successes, go to form our self-image. The image we hold in our mind and soul is the foundation upon which our personality, behaviour, and circumstances are built. Today we hear much about positive thinking, the medicine to change your life. Jesus warns against sewing a patch of new cloth on old garments because it pulls away and tears more. In the same way, positive thinking alone cannot be used as a crutch for changing old scars affecting your self-image. Positive thinking will only work for you when it is consistent with the image you hold in your mind.

Scars we suffer affect us spiritually, hence our good or bad self-image.

In the 1960s, Plastic Surgeon Maxwell Maltz, M.D., noted how superficial scars people experienced from accidents in life significantly affected their mental picture of themselves. Often their appearance would make them ashamed and depressed, but after plastic surgery, their whole personality changed for the better. He also noted, sometimes, even after surgery had changed their physical appearance, their mental picture of themselves and their personality would remain the same. He realized that people's scars are from mistakes and failures they identified with, concluding that "I am a failure." Maltz realized even though our Creator engineered us for success, the scars we suffer, deeply affect us spiritually, hence our good or bad self-image. The worst and greatest scars were experienced by Jesus for our sins, so we might have new life and spiritual growth when we trust Him as Lord of our lives. 1 Peter 2:24, *"He Himself bore our sins in His body on the cross, so that we might die to sin and live to righteousness; for by His wounds, you were healed."*

Regardless the emotional scars you have, Jesus will heal you when you trust Him and ask for His help to become whole and not a failure anymore. Then you can confidently say, *"My Lord and my God."* What emotional wounds do you need to bring to Jesus today?

Prayer: *Dear Lord, please help me to trust You to change the emotional scars of my life, so that I can live for You… to be who You want me to be. Amen*

DAY 280
HANDS OFF

2 Chron. 20:12,15, *"We do not know what to do, but our eyes are upon you. ….. Do not be afraid or discouraged. For the battle is not yours, but God's"* NIV

In 1 Chron. 13, we read how Uzzah lost his life simply by laying his hands upon the ark of God. He did it with every good intention to stop it tumbling as the team of oxen carried it along, but he touched God's work with overbearing confidence and died. Much of our life as Christians consists of leaving things with God. When we wholly trust something to God, we must keep our hands and suggestions to ourselves. God will do a far better job than we can.

Throughout my life, there have been times when I faced what seemed an impossible problem, and I often wished it would go away. That is not the way of life, so I had many sleepless nights because I would pray asking for God's help, but I would continue to sort out a solution for myself. Why do we always think we have the answer if only God would listen? We tend to treat God like someone who is supposed to go, fetch, and deliver our requests. Regrettably, we do not understand the true nature of prayer and what is even more tragic, we don't even know that we don't know! LET GO AND LET GOD!

We treat God like someone who is supposed to go, fetch, then deliver.

We must understand God requires us to bring our problems to Him, stop worrying, and let Him take control. Then look forward in expectation and be thankful that He has already heard and answered our prayer. We must have faith to believe whatever must happen for our benefit will occur. Then we will be able to improve our quality of life. In Philippians 4:6, Paul tells us, *"Do not be anxious about anything, but in everything, by prayer and petition, with thanksgiving, present your requests to God."* Only then can we be at peace while we await with expectation. Sometimes we receive what we ask for, but often when the answer materializes it is so much more than we could ever have imagined. Clarence Smithison once said, *"Faith is the ability to see the invisible and believe in the incredible,"* and that is what enables believers to *"receive what the masses think is impossible."*

I am perplexed. I say, 'Lord, make it right!
My trembling hands may shake, but yours Lord, make no mistake.'

Unknown

DAY 281
NEVER FORGOTTEN

Isaiah 49:15, *"I will not forget you."* NIV

Sometimes when we get up to face our day, we can genuinely feel forgotten. This was exactly how I felt one morning as I came to spend time in my Lord's presence. Today, was the first anniversary since my husband had gone home to heaven. After nearly 54 years of living and working together, times like this can really bring us low.

> His scars from the nails bear the names of each of us.

As I opened my Bible to read about when God restored Israel, I read, *"Can a mother forget the baby at her breast and have no compassion on the child she has borne? Though she may forget, I will not forget you."* It seems impossible that a mother could forget, but unfortunately, rare though it be, we know that this is indeed true. Far above the love of a mother is God's love for each of us, yes, even for me on this day. What comforting words to know that God never forgets us? I sat down, and as I let these words minister to my heart, He lifted me to face the day ahead.

In verse 16, God even tells us, *"I have engraved you on the palms of my hands."* Yes, His scars from the nails that fixed Him to the cross bear the names of each of us. What love and peace He gives even on our worst days. He is closer to us than anyone on this earth because His Spirit is within us to comfort and restore us each day. After time with God, I rose, and with the Psalmist, was able to say, *"This is the day the Lord has made; let us (me) rejoice and be glad in it."*

My friend, come to Jesus and then go forward in life knowing that God said to you, *"I will not forget you."*

Prayer: Thank you Father, that You never forget me. All I have to do is come to You knowing You will comfort and bring peace to my heart. Amen

DAY 282
SELF SACRIFICE

2 Peter 1:3, *"His divine power has given us everything we need for a Godly life through our knowledge of him."* NIV

There were two porcupines who lived in Alaska. When they needed to get warm, they got close to each other, but naturally, they needled each other. When the hurt became unbearable, they would move apart, but then they got cold again, so once more they tried getting close, only to find that they needled each other again. Life for them was either hot or cold.

Isn't this just like us, especially in our families? Our personality differences irritate and hurt each other even though we love them and desire to be close. We must work at our relationships by asking God to show us where we need to change so we can show Christ-like qualities of love, understanding of each other's views, and compassion to have a forgiving spirit. Let us strive to,

> *Build others up by seeing them through the eyes of Jesus.*

"Be completely humble and gentle; be patient, bearing with one another in love" (Ephesians 4:2).

Jesus' love and compassion teach us that these things are possible even in our families. Though foreign to our nature, understanding and self-sacrifice can be part of our character as we wait on the Lord for His Spirit to reveal them through us. Can you imagine how the home atmosphere would change if we all had an attitude of self-sacrifice, showing as total unselfishness? This does not mean letting others walk all over us but building each other up by seeing them through the eyes of Jesus. They, in return, will understand and love us more.

Self-sacrifice, as Jesus demonstrated, can change, and transform our relationships at home and work, especially for those who don't yet know Jesus. He wants us to take our eyes off our needs, have self-control, and be gentle, kind and loving. Then we will reflect Jesus, seeing change in ourselves and our loved ones. Have you shown love to those closest to you today?

Prayer: *Lord, I come and humbly ask that You change me from within so that I might have self-control and freely show love and compassion to those I love. Amen*

DAY 283
STRENGTH IN GOD'S GRACE

2 Timothy 2:1, *"Be strong in the grace that is in Christ Jesus."* NIV

Abraham Lincoln was commander-in-chief of the Union armies during the American Civil War, where the penalty for desertion was execution. Lincoln had great empathy for the soldiers who had lost their nerve and given into fear in the heat of battle. He pardoned them despite the frustration it caused the Secretary of War. His empathy endeared him to his soldiers, resulting in them loving and wanting to serve Lincoln even more.

We must know our strength comes from God's grace.

When Paul wrote to Timothy, he told him to be strong in the grace of Christ because Paul knew without God's unmerited favour, Timothy would be unable to endure the hardships of living his Christian life and staying obedient to the Saviour. Paul told him *to "Do your best to present yourself to God as one approved, a workman who does not need to be ashamed and who correctly handles the word of truth."* (v.15)

Living our Christian life today is no different, for to live as Christ's soldiers, we need to know where our strength comes from, drawing daily on God's grace. When we depend on Jesus, who is full of grace, our trials become lighter, and we find peace as we trust in God, even when our journey is painful and wrought with daily problems.

We must always be aware, *"God's grace IS sufficient for all our needs."* (2 Cor. 12:9). This is fact, and we must be careful not to turn His grace into hope or prayer but accept it as reality. Only then will we find the power we need as we believe and take God at His word.

How can the grace of Christ become a strength for you to serve Him as Timothy did? Pauls calls us to be set apart for Christ, by pursuing faith, love and peace, and to serve Him out of a pure heart. (v.22) God will reward our faithfulness to Him.

Prayer: *Dear God, please strengthen me in the grace of Christ, that I may serve You faithfully every day. Amen*

DAY 284

SIMPLY OBEY

John 12:46, *"I have come into the world as a light, so that no one who believes in me should stay in darkness."* NIV

Jesus makes a deep impression on us of what is right, convicting us of sin and God's will for us. How can we know Christ better, and there is only one answer; believe He loves you, believe He died on the cross to save you, and believe He is prompting you by His Spirit to follow Him for a better and holier life. Before we entrust our lives to any leader, we like to know about them, regardless of their promises of better days ahead, but Christ tells us to obey Him first, and He will undertake as we put our trust in Him.

Astronaut Frank Borman on the first space mission to circle the moon, was unimpressed with the drab pockmarked surface. He became bored and tired until one exhilarating moment when the earth rose from behind the moon, reflecting the bright rays of sunshine on its surface. When we trust and surrender to Jesus, the light of His love will be reflected on others to inspire them. *"The light of God's love shined within us when he sent his matchless Son into the world so that we might live through him"* (1 John 4: 9).

> *The best way of understanding Jesus is simply obeying His word.*

Hear Him say, *'don't shirk from what I have asked of you,'* or *'you must bear your cross for Me,'* or *'finish well the job I have given you to do?'* You may not have associated it with Christ, yet do not doubt it is His will and you will be blessed for your obedience. Only through obedience will you know Him and be led on to greater works for your God. Mary told the servants at the wedding, *"Whatever He says unto you, do it!"* She knew there was no better way of understanding Him than obeying Him. Our greatest joy comes as we allow the light of His Spirit to shine through us.

Jesus said, *"You are going to have the light just a little while longer. Walk while you have the light, before darkness overtakes you"* (John 12: 35). What is our problem? We can believe amazing things about space, yet we fail to go all the way in our belief of our Creator. Hear Jesus say, *'my child, believe, and you will find Me!'*

Prayer: *Lord, help my unbelief that I might forsake everything I am, both great and small, for Your love and guidance. Amen.*

DAY 285

THE DIVINE ART OF COMFORT

Isaiah 40:1, *"Comfort, comfort my people, says your God"* NIV.

Some people have a God given ability to come alongside others in times of need. Our world is full of hearts desperate for comfort. As a child I lived in the country, and my mother would often walk for miles to help another mother to be able to care for their child's sickness. She seemed to have an innate understanding of just what to do.

> *Jesus loves you just as you are; your struggles, sufferings and tears become His pain.*

God calls us to extreme costly training. Those who bring comfort have usually gone through struggles and tears as they learned through their own problems to become a comforter for their Lord. They have learnt to be comforted by the Spirit of Almighty God in their own darkest hour so they can comfort the aching heart of those in need. Only through the lavender flowers being crushed, is the sweet perfume released into the air, and so it is for those who comfort others.

Do not become distressed and wonder why you are passing through unbearable sorrow. It is a unique experience to realize that Jesus loves you as you are and that your struggles, sufferings, and tears become His pain. Psalm 27: 14 says, *"Wait for the Lord; be strong and take heart and wait for the Lord."* As time passes, God will bring many others in need of comfort to you so that you can tell them how you suffered and were comforted by your Lord. As you tell others how the Lord wrapped His arms around you and lifted you above your suffering, you will have the great pleasure of seeing hope in them as they too, trust Him for comfort.

God has called you to suffer, so praise your Heavenly Father for the suffering filling your life with an abundance of experience and helpfulness for others. God comforts us so we can become comforters to others, never so that we can be comfortable.

Prayer: *"Hear my prayer, O Lord; let my cry for help come to you. Do not hide your face from me when I am in distress. Turn your ear to me; when I call"* Psalm 102: 1-2.

DAY 286
GOD OR ME

Ecclesiastes 2:10-11, *"I denied myself nothing my eyes desired; I refused my heart no pleasure... Yet when I surveyed all that my hands had done and what I had toiled to achieve, everything was meaningless, a chasing after the wind."* NIV

Life for the majority, is all about Me, my popularity, my self-image, my self-esteem and my self-realization. With modern technology of many instant platforms, we are continually bringing ourselves to the fore as we post our hour-by-hour activities whilst failing to interact personally with friends and relations.

Unfortunately, our focus on self has led our society to a personal fulfilment world of pleasure and emotion. We spend hours stimulating our bodies through sport, diet and workouts but spend very little or no time on the condition of our souls and mind.

Beware of the religion of self and the material world.

Whilst physical exercise is important for a healthy body which is the temple of the Holy Spirit (1Cor.6:19), in our search for health, we often try to turn our bodies into eternal youth. Paul warned us in Philippians 2:3, *"Do nothing out of selfish ambition or vain conceit, but in humility consider others better than yourselves."* By lavishing ourselves with everything and placing so much emphasis on self, without realization we are being manipulated by the pleasures of the world and are not thinking about our spiritual relationship with Jesus or love and care for others.

Let us beware of the religion of self and the material world, which is gaining new ground every day, and let's begin to focus on the words of the teacher in Ecclesiastes 12:13-14, *"Now all has been heard; here is the conclusion of the matter: Fear God and keep his commandments, for this is the duty of all mankind. For God will bring every deed into judgment, including every hidden thing, whether it is good or evil."*

Is your life reflecting the God you serve?

Prayer: *Dear Father, please help me to keep myself from vain conceit and each day humbly seek to help others for You. Amen*

DAY 287
SET FREE BY THE SON

John 8:36, *"So if the son sets you free, you will be free indeed"* NIV.

When we think of someone being set free, we tend to think of those who have been in bondage to substance abuse or some form of addiction, but each of us has our demons that we try to hide. We live in a world of fear, jealousy or anger, just to mention a few. Some of those serving time in prison are freer than some of us. *"In the same way, count yourselves dead to sin but alive to God in Christ Jesus"* (Rom. 6:11). The great preacher D.L. Moody once said, *"I have little sympathy that Jesus saves us, just to leave us in a 'prison'. He has come to deliver us from our temper, passions, and lusts."*

> **Jesus has come to deliver us from our temper, passions, and lusts.**

Are you a professing Christian but are still enslaved to sin in your life? How often do you lay awake at night tormented by memories of things like temper, fear, or jealousy that you have tried to change but could not? Do you often feel chained by such emotions? If you want victory over your sins, you must know Christ more deeply, for He is the only one who can release the hold and grief you suffer from these demons.

When you accept Jesus as your Saviour, He forgives the past. You must accept that He has forgiven your past and not allow the torment to continue, and when temptation comes, ask God to fill you with His power to overcome and to have the freedom that He died for and longs to give. Only then can your darkness within become light, and your guilt become a confirmation of your glorious liberation when you are truly set free from prison, knowing that you don't have to fear what tomorrow will bring.

Praise the Lord, Jesus has set you free from the past and in Him alone, you can know total freedom.

Out of my bondage, sorrow and night,
Jesus, I come, Jesus, I come;
Into thy freedom, gladness, and light,
Jesus, I come to thee.

William T. Sleeper 1887

DAY 288
DON'T PUT OUT THE FIRE

1 Thess. 5:19, *"Do not put out the Spirit's fire."* NIV

When we receive forgiveness of our sins through trust in Jesus, God fills our souls with the Holy Spirit. In Romans 8:9, Paul writing to the church says, *"You are not living the life of the flesh, you are living the life of the Spirit, if the Holy Spirit of God really dwells within you."* If we receive the Holy Spirit at the time of Salvation, what is happening in us that Paul is saying *"if the Holy Spirit really dwells in you."* Where have we gone wrong?

As God's children, the Holy Spirit always lives in us. He is our Comforter that came to live within when we were born again. We often want to have control rather than allow the Spirit to guide us in how we live. When we are unforgiving, or we doubt, don't tell the truth, or worry, this grieves the Spirit because we fail to delight in the peace and joy, He desires to impart to us. When we grieve Him, it is like we put out the fire of His ministry in our lives.

> *Continually surrendering to God, or you will miss the breeze.*

Our soul is the centre of our personality. From our soul we look at two worlds, the material world through our organs of touch, sight, smell, taste and hearing, and to the spiritual world, through our conscience and intellect. From one, we can descend to the material and through the other, ascend to a relationship with our Creator God. We must make a choice. The voice of the Spirit as He speaks to your soul can be as gentle as a breeze, but unless you continually surrender to God, you may miss His voice. Is there something God has spoken to you about, yet you continue to go your own way? If each time the Spirit speaks, you ignore Him, eventually He stops speaking.

Whatever is 'prompting' your soul to change, deal with it through the power of the Holy Spirit within you. He can lead you to walking and living daily in Him to enjoy love, joy, peace, patience, kindness, goodness, faithfulness, gentleness, and self-control, that He longs to give you. Paul says in Galatians 5:16, *"I say then: Walk in the Spirit, and you shall not fulfil the lust of the flesh."*

Prayer: *Dear Lord, forgive me and lead me by Your Spirit. and help me not miss what You are saying to me each day. Amen*

DAY 289
THE POWER OF STILLNESS

Romans 15:33, *"The God of peace be with you all."*

Psalm 46:10, *"Be still, and know that I am God."* NIV.

Something that has always struck a chord within me is when singing songs of worship; suddenly, there is an emphatic pause. Not being a musical person, I will often start singing again before the right time, but the pause is there with a purpose. It allows the singers to shift their attention from one event to the next and also help us remember the tune and lyrics. In life, we experience a pause in nature just prior to the storm erupting with force.

Pauses in life make us aware of something to come.

We all need to pause! These pauses in life make us aware of something to come. When the Psalmist bids us to be still, we experience the source of all strength when we wait in the quietness and confidence of the presence of Almighty God. It is a time of peace where the tranquil nature of our Lord invades our life. A place where we can dwell alone with God in eternal stillness. *"My peace I give to you. I do not give to you as the world gives. Do not let your hearts be troubled and do not be afraid"* (John 14:27).

Regardless of the business and movement of the world around us, we must be on guard lest we rob ourselves of that place where we can dwell alone with our Lord in stillness, that place where we experience the deep peace God longs to give. Guard your soul against unconfessed sin, worry, and lack of control over selfishness and anger, because these are the things that will destroy God's peace in our lives. *"Let the Peace of God rule in your hearts."* Your desire for God's peace, must act as your umpire in the conduct of life.

Having *"made peace through his blood, shed on the cross,"* (Col. 1:20), be still and listen for the gentle whisper of your Lord, who alone can bring God's peace to guard your heart and mind.

Prayer: *Lord, I humbly ask that Your Peace will guard my heart and mind and rule within me, that out of Your Peace, I will move forward to serve others for You. Amen*

DAY 290
THE KINGDOM TO COME

Psalm 2:6,12, *"I have installed my king on Zion, my holy mountain... Blessed are all who take refuge in him."* NIV

This Psalm is about the reign of Christ, and in the first three verses, we see the nations of the world planning revolt. Throughout history, nation has fought nation, but combined, there's always been denial of the authority of Jesus. No matter how rebellious humanity is, we will never alter the Divine Purposes of God.

Think back two thousand years ago, Jesus said to a group of ordinary men, *"Follow me."* Imagine being one of them; like us, they had jobs, families, and friends, and none of them probably expected their life to change so quickly and completely. Over the next three years, the teaching and wisdom of Jesus, His authority and power, and finally, His death and resurrection would forever shape every aspect of their lives. Sadly today, many who claim to be followers of Christ believe that they can be a follower of Jesus without being like Him... a follower who doesn't follow. They want to know Jesus and not change anything about their lifestyle. Being a follower of Jesus isn't hard, but it affects everything about you. Luke 6:14 says, *"Everyone who is fully trained will be like their teacher."* At this point in time, would you call yourself a faithful follower of Christ?

> There has always been a denial of the authority of the Messiah.

Following Jesus is not about rules but about loving and enjoying life with Him. *"If you love me, you will keep my commandments"* (John 14:15). Love for, and obedience to Jesus cannot be separated. The Sonship of Jesus is an eternal fact, and as He ascended to His Throne in Heaven, He called for His followers to change the world through the indwelling Holy Spirit, bringing all praise and glory to God. For those who are rebellious it is madness to dream of doing our own thing and ignoring God's purpose for us. *"Serve the Lord with fear and celebrate his rule with trembling... or he will be angry and your way will lead to your destruction"* (Psalm 2:11-12). If you are not following Jesus, take His outstretched hand in love and forgiveness, and shelter in Him from the judgement to come for the disobedient.

Prayer: *You have commanded that I love you with all my heart and soul, all my mind and strength. Lord, grant me the perseverance to obey You. Amen*

DAY 291
REFINED FOR GOD

Malachi 3:3, *"He will sit as a refiner and purifier of silver; he will purify . . . and refine them like gold and silver. Then the Lord will have men who will bring offerings in righteousness."* (NIV)

> He sat by a fire of seven-fold heat, as He watched the precious ore,
> Closer He bent with a searching gaze as He heated it more and more,
> He knew that you could stand the test, and He wanted the finest gold
> To mould as a crown for the King to wear, set with gems of a price untold.
> So, He laid your life in the burning fire, though you would have said to Him 'Nay,'
> And He watched the dross that you had not seen, as it melted and passed away.
> The gold in your life grew brighter still, but your eyes were so dim with tears,
> For you saw but the fire -- not the Master's hand,
> as you questioned with anxious fear,
> Yet your gold shone out with a richer glow, as it mirrored a Form from above,
> That bent o'er the fire, though unseen by you, with a look of ineffable love,
> As He waited there with a watchful eye, with a love that is strong and sure,
> And your life did not suffer a bit more heat, than was needed to make it pure.
>
> James M. Gray

> *Only love would allow us to go through the trials of life.*

From these beautiful words, we can understand how valuable we are to our Heavenly Father. Only love that would dare to die to redeem us would allow us to go through the trials of life, so that we are fit to be jewels in the Master's crown. His love will always extinguish the fire in our lives when we are His dear children. Let us look to Jesus, our wonderful friend and see Him reflected in our lives as He removes the dross.

Prayer: Thank You Lord Jesus, that Your love and grace are always sufficient for all my needs. Refine me that I will be fit for Your crown. Amen.

DAY 292
JESUS EQUALS LIFE

Hebrews 1:3, *"The Son is the radiance of God's glory and the exact representation of his being, sustaining all things by his powerful word. After he had provided purification for sins, he sat down at the right hand of the Majesty in heaven."* NIV

Jesus is an exact replica of God and came to reveal God to us. When we look at the life of Jesus and what He did, we see what God is doing. John 5:19 says, *"Very truly I tell you, the Son can do nothing by himself; he can do only what he sees his Father doing, because whatever the Father does the Son also does."* Jesus is full of God's compassion and speaks His words, for He is God.

When Naaman, captain of the army of the King of Aram, was sent by the King's maid to the prophet, he told Naaman to bathe in the Jordan river to receive healing from his leprosy. He at first refused because, to him it seemed foolishness. However, when he humbled himself and bathed, imagine how stunned he must have been when he was healed. We serve the same God, who healed Naaman, and yet if God told us to do something that we saw as foolishness, I wonder if we would obey, ignore, or even argue with God?

> Allow God to break you so He can make something beautiful of you.

To have the fullness of life that Jesus gives, we must be willing to obey. Before we can have life, there must be death. Jesus had to die to give you and me eternal life, and we must be prepared to allow God to break us from our old ways so that He can make something beautiful of us.

Sometimes being broken means experiencing grief, disappointment, or sickness, all of which we see as tragedies, but the Lord of life sees them as opportunities to be used for His glory. Only after we experience brokenness can we know the love of Jesus in all its abundance as we surrender to His leading in our lives.

Are you prepared to allow the Lord to break you, so you can experience the fullness of life in Jesus?

Prayer: *Jesus, forgive me for all the times I have said no to You. Please help me to be willing to obey Your leadership in my life. Amen.*

DAY 293
TRUE RELIGION

Matthew 15:16,18, *"Jesus said, "Are you still so dull? The things that come out of the mouth come from the heart, and these make a man unclean"* NIV.

Jesus confronts His disciples with what it means to have 'true religion.' In the very fact of their ignorance, they appeared innocent. This is like so many today. Most people haven't done anything they consider sinful, like mentioned in verse 19 – sexual immorality, theft, slander etc. They remain in what they believe, a pure state of mind, believing they are innocent, but are really ignorant that we are born sinners and need the forgiveness of Jesus.

We do not have to remain ignorant and miss God's gift of eternal life.

Like His disciples, we are afraid of what Jesus' death reveals within each of us. We prefer to remain ignorant and innocent whilst appearing pure rather than giving Jesus complete control of our life. Whilst ever we choose to take refuge in our innocence, we are heading for eternal disaster and death. The only thing to protect us from eternal death is the safety of Jesus's blood shed for us when He took our sin and willingly died for our forgiveness.

True religion is a personal growing relationship with Jesus through the Holy Spirit and trusting your life to Him. Jesus showed us how to have a personal relationship with God when He lived on earth. He prayed, attended the Synagogue and Temple services, constantly referring to Holy Scripture and lived in unbroken fellowship with His Father.

If constant fellowship with His Father was necessary for Jesus, how much more for you and me. We can have the Divine Nature that Christ had through the Holy Spirit. We do not have to remain ignorant and miss God's gift of eternal life but ask forgiveness and live our lives for Jesus. Psalm: 40:4 says, *"Blessed is the man who makes the Lord his trust."*

Prayer: *Here I am, Lord, in my sin and ignorance of what You did for me. Please forgive me and fill me with Your Holy Spirit, and take my hand and lead me to experience Your peace in my life. Amen*

DAY 294
LOOK BACK

Deuteronomy 8:2, *"Remember how the Lord your God has led you all the way."* NIV

When we accept Christ as Saviour, our Christian life and faith begin without certain evidence of God at work in our lives, but as the years pass, we know and understand the leading of God's Spirit. It is an excellent exercise to look back and see how God has brought together the many facets of our lives to bring us to where we are today.

In Deuteronomy 9, God reminds the Children of Israel to look back, to remember who led them and fed them for forty years as they wandered in the desert, despite their distrust and grumbling. Likewise, He will surely supply our needs and care for us, to find when we allow Him, there will be no lack in our lives. Look back on your life...

> Look back and be amazed at what the Lord has done in your life.

Its sins and backslidings – leave them behind and go forward in new life in Christ. **Its discipline** – sent to correct and strengthen. **Its trials** – to allow God to deliver so that we may glorify Him. **Its loneliness** – to enable His love and peace. **Its temptations** – to know God's protection. In all your life experiences, God has been humbling you and testing you (v.2), teaching you (v.3), caring for you (v.4), and disciplining you (v.5). Jesus has done all this to make you the person you are. Romans 8: 27-28 *"The Spirit helps us in our weakness... The Spirit intercedes for the saints... In all these things God works for the good of those who love Him."* The living Lord Jesus is praying for you today.

Yes, it is good to look back and see what the Lord has done, so give praise and commit yourself to serve and worship Him. Put your hand in His and walk with Him to bless the world around you.

Prayer: *Lord God, be with me yet; don't let me forget – please don't let me forget! Amen.*

DAY 295
AMBITIOUS FOR CHRIST

2 Corinthians 5:9, *"We make it our goal to please him, whether we are at home in the body or away from it."* NIV

When we know and obey God, we have meaning and purpose to our lives, giving us opportunity to be ambitious within the sphere of our faith. The natural abilities the Lord has given us, He will direct to worthy actions, so we don't have to aim for the world's applause. We must motivate ourselves to be ambitious for those things worthy of holy achievement. *"Make it your ambition to lead a quiet life... and work with your hands."* (1 Thess.5:11)

Obeying God gives purpose to life.

Ambition in our daily work requires us to quietly mind our own business and work diligently with our hands to do the best job we can. What we do is unimportant, but our attitude to what we do is what matters. The early Christians had great expectation of the end of the world taking place in their lifetime. This often resulted in surrender of their occupations, making them restless instead of living ordinary lives and showing Christ's love to others. Let us be careful not to let the unrest of our world today, whether social or pleasure, cause us to stop living our life every day for Christ. We must be ambitious to please God, because on judgement day, He will weigh the worth of our mortal life. Day by day, the Lord judges our character and looks at the worth of our life both here and after death. We must endeavour to be well-pleasing to Him both in this life and the next.

The ambition of our Christian life should always be to share the good news wherever possible. We are surrounded by people from all walks of life who do not know that God loves them. Our greatest ambition is to bring them to Christ, whilst remembering what we do for God must always be by the power of the Holy Spirit working through us. *"I will not venture to speak of anything except what Christ has accomplished through me."* (Rom.15:18) If we are to achieve our ambition in Christ's work, we must please Him, by spending more time in His Word and His presence.

Prayer: *Give me grace, dear Lord, to be ambitious and work while it is still day and there is opportunity to share Your love with others. Help me to be aware of the work of Your Holy Spirit within me as I care for those around me. Amen*

DAY 296
DEPENDENCE ON GOD.

Psalm 28:7, *"The Lord is my strength and my shield: my heart trusts in him, and I am helped"* NIV.

David knew where his strength and power came from when he cried out to God as he was being pursued and was alone for so long. As Christians, we are also strengthened by the Holy Spirit in our inner being, but we often fail to acknowledge God's strength and draw on it. The strength and power that is ours in Christ can never be exhausted.

When Moses blessed the tribe of Asher, he said: *"As your days, so shall your strength be."* When God blesses us with spiritual strength, we will be strong in our will, our affection, our ideals and our achievement.

We can rely on the Lord to give the necessary strength to go on.

When we go through life's trials, we can always rely on the Lord to give us the necessary strength. He will give us strength to overcome our difficulties and not be afraid, and strength that can only come from Him when our life is filled with sorrow and pain. Sometimes we need God's strength to just stop and meditate on His word to receive what He has for us.

When a tiny baby or child suddenly takes ill or has to have major surgery, the parents feel powerless, and their only resource is to rely on the strength of their God. To have to sit and wait requires tremendous power from God.

Why do we fail to draw on the strength and power our Lord waits to give us? We must come to our Lord in complete surrender and ask Him to take care of our situation instead of trying to work it out ourselves. He will then bless us with His strength and power.

Prayer: *Forgive me Lord, for so often trying to achieve in my strength when you want to help me. Lord, I surrender myself to you and ask you to take care of every situation in my life.*

DAY 297
SLOW BUT VICTORIOUS

Matthew 13:32, *"Though it is the smallest of all seeds, yet when it grows, it is the largest of garden plants and becomes a tree."* NIV

Through technology of our age, we see people like recording artists, rise to the top of the charts very quickly. We have become obsessed with being successful and becoming rich. Even the products we purchase are not made to last, so we have become a society where we just buy another. The big and dramatic, or the quick fix, is what life for so many has become. In Psalm 78:2, we read prophecy about Jesus, *"I will open my mouth in parables."* Jesus used parables to help the people understand the life He wanted to impart to them through His salvation. In this parable, Jesus talks of the smallest of all seeds growing into a large tree. Just what did He want them to understand?

God can make something great of you, just as a large tree can grow from a small seed.

This parable is a comparison of God's kingdom. God takes something like a mustard seed and gradually makes something like a great tree, or he takes a person, someone of insignificance, and makes them, over time, someone filled with God's love and compassion for others. Someone who others want to come to, to help them find God's love for them, just as the large tree grown from the small seed shelters the birds of the air. Unlike products today that don't last, when we grow our lives in Christ, we will continually help others.

God's kingdom is also like Jesus. His life on earth was humble, helping and healing others. Like the seed that was buried to become a great tree, Jesus also died, was buried, and rose to be victorious over death and since then has been building His kingdom through those who shelter in His love and extend His salvation to others. It is our Lord who gives the shelter, not us; we are only like the branches that others can come to the Lord through. What seemingly small thing can you do that will encourage and bless those around you?

Prayer: *Thank You Lord, that you would consider using me to bless and encourage others. Help me see little things I can do to build Your great kingdom. Amen.*

DAY 298

HE LIVES! HE LIVES!

Daniel 6:20, *"Daniel, servant of the living God, has your God, whom you serve continually, been able to rescue you from the lions?"* NIV

Our God is the living God of today, just as He was thousands of years ago... since before the beginning of time! Our God is still Sovereign and power beyond our understanding, He still has the same everlasting faithful love for each of us who love and serve Him, and He will still do for us just what He did for those like Daniel. Through the Scriptures, numerous verses tell this, yet it often seems that this is the very thing we lose sight of in our daily life.

In our darkest moments, let us never lose sight that He is still the living God, and we can come confidently to Him for deliverance. When we trust without doubt, we can be assured that in the greatest difficulty, the most challenging trial, the deepest sorrow or even man's persecution, He will sustain us by His grace and give us peace.

> **Talk to your Saviour as easily and naturally as if to a friend.**

Isaiah 41:10 says, *"Fear not, for I am with you; Be not dismayed, for I am your God. I will strengthen you. Yes, I will help you, I will uphold you with My righteous right hand."* This must be our hope for ourselves and also for humanity.

Daniel served God faithfully. He walked and talked with God as we would with a close friend because He knew without a doubt God was beside him. This must have been a comfort for Daniel to know that regardless of how he felt, God was with him. I wonder if he was amazed when Jesus revealed His presence by shutting the lion's mouths. What an amazing God we serve.

Is Jesus so real to you that He is continually in your thoughts? Do you talk aloud to Him throughout your day when you are alone, at work, driving your car, at home or anywhere else? Talk to your Saviour as easily and naturally as if to a friend until the reality of His presence becomes part of your everyday life.

Prayer: *My Jesus, I am grateful that You live within my heart. Help me to make You part of my every thought and every action until Your presence becomes a moment-by-moment reality for me. Amen*

DAY 299
TROUBLESOME ME

Romans 7:19,25, *"For I do not do the good I want to do, but the evil I do not want to do - Thanks be to God, who delivers me through Jesus Christ our Lord!"* (NIV)

It has been said with wisdom, *"The person I have the most trouble with is the person I see every day in my mirror."* Which of us has not grieved over our own spiritual shortcomings? We will experience this grief if we have not yet learnt the full power of the Holy Spirit within.

> *Just as Satan doesn't have power to cast out Satan, man's will cannot put off its own evil.*

No one was more conscious of this than Paul. Let us not take comfort in that but beware and careful not to allow ourselves to become trapped in Satan's snare of despair, which hinders us having the benefit of the unlimited grace of God. Just as Satan does not have the power to cast out Satan, man's will cannot put off its own evil.

When we learn to come to our Heavenly Father every day, handing over our inner selves to the Holy Spirit, we can become *"more than conquerors through him who loved us"* (Romans 8;37). Whilst ever we try to fight the conflict in our own strength, we will experience the ups and downs of our lives that Paul speaks about; continuing to do what we don't want to do. Who has not experienced failure again and again, despite your endeavours and strenuous desire to conquer your problems?

There is only one way to get rid of *"troublesome me."* We must know that the Spirit of Jesus is prepared to renew us inwardly day by day (2 Cor. 4:16) and set us free from sin that chokes us within. For each of us to experience the power of the Holy Spirit in overcoming, we must have daily renewal. Every day, we must seek by faith a fresh infilling of the Holy Spirit that our Heavenly Father delights to bring to us.

Prayer: *Dear Lord, may I live very near to You each day, not by my own energy or resolution, but by the indwelling of the Holy Spirit. Teach me the benefit and amazing experience of abiding in You continually. If I stray, please recall me before I go too far. Amen.*

DAY 300
CO-OPERATING WITH GOD

Luke 5:7, *"They signalled their partners in the other boat to come and help them, and they came and filled both boats so full that they began to sink."* NIV

How exciting it would be when you went fishing if the boat was so full it couldn't hold your catch. For a person who likes fishing, there is nothing like the thrill of the catch. You want to continue fishing because you cannot see just what is there and always hoping for bigger and better fish. If only, as Christ's fishermen, we got so excited, that we were out there living and witnessing for our Saviour each day. But this work requires co-operation.

Firstly, the disciples had washed their nets, so they were prepared with clean nets ready to fish when Jesus told them to set sail to catch fish. We must always be prepared with pure hearts to respond to the Lord's command. *"Those who cleanse themselves... will be instruments for special purposes, made holy, useful to the Master and prepared to do any good work."* (2 Tim. 2:21)

> We must obey, even when Jesus asks something that doesn't make sense.

Even with a small task, we must be ready to obey. Jesus told Peter to only go a little way offshore. Maybe He was testing Peter's trust, because He knew the demands that Peter would have on his life later on. Peter didn't fail, and immediately made his boat available to the Lord. Likewise, when we offer Jesus our life to use in His service, He won't fail to supply our every need.

Even though the disciples had fished all night and caught nothing, they did not hesitate to obey, even against their better judgement. Nobody knew those waters better than the fishermen, but Jesus knew the blessing they would receive through obedience. *"At Your word, I will let down the nets!"* We must never fail to obey, even when Jesus wants us to do something that just does not make any sense.

So many fish! They called others to come and share the catch. Sometimes we need the help of our brothers and sisters in Christ. We can share the joy of seeing other saved by working together for God. Let us commit to co-operating with God, as together we work for the salvation of others.

Prayer: *Dear God, help us to be prepared to allow You to work through us so we might see those around us come to know You as their Saviour. Amen*

DAY 301

TIMES OF SORROW

2 Timothy 1:12, *"I know who I have believed, and am convinced that He is able to guard what I have entrusted to Him for that day"* NIV.

There comes a time in life when we must say goodbye to those we dearly love, even though, as Christians, we know that we will meet again in the future. I would like to share my experience with you in hopes that it may help you in your hour of need. For eight plus years, I watched his health deteriorate. There were times of frustration when I could see something that would help, but he failed to comply. There were times of sadness as I watched him struggle to move about. Times when I wanted a break from it all. During these times, I shed many tears before God as I asked His help to cope with everything. In all this, the most important thing was I learnt more deeply how much I needed the courage, love and self-discipline Paul talks about. *"God did not give us a spirit of fear, but a spirit of courage, of love and of self-discipline."*

> We know that we will meet in the future.

Sadly, his last two years he spent in care as I could no longer manage at home. This was partly relief but also a feeling of failure and guilt; I had always managed, so why a problem now? God has a plan and always sees the big picture. For both, those years proved to be for our spiritual growth. Each day as I visited, we read God's Word and prayed together as God showed us both things we had not seen in His Word before. It was a time of being dependent on God, which drew me closer to Jesus. Each day I saw God's amazing love and grace in our lives as He prepared us for the parting that was to come.

Not all of us have time with the Lord beforehand. For me, it was special and different to when my dad was suddenly taken in an accident. I became more aware of Jesus with me, so it was almost as though Jesus stepped in to fill the gap when the final day came. Yes, I still missed my husband and grieved, but Jesus was there to take the weight to help me through. If you have lost a loved one, I grieve with you and pray God to strengthen your faith. In your grief, know that just as God gave me comfort and peace, He can do it for you. I cannot explain my experience, except to say, *"God's grace is sufficient for you, for God's power is made perfect in weakness"* 2 Corinthians 12:9.

Prayer: *Thank You Lord, for Your comfort in times of sorrow. Amen*

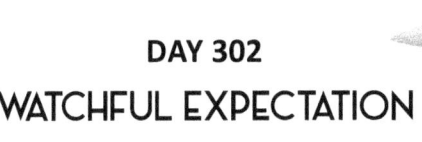

DAY 302
WATCHFUL EXPECTATION

Psalm 62:5, *"My soul, waits silently for God alone, for my expectation is from Him."* NKJV

Consider Paul when he went from Damascus to Jerusalem to proclaim the gospel to people he had persecuted. In Acts 22:17-21, we read how some were telling him to stay, and others were telling him to go, or he would be killed. As he went to the temple alone to pray and wait on God, he clearly heard the Lord tell him, *"Go; I will send you far away to the Gentiles."* Paul did not expect the Lord to speak these words to him, for he thought God would have him convert the Jews.

We must expect and be watchful on our part, so we receive the help we desire. If we are not alert to God, watching for our Lord's coming, and His hand at work in daily events of life, we will miss His voice to us. Imagine if you were to go to your bank to receive cash, you walk in, lay your card down on the teller's desk and then pick it up and walk out without having received the cash; people would think there was something wrong with you. The bank is there to receive your card and give you money, and under normal circumstances, you do not leave until you receive your request. When we plead God's promises before His throne, we must have common sense and expect God's answer, just as Paul did.

> **We must watch for God in the daily events of life.**

Many of us play with prayer, for we do not expect an answer. Our Heavenly Father wants us to do business with Him when we pray and expect to hear from Him. Like when Paul went to seek God's response to his prayer and did not expect the answer he received, we must come to realize that when God answers differently than we ask, He is doing something better for us than we could imagine. We must be like Paul and obey, knowing that God will not ignore our expectations but that we will hear from Him. John 8:32, *"And you will know the truth, and the truth will set you free."*

Prayer: Thank You Father, that you are ever waiting to do business with me, showing and teaching me Your ways. Help me to pray with expectation and be watchful for Your answer. Amen

DAY 303
FROM DARKNESS TO LIGHT

Luke 18:41-42, *"What do you want me to do for you?" "Lord, I want to see,"* he replied. *Jesus said to him, "Receive your sight; your faith has healed you."* NIV

What is it in your life that disturbs you most, that thing that you want changed but you seem powerless to do anything about? Perhaps it's a habit that needs change, maybe sin or illness, or even a bad relationship that you just can't let go.

God can do the impossible as naturally as one breathes.

Like the blind beggar, who, even though he could not physically see, possessed spiritual insight to recognize who Jesus was and called out, never let go of the disturbance that causes you pain until it brings you face to face with Jesus Himself. Even when common sense says, "What you want and ask is impossible." Do not listen to your common sense because you will remain exactly where you are. Just as when Jesus asked the beggar, *"What do you want me to do for you?"* the beggar had the faith to believe in the impossible and did not hesitate to accept the power of Jesus to heal. If in its present form, your disturbance is not something impossible for you, then it is not a genuine disturbance. Our God can do the impossible in our lives.

When we have the spiritual insight to realize and see Jesus as the Almighty, He does the 'impossible thing' within us as naturally as breathing. The impossible thing each of us face is to be so in touch with our Lord that nothing remains of our old life. Our agony comes because we won't obey, we won't believe, we won't cut the chord with our disturbance, and we just prefer to keep worrying about it.

What is your disturbance that you need to put in Jesus' hands? Seek God's help today.

Prayer: *Dear Lord, take from me anything that's stopping me from coming face to face with You, that I may gain the spiritual insight to believe in the impossible. Amen*

DAY 304
STAND STILL AND SEE

Exodus 14:13, *"Stand firm and you will see the deliverance the Lord will bring you today"* NIV.

God gave this command to Moses as the Israelites stood on the shore of the Red Sea in great fear of the Egyptian army pursuing them. These words are also the command God gives us when we face impossible difficulties.

When we have no way to retreat or move forward and feel defeated, our Lord's word to us is *"Be still before the Lord and wait patiently for him; do not fret when people succeed in their ways"* (Psalm 37:7). It is at such times that Despair whispers, "give up," but God wants us to be cheerful and courageous, rejoicing in His love and faithfulness as we wait for His overcoming power.

We hear Cowardice say, *"go back to your old ways; being a Christian is just too hard, and God isn't answering your prayer."* If you are a child of God, you cannot risk following Satan back to the worldly ways. Your Lord has said, *"I will strengthen you and help you; I will uphold you with my righteous right hand"* (Isaiah 41:10). He wants to lift you from strength to strength, even strengthening you while you wait patiently for His answer.

> In times of uncertainty, or doubt, you must wait for your Lord.

As you wait, do you hear your mind telling you to *"stand still and wait is sheer idleness."* Too often we take this road instead of waiting for God, who will not only help but will come through and do. *"Now to him who is able to do immeasurably more than all we ask or imagine, according to his power that is at work within us"* (Ephesians 3:20). Your boastful faith tells you to march into it and expect a miracle, but faith doesn't listen to your presumption, or despair, or cowardice, but to God, as He says, *"be still."* Keep yourself alert, expecting further orders, patiently awaiting God's direction, and it will come as it did to Moses when He said, *"Go forward."* In times of uncertainty or doubt, you must wait for your Lord without any force or action on your part.

> *Be quiet! Why are you anxious about your tangled ways?*
> *God knows them all. He gives speed, and He allows delays.*
> *It's good for you to walk by faith, so just trust awhile*
> *Then you shall reap the full sunshine of His smile.*
>
> Unknown

DAY 305
I AM COMING!

John 14:3, *"I will come again and will take you to myself, that where I am you may be also."* NIV

Throughout history, it has been revealed and told to humanity that Christ will return to earth to take those who love him to heaven. Jesus made it clear to his disciples He would come back but the day and hour are unknown to anyone. In the 21st century, we have become very complacent about Christ's return. Civilization has seen many great disasters, wars, and terrorism, yet Jesus still lingers. I clearly remember my mother-in-law telling me she nearly didn't get married because everyone was sure of Christ's return after the Great War (1914 -1918.) People have tried to predict this event, but we can be sure that each day is one day closer.

The question is – Are you ready?

More important than when is the question: Are you ready? Yes, you say, I have accepted Jesus as Saviour, but when you stand in His Holy Presence, will you feel completely satisfied with the life and love you had for Jesus here on earth? Some time ago, when driving, a song was playing speaking of the day Jesus would come for me and if I would be ready. Would I be living so close to Him that I would not have to worry about standing before Him and giving account of my life? As I drove, my heart overflowed, and tears filled my eyes as His Spirit touched my life. That day I decided I would make every effort in my relationship with Christ to get closer to Him so when He returned or called me to heaven, I would be living my life each day walking in His presence.

Life since has not been easy, there's troubles, pain and grief, but Jesus has been faithful in everything. Luke 12:40 says, *"You also must be ready, for the Son of Man is coming at an hour you do not expect."* You can have peace, joy and happiness each day living close to Jesus. Imagine your life glowing with God's presence, so everyone wants to experience the life you have? I encourage you to decide now to live close to Jesus each day that remains for you, so on His return, you will not wish you had lived more or done more but He will say, *"Well done, my good and faithful servant."* Read, Matthew 16:27.

Prayer: *Praise You Jesus, for the assurance You are returning to earth. Amen*

Success is knowing your purpose in life, growing to reach your maximum potential, and sowing seeds that benefit others.

John Maxwell

"But blessed is the one who trusts in the Lord, whose confidence is in him."

Jeremiah 17:7

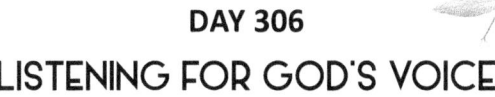

DAY 306
LISTENING FOR GOD'S VOICE

Genesis 3:8-9, *"They heard the sound of the Lord God walking in the garden in the cool of the day, and the man and his wife hid themselves from the presence of the Lord God... God called to the man, "Where are you?"* NIV

Above all other sounds in the Garden of Eden, Adam and Eve could distinguish the voice of the Creator, and being afraid because they had sinned, they tried to hide. Also in 1 Kings 19:9, we find God speaking to Elijah, *"What are you doing here?"* Elijah pleads his case with God, about how zealous he had been for God, but how the Israelites had rejected God's covenant. In both cases, they heard God speak and they recognized His voice.

Some years ago, each morning a Shrike Thrush came to our bedroom window and woke us up early in the day. He was very gregarious because I had encouraged him by whistling to him when gardening. His song has remained with me, and today although I reside elsewhere, in the early morning, the notes from a Shrike Thrush some distance away seem to be the first bird song I hear. Within a few minutes, the other birds join in, and then it becomes hard to hear him above their calls and chatter. I hear him because my ear knows his song.

> When we are humble and come to God, we will hear His voice.

God needs us to be quiet, or we will miss His voice because of all the other voices inside our minds. In 2 Chronicles 7:14, God spoke to Moses, telling him, *"If my people... will humble themselves and pray and seek my face... then I will hear... and forgive their sins."* If we are humble before God and come to Him in the quiet, we will hear His voice. Maybe He is calling you to do something particular for Him, like encouraging or showing care to someone, or perhaps you heard Him speak to you, telling you that you need to come and ask Him to forgive your sin and let HIm bring salvation into your life.

Despite God's power and holiness, He loving presence is with us when we are His. The important thing is that when we hear His voice, we obey.

Prayer: *Dear Lord, please forgive my sin, fill me with Your love, and always help me to be attentive so I don't miss hearing Your voice. Amen*

DAY 307
WALKING WITH JESUS

Colossians 2:6-7, *"Just as you received Christ Jesus as Lord, continue to live your lives in him... overflowing with thankfulness."* NIV

Do you realize just how vital your daily walk with Jesus is for your spiritual wellbeing and how you display what Jesus means to you? What we are inside is worked out through our behaviour, which is often the only 'view' of Jesus that the world experiences. *"You show that you are a letter from Christ... written not with ink but with the Spirit of the living God"* (2 Cor.3:3). We need to learn to live each day so that our life pleases God and blesses others.

Only through Jesus will we conquer our bad habits.

When we give our lives to Jesus, we must remember we have asked Him to be the Lord of our life. At first, it is a matter of taking small steps, of just committing to learning more about Jesus by reading His Word and speaking to Him each day in prayer. It can be of value if you have someone to mentor you on your spiritual journey, for often this is when we fall away and return to our old lives. As you look to Jesus each day for the spiritual strength and grace needed in every circumstance, it will become as natural for you as any other daily experience. You will receive by faith God's grace and the Spirit will work into your life a tenderness and care for others.

Having Jesus close as your daily companion makes it possible for you to sacrifice your affections of the 'self-life' you lived, before you came to Jesus. Self-will will intrude on your behaviour and conversation unless checked, and you will find it drags your character and your spiritual life down until Jesus means little to you. *"Those who belong to Christ Jesus have crucified the flesh with its passions and desires"* (Gal.5:24).

For each of us, the only way to stop this happening is to allow the Holy Spirit to have complete control of our life, as He makes our spiritual walk more effective and precious every day. Only through Him will we conquer our bad habits, to not only experience deliverance from the self-life, but make us a refreshing balm that will please God and benefit others.

Prayer: *Lord, give me strength each day to make time with You so that Your Spirit might work within me, guiding and directing my steps so that my life might please You and bless others. Amen*

DAY 308
CALLED TO SERVE

1 Timothy 4:14-15, *"Do not neglect your gift. ……. Be diligent in these matters, give yourself wholly to them."* NIV

In this day and age, we see from the very young right through to the elderly, day after day, people jogging, walking and going to the gym to keep their body physically fit. They make sure that all of their muscles are brought into play but spend little or no time developing the resources of their spirit and soul.

Paul tells us in 1 Timothy 4:7-8, *"For bodily exercise profits a little, but Godliness is profitable in all things, having promise of the life that now is and that which is to come."*

Our verse today warns us not to neglect the gifts we have been given to help others. We need to give 100% in our service, just as much as we do to keep physically fit. Serving others will bring character and spiritual growth to our life, which will last eternally.

Serving others will bring character and spiritual growth to our life.

You may be filled with the thought that there isn't much you can do. It doesn't require money, special equipment or materials to pray for someone, to be helpful to someone, to show kindness, or to give thanks to God and praise Him. The fact is, it isn't about what you do, but how you do what you do that God blesses.

We must stir up our souls for God. When we do, His grace will reveal itself, and we will be examples in our conduct, love and faith (verse 12) so that others will be drawn to our Saviour. Right now! We need to begin with what we have and just where we are.

Prayer: *Heavenly Father, thank You for Your gifts in my life. Please give me the courage to step out and serve You showing love and kindness to others and most importantly please help me to always speak of Your love when the opportunity arises. Amen.*

DAY 309
GOD OF JUSTICE

Psalm 13:1, *"How long, Lord? Will you forget me forever? How long will you hide your face from me"* NIV.

What is justice or injustice? At some stage in life, we all face injustice when we have been mistreated. Years ago, Dr Martin Luther King sought justice for the American people of his culture and stood and proclaimed that the time had come for the people of the United States of America to lift themselves from racial injustice and become brothers and stand together as equals. Still today, people all over the world, are treated with injustice because of social division.

Jesus is your spiritual lifeline, and you can know that you are loved.

Bringing justice in a situation can take a long time, even centuries, to prevail. Even here in Psalm 13, David is asking the same question we ask today. *"How long?"* Perhaps you are facing injustice in your own life, which can be challenging as you face tension, confusion, bullying or abuse. In Psalm 13, we find the remedy that David used; he focused on all he knew of God's love, reminding himself of the blessings he had received. *"But I trust in your unfailing love; my heart rejoices in your salvation. I will sing the Lord's praise, for he has been good to me"* (verses 5-6).

Unlike David, today, we have the added blessing of experiencing a personal relationship with Jesus as our Saviour, who died that all might be equal and indeed are equal in the sight of God. *"There is neither Jew nor Gentile, neither slave nor free, nor is there male and female, for you are all one in Christ Jesus"* (Gal.3:20). Even when justice for you is a long time coming, cling to God's love which will never fail, as you trust and rest in Him not just for today but permanently. Jesus is your spiritual lifeline, and you can know that you are loved.

Prayer: *Loving Jesus, help me to draw close to You and know Your love even in the darkest and longest injustice. Please keep me trusting You, talking to You, and leaning on Your promises. Amen*

DAY 310
SHINING LIGHTS

Matthew 5:16, *"Let your light shine before others, that they may see your good deeds and glorify your Father in heaven."* NIV

When I was just a child, we climbed round and round the steps of the lighthouse situated on the hill at Byron Bay in New South Wales. When we got to the top, I was stunned by the size of the light, but at night, I was also fascinated as we watched the flash go out to warn ships at sea. They needed that warning, and that is why Jesus used the illustration of being the light of the world for Him as we let our lives influence others in positive ways.

To be a light for Jesus is truly a privilege, as the power of the Holy Spirit within us shines out to those we know. Do those you mix with each day know that you are the person they can feel free to come to for help when trouble comes their way, or are you hiding your light away? We are called to live as beacons of God's love, hope, and care, taking the opportunity to share the saving grace of Jesus as we serve in His name.

The greatest gift to those around you is to shine God's love and care.

Often our good intentions can be rebuffed by those we try to help. Wherever God leads us, let us bless others in the name of Jesus, have patience, and show consistent love as we demonstrate a prayerful influence that will finally prevail, because shining forth from your life and mine will be the greatest light of all – the light of the Holy Spirit.

There is no doubt that many of us have been helped by fellow believers throughout our lives. Likewise, let us keep our light burning, by being filled with the Spirit, so that we may brighten the lives of others, that they too, may glorify our Heavenly Father. How can you be Christ's light today?

Prayer: *Dear loving Father, I will let my 'light' shine for You. Please fill me with Your truth and love so that I might shine forth for You each day. Amen*

DAY 311
DOWN IN THE VALLEY

Psalm 42:11, *"Why, my soul, are you downcast? Why so disturbed within me? Put your hope in God, for I will yet praise him, my Saviour and my God."* NIV

Are you like King David, a man of many moods, often finding himself gloomy, discouraged, and depressed? Do you look at the world and feel there is no hope? David often complained to God, *"Lord, how many are my foes! How many rise up against me! Many are saying of me, God will not deliver him."* (Psalm 3: 1-2) Sometimes it seems that God is deaf, but this is not true. Our disturbed hearts are never the fault of God or His promises.

> Sometimes, it seems that God is deaf, but this is not true.

To understand why we can be a person of moods, we must first remember we are still human, and even if we are born again, we still have to contend with our humanness and all its faults. On top of this, Jeremiah tells us that our heart is deceitful beyond understanding. In other words, we are subject to varying emotions and can be highly sensitive.

We must also remember that when we are born of the Spirit, we still must contend with the flesh. John 3:6 says, *"Flesh gives birth to flesh, but the Spirit gives birth to spirit."* Thankfully, we do not have to contend with our old nature alone, for once we accept Christ as Saviour and trust in Him, we have the indwelling of the Holy Spirit. Even Elijah, after victory over the prophets of Baal, still became depressed and wanted to die. We are to be aware that we must constantly come to Jesus for His help to overcome.

For some, our moods are part of our nature, or may be caused by physical weakness or illness. Whatever the cause, we must remember that Jesus understands and takes this into consideration, and understanding your victory over your depression or mood may be more difficult. We must always be careful not to use these causes as excuses but face our issues squarely and come to Jesus, remembering that God's promises are more dependable than any of our feelings. *"Put your hope in God, for I will yet praise him, my Saviour and my God."*

Prayer: *Dear Lord, forgive me for my moods which take my eyes off You, so I see only myself. Please help me to remember when I am overcome with despair or weakness to look up and seek You and put my trust in You. Amen.*

DAY 312
THE PRINCIPLE OF VICTORY

1 John 5:4, *"For everyone born of God overcomes the world. This is the victory that has overcome the world, even our faith."* NIV

If we permit ourselves, it is very easy to find things every day that rob us of peace of mind, which is our victory. Our adversary is in the business of trying at every turn to deceive and ruin our lives. This verse clearly states that our victory comes through the power of our faith in Christ. Have you ever been so angry with someone that you wanted to walk out, never to speak to them again, but you continued the relationship and communicated God's love to them? Have you given care to someone unlovable and seen a transformation in their life? This is the kind of power and victory we have when we trust ourselves to God each day.

I am always amazed at the tremendous force and power used to tunnel under a city or river to make roads. This kind of power is obvious to us, but there is a quiet power like that built into a tiny seed that enables it under the right circumstances to burst forth into a beautiful tree. Like the seed, your faith can overcome as you believe in the power of God through you, no matter how terrible or what trouble comes. By quickly lifting your heart to God in absolute trust, you can bring about change. Does this make you excited about what God can do in your life, so that we want to stop worrying about our situation, become gentler and kinder, and reach out to help others?

> God is still on the throne and can turn our defeat into victory.

Let us remember that God is still on the throne and is here to turn our defeat into victory, even in a split second if necessary. We must not forget that through faith, we have God's power to overcome the world, so let's accept it and see victory and peace in our lives. *"Thanks be to God! He gives us the victory through our Lord Jesus Christ."* (1 Cor. 15:57.)

O victory in Jesus, my Saviour, forever.
He sought me and bought me with His redeeming blood;
He loved me before I knew Him, and all my love is to Him,
He plunged me to victory, beneath the cleansing flood

Eugene Monroe Bartlett Senior (1885-1941)

DAY 313
SANCTIFICATION

1 Thess. 4:3, *"For this is the will of God, even your sanctification"* NIV.

Close your eyes and visualize Jesus standing right next to you. Suppose He asks if you are happy and satisfied with your life – with your relationship with God; what would you answer? Suppose He said to you, *"My child, I love you, and you are aware of that, but to have the happiness I have promised, you must die to self that you might live."* John 12:25 tells us, *"The man who loves his life will lose it, while the man who hates his life in this world will keep it for eternal life."*

> *Sanctification calls for us to both die and live.*

Sanctification calls for us to both die and live. It is the renewal of our fallen nature by the Holy Spirit through faith in Jesus Christ. We are sanctified therefore, when we live our life here on earth following God's will and purpose for us. When the Holy Spirit shows us the importance of sanctification, there is always something in the human nature that tugs against what Christ wants for us and the struggle within begins. We are aware of and desire the happiness that comes when we die to ourselves setting us apart to live for God, but often we find ourselves returning to our old condition.

We must ask, *"Am I willing to allow the Holy Spirit to strip me of everything, that I might be a slave to Christ?"* In speaking to the Christians in Rome, Paul says, Romans 6:19, *"I am using an example from everyday life because of your human limitations. Just as you used to offer yourselves as slaves to impurity and to ever-increasing wickedness, so now offer yourselves as slaves to righteousness leading to holiness."* It is the Holy Spirit who makes us more like Christ, and our part is to continually turn from sin and trust Jesus.

Sanctification means being made one with Jesus, not something the Spirit puts into us, but the Spirit living in us and changing our lives to be holy. We shall never be holy until we allow Him to break and remake us. This is the joy and happiness our God longs for each of us.

Prayer: *Dear Lord, I come to You asking for Your sanctification to be real in me. Draw me to yourself and teach me Your way, keeping me from falling back to the old habits and condition that fills my life. Amen.*

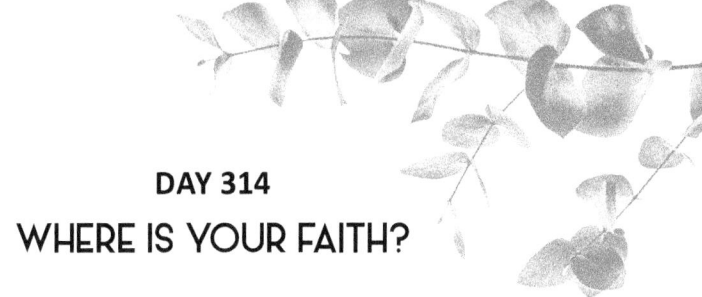

DAY 314
WHERE IS YOUR FAITH?

Judges 6:39, *"Then Gideon said to God, "Do not be angry with me. Let me make just one more request. Allow me one more test with the fleece."* NIV

Gideon wanted to be sure of God's will, so twice he asked God to make the fleece first wet, then dry and the ground covered with dew. Like Gideon, we often find it hard to believe unless we have a sign from God or an emotional feeling. It is as though we need this affirmation before we can trust our Heavenly Father, not to say that sometimes this can be how God does speak. Much more significant is our faith when we can trust God without requiring feelings. When favourable circumstances, emotions, and human common sense all appear to urge us to believe to the contrary, we must believe and trust God and His Word, which is the ultimate truth we follow.

Yes, we must trust, like Paul when he was on board the ship on his way to Rome and the storm broke. Acts 27:20 tells us, *"When neither sun nor stars appeared for many days and the storm continued raging, we finally gave up hope of being saved."* We can only imagine what a terrifying experience this must have been for both Paul and the crew who sailed with him. Paul sought the Lord with courage that God would prevail and save them; he boldly proclaimed, *"Keep up your courage men, for I have faith in God."* We need this kind of faith in our lives. Is your faith filled with this trust and courage in your God, who will not fail you in the trials of life?

> Have faith to trust when everything appears to bring disaster.

Even though I knew that God had promised that He would never leave me, it was a most blessed experience in life when I reached a stage in my walk with the Lord, where even though things would not always go the way I wanted, deep within I knew, and I knew that I knew... that Jesus loved me and would always honour His promise.

May our God help us to have the faith to fully trust His Word when everything else appears to bring disaster to our lives.

Prayer: *Father, please help my unbelief and help me to trust Your Word that tells me You will never leave or forsake me. Amen*

DAY 315
PAYBACK TIME

Matthew 5:39, *"I tell you, do not resist an evil person. If anyone slaps you on the right cheek, turn to them the other cheek also"* NIV.

Whenever we're confronted verbally, we are tempted to respond in the same way, blame for blame. Blame is a natural response of most, for when attacked, we immediately want to protect ourselves, and so we retaliate in the same way. Even though this is the natural way for most, it may not be the best, as it is not the thing mature Christians do. As a child of God, we need to control how we respond to any attack on us, because if we are not in control, the situation can turn into an argument, or alienation. *"Do not repay anyone evil for evil"* (Rom. 12:17). We may feel humiliated, by giving up our right to retaliate. The world calls this cowardly; and we do not like to be labelled. Still, when it comes to our spiritual life, we must take control of our actions and have tight rein on our tongue, speaking out of maturity rather than hurt and anger, which is a good indicator of our relationship with Jesus. *"Those who consider themselves religious and yet do not keep a tight rein on their tongues deceive themselves"* (James 1:26).

> **By turning the other cheek, we reveal the character of Jesus.**

If we are insulted, we can easily resent the other person rather than stop, think, and perhaps say something like, *"I'm sorry you feel that way, and it upsets me to think that you would speak unkindly to me."* Often this can take power away from them, giving an opportunity to hear, react and deal with the situation in an equable way, although in saying this, sometimes you have to leave it to be resolved later. Try to overlook the resistance, and remember, *"A man's wisdom gives him patience; it is to his glory to overlook an offense"* (Proverbs 19:11).

In the Sermon on the Mount, Jesus taught, we must never look for justice but must never fail to give it. By turning the other cheek, we reveal the incredible character of Jesus. Never look to them to do what is right and mature, but rather do what is right and mature yourself as a follower of Jesus.

Prayer: *Forgive me Lord when I have spoken in anger. Help me to stop and think about how You would answer and help me to pour water on the fire to put out flames and maintain good relationships. Amen*

DAY 316
GIVE JOYFUL PRAISE

Psalm 100:1-2, *"Shout for joy to the Lord, all the earth. Worship the Lord with gladness; come before him with joyful songs"* NIV.

When I hear these verses, it makes me think of a little ornament I was given a long time ago when a friend and I made up a song to honour people of our church who worked together to build a new sanctuary. On it was printed, "make a joyful noise unto the Lord," which was totally applicable because neither of us could sing a note, so it could only be a joyful noise. Still, a joyful noise it was and a night everyone remembers with praise and thanksgiving.

This Psalm is about giving praise through joyful worship, not just having a thankful heart but expressing our thanks in song to our Heavenly Father. One little birdsong can start the whole bush singing, just as when we sing and worship in loving adoration, it is contagious and start everyone praising God. Let us be careful not to hinder the gladness of praise by being dull, gloomy and depressed. If we love the Lord, we should serve Him with gladness of heart; even if we can't sing well, we can 'make a joyful noise' that our Lord loves and accepts from us. Regular church attendance cannot be emphasized enough because it is here that we can lift our voices as one in praise and worship. Let us *"enter his gates with thanksgiving and his courts with praise"* (v.4).

> Be careful not to hinder the gladness of praise by being dull.

Despite the pain and sorrow in our world, our God is indeed good. We need to believe in God's goodness and affirm His blessings in praise, for His goodness, mercy, and truth endure to all generations. We can be comforted by knowing that His mercy and love are everlasting, for if it were anything less, we would be justified by despairing. However, it is for all generations from when this Psalm was written, still today and forever more. It is an excellent exercise to praise God at the end of each day for all His blessings.

*What blessing has your Lord bestowed on your life
that you can praise Him for today?
Bless the Lord, O my soul, and all that is within me,
Bless His Holy Name.*

Andraé Edward Crouch

DAY 317
ROOTED AND ESTABLISHED

Ephesians 3:17-18, "I pray that you, being rooted and established in love, may have power . . . to grasp . . . the love of Christ." NIV

When you want to propagate plants, you take many cuttings from one healthy plant, and after dipping each cutting into honey or striking mix, you plant them in propagation mix. The special blend is to help the cuttings develop robust root systems. Within a few weeks, the cuttings have developed roots, and then the buds on the side of the cuttings begin to grow into a new and healthy plant to produce many flowers.

Jesus is our place of belonging, our reason to celebrate life and hope forever.

We need to develop strong spiritual roots to grow into people with strong faith so that we do not wither or wilt under the struggles of life. In Ephesians 3: 17, Paul tells us to be rooted and established in the love of Christ. This is a beautiful picture of what our lives can be when we belong to Him. God, as it were, adopts us into His family through Jesus our Saviour, being able to bring purpose and peace into our lives even despite our problems. Jesus is our place of belonging, a reason to celebrate life and hope forever.

Each night before bed, I pray the prayer that Paul prayed for the Ephesians. As a mother, I have made this my prayer for my family members. When you pray this prayer for others, you will allow the Holy Spirit to work in their lives so that they will be rooted and grounded in the love of Christ, *"to grasp how wide and long and high and deep Christ's love is, and to know this love that surpasses knowledge, that they may be filled to the measure of all the fullness of God."*

Prayer: *Thank You dear Lord, for Your love for me. Help me to understand just how great that love is, and may Your love grow in my life to produce the beauty of Christ to the world in need. Amen*

DAY 318
NEVER ALONE

Ecclesiastes 4:9-10, *"Two are better than one... If either of them falls down, one can help the other up."* NIV

Loneliness is where negative emotions affect anybody, rich or poor, child or adult, to feel empty, worthless, and alone. Lonely people crave contact with others, yet they can be surrounded by them. Sadly, we can be unaware that someone close to us feels this way. Take a husband and wife who lived together for 50 years, and suddenly one passes away; or a child at school who just doesn't seem to fit in with anyone. Loneliness can even shorten our life span. We can have everything, and still be lonely and long for companionship.

To overcome loneliness, we require meaningful relationships. Think of Moses, a man who basked in favour at Pharaoh's Palace for forty years but then spent forty years in exile, poverty, and heartbreak, tending sheep. As he watched over the flock, he probably felt lonely and perplexed, but he wasn't alone. Suddenly, a common bush burst into flame, *'And the angel of the Lord appeared to him in flames of fire from within a bush... God called to him from within the bush "Moses! Moses!" And Moses said, "Here I am"* (Exodus 3: 2,4). Moses was not alone!

> **To overcome our loneliness, we need meaningful relationships.**

If you are lonely, realize that God is just as much there with you as He was with Moses. There is no one better to have as your companion and to build a relationship with than Jesus, your Saviour. Take this to your heart, lonely and down-cast soul, and be of good cheer, for the God of Creation is with you, even when you are at the end of yourself. He takes you in His arms and concerns Himself with your need. *"Though the mountains be shaken and the hills be removed, yet my unfailing love for you will not be shaken, says the Lord"* (Isaiah 54:10). Find your encouragement in the reality that you are never truly alone because Jesus' Spirit is always with you.

> *No, never alone,*
> *No, never alone.*
> *He promised never to leave me,*
> *Never to leave me alone.*
>
> Anonymous

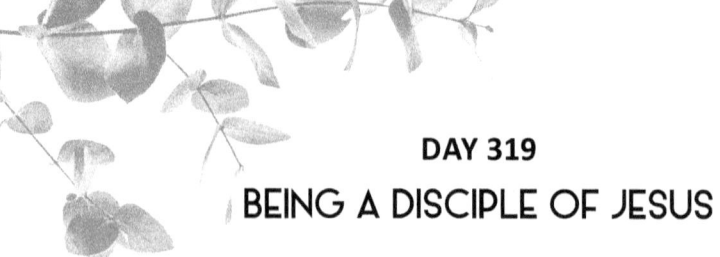

DAY 319

BEING A DISCIPLE OF JESUS

Luke 14:26,33, *"If any come to Me and do not hate even their own life... he cannot be my disciple. In the same way, any of you who does not give up everything he has, cannot be my disciple."* NIV

In bible times, to be a disciple meant not only being a follower of a teacher but also imitating the teacher you followed. To be one of Jesus's disciples was no easy walk in the park. They had to follow Him and learn about Him, which often meant that they found themselves in very uncomfortable situations.

> **The closest relationship we can have, is with Jesus our Saviour.**

Discipleship means to be dedicated, having a passionate devotion to one person. We are not expected to dislike our loved ones, but our dedication and love for Him when compared with everyone else, means we live as though everyone else takes second place. The closest relationship we can have, is with Jesus our Saviour. We must ask ourselves if any other relationship we have clashes with the claims of Christ.

For us to be passionate disciples of Jesus, we must be filled with and walk each day with the Holy Spirit. In Luke 9:23, Jesus said, *"If anyone would come after me, he must deny himself and take up his cross daily and follow me."* Genuine love for Jesus can only be found through living in the Spirit. How can we achieve a life lived in the Spirit? The only way is to allow the Holy Spirit to control your whole personality by being in a constant relationship with Jesus. Then the Holy Spirit will give you love, and devotion to Jesus Christ like you cannot imagine.

When we are filled with devotion and love for Jesus, our thoughts and actions naturally align with God's will for us. Living in God's will, gives joy and sparkle to being a disciple of Jesus.

Prayer: *Father God, thank You for calling me out of darkness and into a life lived in the Spirit. Please help me to stay close to You so that I am truly a disciple of my Saviour, Jesus. Amen.*

DAY 320
TAKE COURAGE

Acts 27:23-24, *"Last night an angel of the God to whom I belong and whom I serve stood beside me and said, 'Do not be afraid, Paul. You must stand trial before Caesar; and God has graciously given you the lives of all who sail with you'"* NIV.

Courage is the opposite of fear, and we know that fear is an emotion we feel when faced with danger, whether real or imagined. Typically, when we fear, we want to fight back, and our body instantly wants to lash out or run away, so we don't have to face our situation. Paul had learnt to detect and hear the voice of God, and if we are to understand courage, we need to be like Paul and have an obedient will, an ear to listen to God. Because Paul was focused on God, the angel sped to him and gave him hope.

If you and I want angel help, we need to be able to say with Paul, *"An angel of the God to whom I belong and whom I serve, stood beside me"* (v.23). His help came because he was obedient to the Lord. We must ask ourselves if we really are obedient to God. Our prayer of faith must believe that God will answer. What a blessing if you and I were to pray for all those who 'sail in our ship of life,' that they might find Christ as their Saviour, for this is what God requires of us.

> We must be calm and let God's peace and stillness rule within us.

Paul had assurance God had answered, but the storm did not suddenly cease. No, Paul acted with courage in the face of fear to do what he could, depending on God's guidance. When it comes to the crunch in a stressful or fearful event, we must be calm and let God's peace and stillness rule within us as we stay in constant contact with Him.

We know we will encounter many storms before we arrive on the fair shore of heaven. If we can rest, knowing the Lord is with us, staying calm and focused, He will give the courage we require for every situation. *"God is our refuge and strength, an ever-present help in trouble. Therefore, we will not fear, though the earth gives way and the mountains fall into the heart of the sea"* (Psalm 46: 1-2).

Prayer: *Dear Lord, give us faith to trust You for courage we need in every situation. Help us stay close to You so that we might have angel help. Amen.*

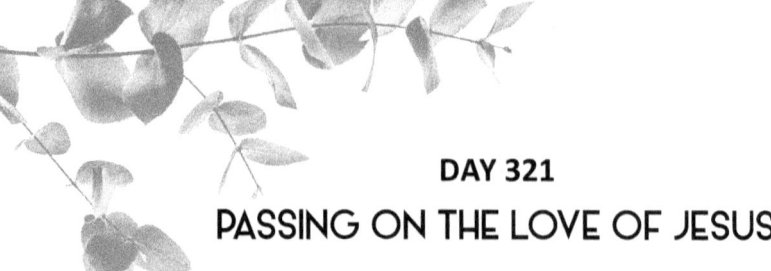

DAY 321
PASSING ON THE LOVE OF JESUS

2 Timothy 1:5, *"I have been reminded of your sincere faith, which first lived in your grandmother Lois and in your mother Eunice and... now lives in you also."* NIV

As we age, we look at life wondering what we are passing on of value to benefit our children, and grandchildren. Most of us, think about what we will leave them in monetary value, but far more significant is what we leave them of spiritual value for their life ahead. Just as any mother or grandmother dearly loves her family, in the passage that surrounds our verse today, Paul valued the sincere faith that Timothy's mother and grandmother had instilled in Timothy, who had come to know Jesus as his Saviour. No matter who we are, our faith must be of spiritual value.

Life is not about you but about God.

In verse 6, Paul encourages young Timothy to stay focused and *"fan into flame the gift of God, which is in you."* Each of us, both young and old, must continually fan the flame of our faith and keep our focus on Christ. In verse 9, Paul also reminds Timothy that he is to lead a holy life. Like Timothy, we are set apart for God's work. Life is not about us but about God.

Maybe Timothy no longer had a father because Paul refers to him as his "dear son." For those who belong to Jesus and don't have parents or grandparents, be encouraged and seek out someone like Paul within your church family to help and mentor you to embrace the gifts God has given you, and for those of us who are parents and grandparents within the church, we should likewise encourage our young people in their walk with God. We must always be on the alert to build each other up in our walk of faith.

If you are a parent, whether young or old, what spiritual legacy would you be able to leave your children today?

Prayer: *Father God,*

This life, this beauty belongs to me,
For God has placed it all there
But it isn't mine to hold selfishly,
It's only mine to share.

DAY 322
LIVING FOR GOD

1 Thess. 2:8, *"We cared for you. Because we loved you so much, we were delighted to share with you not only the gospel of God but our lives as well."* NIV

The people in Thessalonica began questioning Paul's motives, so he endeavoured to explain, to squash their talk. In life, we are frequently praised by the applause and approval of our friends and work colleagues, and because we desire to build ourselves up in their eyes, we can easily make the wrong choice. You may have been successful in your life and have a cabinet full of trophies displaying all your achievements in the sport, business, or hobbies. Whilst these are to be admired, we must not forget where our ability came from and acknowledge Jesus. *"My help comes from the Lord, the Maker of heaven and earth"* (Psalm 121:2).

While the world tells us that we need to approve of ourselves and love ourselves, Paul shows us in his example that our priority is to love God and then others. When we long for the approval of others, it is really an extension of wanting support for self-gratification. A good self-test is helping and encouraging someone without telling anyone else what we have done... and leaving it in God's hands. Paul lived for God's approval, where the consistency of his faith lined up with his pattern of living. He cared for the church and loved them so much that he wanted to share the gospel and minister to their needs by sharing his life. He looked for the approval of God.

Seek to live lives approved by God and experience His blessing.

We receive God's approval when we accept Jesus as the sacrifice for our sins. From then on, our choices are about God and His will for us. We must choose faithfulness to God and follow Paul's example to care about others and share the life-giving gospel with them, giving of ourselves by encouraging, comforting, and loving them for Jesus, without any praise. As we seek to live lives approved by God, we experience the blessings of God, which will far outweigh approval of others. What kind of impact is your life having on others?

Prayer: *Thank you Lord, help me to honour You with the choices I make, and for loving me through my life, teaching me to seek Your approval. Amen*

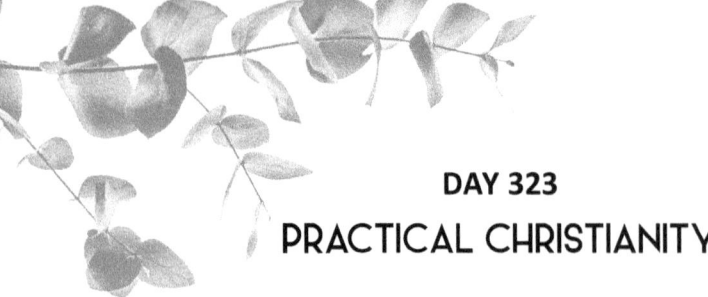

DAY 323
PRACTICAL CHRISTIANITY

James 2:26, *"For as the body without the spirit is dead, so faith without works is dead also."* NIV

James, the brother of Jesus, was respected in the early Christian Church for his saintly life. Unlike Paul, who, taught about doctrine and on the life of Christ and the resurrection, James teaches more about what Jesus instructed the early Christians to do in the conduct of their everyday life.

> There must be a balance between the faith of a man and his works.

Many people in the early church believed in Christ and would often pride themselves in the accuracy of their creed, but James is very outspoken in saying this was not enough to save a man's soul. Today many think that if they believe in God and do good works, they will have a home in heaven. Whilst Paul clearly states that it's our faith in Jesus that gives salvation. Eph.2:8-9. *"For it is by grace you have been saved, through faith- and this not of yourselves, it is the gift of God. – not by works, so that no one can boast."* He also says that there must be a balance between the faith of a man and his works.

Therefore, our commitment to Christ is measured not by our lip service only but by our whole life. Our Saviour needs us not to just say something but to serve others for Him. To be effective disciples of Jesus, we must build our relationship with our Lord through the constant reading of God's Word and prayer; otherwise, our motives will prevent genuine service.

To truly be what God calls us to, we must have a faith that is rooted in our Lord so that like any fruit tree, we are being fed and growing whilst at the same time producing the fruit that our Lord calls us to. We must always be prepared to bear the burdens of those we encounter, encouraging and showing love to the weak, and reaching out with unselfish action to all. Even when our efforts are ignored, we must maintain our standards, and love in the name of Jesus.

"Our faith justifies us as a Christian; whilst our works justify our faith." John C. Maxwell.

Prayer: *Help me Lord, to grow in faith and love others, please keep me from unkind words or where there is an opportunity to show Your love. Amen*

DAY 324
SPIRITUAL LOVE

1 Corinthians 13:13, *"And now these three remain: faith, hope and love. But the greatest of these is love."* NIV

As we think about this verse, let's dwell on love as a fruit of the Spirit within, not as work. With work, there is a strain on the muscles and emotional stress, but fruit is a natural product of the plant, so when our life is filled with the Holy Spirit, we are filled with love for our unsaved brothers and sisters. Only when we are filled to overflowing can we show spiritual love to all humanity.

We must also be conscious of love in contrast to the emotion of love. We should always love, even though the feeling of love is not always possible. We love with our mind and strength, but not necessarily with the emotion of our hearts. Therefore, we can love by determining to put our thoughts and energies into service or work, without having the sweet glow of heart felt love from the Holy Spirit. Paul shows us that all gifts are of little worth without real love as inspiration from the Spirit.

> Love is full of trust, always hopes and patiently endures.

God is Love. So, what is this special love that comes from the overflow of God's Spirit within? It is patient and kind, never envious or jealous; does not put oneself forward or is self-assertive; never boastful, proud, or behaves unbecomingly. It is not assertive, blazing in passionate anger and does not brood over wrongs. Love finds no pleasure in injustice done to others but joyfully sides with the truth. Love knows when to be silent; being full of trust always hopes and patiently endures.

These high ideals seem impossible to achieve. We must believe and know that God baptised us with this love when we asked Jesus to be our Saviour. Let us ponder each aspect of God's love within us and stop striving to achieve it in our own strength, and by God's unending love and grace for us, allow His Spirit to work out His love in our lives.

Prayer: *O Lord, my love is a feeble spark; I want it to be a flame for you. Breath your Spirit into me, until Your love flows from me to others. Amen.*

DAY 325
BEING THANKFUL

John 11:14, *"Then Jesus looked up and said, 'Father, I thank you that you have heard me"* NIV.

For many, we pray to our Father and then wait for an answer. If we receive a favourable response, we thank God for hearing and answering our prayer. This, however, is not the order of our Heavenly Father, where giving thanks precedes the answer. Before the raising of Lazarus, Jesus gave thanks for the miracle of resurrection He and His friends were about to see. To be thankful before the answer comes, is true faith and belief in the unexplainable power of the God we serve. Faith that enables gratitude to break forth before the arrival of an answer is the essential preparatory need for obtaining the answer and the work of the Holy Spirit.

God is pleased when we come with a thankful heart.

As children, my sister and I had a pet dog that we loved dearly. We lived on a farm where dad laid poisonous baits for wild dogs who killed the livestock. Although very careful to make sure his neighbours knew to keep their pet dogs safe, one day our dad forgot to shut the door of the shed where he had prepared the baits, with the result our beloved 'Toby' took and ate one of the baits. Despite our parent's actions, our pet collapsed as she writhed in pain. Dad carried her limp body, laid her in the downstairs laundry and shut the door.

When time for bed, my sister and I knelt and asked Jesus to heal our dog with total expectation of seeing her the following morning. Dad rose early to bury our pet, only to find her fully recovered and leaping excitedly when he opened the door. This experience has forever imprinted on my mind the importance of belief and thanks to a God who understood the prayer of two little girls. We are told to come with thanks before God's throne. Nothing pleases God more, and nothing blesses us more, than when we come with a thankful heart to our loving Heavenly Father. Psalm 107:8-9 *"Let them give thanks to the LORD for his unfailing love and his wonderful deeds for mankind, for he satisfies the thirsty and fills the hungry with good things."*

Prayer: *Thank You Lord, for making me aware to come to You with a thankful heart, believing in Your power to perform miracles. Amen*

DAY 326
BEARING FRUIT

John 15:5,8, *"I am the vine; you are the branches. If a man remains in me and I in him, he will bear much fruit... This is to my Father's glory."* NIV

As a gardener, I love the time of year just before the spring, as the weather warms, when it is time to prune. I carefully examine each bud on the bare stem, choosing a plump one to cut at an angle above it. I wait patiently to see what will happen as the sap returns, bringing food and warmth to the bud. It is exciting to see the new shoot start to develop, then new growth and finally a beautiful rose or some other flower.

In our spiritual lives, God is the gardener, Jesus the vine, and you and I the branches that are to bear the fruit. Jesus says, *"Remain in me, and I will remain in you. No branch can bear fruit by itself."* Just as in nature, the branch must be attached to the plant so that the nourishment can grow the fruit or flower, so likewise, if we do not remain in Jesus to receive spiritual food for our soul, we cannot be of any use to God. Here Jesus warns us that if we are unwilling to allow the Holy Spirit to prune and change us from just being someone who believes in Jesus, we will be in danger of being cut away. In our Christian walk, we either grow by letting Christ prune us of the things that stop growth, or we die spiritually. These may seem harsh words, but they were spoken to the disciples by Jesus.

> *Pruning can be painful but is always profitable.*

In our lives, God must often do some intense pruning for us to bear fruit for His Kingdom. Do you need pruning, and are you willing to submit to being pruned? When was the last time you felt God's love pruning your life? Pruning can be painful but is always profitable. In James 1:2-4, we read, *"Consider it pure joy, whenever you face trials of any kind, because you know that the testing of your faith develops perseverance... So that you may be mature and complete, lacking nothing."* Even the desire to yield to God's pruning, requires His help.

Each day, we must ask God for a fresh infilling of the Holy Spirit so our growth will genuinely bear fruit as we serve others for Him. God will bring opportunity and events into our lives so we can bear the fruit He requires.

Prayer: *Dear God, help me be willing to allow the Holy Spirit to change and grow me so You can use me to help bring others to Salvation. Amen*

DAY 327

GOD'S CHOSEN

Matthew 20:1, *"For the kingdom of heaven is like a landowner who went out early in the morning to hire men to work in his vineyard."* NIV

God, our Father, weeps over the souls of men and women around us who do not know Him as Saviour. Each day He comes to us and says, *"Go work for the harvest is ripe, and I need you to show compassionate love and to even tell humanity that I love them and died for them."* Even though we know that God could do it, for some unknown reason, He must have the cooperation of each of His children.

> **He needs your faithful prayer for humanity.**

He comes to you, young men and women and tells you that He needs you to tell others about what He has done in your life. He gave you skills that He wants to use, perhaps to be a children's or youth leader or even to go into full-time ministry. Maybe your chosen field is in medicine, teaching or some other profession. Whatever your choice, can you hear Him say, *"I want your help harvesting the souls who need Me?"*

He comes to you who are in the middle and the latter years of your life. Perhaps He has given you success in business and now says, *"Go and use your money, your time and your influence for Me."* Even when you have fewer days ahead than what is behind you, He needs your help. He needs your faithful prayer for humanity that His Spirit might draw them to Jesus. While here on this earth, we are needed to bring others to Christ.

Let us not make excuses that will be to our detriment when we stand before the Throne of God. When we say yes to Him, we can know He will lead and provide. Can you hear the urgency in His voice and answer in your heart, *"Here am I, send me?"*

Prayer: *Dear Lord, accept my hands to work for You and my lips to speak for You. I am willing to serve you here on earth, so please guide me in Your service. Amen.*

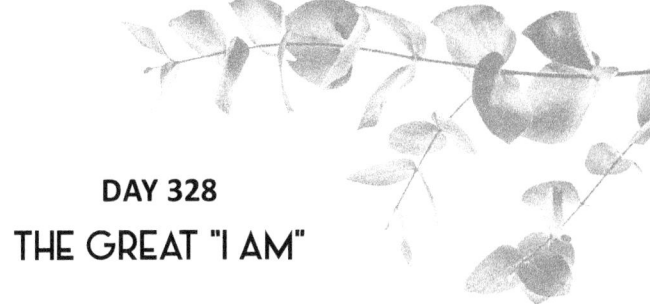

DAY 328

THE GREAT "I AM"

Exodus 15:11, *"Who among the gods is like you, Lord?... majestic in holiness, awesome in glory, working wonders?"* Exodus 3: 14, *"God said to Moses, "I am who I am."* NIV

It fascinates me that our body is so created that nearly 100 trillion cells all work together to make us who we are. It doesn't matter how much we know about Creation and how awesome our God is; we must keep being reminded because we continually forget who God really is and think He is there just to obey our beck and call. Due to the business of life, it can be easy to get out of bed and start our day without any thought of God, but we must constantly remind ourselves that we need Him every day.

We make excuses that whatever a person thinks about God is fine; but **God is Holy**. We don't have any right to decide anything about God because when Moses questioned God, he was clearly told, "I AM WHO I AM." Holy means set apart so there is no way we can really know who He is, and no one can compare with Him. What an experience is ours to worship a God who we cannot exaggerate.

> We are arrogant to believe God owes us an explanation.

He is eternal. Time is irrelevant in God's world. For us, life began at a specific time, but not for God. How can we understand, or think we have a right to limit God to our ability to comprehend? He was always here, and Psalm 102:27 says, *"Your years will never end."* I get confused when I think of eternity and living with God in heaven, yet for those who believe, that is what we will experience.

"Nothing in all creation is hidden from God's sight" (Hebrews 4:13). Our God is **all-knowing** and **all-powerful**. He knows our thoughts before we think them, and yet we dare to question His dealing with us. We are arrogant if we believe the God of the Universe owes us an explanation for what He does. Despite our forgetfulness, what comfort to know the God of all Creation loves us so much that He wants to fellowship with us for eternity. Take time today to praise and worship His glory and majesty. Ask yourself, *"do I really know God as my loving Heavenly Father?"*

Prayer: *Father, even though we dwell in a temporal world, enable us to appreciate Your Holiness, being mindful each day to worship You. Amen*

DAY 329
COMMIT AND LEAVE

Psalm 37:6, *"He will make your righteous reward shine like the dawn, your vindication like the noonday sun."* NIV.

Whatever is pressing on you and causing you anxiety or distress, go and spill your heart, everything, and every word to your Heavenly Father. Put the whole matter into His hands, and experience freedom from the cares of this world. *"The salvation of the righteous comes from the Lord; he is their stronghold in time of trouble"* (verse 39).

> *If there is the slightest doubt about God's way, faith will not have anything to do with it.*

When you are suffering, or have any difficulty in your life, acquaint your God with it; yes, burden Him with it and be done caring about the situation. Be quiet, go about your day with diligence and dependence on your Lord, and *"call on Him in the day of trouble; He will deliver you"* (Psalm 50:15).

To commit your way to God, you must believe that His way is the best for you. If there is the slightest doubt about God's way, faith will not have anything to do with it. Your commitment must be continuous, not just a single act when times are tough. Even when God's guidance seems to make no common sense or is an unexpected path to take, be sure not to take the reins from Him... let Him guide and lead you.

We often remain anxious and fearful because we have not left our problems with the Lord. We take it to Him... and then we take it back again... and so remain in the same place spiritually.

Are you willing to allow God to judge all your ways, especially your habits and views?

> *Construct a fence of trust around today.*
> *Fill every moment with loving work, and therein stay,*
> *Don't look toward what may come tomorrow;*
> *For God will help you bear the joy or sorrow.*
>
> Mary F. Butts

DAY 330

FOCUS

Acts 3:4,5,16. *"Peter said, "Look at us!" So, the man gave them his attention.... By faith, in the name of Jesus, this man whom you see and know was made strong."* NIV

As Peter and John were about to enter the temple, the beggar asked them for money. Peter, having no money, but knowing that he had the power of the Holy Spirit within him, asked the beggar to look at him. There is every possibility that Peter asked this, so the beggar would stop looking at his own need for money and see the reality of having faith in God. Peter said, *"In the name of Jesus Christ of Nazareth, walk."* (v.6). So, what happened for the beggar? His focus on having faith in God enabled him to rise and walk. (v16)

Our attitude to faith in God, can often achieve very different results, but it is absolutely necessary for success. The amazing thing is that faith is possible even when we are somewhat ignorant. Many of the great men of the Old Testament acted in faith to conquer kingdoms, administer justice etc., even though they were unaware of the truth that the gospel has revealed.

> Faith in what we can't see is absolutely necessary for God's power to meet our needs.

Faith in what we can't see is vital for God's power to meet our needs. When we focus on the power of God and entrust our soul and destiny to His will, we will know that He can do better for us than we could ever do for ourselves... this is faith. Hebrews 10:23, *"Let us hold unswervingly to the hope we profess, for He who promised is faithful."* Focus and faith obtain blessings.

Are you focused on something apart from God? What difference would faith with focus make in your life?

Prayer: *Dear Lord, keep my focus from wandering from You, and help me to know Your power in my life. Amen*

DAY 331
OUR ALL-LOVING FATHER

Psalm 30:5, *"Weeping may stay for the night, but rejoicing comes in the morning"* NIV.

It is a memorable moment in our life when we become aware that the Almighty Sovereign of the universe is our all-loving Father. We spend our nights with doubt and worry, but when morning comes, and we become aware of His love for us, it is like the light within is turned back on. With no longer fear and anxiety we know we have the assured hope of living with Him.

We are no different to Thomas, who, after a week of disbelief and doubting that Christ had risen from the dead, stood facing Jesus, only to learn that Jesus' heart was full of sympathy for His disciple. *"Then he said to Thomas, Put your finger here; see my hands. Reach out your hand and put it into my side. Stop doubting and believe"* (John 20:27).

The Almighty Sovereign of the universe is our all-loving Father.

Our weeping comes because we try in every way to solve our own problems. When you believe that Jesus is interested in dealing with all the mysteries and problems of your life, the joy comes when you open your heart to Christ. We will never understand God's ways and even less the mysteries of life. Whenever we catch a glimpse of His objective for our lives, joy fills our hearts with praise and thanksgiving. Dare to give praise openly, even if those around you wonder in amazement at your outburst.

The glorious joy for those who believe is that soon Christ will come for His own. On that day, the power of the prince of this world will be broken and his reign will end. The prophesies told in Scripture will be revealed, and we who are God's children will lift our hands in praise to the King of the Universe. On that glad morning, we will see the radiant faces of our loved ones who have gone before welcoming us on the other side, and it will be a morning filled with the Joy of the Lord that will last for all eternity.

We must keep reminding ourselves that during our trials, we can know that it isn't a life sentence, for Joy will come in the morning when our Lord returns.

Prayer: *Dear Lord, when the night is dark and filled with trouble, come to me, that I will find the Joy and peace that only You can give. Amen*

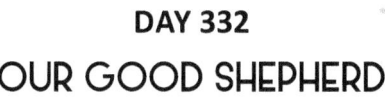

DAY 332
OUR GOOD SHEPHERD

Heb. 13:20,21, *"Now the God of Peace, that brought again from the dead our Lord Jesus, that great Shepherd of the sheep, through the blood of the everlasting covenant, make you perfect in every good work to do His will"* NIV.

What a comfort to us to know that our Heavenly Father is *"the God of Peace."* He is the Creator, the giver of peace, and we can trust Him for His love, patience, faithfulness, and gentleness. He will not bruise us but encourage us to never be afraid but trust and love Him as our Saviour, our God of Peace.

Our God *"brought again from the dead our Lord Jesus, that great Shepherd of the sheep."* Jesus knew His mission before He came to earth and never flinched from carrying it out, so that we could have a personal relationship with our God. He knew that the Father was waiting to welcome Him to Heaven, and that God's Everlasting Arms beneath Him would raise Him to life again, that we would no longer be cursed by eternal death. God did not fail Him, and neither will He fail us.

> We need not be afraid of God, for He is our God of Peace.

The good Shepherd, our Lord Jesus is our great and loving God. Many sheep, through the attractions of this world have strayed, but the Good Shepherd seeks them, to bring them back to the fold. Jesus said, *"I give them eternal life, and they shall never perish; no one can snatch them out of my hand"* John 10:27.

God's promise and the blood of the Cross seals our Salvation. We know with humility that our names are written in the Lamb's Book of Life. We are saved to save others, making our calling sure, serving our Lord, and then *"we will receive a rich welcome into the eternal kingdom of our Lord and Saviour Jesus Christ"* (2 Peter 1:11). Are you one of the lost sheep that Jesus Is looking for?

Prayer: *Thank You Father God, for sending your Son to die so that we might be forgiven and enter a personal relationship with You, the God of Peace. Amen*

DAY 333
GOD KNOWS THEIR NEEDS

Psalm 84:3, *"Even the sparrow has found a home, and the swallow a nest for herself, where she may have her young – a place near your altar, O Lord Almighty, my King and my God."* NIV

Parents spend many stressful hours caring for and disciplining their children to grow up to be responsible God-fearing adults. For some, these years have not been easy as our teenage children make unwise decisions for their lives. Proverbs 22:6 tells us, *"Train up a child in the way he should go, and when he is old, he will not depart from it."* Often when our children are going through their teenage years, we wonder if these words are true.

> **We need to ask God's guidance in rearing our families.**

Over time, I have enjoyed watching little birds who frequent my garden, build their nests. It amazes me the care they take to provide the right place for their young. I have noticed that even the birds discipline their young. They chirp away and then suddenly, if I approach the area of their nest, one chirp from the parent and there is immediate silence. Once, when finches were teaching their babies to fly, one took fright and got stuck behind a box in the garage. I carefully caught the fledgling and placed it back in the nest to the delight of the parents. What a memorable experience to have.

Just as the finches needed help, so do we as parents. We need a place near God's heart, where we can share our struggles and ask God's guidance in rearing our families. God gave us our children, and He loves and cares for them beyond understanding. We must do our part, setting an example of living close to our Saviour, always being willing to listen and guide, even when it hurts. Surrender yourself and your family each day to the Lord because He knows them and what they need far better than you. Can you hear Jesus say to you: *'My child, why are you worrying and confusing yourself when you can leave your concerns about your children to Me? Let your mind be peaceful; so, I say to you to truly surrender yourself to Me, and I will take care of every concern for you and resolve all your difficult situations.'* Is there something that you need to surrender to Jesus today?

> *'What a friend we have in Jesus, all our sins and griefs to bear,*
> *What a privilege to carry, everything to God in prayer.'*
>
> Joseph M. Scriven

DAY 334
JERUSALEM

Luke 18:31, *"We are going up to Jerusalem."* NIV

We start our Christian life when we accept that we are a sinner in the sight of God and ask Jesus, who died to save us, to be our Lord. Here, we begin our journey with Christ, and end with Him when He calls us home or returns to claim His own. Unlike our natural life, where our ambitions change over the years, our beginning and our end are the same... our Jerusalem, through our Lord Himself.

During these years, our goal must be to trust, follow and grow to become more like Jesus. Our aim must be, not just to be helpful or to win the unsaved but to 'do' God's divine will. Jerusalem is the place where Jesus began his ministry, and it was the place where He surrendered to His Father's will when He died on the cross. Unless we are prepared to go with Jesus to the cross, we will have, at best, a weak and poor relationship with Him. When Jesus went to Jerusalem, knowing He was to die for the sins of humanity, He did not allow anything to discourage Him in any way. Our Lord did not favour anyone on His way to fulfil the purpose for which He was born.

Our goal must be to trust, follow and grow to become like Jesus.

Luke 6:40 says, *"The disciple is not above his teacher: but every one when he is perfected shall be as his teacher."* Works of the Spirit will be evident in our lives as we are made perfect in Christ; we will bless others in the name of Jesus, some will be thankful, but the majority, as in the day of our Lord, will show gross ingratitude. Through all this, let us not be deceived or deflected from our goal to reach our destination. As it was for our Saviour, it will be for us on our way to Jerusalem.

When Jesus reached Jerusalem, they crucified Him, and Calvary became the gateway to our salvation. Thankfully for each of us, walking the road to our Jerusalem, our life will not end in crucifixion, but by the grace of our Lord, our way will end in glory. Until then, we all travel our road up to Jerusalem.

Prayer: *Heavenly Father, let the glory of the Lord fall upon us as we travel our road of life so that those who pass by may be drawn to the Cross of Christ and be saved. Amen*

DAY 335
OUR LOVING GUIDE

Job 23:10, *"But he knows the way that I take; when he has tested me, I will come forth as gold"* NIV.

The story of Job, who God allowed to suffer at the hand of Satan, is played out repeatedly in our lives. Often in the affliction of life, when Satan seems so busy, it can be challenging for us to see the hand of our loving Lord at all. When we think that He has abandoned us, this is often the very time when He is right there directing our path. *"When my spirit grows faint within me, it is you who watch over my way"* (Psalm 142:3).

> **No trial comes to the believer without some wise and loving purpose.**

No trial comes to the believer without some wise and loving purpose which we may never see this side of heaven. As parents, we deal each day with our children in the same way, for we know that unless we administer discipline to the ones we love, they will not achieve their best life. Our love is tender enough not to inflict unnecessary punishment but strong enough to do what is needed.

Time after time, in our hour of trial, when some circumstance seems to ruin our lives, we speak of it as providence, but what is providence? When we speak of providence, let us be careful lest we dethrone our living, directing and loving God from being the Sovereign of His earth and our lives. He is our ever acting, personal guide, and we can trust that nothing will pass His tender and compassionate eye that He does not intend for our good.

God is the secret of all the mysteries and misunderstood happenings of your life. *"The Lord gave and the Lord has taken away"* (Job 21:1). You must be like Job, who saw God's hand even when everything was taken away. When we can see God in everything that affects our lives, and we are at our lowest, like Job we will be able to find the faith to say, *"Though He slay me, yet will I trust Him."* What is happening in your life that you need to hand over to God?

Prayer: *Father, forgive me for trying to do things my way when You simply want to direct me in Your path for my life. Help me to trust Your guidance, even when everything seems to be against me. Amen*

DAY 336
BLESSING FROM GOD

Matthew 5:10, *"Blessed are those who are persecuted because of righteousness, for theirs is the kingdom of heaven."* NIV

Great servants of God are introduced to the world in many ways. Some rise gradually and with majesty, like the rising of the sun, from childhood to adult life and usefulness. Others are like a flash of lightning on a dark night, charged with a message irresistible to humanity's ears. Such men were Elijah and John the Baptist, and such was Stephen.

Little is known of Stephen's beginnings. He was almost certainly a Jew and likely had known Jesus, which enabled him to recognize Jesus in glory. But of his childhood and education, we know nothing, having only the record of his speech on that last day. Acts 7:8 tells us, that he was *"a man full of God's grace and power, doing great wonders and miraculous signs among the people."* When he was taken before the Sanhedrin, the men of Jewish power; as they looked at him, they *"saw that his face was like the face of an angel"* (Acts 6:15). After delivering his speech, he was filled with the Holy Spirit and looking up to heaven he saw the glory of God.

> God's love and blessing is within the reach of everyone.

In Matthew 11:6, Jesus said, *"Blessed is the man who does not fall away on account of me."* The wonder of God's love is that this blessedness is within the reach of each of us. We are often tempted and do not fully understand the mysteries of God's dealings with us. Like Stephen, if we refuse to give into the temptations of this world and daily come into Christ's presence, learning, and growing closer to God through the work of the Holy Spirit in our lives, then the peace of God that Stephen experienced will also keep our hearts and minds. Oh, the joy... that we too will enter heaven beholding the face of Jesus our Saviour. In your last hours, will your face shine with the love and light of Jesus?

> *He heeded not reviling tones, nor sold his heart to idle moans,*
> *Though cursed and scorned and bruised with stones.*
> *But looking upwards, full of grace, he prayed, and from a happy place,*
> *God's glory smote him on the face.*
>
> Tennyson.

Being a Christian is more than just an instantaneous conversion it is a daily process whereby you grow to be more and more like Christ.

Billy Graham

"Whoever believes in the Son has eternal life but whoever rejects the Son will not see life, for God's wrath remains on them."

John 3:36

DAY 337
GOD'S POWER IN LIFE

Psalm 8:3-4, *"When I consider your heavens... what is man that you are mindful of him."* NIV

We may know about God, but do we know Him as our constant companion? When Jesus was on earth, He constantly referred to the loving and reverent fellowship that the holy men of the Old Testament had with God, as He moved them by the Holy Spirit to write and speak. These men of God were mostly ordinary people like you and me, yet we stand in awe of what God achieved through them. Consider, if we are like them and God is still the same today as He was then, are we falling short?

Today, we think we are too busy, or we don't understand the Bible, and yet Charles Spurgeon once said, *"Nobody ever outgrows Scripture; the book widens and deepens with our years."* The truth is, God will speak to us when we take time to listen to His words in scripture. In Psalm 119:30, we read, *"The unfolding of your words gives light; it imparts understanding to the simple."* How true these words are, and this has been the experience of those who have read, digested, and studied the scripture. God uses the words to restore our trust, give us wisdom in the decisions of everyday life, help the sad heart rejoice, and give understanding to reality and sincerity in helping others.

> You can only know God by listening to what He says.

When we read our Bible, the words we read will purify our hearts and minds. We need to make it a daily exercise, allowing God to speak to us, and then we can respond to Him in prayer. If we are to know the power of God in our lives, we must follow the great preachers of the past who were able to speak the Word with boldness because the truths of God's Word inspired them.

The Psalmist asks in Psalm 119:169, *"Give me understanding according to your Word,"* We must read and study Scripture If the love of our Heavenly Father is to flow from us to others. The more we read our Bible, the closer God will be to us, and the greater will be the power of the Holy Spirit within us.

Prayer: *Lord God, teach us to read, mark, learn and meditate on Your words, so we can lead others into a proper understanding of You. Amen*

DAY 338
THE COST OF FOLLOWING JESUS

Mark 8:34, *"Whoever wants to be my disciple must deny themselves and take up their cross and follow me."* NIV

Simon Peter urged Jesus to save Himself from suffering, but He answered that this could not be. He went on to make the disciples understand that if anyone was to follow Him, they must deny their own choices, will and pleasures if they wanted to reach the highest life for themselves.

It is the 'here and now' that matters.

In today's culture, we follow someone on social media without thinking, so often finding those we follow can lead us to sin and failure, often to the detriment of our life. Jesus tried to make it clear that following Him was not about getting a ticket to heaven but a commitment to do life every day with Him. He added the importance of commitment on a daily basis. *"Deny oneself and take up their cross daily"* (Luke 9:23).

What does this mean for your life? To deny ourselves involves constantly refusing to gratify our self-life, regardless of how rejected or humiliated we feel. When we live for the fulfilment of building a warm nest, avoiding discomfort, making money for our enjoyment and inventing schemes for our pleasure, we will become disappointed and miserable. We must be careful not to become caught up in self-gratification.

How many have done these things only to lose their own soul? Jesus asks, *"What good is it for a man to gain the whole world, yet forfeit his soul?"* (v.36). It is the 'here and now' that matters, even though when we refuse to choose the views of the world it will bring upon us criticism, dislike and even hatred.

How can our Lord use us in the great future He has for our world if we fail Him in the limited sphere of our day-to-day life? What is important to you, the approval of man or the blessing of God... with eternal life thrown in.

Prayer: *Dear God, we have disappointed ourselves and made life choices that have not filled us with the water of life to quench our thirst. Help us to choose to walk in Your way every day. Amen*

DAY 339
THE WISDOM OF LIFE

1 Samuel 16:7, *"The Lord does not look at the things man looks at. Man looks at the outward appearance, but the Lord looks at the heart."* NIV

In God's kingdom, what matters is your will, heart, mind, and your spiritual growth. The things man sees on the outside are social media, profession, friends, and our home and car, but they don't define who we are. Even though things carry value to those around us, they are unimportant when we look at them in the light of God's kingdom. At the heart of God's Word, our hidden strengths are what will get us through life. When we look at King David life, we see it as a miracle, but really, it is a moral story showing strength, boldness and confidence whilst being a servant of God. Throughout his life, we see time and again how David brought honour and glory to God.

While David, Jesse's youngest son, was a shepherd God was preparing him for anointing by Samuel to become king of Israel. At his anointing, we read, *"From that day the Spirit of the Lord came upon David in power."* (v.13) We pick up where the Philistines are gathered to fight Israel. Goliath came forward, like a conqueror and destroyed any confidence the Israelites had. Meanwhile, David appears filled with God's Spirit, and boldness, making his brothers angry because they were fearful. How dare David be so cool! They try discouraging him by trying to destroy his faith and said in v.25, *"Do you see how this man keeps coming out."* *(Don't be silly, you'll be killed.)* David had strong faith from mediating on God's words while tending the sheep. He said to Saul, v.37, *"The Lord has delivered me from the paw of the lion and the bear, and will deliver me from the hand of this Philistine."*

Our hidden strengths are essential to get us through life.

Today people are discouraged, unsure and uncertain of themselves. We must encourage them that their strength is in God, who wants us to be strong and courageous for Him. Do not let the words of others discourage your spirit; encourage yourself with the words of scripture and prayer. You have what you need to overcome within your soul – the Holy Spirit, the wisdom of your life. Slay your Goliath through the power of the Spirit within and know God is training you for His service.

Prayer: *Father God, by the power of Your Spirit, fill me with courage and boldness to be your witness in the world today. Amen*

DAY 340
TRIUMPH OVER DEATH

Rev. 1:17-18, *"Do not be afraid, I am the Living One; I was dead, and now look, I am alive for ever and ever! And I hold the keys of death and Hades"* NIV.

In Acts 2, when Peter addressed the crowd, he explained that Jesus was raised from the dead, free from the agony of death because death could not keep its hold on Him (v24). Even though Christ suffered bitterly, it did not stop His love for humanity, even for those who crucified Him. He died not only to overcome sin but that through His death, we who have given ourselves to Him need not fear the terror of death.

> Even though Christ suffered bitterly, it did not stop His love for those who crucified Him.

What makes us fear death? It is a mystery, but a mystery that we need not fear, for Christ showed us that it is only the door to a far better life. We will be the same spirit, living in a different environment, where we will hear the voices of those gone on before us as we fellowship with them. To die in this life is to be welcomed by Him. *"You will receive a rich welcome into the eternal kingdom of our Lord and Saviour Jesus Christ"* (2 Peter 1:11). We also need not fear the loneliness of death, for Christ has told us that as we pass through the dark valley, we will be aware of His presence with us. We know He is within us here, and death will not separate us, not even for a second, from the love of our God. When Jesus died, He died alone, for the Father could not bear to look on the sin He took for us, but none of us has to pass through that experience. He said, *"I will come again, and receive you unto Myself."*

We need not fear what is beyond, for the curse of sin has been put away forever through the death of our Saviour. What others call death, let us consider as a 'sleep', where our spirit leaves our body, and we awake with fresh energy in the Eternal Morning filled with exceeding joy as we are presented before Jesus, the faultless Lamb of God. *"To him who is able to keep you from stumbling and to present you before his glorious presence without fault and with great joy"* (Jude 24).

Prayer: *O God, may I trust You so much, that when my time on earth is done my faith will be stronger than ever. Grant that I will not fear the mystery of death but rejoice that I will be in Your presence. Amen*

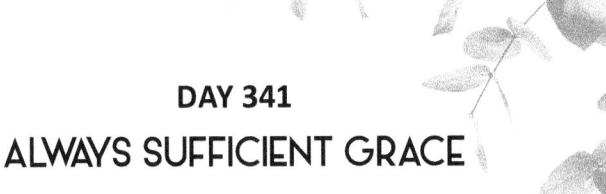

DAY 341
ALWAYS SUFFICIENT GRACE

2 Corinthians 12:9, *"My grace is sufficient for you, for my power is made perfect in weakness."* NIV

Here we read that God's grace is sufficient for all our needs, and even though we know that's true, taking God at His word can often mean a different set of circumstances. Even though we may be sure and believe, it is often very different when pain and sorrow come. We ask, do I really accept His all-sufficient grace, or do I doubt that I will know His power within me?

When we look back at our forebears who endured horrific persecution in the two world wars, we ask, how did they do it? For years their lives seemed helpless as they sort to survive on food rations and often scraps throughout Europe and England. They were brave people, but God's grace was sufficient in their defenceless state, and His power was made perfect in their weakness.

It would seem when need arises, God's overflowing favour of grace is there for us.

Paul endured some form of pain throughout his life, relying on the Lord, who gave him the power of endurance to continue bringing the good news to thousands and helping establish the early church.

While in conversation with my doctor, he once told me how throughout his years in practice, he had experienced some of the most pleasant and contented natures in those who suffered from disabilities. It would seem that when need arises God's overflowing favour of grace is there for us to draw on.

When Jesus is our Lord, suffering brings out the special graces that the Spirit fills us with. We must believe, and be strong in Christ, despite our shortcomings. Each of us can know the perfect peace offered through God's grace as we allow Him to be strong in us where we are weak. God's grace is there right now; we only need to ask and be blessed.

Grace, grace, God's grace,
Grace that will pardon and cleanse within.
Grace, grace, God's grace,
Grace that is greater than all our sin.

Julia H. Johnston

DAY 342
GOD HAS PROMISED

2 Peter 1:4, *"He has given us his very great and precious promises, so that through them you may participate in the divine nature."* NIV

When God accepted you and me as believers, He gave us the Holy Spirit within, and also His precious promises so that when faced with the trials of life, we can trust Him to see us through and grow us in His divine nature. When a shipwright builds a yacht or any sea-going vessel, he builds it to withstand a hurricane's power; otherwise, it would be a foolish captain who would trust its ability. God doesn't make mistakes, and we can be sure He will be faithful to what He promised. He has given us life jackets, encased in *"His divine power for a life of Godliness through our knowledge of him who called us by his own glory (His very presence) and goodness"* (2 Peter 1:3).

> **We can be sure that He will be true to what He promised.**

Christ wants us to use His power in our lives and not just talk about it. He longs to bless us so that we might appreciate just how great our God is and praise Him. We need to realize and make more use of the power of God within us, by taking God's promises and applying them daily in our own lives.

We must stop viewing God's promises as though they are for someone else and instead use them every day as a source of comfort for the very situation we are going through. Trust Jesus whenever you need His comfort because God cannot say no to something He has promised. *"Not one of all the Lord's good promises to Israel failed; everyone was fulfilled"* (Joshua 21:45). Find God's promise for you today and trust Him in it.

> *God has not promised skies always blue,*
> *Flower-strewn pathways all our lives through;*
> *God has not promised sun without rain,*
> *Joy without sorrow, peace without pain.*
> *But God has promised strength for the day,*
> *Rest for the labour, light for the way,*
> *Grace for the trials, help from above,*
> *Unfailing kindness, undying love.*
>
> Annie Johnson Flint

DAY 343
THE GREATEST LOVE

Luke 23:34, *"Jesus said, "Father, forgive them, for they do not know what they are doing."* NIV

Years after World War 2, in the Ravensbruck concentration camp where some 50,000 women lost their lives, a crumpled piece of paper was found, and written on it was a prayer asking the Lord not to remember the suffering the German soldiers had inflicted on her. Instead, to remember the camaraderie, loyalty, courage, generosity, and greatness of heart the prisoners had learned because of suffering; asking that on judgement day there be forgiveness for those who had persecuted them. This prayer showed the inexpressible grace required of the writer to seek God's forgiveness for her oppressors.

Jesus left the glory and splendour of heaven knowing that He was destined to die on the cross for the sins of every man, woman, and child throughout history. As He hung there with two criminals, one either side of Him, He even spoke words filled with love and compassion, assuring the one criminal that because of his faith, he would be with Him in paradise. As he agonized, He looked below at the soldiers who had crucified Him, together with the people who had accused Him unjustly, asking God to forgive them... and from the cross, He poured out redeeming love, sufficient for them and the whole human race. Enough love for you and enough love for me.

> We only need to ask forgiveness to know His redemptive love.

If any of us had to pay the penalty for our sin and hang on a cross, it would be more than likely there would be no love whatsoever in us. Here, we witness the Son of God with increased love for those who wronged Him. That same love is still being poured out today for yours' and my sin. We only need to ask forgiveness to know His redemptive love within our very being.

Without the amazing, unfathomable love of Jesus, there would be no heaven, no bird song, no flowers along life's path, and the ocean would be dry. Without Jesus, you and I would be eternally lost to be dammed in hell. There never was and never will be any greater love than the love of Jesus. *"Greater love has no one than this: to lay down one's life for one's friends"* (John 15: 13).

Prayer: *Dear Lord, all I can do in thanks for Your great love, is offer You my life and let it be Yours. Amen*

DAY 344
OUR LORD'S SURPRISE VISIT

Luke 12:40, *"You also must be ready, because the Son of Man will come at an hour when you do not expect him."* NIV

When Jesus came to earth as a baby, He was not recognized as the long-awaited Messiah. Even though His coming was prophesied through the Old Testament, He was still rejected. He taught in the temple and then gave His life for our sins so that through acceptance and forgiveness, we could have eternal life, but He was not acknowledged as the Messiah, and for many today, He still isn't.

> *Ignore anyone who would hinder your expectation of Jesus Christ.*

Since His ascension to Heaven, through the Holy Spirit, He comes to us at any time, and we must always be ready to listen to Him. He comes to us through different ways and experiences, and if you have been someone who has experienced the very presence of the Lord, praise be to God. Maybe you are still longing for just such an experience.

We can face a battle about being ready because we allow ourselves to become absorbed in our lives, like work, family, sport, entertainment, success or anything else that takes our focus away from expecting at any moment to meet Him. It has nothing to do with our denomination or teaching, but we must be prepared, or we may miss Him. In Matthew 25, we read the parable about the ten virgins, five who were ready and five who were unprepared. *"But while they were on their way to buy the oil, the bridegroom arrived."*

To always be prepared, you must keep yourself true to God by being intently focused each day through your personal relationship with Jesus. You must move from being 'religious' to setting your heart on being spiritually in tune with Jesus 100% of the time. You must set your heart on expecting His return so that when He appears to you in your present life or returns to take you home to Heaven, it will be as though you are the only one. You must trust only Jesus and ignore anyone who would hinder your expectation of the presence of Jesus Christ.

Prayer: *Dear Lord, may my expectation of seeing you each day keep me focused on my relationship with You, so I will not miss You when You come to me. Amen.*

DAY 345
HIS DISCIPLINE

Hebrews 12:5-6, *"The Lord disciplines those he loves... endure hardship as discipline."* NIV

Discipline involves correction and training. Without doubt, the most disciplined body of people is the armed forces. As they train and are corrected, we see an elite group of people who, through the discipline they have received, are self-controlled, obedient, and upright citizens. Could you imagine the chaos if these same men and women were to go into conflict, without a commanding office and not having been trained in discipline?

The Bible has a lot to say about the necessity of discipline from a child of young age to adulthood. Proverbs 15:32 says, *"He who ignores discipline despises himself, but whoever heeds correction gains understanding."* Proverbs 19 tells us, that in disciplining our children, we bring hope and not death, and accepting instruction will bring wisdom. We are also advised to train a child in the way of the Lord and in Proverbs 23:13, *"If you punish him with the rod, he will not die."*

> We listen to everyone except our God on this important subject.

Where have we gone wrong? Today we have so many undisciplined children and adults who please themselves with when and what they do. Satan is deceiving us, as we listen to everyone except our God on this important subject. Many of us today let our children decide what they need and want to do when they cannot decide with constructive understanding. Hebrews 12:7-8 says, *"God is treating you as sons. For what son is not disciplined by his father?"* From these words, God requires us to discipline our children or suffer the consequences.

As adults, God disciplines us. *"All discipline seems painful rather than pleasant, but later it yields the peaceful fruit of righteousness to those who have been trained by it"* (Heb. 12:11). God disciplines us because He wants us to share His life with Him. What a difference when we see the trials of life as discipline from God, training us to be holy. So, let's rejoice at being disciplined, and let's not forget to discipline our children for the glory of God.

Prayer: *Please give me understanding and the ability to discipline my children so they grow to be citizens of the Kingdom of God. Amen*

DAY 346
STRENGTH FROM GOD

Psalm 28:7, *"The Lord is my strength and my shield; my heart trusts in him, and he helps me"* NIV.

Each of us has within a God given strength, our character, which makes us able to live with determination and decision. We are *"strengthened with power through his Spirit in our inner being"* (Eph.3:16). It is as though when the strength of character is required, the power of the Holy Spirit within us, gives a strength that cannot be exhausted. In all the circumstances of life when we come to the Lord, He gives us strength to go on.

Our spirit gets crushed by defeat or a wrong choice.

The struggle of everyday life can quickly depress our spirit. Often, our spirit is crushed by defeat or wrong choice, and the road to victory seems to have no turning. Like David, we must claim God's strength as we trust and shelter in Him, for He has promised to help us even when we ask why! He alone can give us the strength to climb over the difficulty of a broken marriage, bankruptcy or financial failure, abuse, illness, and every other circumstance we may encounter.

We also grow faint when we come to the drudgery of each day, we just can't get ahead, and all is closing in around us. Jesus is there to give us the courage to face another day, as He did for Joshua when he had to lead the children of Israel. *"Be strong and courageous. Do not be afraid; do not be discouraged, for the Lord your God will be with you wherever you go"* (Joshua 1:9).

In the seasons of life when we are physically frail from age or illness, and forced just to sit when our mind knows and wants to do something constructive, or during times of grief, nothing can explain the strength that comes from God as He gives us His peace.

In all of life, as we wait on our God for the strength to overcome, we can say with David, *"My heart leaps for joy, and with my song I praise him"* (Psalm 28:7).

What do you need God's strength for in your life?

Prayer: *All-powerful God, when I am weak, then You are strong. Please give me the strength to face every situation that comes to me in life. Amen*

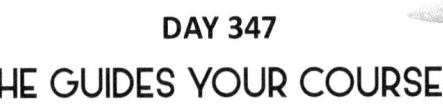

DAY 347

HE GUIDES YOUR COURSE

Isaiah 30:21, *"Whether you turn to the right or to the left, your ears will hear a voice behind you, saying, "This is the way; walk in it."* NIV

> *Lord Jesus, touch us with your skilful hands.*
> *Don't let the music that's in us die!*
> *Mould and polish us to bring forth,*
> *Your life and love that in us lies.*
>
> Unknown

When we have prayed for God's help, we sometimes wonder why He didn't help us sooner, but it is not His order, for, firstly He has to adjust us to the trouble we are facing in order that we can learn from it. *"I will be with him in trouble, I will deliver him and honour him"* (Psalm 51:19). Your Lord will be with you in your trouble, but then He will take you beyond it, but not until you have stopped being restless and become calm and quiet in His presence.

Our problems, like storm clouds around us can become dark and over-bearing, and we can wonder just where our God is, but let us remember that many civilizations have preceded our generation. God, in His wisdom, held those He loved in the hollow of His hand and brought

> **Never count yourself forgotten by God.**

them through a break in the clouds to the sunshine of better things. We must never doubt that the clouds will break, nor dream that wrong will prevail over right, and most importantly, never count yourself forgotten by God.

There are two ways to overcome our problem. One is to try to get rid of it by fretting and worrying, making our own plans that can or may not work out. The other is to recognize the problem as a challenge from God to claim from Him a greater blessing than we have ever experienced before and delight in His Divine grace. The Lord may seem asleep, oblivious and uncaring to our problem, but let us, always remember that He is round about us ever guiding our course. Listen, and you will hear Him say, *"This is the way, walk in it."*

Prayer: *Lord, help me always to recognize Your Sovereignty and wait on You. Amen*

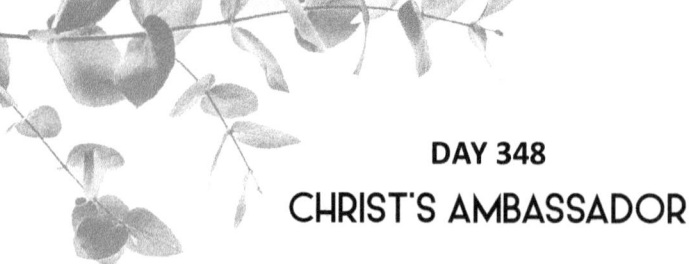

DAY 348
CHRIST'S AMBASSADOR

2 Corinthians 5: 17,19,20, *"Therefore, if anyone is in Christ, he is a new creation... He has committed to us the message of reconciliation. We are therefore Christ's ambassadors, as though God were making His appeal through us."* NIV

An ambassador is someone who goes to another country or area to represent their country or someone. There is a sense of power being able to make a deal or bring peace and reconciliation during unrest.

> *Your Heavenly Father sees the little acts you do for Him.*

Today, there is great unrest throughout our world with people being affected by a pandemic, which causes worry, stress and even death for many. In such times Jesus has called us to be His ambassadors, to bring hope and point men and women to the Saviour, who can bring them peace in a hurting world. In Christ's service, some of us plant the seed, some care for the growth, some trim and train, and some reap the harvest. Then there are those who go to the hard soil and till it for the Sower, softening someone's heart to the things of God, but all are Christ's ambassadors.

If you are elderly, do not give up being God's ambassador because your wisdom and life experiences can influence young people for Christ. There is nothing more significant than to use the experiences that we have, to hand on to others especially young adults. Paul was God's ambassador, carrying the Lord's name in peace and love. You must recognise that God has made you a new creation, allowing His love, brotherly kindness, and peace to flow from you to others. Humanity looks at the big and important things, but your Heavenly Father sees the little acts you do for Him. As God's ambassador, you bear His name and your example is what the world sees, so be encouraged to continue to notice those who need help. Encourage and pray for them, and so fulfil your calling to reconcile the world to your God and Saviour.

> *We said that we would hold the Christ light,*
> *If any of our brothers are afraid.*
> *That we will reach the hand of service,*
> *Let's not forget the promises we've made.*
>
> K. Cameron-Smith

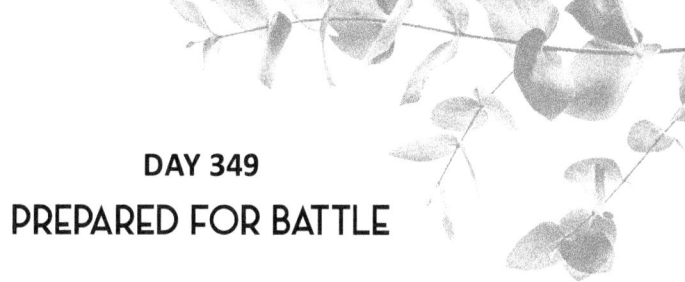

DAY 349
PREPARED FOR BATTLE

Ephesians 6:13, *"Therefore put on the full armour of God, so that when the day of evil comes, you may be able to stand your ground"* NIV.

We must recognize we are engaged in a battle with unseen evil spirits and demons who are fiercely involved in our lives. As we live spirit-filled lives, we will have to fight battles. One of these battles is the fight to preserve strong marriage and family relationships. This chapter teaches about obedience of children and about the responsibility of fathers. Today we see many families broken through divorce, where the children are disobedient, having little or no respect for the single parent and too often where either the mother or father takes no responsibility in raising the children.

We read, *"Be strong in the Lord and in His mighty power."* (v.10) These words can give hope when Satan is continually using discouragement to destroy our lives. Even though we witness so much of this happening, we can have strong marriages. Paul tells us to put on the armour of God. The *belt of truth* speaks of peace of mind (Phil. 4:7); the *breastplate of righteousness* is the surety of your salvation; feet fitted with the *gospel of peace* comes from walking every day in the Holy Spirit; *the shield of faith* is your trust in God; *the helmet of salvation* and *the sword of the Spirit*, is to know, read and meditate on God's Word. Praying in the Spirit (v.18), gives us the power to fight against the evil forces that try to destroy our families. This power is the same power that raised Christ from the dead.

> Fight to preserve strong marriage and family relationships.

Allow these verses to be a source of strength for you. I remember my dad bringing the Bible to the breakfast table each day and reading to the family. This may not be possible in your home, but I encourage you to read God's Word as a family and with your partner to experience God's blessing on your marriage and your family. In my life there were times when had It not been for the wisdom and strength gained through putting on the armour of God, life would have been difficult. Your marriage and family are worth the battle, and you have the power of the Holy Spirit within you.

Prayer: *Dear Lord, help me take this important step in my marriage and family, so that we may grow together in Christ every day. Amen*

DAY 350
KNOW THE TRUTH

2 Timothy 1:12, *"I know whom I have believed"* NIV.

Paul found the people in the church at Ephesus (Acts 9) in total disagreement about what was right or wrong in their belief. Today, we are seeing great confusion among believers regarding our present world situations. Are we listening to man or to what God tells us in His Word?

God tells us, we must not live in fear. *"For God has not given us a spirit of fear, but of power and of love and of a sound mind"* (2 Timothy 1:7). As believers, we have the Holy Spirit within us, and we are to trust God. We must be careful making decisions if we are fearful, for this is when the evil will confuse us. We need to pray (Psalm 56:3); think logically and clearly with the help of the Holy Spirit (1 Thes.5:21); and instead of allowing confusion from the news or social media, read our Bible to hear what God says (2 Cor.5:1).

> **We must use wisdom and discernment lest we be deceived.**

We are told not to fear and use wisdom and discernment lest we be deceived. *"Dear friends, do not believe every spirit, but test the spirits to see whether they are from God, because many false prophets have gone out into the world"* (1 John 4:1). Our God is not a God of confusion, so we need to trust God's Word and stop listening to the words of this world. We must be careful not to become slaves to those in control of this world, but rather stand firm and choose freedom. *"Don't you know... you are slaves to the one whom you obey"* (Romans 6:16). When we, through trust and prayer stop living in fear, pray for discernment and choose freedom, we can expect persecution, for we have a powerful enemy. We see persecution around the world, but we can also expect it. *"If they persecuted me, they will persecute you also"* (John 15:20). In Romans 8:28, Paul tells us that everything works for our good.

We must hold fast to God and each other in troubled times and share God's good news. We must all pass from this earthly life, but what of the life after that? Hold fast, so that you are not deceived. Trust and pray, enduring to the end, that you may behold the glory of your Heavenly Father whilst being able to say, *'I know whom I have believed.'*

Prayer: *Lord, help me to live each day with the freedom that trusting in Jesus gives me. Amen*

DAY 351
YOUR CHOICE

Matthew 4:4, *"Jesus answered, "It is written: 'Man shall not live on bread alone, but on every word that comes from the mouth of God."*

Matthew 6:33, *"But seek first his kingdom and his righteousness, and all these things will be given to you as well"* NIV.

When Satan tempted Jesus in the desert, he said, *"Make these stones into bread."* Imagine how hungry Jesus felt after fasting for 40 days? I guess Satan thought he had the victory until Jesus replied, *"Man does not live by bread alone."* What would you choose if you were in a similar situation? This question comes to everyone and must be answered by each of us. Most of us, would find difficulty not to choose sustenance for our bodies and life. But according to Christ, this must be secondary.

Whether in the loneliness or busyness of life, the Devil comes to all, convincing us that it is more important to live. We must make money for bread, a home, a new car, or a business, leaving the consideration of purity, truth, thankfulness, worship of a Holy God and life after death to come in second place. Satan will say, *"Make these stones into bread."* At that exact moment you will hear Christ say, *"But seek first his kingdom and his righteousness, and all these things will be given to you as well."* God gives each of us a choice to choose between Him and the things of this world.

> God gives us the choice between Him and the things of this world.

We tend to take hold of the materialistic when Satan says, *'you deserve it,'* or when it comes to love, he tells us to delight in it apart from God's command. We seek knowledge in ways not clear in God's word. God gave us these strong desires, and He knows we need each of them, but He is more than these and will meet all our needs. Leave the responsibility of your life in God's hands. Isiah 49:23 says, *"Those who put their hope in me will not be put to shame."* Even if there is only a breath between you and death, dare to wait on Him to supply all your needs according to His riches in glory. What a glorious victory awaits those who commit their way to the Lord; trust in Him and are assured that He will do it.

Prayer: *Lord, give us the grace to seek first Your Kingdom and its righteousness, in the sure and certain faith that all will be well. Amen*

DAY 352
ARE YOU PREPARED?

Isaiah 11:1-3, *"A shoot will come up from the stump of Jesse... The Spirit of the Lord will rest on him - the Spirit of wisdom and of understanding, the Spirit of counsel and of might, the Spirit of the knowledge and fear of the Lord - and he will delight in the fear of the Lord."* NIV

In Isaiah's time, one king just replaced another. It was a time of cruelty and battle, but God chose Abraham's family to bring to them a king – a Saviour who would reign with love and peace. In Isaiah 9:6, he prophesied, *"For to us a child is born, to us a son is given, and the government will be on his shoulders. And he will be called Wonderful Counsellor, Mighty God, Everlasting Father, Prince of Peace."* For us who live today, this is our Lord Jesus, who was born at Christmas to the virgin Mary with Joseph as his earthly father and God as His Spiritual Heavenly Father.

Spend time living in the pure air of Holy Scripture and prayer.

For years, the Jews waited and prepared for the coming of the Messiah. However, when God did send the prophesied Messiah, the Jews would not acknowledge Him as the Saviour they had waited so long for. Even when Mary took Him to the temple and Simeon, the High Priest, filled with the Holy Spirit knew from God, this Holy baby was the 'stump' of Jesse who would save God's people, they still did not believe. Simeon had waited all his life, for God had told him that he would not die before the Messiah was born. Luke 2:30 *"For my eyes have seen your salvation."* Simeon was prepared and would not be deceived by anyone. Are you eagerly waiting, and prepared as much as you can be for the second coming of Jesus? To be ready, we must breathe each breath in the fear of the Lord. We all know the difference between putrid and the fresh air we inhale as we stand on a beautiful beach. We must be prepared by living in the pure air of Holy Scripture and prayer.

The Holy Spirit wants to bless us with wisdom and understanding. We need counsel and direction as to our life purpose, and strength to do what God requires of us, being students in the knowledge of our Heavenly Father so that when our Saviour returns to bring the life of blessedness and peace that He has promised, we will be ready and will not be deceived by Satan.

Prayer: *Lord Jesus, fill us with Your Holy Spirit, and help us not to be deceived but prepared for a new life when You reign for all eternity. Amen.*

DAY 353
SONGS OF PRAISE

Luke 1:46,47,68, *"My soul glorifies the Lord and my spirit rejoices in God my Saviour. Praise be to the Lord, the God of Israel, because He has come and has redeemed his people"* NIV.

These words from Mary's prayer and Zechariah's song have stirred our hearts for centuries. We may not be able to put our joy and triumph as eloquently or musically, but God understands when our hearts are open to the worship and praise of our Heavenly Father.

When God blesses our life, we often feel unworthy, but God will do for the most unworthy of us just as much as He will do for His saints. Why, we ask, and the answer comes because He blesses us for His Name's sake. *"Holy is His Name."* In other words, we cannot account for the power and love of our Father except to say that it is part of His wonderful character.

> Nothing excites our faith as much as when we speak God's Word.

Through the centuries, Kings and Presidents have been dethroned because of pride and arrogance, while many lowly people have been lifted to places of authority by God. When we genuinely seek each day to grow our faith in Jesus and do what God requires of us, we will be blessed. *"Blessed are those who hunger and thirst after righteousness, for they shall be filled."* (Matt.5:6) Whoever is humble and filled with faith will be blessed by God.

We must be careful not to miss any opportunity that God gives us to share the Gospel with those we come in contact with. Nothing excites our faith as much as when we speak God's Word and are able to tell someone just how much Jesus loves them. Then like Mary, we will say: *"My soul glorifies the Lord."*

Prayer: *Dear Lord, I pray for wisdom in all my relationships today. Please grant that I may cause no one to fall but that my words and actions will draw those I come in contact with to the cross of Jesus.*

DAY 354
PRAYER THAT OBTAINS

John 15:7, *"If you remain in me and my words remain in you, ask whatever you wish, and it will be done for you."* NIV

When Jesus prayed, He expected answers to His prayers, and when He was on earth, He led people to feel that they could obtain answers through prayer; otherwise, what would be the use of prayer, and why would He have taught us throughout His Word how we are to pray. *"And whatsoever ye shall ask in my name, that will I do, that the Father may be glorified in the Son."* (John 14:13)

> If our prayer is to prevail, it must always bring glory to the Father.

We all know someone who, through prayer, has received or been helped and we have probably wondered how they learned the secret that we often feel had eluded us. Our problem is that we so often ask amiss. Much has been written on prayer and how to pray, but if our prayer is to prevail, it must always bring glory to the Father. Jesus lived and died to bring glory to the Father (John 14:13), and He lived to bring humanity to understand and know the Father. The way you and I can bring glory to God through prayer is to constantly be praying for the salvation of those we come into contact with each day, for our Lord wants us to bear much fruit. (v.8)

Our prayer must be in Christ's name. In other words, our prayer must not be according to our will and nature but according to the will of the Father. It is not enough to just mention the name of Jesus at the end of our prayer, for we must allow the Holy Spirit to produce the blessings that the Lord would have us utter.

We know that God doesn't make promises that He doesn't keep. These verses do not necessarily mean that God will answer every prayer, but He promises He will respond as we long to become closer to Him. As we hunger for spiritual growth, He will satisfy us. Change takes time, so don't give up, but keep asking God to make you holy even as He is holy.

Prayer: *Lord, all that we desire is known to You; help us to ask for what Your Spirit has awakened within us, that we will bring glory to Your name. Amen*

DAY 355
CHOSEN BY GOD

Luke 6:13, *"He called his disciples to him and chose twelve of them."* NIV

When the Lord chose His apostles, they spent the first few years learning from Jesus as they lived and worked together. They were not chosen for comfort and joy for themselves. He taught them the blessing of being poor, hungry, hated and insulted so that God could achieve the great purpose of Salvation in people's lives. He transformed their perspective and attitude each day until they were masters at serving their God and bringing the people of their day to experience God's love through Jesus the Saviour.

As we travel through life with Jesus, we will find He explains mysteries and things unknown to the ordinary man that excites our hearts, and we know within our inner being that we have heard from our Lord. The more we place our trust in Him, the further He will lead us beyond our knowledge until we experience things only known to Him. He draws us closer to Himself and reveals the eternal things of His purpose for humanity. A place in our life where we no longer live for position, money or the pleasures of this life but in complete trust for God and His purposes alone.

> **He explains mysteries unknown to the ordinary man.**

We are not called just to be sure of our eternal destiny, nor to be sheltered from the problems of this life, but to go and serve God and man, looking for those whose hearts will trust Him for all He desires to do in their lives. The great evangelist D.L. Moody's ministry began when he overheard the words, *"The world has yet to see what God can do with a man fully consecrated to him."* His response was – *"By God's help, I aim to be that man."*

Is your heart set on Jesus, and will you trust Him for all He desires to do in and through you? Such was the life of Moody, and such can be your life and mine, providing we always bring the praise and glory to our Lord, for it is rightfully His. *"Whoever serves me must follow me; and where I am, my servant also will be. My Father will honour the one who serves me."* (John 12:26)

Prayer: *Thank You dear Lord, that You want us to be Your disciples. Give us teachable hearts, listening ears and complete trust so that You can mould us into workers in Your fields of sacred ministry. Amen*

DAY 356
THE TRANSFORMED LIFE

Genesis 32:1,24, *"Jacob went on his way, and the angels of God met him... So, Jacob was left alone, and a man wrestled with him till daybreak"* NIV.

As a child of God, there comes a time in our spiritual growth when we shall meet with the angels of Heaven as we come to our crisis hour. We do not see our helpers or hear the beating of their wings, but they are indeed present. Psalm 34:7 says, *"The angel of the Lord encamps around those who fear Him, and he delivers them."* Oh! What comfort for us to know that this is so. If we reckon on their presence with us, God will bring us to an experience with Him before which everything else will be insignificant.

God will wrestle with us to break our stubbornness and lack of faith.

When God wrestled with Jacob, He was pressing the old life from Jacob. God will wrestle with us to break our stubbornness and lack of faith until we cannot hold out any longer, and like Jacob, we fall into the arms of Jesus. We must surrender our self-life and let go of what holds us to the physical and material of this world before God can bless us with a new life where we know that we cannot let Him go. In that hour, we will understand that only our Heavenly Father can satisfy our needs, and we will fully surrender to Him and the highest and best He has for us.

Is God leading you to this never to be forgotten experience with Him? Are you experiencing a deep trial or an impossible situation? God knows how to guide you through to a life of surrender and trust, a life where you will die to self and through Him will have victory. Like Jacob, when you admit who you really are, there will be a spiritual turning point in your life from where you will go forward, walking daily in the Spirit of God.

Turn to the God of Jacob and cast yourself helplessly at His feet. Die to your own will and rise like Jacob into God's wisdom, strength and all-sufficiency. There is no way out but to come into a new and higher experience with God. Let Him make you into Royalty today.

Prayer: *Lord, I am all weakness, but You, the Almighty God, can fill me with Your strength. Make me leave all that will hinder my walk with You, and help me to trust my life to You – through Jesus, my Saviour. Amen.*

DAY 357
FOLLOW WITH HUMILITY

James 4:10, *"Humble yourselves before the Lord, and he will lift you up"* NIV.

Living near a major Airforce Base, three fighter jets often fly over on their way to a display or just for practice, always flying in formation so close together that I am always amazed they don't collide. I ask myself, *"How can they do it?"* for it is very impressive, and their precision is amazing.

Every time these jets fly over, I look up and wonder, how can they fly so close without touching each other and crashing. Thanks to technology and the obvious reason of trust, as the two pilots following have complete faith in the lead pilot, travelling at precisely the correct speed and trajectory. The wing pilots surrender any desire to switch directions or question their leader's path, getting into a formation and closely following, with the result of forming a powerful team.

> Jesus is our pilot; with Him we are in the best position for our lives.

The path that Jesus took was no different, for He denied Himself all praise and was obedient to His Father. For us, this lifestyle of Christ can be tough to understand or follow. Having been born again, with the Holy Spirit in our lives, God invites us to give up our selfish desires and trust in Him. Jesus is our lead pilot, and we are in the best position, with Him in control. We must humble ourselves and allow Him control if we want to experience the greatness of being part of His team. Imagine what a collision would occur if one of the wing pilots became proud and wanted to take the lead, much like our lives, when we try to control everything for ourselves, nothing seems to go right.

Humility is not thinking less of yourself, it's thinking of your Lord more than yourself, for we will all be humbled before God. Philippians 2:10-11 says... *"at the name of Jesus every knee will bow—in heaven and on earth and under the earth - and every tongue will confess that Jesus Christ is Lord, to the glory of God the Father".* You can walk in humility now and experience God's blessing or continue to want control and lose being lifted and loved by your Lord.

Prayer: *Help me Lord, to humble myself and allow you to control my life so I can experience the blessings you have for me each day. Amen*

DAY 358

KNOW THE FATHER

John 14:8-9, *"Philip said, "Lord, show us the Father and that will be enough for us." Jesus answered: "Anyone who has seen me has seen the Father."* NIV

The three years that Phillip had spent with Jesus had a remarkable influence on him. Even though he knew Jesus as the long-awaited Messiah, he was still eager to know God the Father. He mistook who Jesus really was when he said, *"Show us the Father."*

There is an eternal difference between knowing 'about' Jesus and knowing Him personally.

A case of mistaken identity can be embarrassing when you see someone you think you know only to find it is not so, but Phillip's request did not seem like a mistake to him. The problem was that he hadn't fully appreciated just who Jesus was. He even missed the point in question when Jesus replied, *"Don't you know me, Philip, even after I have been among you such a long time? Anyone who has seen me has seen the Father. How can you say, 'Show us the Father'?"* I have often wondered if Phillip felt confused by Jesus' remark.

The only way Phillip could see the Father was through the visible human form of Jesus, who was filled with wisdom, love and purity. Christ reveals the Father to us as He answers our prayers and communicates with us through the Holy Spirit, who abides within those who love Jesus as Saviour.

To understand who God is in character and personality, we need to look at Jesus, who always shows kindness, love, and mercy. God is beyond our understanding but comes to make His home with us through the Holy Spirit. The Father's dominion, might, and majesty are revealed to us as the love of Jesus fills the whole universe. How well do you know God the Father? To understand the Father, you must get to know Jesus through communion with Him, reading His Word and praying. There is an eternal difference between knowing 'about' Jesus and knowing Him personally.

> More about Jesus let me learn,
> More of His holy will discern.
> Spirit of God my teacher be,
> Showing the things of Christ to me.
>
> Eliza Edmunds Hewitt

DAY 359
THE EMPIRE OF CHRIST

Isaiah 9:7, *"Of the greatness of his government and peace there will be no end. He will reign... over his kingdom, establishing and upholding it with justice and righteousness from that time on and forever."* NIV

What does the word Empire mean? Think of the British Empire, comprising many countries over which the King is Sovereign, or the Empire over which Christ is Sovereign being all those from every nation who have given our lives to Jesus. He will rule forever and differently than an earthly King.

Isaiah foretold the birth of Jesus as the one to be sent by God to save humanity. However, Israel continued their sinful ways, looking for a warrior king, and not acknowledging Jesus as Messiah. Whether we recognise Jesus as God's Son, is irrelevant because every human who has ever been born is answerable to Christ as Saviour. When Jesus was on earth, He proclaimed, *"I am the light of the world. Whoever follows me will never walk in darkness but will have the light of life"* (John 8:12). He is King, and after He died and rose victorious over sin, He ascended into heaven to rule His Empire.

> **He is Wonderful Counsellor, Mighty God, Everlasting Father and Prince of Peace.**

"To us a child is born!" (v.6) –

He is our *Wonderful Counsellor*. You can tell Him all your problems and ask His counsel, for He will never mislead you.

He is the *Mighty God*. There is no other more excellent, for He has dominion over the whole universe.

Our *Everlasting Father*. There is no other more loving, faithful father who will care for His children forever.

He is the *Prince of Peace*. *"My peace I give you. I do not give to you as the world gives. Do not let your hearts be troubled . . ."* (John 14:27).

Allow Him to be everything to you, reigning in your soul and bringing you peace, joy, and love. Because our souls are infinite, it will take eternity for us to understand the greatness of being a citizen of the Empire of Christ. Are you a citizen of Christ's Kingdom? Come to Christ today and give Him the governance of everything that concerns your life.

Prayer: *Thank You Lord, for sending Jesus and all He has done and will do for us, for Your love that never lets us go and for Your arms to protect. Amen*

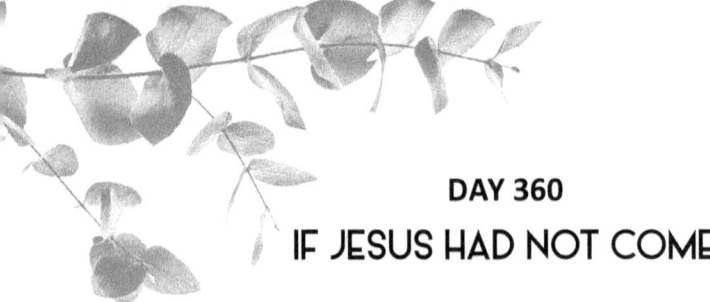

DAY 360
IF JESUS HAD NOT COME

Matthew 1:23, *"The virgin will conceive and give birth to a son, and they will call him Immanuel... God with us"* NIV.

Can you imagine what our Christmas Day would be like if Jesus had never been born? We would wake to just another ordinary day. There would be no excitement from children eagerly waiting to see what presents they have been given. There would be no decorations, no family get-together, no cuddles for each other, and nothing to gladden our hearts and more than likely; we would be bitter and selfish, thinking only of ourselves.

> *Rejoice and be especially glad today because "He has come."*

Then walk outside, and you would find there would be no church to go to and worship with your friends on such a special day, celebrating Jesus' birthday. You would open your Bible, and it would finish at Malachi, and every book about the Saviour of the world would have disappeared. When you met with someone who was sick or in need, there would be no compassion and care, instead a feeling of having been made to do something that you didn't really want to do. There would be no hope for us, for sin would swallow up death, meaning eternal separation from our loving God.

Let us rejoice and be especially glad today because "He has come." Let us meditate on the words of the angel's proclamation, *"I bring you good news that will cause great joy for all the people. Today in the town of David a Saviour has been born to you; he is the Messiah, the Lord"* (Luke 2: 10,11).

> *"There's a song in the air!*
> *There's a star in the sky!*
> *There's a mother's deep prayer,*
> *And a baby's low cry!*
> *And the star rains its fire*
> *While the beautiful sing,*
> *For a manger in Bethlehem cradles the King."*
>
> Josiah G. Holland

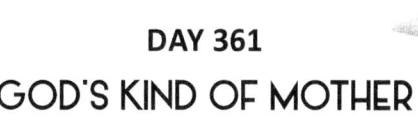

DAY 361
GOD'S KIND OF MOTHER

Proverbs 31:26-27, *"She opens her mouth with wisdom, and loving instruction is on her tongue. She watches over the ways of her household, and does not eat the bread of idleness."* NIV

> *I went for a walk down memory lane, and there on the wall of my mind,*
> *Hung a picture of someone I hold very dear, a woman, one of a kind.*

This is a tribute to my mother, a unique woman, one of a kind. She was a farmer's wife, an extremely hard worker who was always there to encourage and support him. To the women who lived around her, she was the one person to whom others would come with sick children or worries to unburden themselves... she found time for everyone. My mum cooked, cleaned, and sewed whilst opening her home to others, but the fondest memory is that every morning and night, she knelt beside her bed and prayed for her family.

We have the privilege to enrich those we love with the Scripture.

I am confident that as Mary held baby Jesus, she experienced that bond of love a mother feels when she is given her newborn to hold for the first time. We can only imagine how Mary felt each day throughout his life, knowing He would be crucified. *"But his mother treasured all these things in her heart"* (Luke 2:51). What trust and love she must have had in God to willingly give her son to die on the cross, and I wonder if deep in her heart she knew that He would live again. Her obedience is beyond comprehension.

Being a mother is a special calling requiring courage and strength to discipline our children, to teach them God's ways, and even sometimes to show love and patience when they are out of control. Within each mother, there is a God-given bond of love that cannot be broken, regardless of their child's faults. Mothers appreciate the great privilege it is to enrich those we love with words of Scripture and pray for them. They grow and change, often leading different lives than we wish for them. Mothers, I say to you, that the most excellent work we can do in their lives is to bring them to God's throne daily, covering them with God's blessings as we pray for them. May God bless you in your role as a mother.

Prayer: *Thank You Lord for the memories we have of our mothers, that help us see something of Your love Heavenly love for us. Amen*

DAY 362
PREVAILING PRAYER

Acts 4:31, *"After they prayed, the place where they were meeting was shaken. And they were all filled with the Holy Spirit and spoke the word of God boldly."* NIV.

The Holy Spirit is our communicator between heaven and earth, helping us to ask within God's will, as He reveals the thoughts and desires of our Father. It is as though our prayer is borne by the Spirit to the heart of God. We know our thought waves can reach Jesus, but we must be in tune with Him through the Spirit for His thoughts to reach us. In John 16:14-15 Jesus says, *"He (Holy Spirit) will bring glory to me by taking what is mine and making it known to you. All that belongs to the Father is mine. That is why I said the Spirit will take from what is mine and make it known to you."* The Holy Spirit brings glory to Jesus, and Jesus brings glory to God the Father.

> *What peace knowing God is doing better than we can ask or think.*

When we are in tune with the Spirit who dwells within us, we can come boldly to God's throne. We come in prayer, having fellowship with Him, a special time of contact with Him, having a yearning to not just know about Him but a deep hunger that can only be satisfied by communion and love.

Then there is a prayer of request. Often this is the prayer we pray more than any other, but as life advances, we are content to leave our needs and ourselves to the wisdom of our loving Father, who knows best for us, *"So we say with confidence, "The Lord is my helper; I will not be afraid. What can mere mortals do to me?"* (Hebrews 13: 6) What peace we can have knowing that God is doing for us even better than we can ask or think. Praying the prayer of intercession for the salvation of others is probably nearest to the mind of God, as He desires to see men and women come to know Him. Also, we bear with Him the burden for souls controlled by the evil powers. At these times, we must watch and pray that we are not tempted ourselves.

God has called us to come to Him, desiring communion with Him and interceding on behalf of others. What a privilege this is, but also a responsibility to be aware of as we pray in the Spirit.

Prayer: *Lord, please remove anything that hinders me from giving myself to You, with grace to obey You in all things, always in prayer for others. Amen.*

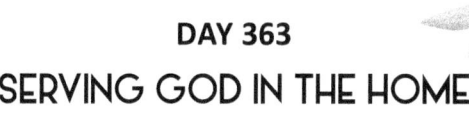

DAY 363
SERVING GOD IN THE HOME

Romans 12:11," *Never be lacking in zeal, but keep your spiritual fervour, serving the Lord."* NIV

In our Christian walk we are continually reminded that our purpose in life is to serve the Lord with a happy heart. To serve the Lord when we are encouraging and helping in the church to win others for Christ, can be a relatively happy time. Even though many don't want to become involved in the things needing to be done within the church, there is always a certain amount of praise for what we do, as well as acknowledging and praising God.

Now, let us look at the other end of the spectrum. Are you sick of cleaning, washing, and cooking a meal your family consumes in minutes? Or, you may be an elderly couple where one is ill and needs constant care, and all you do the whole day is clean up and help your partner with the basic physical needs of life. Or, every time you turn around, there are more dirty dishes or a pile of washing that never seems to end. Perhaps your intentions are well-meaning, but little children are demanding of your time, and before you know it, there are more demands on you than you care to admit.

Be encouraged, take the task in hand and do it with pride.

Our life of service in our family often brings little or no thanks for what we constantly do. Your life seems to have no purpose, so you begin to let things slide until everything folds around you, and you find yourself in tears calling out to God. Listen and hear what Jesus said, *"I tell you the truth, whatever you did for one of the least of these . . . you did for me."* (Matt.25:40)

Are you answering, *"Lord, even this?"* His answer will always be, *"Especially this, who else is going to do it for me? In all these things, you are serving me."*

Be assured and encouraged, take the task in hand and do it with pride. Don't wait because on the list it is marked for someone else. There is no greater joy than to look upon a clean kitchen or all the house tidy and the washing done and folded. Don't sit any longer just looking at it, for this is the service God has called you to at this time of your life, and He will reward you with joy.

Prayer: *Dear God, please help me to love serving my family while I wait for You to work in me, to give me the joy that can only come from You. Amen*

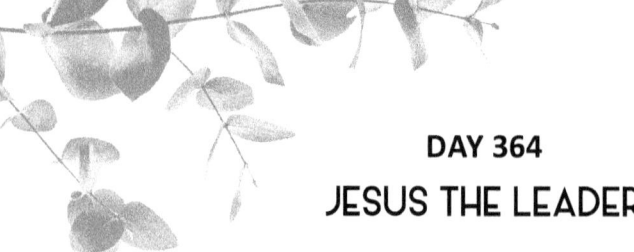

DAY 364
JESUS THE LEADER

Mark 10:43-44, *"Whoever wants to become great among you must be your servant, and whoever wants to be first must be slave of all."* NIV

What attracted people to Jesus? Wherever Jesus went, people were drawn to His authority over demons and His ability to heal the sick, not to mention that He spoke with unrivalled authority. Yet, no one exemplified humility like our Lord. The Pharisees called Him the 'friend of sinners,' but it was his love and humility that attracted people to Him.

> *Humility allows us to live our lives free of pride.*

As followers of Jesus, we must have the same humility in our relationships. When Jesus told the disciples that He was to be crucified (v.33), revealing His purpose for being here, they failed to understand. They believed He was the Messiah, but also thought He would be a great leader who would overthrow the Roman Empire. James and John, wanting to be associated with greatness, asked Jesus to allow them to sit on His right and left hand in glory. The others became indignant, and because of the pride of all concerned, one can only imagine a bitter discussion breaking out. This same situation happens to us when we allow pride to creep into our lives! Jesus answers with feeling, telling them that these places are for those He has prepared.

Putting ourselves first is the way of the world, and if He is to be our leader, we must live our lives by following what He did. He associated with lowliness; he served others and humbled Himself, even dying a criminal's death. *"Being found in appearance as a man, he humbled himself by becoming obedient to death - even death on a cross"* (Phil.2:8).

Everything in our world tells us to promote ourselves, so Jesus's leadership style is counter-cultural to the worldview. Through the gospel, we realize we are sinful and need Jesus, who gives us status because of what He has done for us. Humility allows us to live our lives free of pride as servants of Jesus. We must live as servants because our Christian relationships cannot flourish unless we are humble.

Prayer: *Dear Lord, help us to be humble so the world may see the church of God as the place where they want to find peace and forgiveness. Amen*

DAY 365
JESUS IS WORTHY

Revelation 5:9, *"You are worthy to take the scroll and to open its seals, because you were slain, and with your blood you purchased me for God from every tribe and language and people and nation"* NIV.

I remember singing a chorus, - *"Jesus loves the little children... red and yellow, black and white, all are precious in His sight."* Even though I was taught this, I did not understand because in Australia in the 1950s, there were very few people of other nationalities, and it was rare to see people with different coloured skin to ours, except for indigenous Australians.

When I became an adult, and more people from all over the world came to live in our beautiful country; sometimes, I still found it hard to show the love that God required of me for all people. I prayed about it, and thankfully God has given me love for all His children, regardless of colour, country or creed.

> No one else can stand before the Throne of God for you!

Jesus died for every man, woman and child in our world. We are all equal in God's sight, and what a day that will be when we gather together, people from all nations, around the Throne of God as Jesus our Saviour, breaks the seal of the scroll.

We will sing with the angels as we praise and worship: *"Worthy is the Lamb, who was slain, to receive power and wealth and wisdom and strength and honour and glory and praise!"* (Verse 12).

As believers, the one thing we must do is shed the clutter and baggage that clogs our perspective of that great day. We must eliminate the negatives and concentrate on our own spiritual life because no one else can stand there for us! JESUS IS LORD. Let us be there together, people from every nation, to praise Him.

Prayer: *Father, thank you that no matter who we are, from what country, colour or creed, none of us are excluded from that great day. Teach us to love one another as You have loved us. Amen.*

www.ingramcontent.com/pod-product-compliance
Lightning Source LLC
Chambersburg PA
CBHW070733170426
43200CB00007B/513